MUSLIM WORLD

ISLAMIC BELIEFS, PRACTICES, AND CULTURES

Marshall Cavendish
Reference
New York

Other Marshall Cavendish Offices:
Marshall Cavendish International (Asia) Private Limited, 1
New Industrial Road, Singapore 536196 • Marshall
Cavendish International (Thailand) Co Ltd. 253 Asoke, 12th
Flr, Sukhumvit 21 Road, Klongtoey Nua, Wattana, Bangkok
10110, Thailand • Marshall Cavendish (Malaysia) Sdn Bhd,
Times Subang, Lot 46, Subang Hi-Tech Industrial Park,
Batu Tiga, 40000 Shah Alam, Selangor Darul Ehsan,
Malaysia

Marshall Cavendish is a trademark of Times Publishing
Limited

All websites were available and accurate when this book was
sent to press.

Library of Congress Cataloging-in-Publication Data

Islamic beliefs, practices, and cultures.
    p. cm.
  Includes index.
  ISBN 978-0-7614-7926-0
  1. Islam. 2. Islam--Customs and practices. 3. Islam--
Doctrines. 4.
Islamic civilization. I. Marshall Cavendish Reference.
BP161.3.I785 2010
297.209--dc22
                                          2010008611

Printed in Malaysia
14 13 12 11 10 1 2 3 4 5 6

Marshall Cavendish
Publisher: Paul Bernabeo
Production Manager: Michael Esposito

The Brown Reference Group Ltd.
Editors: Felicity Crowe, Jolyon Goddard, Ben Hollingum,
Sally MacEachern, Henry Russell
Development Editor: Tom Jackson
Designer: Joan Curtis
Picture Researchers: Sophie Mortimer, Andrew Webb
Indexer: Christine Michaud
Senior Managing Editor: Tim Cooke
Editorial Director: Lindsey Lowe

PHOTOGRAPHIC CREDITS
Special thanks to Corbis for their assistance.

Front Cover: Corbis: T. Mughal/epa
Back Cover: Thinkstock: Photos.com.

Corbis: 205, 248; Arshad Arbab/epa 165, 208; Tony Arruza
246; Art Archive 29; Beawiharta/Reuters 160; Bettmann 21, 41,
46, 85, 197, 329; Stefano Bianchetti 45; Alessandro
Bianchi/Reuters 274; Tim Brakemeier/epa 214; David Butow
83; Stehanie Cardinale 276; Christian Charisius 280; Ashley
Cooper 101; William Coupon 128; Rahat Dar/epa 261; Pascal
Deloche/Godong 152; Francoise Demulder 140; epa 99, 171,
295; Alex Grimm/Reuters 283; Antoine Gyori/AGP 79, 135;
Ali Haider/epa 87; Zainal Abd Halim/ Reuters 162; Atef
Hassan/Reuters 174; Historical Picture Archive 8, 37; Jason
Horowitz 126; Alie Jarekji/Reuters 139; Faya Kabli/Reuters
303; Mahmoudreza Kalari/Sygma 292; Ed Kashi 16; Khaled el-
Fiqi 122; Rehan Khan/epa 137, 173; Helen King 93; Kim
Komenich/San Francisco Chronicle 113; Ynnis Kontos 305; JP
Laffont 157; Charles & Josette Lenars 308; Roy Madhur 288;
Buddy Mays 247; Colin McPherson 268; John & Lisa Merrill
211; Viviane Moos 146; Tim Mosenfelder 290; Frederic
Neema/Sygma 109; Kazuyoshi Nomach 19, 69, 104, 119, 127,
150, 176, 200; Gianni Dagli Orti 312; Christine Osborne 33;
Crack Palinggi/Reuters 72; Jason Reed/Reuters 311; Reuters
95, 170, 172, 285, 286, 306, 310; Jeffrey L. Rotman 250; Atef
Safadi/epa 144; Suhaib Salem/Reuters 17; Mohsen Shandiz
130; Jed & Kaoru Share 125; Shepard Sherbell 130, 186;
Smithsonian Institution 63, 65, 198, 213; Ted Spiegel 317;
Stapleton Collection 53; Ramin Talaie 221; The Gallery
Collection 25; Arthur Thevenart 58; Sion Touhig 218; Isabelle
Vayron/ Sygma 149; Bernd Weissbrod/epa 270; Katy Winn 291;
Michael S. Yamishita 75; **iStockphoto:** 15, 32, 50, 143, 184,
195, 203, 254, 255, 256, 264, 273, 277, 278, 294; **Public
Domain:** 299; **Roberth Hunt Library:** 39; **Shutterstock:**
Galyna Andrushko183; Ayazad 91, 178; Can Balcioglu 181;
Lance Belliers 10; Bzzuspaik 233; Joseph Calev 202, 236; Paul
Cowan 158, 232; Sam D. Cruz 48; Daniel Gilby Photography
216; Mudassar Ahmed Dar 192; Distinctive Images 102, 111;
Egypix 114; Ella's Design 179; Ettore Emanuelle Fanciulli 322;
Markus Glenn 244; Javier Gil 224; Godrick 245; Jaroslaw
Grudzinski 190; Javarman 34; Mikhall Levit 81; LiteChoices
228; Holger Mette 222; Evan Meyer 230; Morozova Oxana 240;
Lizette Potgieter 88, 107; I. Quintanilla 320; Jeremy Richards
27; Bernhard Richter 71; Savenkov 188; Camilo Torres 226;
Voyagerix 31; Dana Ward 296; Vladislavs Zarovs 243;
Thinkstock: Photos.com 318, 325, 326; **Topfoto:** 333; Image
Works 330; Roger Viollet 22.

Brown Reference Group has made every effort to contact
the copyright holder for all images included in this book.
If anyone has additional information, please contact
info@brownreference.com.

CONTENTS

CONTRIBUTORS
AND CONSULTANTS

Sulafa Abou-Samra, Visiting Associate Professor, School of Architecture, Prairie View A&M University, Texas

Sikeena Ahmed, Institute for the Study of Muslim Civilizations, Aga Khan University, London

Clinton Bennett, Adjunct Professor, Department of Philosophy, State University of New York at New Paltz

William R. Darrow, Jackson Professor of Religion, Williams College, London

Scott Girdner, Assistant Professor, Religious Studies, Western Kentucky University, Bowling Green

Faiza Hirji, Assistant Professor, Communication Studies, McMaster University, Hamilton, Ontario

Shainool Jiwa, Institute of Ismaili Studies, London

Mohammad Hassan Kalil, Assistant Professor, Department of Religion, University of Illinois at Urbana-Champaign

Omar Khalidi, Collections Librarian, Aga Khan Program for Islamic Architecture, Massachusetts Institute of Technology, Cambridge

Matthew Long, Cincinnati, Ohio

Ron Lukens-Bull, Associate Professor, Department of Sociology and Anthropology, University of Central Florida, Orlando

Baqie Badawi Muhammad, African Studies Program, Indiana University, Bloomington

Shakir Mustafa, Assistant Professor, Modern Languages and Comparative Literature, Boston University

Florian Pohl, Assistant Professor, Department of Religion, Oxford College of Emory University Oxford, Georgia

Zafar Razzaqi, Detroit, Michigan

Dona J. Stewart, Associate Professor, Department of Anthropology and Geography, Georgia State University, Atlanta

Janet Tyson, Fort Worth, Texas

William Youmans, Department of Communication Studies, University of Michigan, Ann Arbor

Kornel Zathureczky, Assistant Professor, Religious Studies Department, Saint Francis Xavier University, Nova Scotia

FOREWORD

You will not find the Muslim world labeled on a map of the globe. Indeed, the very idea of a Muslim world is challenging. It would have to include not only present-day states where Muslims live (including the 50 or so countries where they form a majority) but also all of the places far and wide that have been influenced by Islam, either historically or in terms of ideas and concepts linked to Islam that have been adopted by non-Muslim cultures. The morning ritual of drinking coffee with sugar, for example, links modern Americans to the Muslim world, where the practice originated. The English words "coffee" and "sugar" are derived from the Arabic words *qahwa* and *sukkar*; today the U.S. chain Starbucks serves coffee throughout the Middle East to a young urban clientele who favor caramel macchiatos over traditional Arab (or Turkish) coffee. There are intellectual connections, too. Algebra (*al jabr*) takes its name from a Persian work on math. In science, Islamic scholars such as Ibn Sina and Ibn Rushd (known in the West as Avicenna and Averröes, respectively) were largely responsible for preserving the knowledge of the ancient Greeks and Romans after the fall of the Roman Empire in the sixth century.

For many Westerners, however, the Muslim world remains distant and poorly understood. The 9/11 terrorist attacks in the United States in 2001 and the military campaigns that followed in Iraq and Afghanistan have increased Western awareness of Muslims, yet the information received about Islam is often one-dimensional or based on stereotypes.

The increase of Islamic militancy in western Asia, for example, has highlighted the most negative form of jihad. Originally a word with a range of meanings, including the spiritual conflict between a Muslim's faith and doubts, jihad has been reduced to refer primarily to an Islamic "holy war" against non-Muslims. Extremists have tried to depict terrorism as a broad conflict between their own notions of a Christian West and a Muslim world. The idea that the United States is at war with Islam or Islam is at war with the West creates fear and misunderstanding and contributes to the terrorists' goals.

THE THREE ABRAHAMIC RELIGIONS

The Muslim world is dynamic and multi-dimensional. It does not exist in isolation. Its history has been one of nearly 1,500 years of interaction with non-Muslim regions through trade, politics, or the movement of peoples; indeed, its historical development is inexorably intertwined with the Judeo–Christian perspective that underpins Western culture and heritage.

Islam is one of the three Abrahamic religions. Like Christianity and Judaism, it is part of a spiritual tradition traced to the biblical patriarch Abraham. All three religions developed in western Asia and view Abraham, considered the world's first monotheist, as a progenitor. Although there are differences between the faiths, all three share a belief in a single God, known as Yaweh to Jews and Allah to Muslims. Key individuals (such as Moses and Noah) are found in the holy books of all three. While Muslims revere both the Hebrew prophet

Moses and Jesus, they see Jesus as one of a number of prophets rather than the son of God. They believe Muhammad to be the final and most perfect of God's prophets.

Because Judaism, Christianity, and Islam developed in the same geographical area and coexisted for centuries, it is easy to find commonalities in their doctrines and traditions. Jerusalem is important to all three faiths, and sharing control over this sacred territory has provoked conflict for many centuries. The Crusades, fought over nearly 200 years in the 12th and 13th centuries between the Christian states of Europe and the Muslim-dominated polities around Jerusalem, remain a symbol of Christian–Muslim conflict readily invoked by some Muslims and Christians to provoke new conflict.

A FAR-FLUNG CIVILIZATION

A century after Muhammad's death (632 CE), the area under Muslim rule stretched from the Atlantic Ocean to Central Asia and included peoples of many ethnicities who spoke various languages. Muslims ruled from southern Spain to India, where the white marble Taj Mahal marks a Muslim emperor's grief over the death of his wife. A series of Islamic empires created a cultural legacy that links the Muslim world inexorably to the ideas and philosophies associated with Christian Europe. By the 14th century, however, the Islamic empires had lost much of their territory and influence, beset by both internal and external challenges. Soon Europe surpassed the Islamic world in key technological developments, especially in navigation.

During the Age of Discovery (15th–17th centuries) Europe established control over large parts of the Americas and also Asia and Africa, where many Muslims lived. At the end of World War I, the majority of Muslims came under European colonial rule. By the latter part of the 20th century, many Muslims had organized independent countries, sometimes through rebellion. The legacy of the colonial period, often seen as a period of European exploitation, still influences the opinions of many Muslims toward the West.

DIVERSITY WITHIN ISLAM

Historically, as now, the Muslim community was extremely diverse. By the time of Islam's great empires, the Muslim community had already split into two main factions: Sunni and Shia. A larger number of sects and religious interpretations of Islam also existed, often reflecting local conditions and events. There is no single Islamic law (Sharia). Sharia, better translated as "way" or "path," contains four main schools in the Sunni tradition and two in the Shia. Although the Arabian Peninsula, and Mecca and Medina in particular, are the historical heartland of Islam, most of the world's Muslims are not Arab. The most populous Muslim country, Indonesia (population 230 million), is located in southeast Asia.

Today some 1.5 billion people are Muslim, nearly one-fifth of the world's population. It is impossible to summarize their beliefs, experiences, and opinions. Any attempt to reach a greater understanding of the Muslim world will raise more questions; this work will answer many of them and, ideally, prompt further enquiry.

Dona J. Stewart
Center for Middle East Peace, Culture, and
Development; and Department of Anthropology
and Geography; Georgia State University

Chapter 1

DEFINING ISLAM AND MUSLIMS

Originating from the teachings of the Prophet Muhammad in the seventh century, Islam has since gained more than a billion followers in nations across the world. It is the dominant religious and cultural force among the peoples of northern Africa and western, central, and southern Asia.

Any useful understanding of Islam and the Muslim world must begin with an examination of the religion's core beliefs and practices. These can be found in the revelations made by the Archangel Gabriel to Muhammad—the basis of the work known in English as the Koran—and in the Sunna, the massive body of literature that describes the sayings and actions of the Prophet and deals with every aspect of Muslims' lives.

The Koran consists of 114 suras (chapters) subdivided into varying numbers of verses (*ayat*). Muslims regard the Koran as the infallible word of God. Although they have debated whether it was created and then revealed to Muhammad or if it has existed since the creation of the world, they generally agree about the book's authority, which is reinforced by a long tradition of critical commentary and exegesis (interpretive studies) known as *tafsir*.

The Sunna has consolidated its prestige in Islam because of the need for guidance through a recognized written authority in addition to the Koran. The Sunna has been studied by Muslim scholars since the dawn

of Islam; they developed various techniques to authenticate sayings that were ascribed to Muhammad. Debates continue about the authenticity of a small number of other sayings, and some Muslims fall back on discredited sayings in their attempts to justify various religious, social, economic,

The Sunna has been studied by Muslim scholars since the dawn of Islam; they developed various techniques to authenticate sayings that were ascribed to Muhammad.

or political practices. A key controversy concerns a handful of contentious sayings that demean women and deny their rights. Some Muslims use these sayings to justify the physical abuse of women, but mainstream Islamic thought emphasizes the numerous occasions on which Muhammad stressed kindness and gentle behavior toward women.

This 19th-century lithograph depicts Mecca, the birthplace of the Prophet Muhammad and the cradle of the Islamic religion.

The Koran and the Sunna can be interpreted in numerous ways. The diversity of Islamic traditions across the world, however, comes not only from the different interpretations of the two main written sources but also from interactions between Islam and the preexisting traditions of the indigenous peoples who converted to Islam. This is especially evident in the non-Arab parts of the Muslim world, where the faith has taken root in spite of the fact that the local languages are different from the Arabic in which the holy texts are written.

In some countries, people learn passages of the Koran by heart, and that is often the only Arabic they know. Elsewhere—notably in southern Asia and the Pacific region—the languages used for religious purposes are Malay and its variants rather than Arabic.

THE EMERGENCE OF ISLAM

When Islam first appeared in the seventh century in Mecca, the flourishing commercial city was controlled by a small group of rich Arabs who were polytheists (believers in several gods). The atmosphere

This handwritten version of the Koran was produced on the East African island of Zanzibar. The holy book of Islam plays an active role in the daily life of Muslims all over the world.

THE FIRST MALE CONVERT

One of the most persistent questions in Islam is that of the identity of the first man to convert to the faith after hearing Muhammad's account of his revelations from the Archangel Gabriel. It is accepted by all Muslims that the first convert to Islam was Muhammad's wife, Khadija, but the identity of the first male convert is a controversial topic with opinions often divided along sectarian lines.

According to Ibn Ishaq (c. 704–767), Muhammad's earliest biographer and near contemporary, the original male convert was Ali ibn Abi Talib (c. 600–661), the Prophet's cousin and later his son-in-law. That has become the view of the Shia Muslims, who form the majority in Islam. The Shiites also assert that the first two Muslims to worship in public were members of Muhammad's family: Ali and Muhammad's first wife, Khadija. Shiites believe that Muhammad prayed to Allah at the Kaaba, the building in Mecca that contains a black stone, possibly a meteorite fragment, which,

according to Muslim tradition, was a house of worship first built by Abraham. Over the course of time it had become a center for acts of worship by the pantheists (believers in many gods) who then dominated Arabia. Conversely, the Sunni Muslims (the largest minority Muslim sect) believe that Ali did not adopt the faith by his own free will—he was, after all, only a child at the time. In the Sunni view, the first man voluntarily to call himself a Muslim was Abu Bakr (c. 573–634), Muhammad's father-in-law.

Although no one knows for certain who first decided to follow Muhammad and pledge allegiance to Islam, the date of the religion's foundation may be pinpointed with unusual accuracy for events of that period. Historians agree that the Muslim faith was established sometime between 610, when Muhammad first described his revelation to his closest confidants, and 612, when the Prophet began preaching in public in Mecca.

there was hedonistic (pleasure-seeking), and moral laxity intensified self-centered pursuits. Tribal disputes—both internal and with neighboring peoples—often caused conflicts that lasted for years. Trade with the rest of the region brought Mecca not only material riches but also contacts with Christianity, Judaism, and Zoroastrianism that left strong marks on the emerging Arab Islamic civilization.

For Muhammad, who grew up in Mecca, there was much to learn, and much that he wanted to change. It was in this complex society that the Prophet began preaching a new faith with an emphasis on moral and social responsibility. His message was greeted enthusiastically by the disfranchised and with horror by the rich

and powerful. Islam's birth was anything but smooth, but it came at an opportune time in the history of Arabia.

Muhammad developed into an accomplished, skillful politician and military commander. When the Muslims were weak, he avoided confrontation, as in 615, when he encouraged the migration of many of his followers to Abyssinia (modern Ethiopia), and in 622, when he led the bigger migration known in Arabic as the *hijra* (Anglicized as the Hejira) from Mecca to Medina.

THE INFLUENCE OF MUHAMMAD

Muslims hold Muhammad in a reverence that is rarely understood in the West. They regard the Prophet as a model to be emulated, and so his words and actions, as contained in the Sunna, have become key components of Islamic laws and doctrine. Subsequent Muslim rulers aspired to emulate Muhammad's adaptability when they came to deal with political, social, and military issues. The Sunna is so pervasive in Muslims' lives that it affects not only the central tenets of faith but also small details of life, such as personal hygiene and the treatment of parents, wives, neighbors, and friends.

The speed with which Islam spread was another testament to Muhammad's abilities as a leader. His successors largely abided by the principles he established, spreading Islam with considerable tolerance of the cultures that were being invited to embrace the new religion. In the 100 years that followed the Prophet's death in 632, they brought a vast expanse of the known world—from Spain across Central Asia to India—into a new Arab Muslim empire.

Large communities in western Africa began to convert to Islam from the 13th century, but the most extensive spread of the religion occurred in the late 19th century and the early 20th century, partly as a result of the decline of European colonialism in the developing world.

Muslims are now the majority in about 50 countries, and they form significant minorities in about a dozen more nations in Asia, Africa, and Europe, as well as in the United States, where they comprise 0.6 percent of the population. The Muslim minority in India is currently estimated to be more than 150 million people, which is almost half of the total number of Muslims in all the Arab countries.

With most Muslims today living in non-Arab countries, Islam is constantly interacting with numerous other cultural traditions and is itself changing in the process. For example, U.S. Muslims who were members of the Nation of Islam instituted a form of the religion that was very different from orthodox practices. They had temples instead of mosques, and they considered the founder of the group, Elijah Muhammad, rather than Prophet Muhammad, to be God's messenger. In the late 1970s, the Nation of Islam moved closer to the mainstream, but it still retains some of its distinguishing features, such as an emphasis on African American issues.

Among the characteristics of mainstream Islam that differentiate it from other faiths are its special rituals and demands, notably the five daily prayers, the month-long fast during Ramadan, and the dress code observed by many Muslim women. The mosque, too, does not look like or function in the same way as most churches or temples. Mosques are where Muslims pray, socialize, and study, and they remain a powerful focus for Muslim social as well as religious life.

ISLAMIC BELIEFS AND PRACTICES

The fundamental tenets of Islam are the same as those of Christianity and Judaism. Central to all three is monotheism (belief in a single deity). The Muslim God is Allah, which means "the God" in Arabic. The root of the Arabic word *islam* has several meanings, but those most directly related to the religion are derived from verbs meaning "to submit," and "to profess belief in" or "to convert." It can also mean "to be a member of the monotheistic community;" Muslims therefore often refer to the Biblical Jewish patriarch Abraham as a coreligionist because he was a monotheist (worshipper of one God). *Islam* can also mean "to submit (to God)," and a massive body of Muslim literature supports this sense. Although submission to God has been interpreted in numerous ways, the reading most readily supported by Islamic traditions emphasizes acceptance of God's will and human choice and responsibility. The verb "to reason" occurs more than 50 times in the Koran, which constantly emphasizes the need for reflection and thoughtful choices. Belief in God and the submission to divine will are the keys to the practice of Islam.

Definition of the term *Muslim* depends upon religious faith, but the practical application of the term to individuals also accounts for ethnicity, national origin, color, and class. The flexibility of Islam enables the faith to survive and flourish in sometimes unsympathetic contexts.

One major contributory factor to the success of Islam is its adherents' belief in *ummah* (the worldwide Muslim community). Codified in the Koran, the true purposes of *ummah* are to glorify God, to do what is right, and to help the less fortunate. However, the concept has sometimes been manipulated by fundamentalists for political purposes.

Like all major religions, Islam has several divisions, and these naturally lead to contradictory and competing views. The two main divisions of Islam are the Sunnis, who constitute about 85 percent of Muslims, and the Shia, who form the majority of the rest, and both groups have further subdivisions. Shia Islam developed out of disappointment over the sidelining of Imam Ali, Muhammad's cousin and son-in-law, when the first successor to the prophet was chosen. Ali later became the fourth caliph, but by that time it was difficult to heal the divisions between Muslims. Sects have appeared in Islam

throughout its history. One of the most recent, Wahhabism, appeared in the 19th century. Wahhabis are deeply conservative; their leading members are the ruling family of Saudi Arabia.

THE FIVE PILLARS OF ISLAM

All practicing Muslims believe in the fulfillment of the Five Pillars of Islam: *shahada* (profession of faith); *salat* (ritual prayer); *zakat* (almsgiving); *sawm* (fasting during Ramadan); and hajj (pilgrimage to Mecca). In performing these obligations, it is always the intention rather than the appearance that counts. Fasting to lose weight, for example, is disapproved because the personal benefit that may be derived from so doing diminishes the true, spiritual purpose of abstinence. Universal Muslim recognition of the Five Pillars reinforces the *ummah*.

Muslims profess their faith in the simple declaration, "I bear witness that there is no god but God (Allah), and that Muhammad is the messenger of God," which affirms the oneness of God and the status of Muhammad as his prophet. Professing the faith is fundamental for the rest of the pillars, and its absence nullifies all other practices. The declaration is always a part of daily prayers, and hence it is repeated countless times by observant Muslims. Muslims also repeat the profession of faith outside prayers, at funerals and in nonreligious contexts.

Prayer is next in importance. Muslims pray five times a day. For practical reasons, many Shia Muslims are allowed to combine the two midday and the two evening prayers. Muslims can pray wherever they are—at home, on the road, or in a mosque. They can pray alone or in groups, and all that is needed is a clean spot.

Muslims face toward Mecca when they pray, and people of all ages, ethnicities, and social status congregate at the mosque for prayers. In many places women also attend the mosque; they usually pray in a separate part of the building. The prayers are preceded by the *adhan* (call to prayer), which was traditionally uttered by a muezzin (crier) but which in modern Muslim countries is usually broadcast through amplified speakers from mosque minarets. The prayers include recitations of short passages from the Koran, the glorification of God, and supplications for God's assistance in various matters. The Koran specifies no rituals or times for prayers, but these were established by Muhammad and they continue with hardly any changes.

Zakat means "almsgiving", but the word also means "purification"; consequently, Muslims are required to give generously to help themselves as well as those receiving the benefit. Although the funds generated through *zakat* are to help the needy and to support Muslim institutions, the act of donating is not considered charity but a religious obligation. Muslims do give to charities, of course, but these are actions that are encouraged rather than required as articles of faith. The annual percentage for *zakat* is at least 2.5 percent of a Muslim's assets, not just his or her income, and many Muslims willingly pay a higher percentage. In addition to *zakat*, Shia Muslims pay another percentage, about one-fifth of their income, to maintain religious institutions.

The fast is a yearly obligation in the month of Ramadan, during which Muslims are not allowed to eat, drink, or engage in sexual activity from daybreak to sunset. It is intended to provide Muslims with opportunities to internalize discipline in several forms. To abstain from physical

pleasures is only one aspect of Ramadan. Muslims celebrate the month as an extended occasion for reflection and spiritual growth. Those who cannot fast because of work or illness can make up for the missed days later in the year, and there are other provisions for those who cannot fast at all. It was during Ramadan that Muhammad received his revelation, and the night on which that happened is now known as the "night of Glory." During Ramadan, the fast is broken every day at sunset. It is not unusual for Muslims to stay up for much of every night throughout Ramadan. At the end of the

Muslims profess their faith in the simple declaration, "I bear witness that there is no god but God (Allah), and that Muhammad is the messenger of God."

month, there is a celebration known as Eid al-Fitr (the festival of breaking the fast), a celebration that is a joyous event among Muslims.

The hajj—the pilgrimage to Mecca—is one of the pillars of Islam. All Muslims who are physically able and can reasonably afford to make the journey are required to perform the hajj at least once in their lifetime.

Every year, about two million Muslims congregate in Mecca to participate in hajj rituals such as walking around the Kaaba and throwing stones at three pillars that represent Satan. This action commemorates Abraham's successful resistance of the devil's attempt to dissuade Abraham and his family from disobeying God's commands.

Among other pilgrim traditions are the ceremonial run that commemorates Hagar's search for water in the desert and the taking of water from the well of Zamzam, which represents God's benevolent provision of water for Hagar and her son Ismail (Ishmael), who is regarded as the patriarch of the Arabs.

At the end of the hajj, the ritual slaughter of a lamb symbolizes God's substitution of an animal when Abraham was called upon to sacrifice his son. The white garments that all pilgrims have to wear throughout the six-day event are simple and seamless and are taken by many to symbolize the egalitarian nature of Islam. The ceremonies culminate in the four-day festival of Eid al-Adha.

Although the requirements of the Five Pillars of Islam may seem onerous, it is important to remember that one of the principal attractions of the Muslim faith to generations of willing converts has been its benevolence to those who cannot satisfy its most rigorous demands. Verses in the Koran unequivocally state that Muslims need not overburden themselves.

CONCLUSION

In historical terms, Islam is the most recently established of the world's three great monotheistic religions. In its purest form, its purpose today is the same as it was when it was founded by the Prophet Muhammad in the seventh century: it seeks not to supplant Judaism and Christianity but to supplement them. Monotheism and the line of messengers and prophets who preached it are just a few of the shared principles and heritage

A Muslim prays in the courtyard of a mosque in Delhi, India. In Islam, all acts of worship, apart from Friday lunchtime prayers, may be performed in any convenient location.

ISLAM, CHRISTIANITY, AND JUDAISM

The Koran acknowledges Christianity, Judaism, and Zoroastrianism in ways that include them in a family of faiths that can coexist. The Prophet Muhammad said that his message was not new, and the Koran supports that in numerous references to Moses and Jesus, among others, as earlier messengers who preached monotheism. The Arabic word for God, *Allah*, literally means "the God," a concept that was familiar to pre-Islamic Arabs in spite of their polytheism (belief in many gods).

The common denominator of all these religions is monotheism (belief in a single deity). What sets Islam apart from Christianity and Judaism is its claim to be the true and final message from God. According to the Koran, the revelations received by Moses and Jesus were later corrupted. For instance, the Koran rejects the claim that Jesus was the son of God and dismisses the Christian concept of the Trinity (God the Father, God the Son, and God the Holy Spirit in a single entity).

Among the links between Islam and the Judeo-Christian tradition is the reappearance of several Biblical stories in the Koran: Adam and Eve and the forbidden tree; the infant Moses left on the river and his later encounters with the pharaoh; Joseph and Potiphar's wife; and the life of Mary and the birth of Jesus. The prophets of the Bible are cited reverentially in the Koran, and none is accorded greater respect than Jesus, who—in spite of

the Muslim denial of his divinity—has always been a highly influential figure in Islamic thought. The Koran recognizes Jesus's miracles, and specifically cites those in which he restored the sight of a blind man, healed a leper, and raised the dead.

One whole sura (chapter) of the Koran is entitled "Mary" and retells in detail the story of Jesus's miraculous birth. Indeed, Mary is the only woman named in the Koran, and there are more references to her in the holy book of Islam than in the Bible. The Koran also specifically identifies Jesus and Mary as "a sign for all people" and honors Mary as an example for the faithful to emulate.

Islam has spread beyond its roots in Arabia. The Islamic Center of America in Dearborn, Michigan, which has a mosque and a range of amenities, is the largest facility of its kind in the United States.

Yet, in spite of its strong affinities with Judaism and Christianity, Islam differs from those two religions in many important theological matters. For Muslims, Muhammad brought the final and true message; therefore Muslims consider him the "seal" of all the prophets in the sense that he has given the sole uncorrupted message of God to humanity. While moderate Muslims are content to accept the two preexistent monotheistic religions as evolutionary stages of the final truth, some Islamists claim that the Jews altered the original Torah that was revealed to Moses and that Christians have exaggerated the importance of Jesus for their own ends. Such opinions are highly contentious and have been the source of conflict between Islam and the other faiths.

that bind Muslims to Christians and Jews. Such realization is at the heart of Islam's basic tolerance of other faiths.

Like other religions, Islam has divisions and doctrines, and friction and conflicts between them do occur. These variations of the faith are the natural result of the many diverse cultures among which Islam has spread. Islam may be a monotheistic religion, but it is not monolithic. Certain individuals and groups who happen to have the resources have claimed to speak for he whole of Islam at one point or other.

Such claims need to be scrutinized. It is unfortunate that, in the early 21st century, largely political organizations such as al-Qaeda have made religious claims to justify a terrorist agenda. Islamic traditions over the ages and among numerous cultures have preached moderation and have shunned extremism. Especially in Western Europe and North America, better understanding of Islam will make it more difficult for extremist and fringe organizations to claim that they speak for the entire religion.

See Also

Life of Muhammad 18–21 ❖ Beliefs 48–67 ❖ Peoples of the Book 68–71 ❖ Practices 72–97 ❖ Scriptures and Doctrine 102–123 ❖

Muslim pilgrims throw stones at pillars symbolizing the devil during the hajj pilgrimage at Mena, outside Mecca in Saudi Arabia.

The Life of Muhammad

Muhammad was the founder of the Muslim religion and, as such, one of the most influential humans in the history of the world. He is also known as the Prophet of Islam.

Muhammad ibn Abd-Allah (570-632 CE) was born and raised in the Arabian city of Mecca (in present-day Saudi Arabia). Although Muslims do not regard him as divine, they revere him as the "best of creation" and a role model for all times. His influence may be observed not only in the fact that Muhammad is currently the most popular first name in the world, but also in the way that many Muslims model their conduct on the Sunna (the Prophet's recorded actions, sayings, and teachings).

Every year, tribes from all over Arabia would visit the Kaaba, where each tribe would pray to a particular god or goddess. These pilgrimages were an important source of revenue for the inhabitants of Mecca.

Before the life of Muhammad, the dominant faiths in Arabia were various forms of paganism. Although most Arabs had a notion of a supreme deity, whom they called Allah, they were pantheists who also believed in other gods and goddesses. These lesser deities were often represented as idols and could be found in both private and public locations. The most public place of worship was the Kaaba, a mysterious cube-shaped building in the center of Mecca. Every year, tribes from all over Arabia would visit the Kaaba, where each tribe would pray to a particular god or goddess. These pilgrimages were an important source of revenue for the inhabitants of Mecca. Over time, some Meccans became very wealthy and the gap between rich and poor grew wider. As a result, a social crisis developed in the city.

That was the historical context in which Muhammad was born. His father, Abd-Allah, died before Muhammad was born, and his mother, Amina, died when he was only six years old. After his prominent grandfather Abd al-Muttalib passed away only two years later, he was placed in the care of his uncle, Abu Talib.

As an adult, Muhammad became a merchant and was employed by a wealthy widow named Khadija. Khadija was impressed by Muhammad, who became known as *al-amin* (the trustworthy one). Khadija, who was either 10 or 15 years his senior, decided to propose marriage. The 25-year-old Muhammad accepted her offer, and the couple later had several children.

RELIGIOUS FOUNDATION

The story of Islam begins when Muhammad was 40 years old. Every so often, Muhammad abandoned the hustle and bustle of Mecca and spent time reflecting in isolation. On one occasion, while he was in the cave of Hira on the Mountain of Light (Jabal al-Nur), not far from the city, the Archangel Gabriel appeared and spoke to him about the true nature of God. Scholars now regard this apparition as the earliest revelation of the Muslim holy book, the Koran, which Muslims believe to be the word of God (rather than of Muhammad).

At first, Muhammad did not know how to interpret this incident. He is described as having been afraid and troubled; however, his wife Khadija comforted him and helped him to make sense of his experience. Thereafter, Muhammad received many such revelations throughout his life and came to see himself as a prophet of Allah.

This photograph shows evening prayer at the Mosque of the Prophet in Medina. Around two million pilgrims visit the city annually during the hajj (pilgrimage).

Time line

570 CE	Muhammad is born in Mecca.
576 CE	Muhammad's mother, Amina, dies.
595 CE	Muhammad marries his first wife, Khadija.
610 CE	Muhammad receives a visitation from the Archangel Gabriel.
622 CE	Muhammad leads his followers on the flight from Mecca to Medina.
624 CE	The Muslims defeat the Meccans at the Battle of Badr.
625 CE	The Muslims are defeated at the Battle of Uhud.
627 CE	The Meccans attack Medina.
629 CE	The Treaty of Hudaybiyya brings peace between the Muslims and the Meccans.
632 CE	Muhammad makes his final return to Mecca; he dies in Medina later the same year.

SPREADING THE WORD

The Koran's basic message is that there is only one God; that Muhammad is a prophet in an ancient line of prophets that includes Abraham, Moses, and Jesus; and that there is an afterlife in which people will be rewarded or punished depending on how good or evil, faithful or unfaithful they have been during their time on earth.

Muhammad's claim to be a prophet was rejected by most Meccans, who still believed in numerous gods and goddesses and denied that there was an afterlife. The inhabitants of the city also felt that Muhammad posed a threat to their traditions and their most important source of wealth—the annual visits to the Kaaba made by pilgrims from all over the Arabian Peninsula.

Muhammad, however, did not view himself as the founder of a new faith. As far as he was concerned, he was merely preaching the same message as the earlier prophets. The only differences were the context and the audience. Neither did he hope to end the established Arabian culture, just those aspects of it that he regarded as immoral. For example, he valued the concept of the pilgrimage to the Kaaba because this holy site was believed to have been established by Abraham and his son Ishmael as a place of monotheistic worship. Muhammad aimed to cleanse the Kaaba of the idols that, he believed, were corrupting its original purpose.

ADVANCES AND SETBACKS

Beginning with Khadija, more and more people began to accept Muhammad's message, including his companion Abu Bakr and his cousin Ali, the son of Abu Talib. While some rich people converted to Islam, the religion was particularly attractive to those who had little or nothing. People who opposed existing Meccan practices, such as the killing of female infants and the physical abuse of slaves and others who were weak, regarded Muhammad as a savior.

Threatened by these developments, the pagans of Mecca began to persecute the most vulnerable followers of Muhammad. As a result, Muhammad instructed some of his followers to emigrate to eastern Africa to reside there temporarily under the tolerant rule of a Christian king called the Negus. Meanwhile, tensions in Mecca intensified. Nearly a decade after Muhammad first proclaimed his message, his mission was becoming more challenging. This was especially the case following the death of two important people in his life: his supportive wife Khadija and his uncle Abu Talib, who protected Muhammad despite never having publicly converted to Islam himself. During this difficult period, Muhammad survived an assassination attempt and experienced what he described as a miraculous night journey to Jerusalem. There, he led the previous prophets in prayer, then ascended through the heavens and entered the presence of God. On his return to earth, Muhammad announced what he had experienced and informed his followers of God's decree that Muslims were to pray five times daily.

From Mecca to Medina and Back

With the situation in Mecca deteriorating, Muhammad made a great breakthrough. A group of people from the nearby city of Medina, which was called Yathrib at the time, met with Muhammad and pledged their allegiance to him. Medina had recently suffered a devastating civil war and needed a single unifying leader. Muhammad was invited to fill this role, and he agreed. Shortly afterward, he instructed his followers in Mecca to leave everything behind and emigrate to Medina. There, Muslims, along with Jews and pagans, were finally able to establish the kind of community they had only dreamed of in Mecca. This emigration, or *hijra* (Anglicized as the Hejira), which occurred in 622 CE, now marks the start of the Islamic lunar calendar.

Although the followers of Muhammad had left Mecca, tensions between them and the inhabitants of the city remained. Muhammad had originally forbidden his followers from fighting but, in the deteriorating political climate, he changed his opinion and commanded them to defend themselves.

The conflict between the two sides came to a head during the second year after the *hijra* (624 CE) at the Battle of Badr, where the Muslims, though greatly outnumbered, defeated the Meccans. The Meccans hit back, however, with a victory the following year at the Battle of Uhud in which many Muslims were killed and Muhammad himself was injured.

In the fifth year after the *hijra* (627 CE), the Meccans allied with other Arabian tribes and attacked Medina. The Muslims successfully withstood the siege, thanks to a massive ditch that they had dug around much of the city.

Throughout the Medinan period, Muhammad was also opposed by three local Jewish tribes (there were, on the other hand, numerous Medinan Jews who were quite supportive) and was threatened by people within his own ranks who claimed to be Muslim but were in fact unbelievers. However, Muhammad ultimately succeeded in quelling all opposition.

In 629 CE, Muhammad made peace with the Meccans by the Treaty of Hudaybiyya. However, the agreement was soon broken when the Meccans attacked one of Muhammad's allies. The Muslims—who had now gained many new converts—then amassed an army of around 10,000, occupied Mecca, and restored the Kaaba as a monotheistic place of worship. The Meccans then joined Muhammad and fought alongside him. Eventually, nearly all of Arabia pledged allegiance to Muhammad, who remained based in Medina.

Death and Legacy

In the 10th year after the *hijra* (632 CE), Muhammad again visited Mecca, where he delivered his famous final sermon, which affirmed the rights of women and men, rich and poor, black and white, Arab and non-Arab. Soon afterward, he died at his home in Medina. Muhammad's role as Muslim leader was then taken over by Abu Bakr, the first caliph (successor to the Prophet).

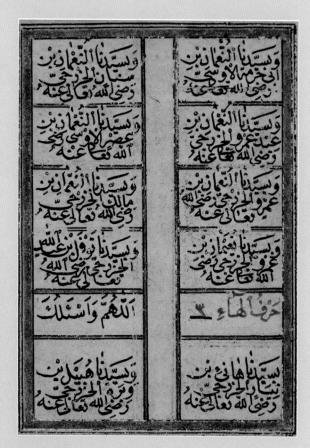

A page from a 19th-century manuscript entitled *Martyrs of the Battle of Badr*. The calligraphy is the work of the artist Ash-Shaykh Muhammad as-Sadi.

Chapter 2

BRIEF HISTORY OF ISLAM

Founded in the Arabian Peninsula in the seventh century CE, Islam later spread across dozens of countries in northern Africa and southern Asia and today has more than one billion adherents. Its influence has ebbed and flowed during the intervening period; ages of expansion and achievement have been interspersed with drastic declines.

Islam emerged in the seventh century CE. The founder of the religion, Muhammad, was born in the Arabian Peninsula, a region on the edge of the Fertile Crescent, a bow-shaped stretch of arable land extending from the Persian Gulf northward to Syria and then south again down the coast of the Mediterranean Sea to Palestine and Egypt. In the Fertile Crescent, some of the earliest civilizations flourished in Mesopotamia (modern Iraq) and along the banks of the Nile River.

The deserts of Arabia had been peripheral to the main centers of ancient civilization, but the Arab peoples who inhabited them were by no means isolated from developments in the surrounding region. By the time of Muhammad's birth in 570, western Asia was dominated by two rival powers—the Byzantine Empire and the Sassanian Empire. The Christian Byzantines, based in Constantinople (modern Istanbul, Turkey), ruled the western territories, including parts of Italy along with Greece and the Balkans, part of the Anatolian Peninsula (modern Turkey), the eastern Mediterranean, Egypt,

and some of the North African coast. The language of the Byzantine Empire was Greek, and its official religion was Christianity.

The Sassanians controlled the eastern lands, including the territories of modern-day Iran, Iraq, Afghanistan, Turkey, and Syria.

The deserts of Arabia had been peripheral to the main centers of ancient civilization, but the Arab peoples who inhabited them were by no means isolated from developments in the surrounding region.

Their Persian-speaking empire—which, in varying forms, had controlled the region for around 1,200 years—relied on a strong bureaucracy and a centralized government to rule their subjects unified by adherence to the religious principles of Zorastrianism (see box). Many of the cultural traditions developed under the Sassanian Empire were later adopted by Islamic rulers.

This 18th-century miniature painting shows the Archangel Gabriel announcing to Muhammad his mission as the Prophet of Islam. Visual representations of Muhammad ordinarily exclude any depiction of his face.

The Byzantine and Sassanian empires shared a long border and fought each other continuously for control of the central part of western Asia. Neither side anticipated that its greatest challenge would be the rise of a new religious power in the relative backwater of the Arabian Peninsula.

At the start of the seventh century, the Arabian Peninsula remained geographically remote—on the fringes of Byzantine and Sassanian territory but beyond the control of either empire. Arabian society was based on tribal or kin-based social groups. Lacking a centralized government, each tribe had to be self-reliant, solving its own disputes and allocating its own resources. In the harsh desert climate, traditional Bedouin society developed values that would later influence the characteristics of Islam. Chief among them were a stringent honor code, an emphasis on hospitality, a strong oral tradition, and respect for horsemanship and bravery in battle.

Mecca was the principal city in the Hejaz, the southwestern coastal region of Arabia that borders the Red Sea. The city was a key staging post for the caravan trade and the site of Arabia's most important pagan shrine, the Kaaba. A small, cube-shaped building, the Kaaba contained in its walls a black stone, possibly a meteorite remnant, which was thought to date back to the time of the creation of the world. Before the advent of Islam, the Kaaba housed hundreds of pagan images and was thought to be the center of the world and the gateway to heaven. Every year, the tribes in the region declared a truce and went on pilgrimages to worship at the shrine.

ZOROASTRIANISM

Based on the teachings of the prophet Zarathustra or Zoroaster (c. 628–551 BCE), Zoroastrianism was the ancient Persians' dominant religion from the fifth century BCE. There are still Zoroastrian communities today, primarily in Iran but also in India, where believers are known as Parsis. A few Zoroastrians also live in North America. As a rule, Zoroastrians do not proselytize or seek converts.

Zoroastrians are monotheists, worshipping a single creator god called Ahura Mazda. Ahura Mazda is associated with the element of fire, which is considered pure and plays a significant part in religious rituals. To Zoroastrians, the universe is the theater of an ongoing struggle between the forces of truth and order and those of deception and chaos. They believe that truth, personified by Ahura Mazda, will ultimately prevail over the forces of darkness, at which point the world will end and all creatures, dead and living, will be reunited in Ahura Mazda. People are important actors in this conflict, for their choices can contribute to the cause of truth. Thus the concept of free will plays an important part in Zoroastrian belief.

Zoroastrianism became the official religion of the Persian Achemenid Empire in the sixth century BCE. Although many of its sacred books were burned by Alexander the Great when he invaded Persia in 330 BCE, the faith itself continued to thrive, becoming a state religion under Sassanian rule. After the defeat of the Sassanians by the forces of Islam, Zoroastrians received protected status, along with Christians and Jews, as *dhimmis* (People of the Book), although in practice many converted to Islam.

The Kaaba was also an important source of power for the city's ruling tribe, the Quraysh, who guarded the shrine. The Quraysh were split into numerous clans that were often in conflict with each other.

THE REVELATION OF ISLAM

Known as the Prophet of Islam, Muhammad ibn Abd Allah was a Quraysh by birth. His father died before he was born and his mother died when he was six years old. He was raised thereafter by an uncle, reducing his status in a society in which family affiliation was a key factor. Even so, he grew up to prosper as a merchant and was hired by a wealthy widow, Khadijah, to manage her business dealings. The two eventually married.

Muhammad's life was transformed around the age of 40 when he began to receive messages from God, delivered by the Archangel Gabriel. According to Muslim tradition, Islam was revealed to Muhammad; in effect, Muhammad became

This map of Arabia and South Asia is one of 33 charts in an atlas compiled by the Venetian cartographer Battista Agnese (c. 1500–1564).

a vessel for the word of God, charged with the task of carrying it to others. The earliest converts to Islam were Muhammad's own family, notably his wife Khadijah. The message itself, teaching submission to a single, all-powerful God, challenged the existing pagan order in Mecca. Muhammad's teachings also contained strong themes of social justice—among them, the equality of all people and the obligation to care for the poor and weak— which greatly appealed to the many people who were disadvantaged in a kin-based society. All adherents to Islam, regardless of wealth or status, were considered to be part of the *ummah* (religious community). In the early days, the *ummah* consisted largely of slaves, craftspeople, and the least powerful members of society.

The merchants who controlled Mecca at first tolerated Muhammad, but relations soured when the Prophet denounced the wealth of the ruling elite and its pagan beliefs, thereby challenging the foundations of Quraysh power. In 622, Muhammad and his small band of followers were forced

MUSLIM SPAIN

For eight centuries, Muslims ruled southern Spain, known in Arabic as al-Andalus. There they created a vibrant civilization famed for its artistic achievements and religious tolerance. The Muslims of the Iberian Peninsula were known to their Christian opponents as *moros* (Moors).

Muslim rule was first established in Iberia in 711 CE by a Berber army acknowledging the overall suzerainty of the Damascus-based Umayyad caliphate. Power subsequently devolved to local Muslim rulers but, in 756, Abd ar-Rahman—a member of the Umayyad ruling family who had survived the slaughter of his relatives when the Abbasids seized control of the caliphate in Damascus— arrived in Spain and proclaimed himself emir (prince) of Córdoba, the region's largest city. Abd ar-Rahman's grandson later expanded Umayyad control throughout southern Iberia and into northern Africa, proclaiming himself caliph, a claim that challenged the Abbasid claim to sole spiritual authority in the Islamic world.

In its golden age in the 10th to 12th centuries, the Andalusian capital of Córdoba had a population of 500,000, making it the largest city in Europe. While the rest of the continent was still mired in the Dark Ages, Andalusia was a global cultural center. Writing in Arabic, scholars made significant advances in such fields as mathematics, astronomy, and medicine. Europeans seeking knowledge came to the city from the Christian lands to the north, attracted by the work of philosophers such as Averroës (Ibn Rushd). There they also had access to works produced elsewhere in the Muslim world by such leading thinkers as the polymath Avicenna (Ibn Sina), which helped lay the foundation for Europe's Renaissance. Perhaps the region's most impressive characteristic was its culture of religious tolerance. Andalusian society included Christians, Muslims of various ethnic origins, and Jews, all at a time when Jews faced persecution in Christian Europe. Al-Andalus was so culturally and economically rich that it was described as "the ornament of the world."

Even so, Iberia's displaced Christian rulers never ceased fighting to regain their lost lands. At one time confined to the extreme north of the peninsula, the Christian forces gradually won back territory in a long struggle known as the Reconquista (reconquest). The process culminated in 1492, when Granada, the last of the Moorish emirates, fell to the Catholic rulers Ferdinand and Isabella, and Muslim Spain was no more.

Indian Muslims celebrate the annual festival of Eid al-Fitr at the mosque at the Taj Mahal in Agra. In the Islamic calendar, years are known as Hejira years because they are counted from Muhammad's flight—*hijra*—from Mecca to Medina in 622.

out of the city and took refuge in the town of Yathrib (modern Medina). Known as the hijra (Anglicized as the Hejira), Muhammad's flight from Mecca marks the beginning of the Muslim calendar.

Muhammad was welcomed in Medina because of his reputation as a talented mediator, and he soon became the leader of the city. He forged alliances with neighboring tribes, and the *ummah* quickly grew. Muhammad also proved a skillful military commander, and under his guidance the Muslims became a dominant force in the region.

In 630, Muhammad returned to Mecca with an armed force and compelled the Quraysh to recognize his authority. Under the rules of war at the time, conquerors typically slaughtered the vanquished and took all their possessions. However, Muhammad spared his enemies, and his magnanimity attracted further converts to his teachings. He destroyed all the pagan images in the Kaaba and rededicated the shrine to Allah. While doing that, the Muslims circled the building seven times, an act that is now repeated by millions of pilgrims each year in the course of performing the hajj (the pilgrimage to Mecca that is an act of faith for all Muslims).

THE RIGHTLY GUIDED CALIPHS

Muhammad died in 632 without designating an heir. The *ummah* needed a new leader—one who would not be a prophet, as Muhammad had been, but rather a caliph (successor) who would guide the community's religious and political life. A dispute broke out among Muhammad's closest companions over who should fulfill the role. One group favored Abu Bakr, Muhammad's father-in-law, while the other preferred Ali, the Prophet's son-in-law. That disagreement created an enduring rift in the Muslim community that persists to this day. One sect, the Sunnis, regard Abu Bakr as Muhammad's legitimate heir; the other sect, the Shiites, believe that the Prophet ordained Ali to succeed him.

Abu Bakr became caliph but he died in 634, only two years after succeeding to the position. Three other caliphs followed him in quick succession: Umar (c. 634–644), Uthman (c. 644–656), and Ali (c. 656–661). Collectively, those four leaders are known as the *rashidun,* or "rightly guided caliphs."

The Muslim community enjoyed great military success under the *rashidun.* In 637, Islamic armies defeated the Sassanians and seized Damascus; four years later, they also captured Egypt. The rapid spread of Islam in the years after Muhammad's death has led many observers in the West to believe that the new faith was spread by the sword, with forced conversion. Actually, the reasons for its success are more complex. Islam's very simplicity—one could become a Muslim merely by professing the faith—was a major factor. At the same time, its message of social justice resonated with the poor and the weak. Muslim merchants also played a part by making it economically advantageous for those involved in trade to convert to Islam. So, even though the military prowess of Muhammad and his successors was an important factor in the growth and consolidation of Islam, it was by no means the defining reason for the rapid spread of the faith.

THE UMAYYAD EMPIRE

After the death of caliph Ali and a struggle for the succession, power passed to the governor of Damascus, who created the first hereditary Islamic empire, that of the Umayyads (660–750). The Umayyad Empire marked a new phase in the development of Islamic civilization.

The Umayyad rulers made Damascus their capital, building the city's Grand Mosque, one of the largest and oldest structures of its type in the world. The Grand Mosque occupies the site of an older Christian church, purchased from its original owners and then demolished.

The Umayyads focused on expanding Muslim territory across North Africa and

CAIRO AND THE FATIMIDS

The Fatimids rose to power in the 10th century in northern Africa, where they wrested control from the Abbasids of much of the region that now comprises Algeria and Tunisia.

In 969, the Fatimids founded a new capital in Egypt, calling it Al-Qahira (meaning "victorious"), a name subsequently transliterated into English as Cairo. The original settlement was a walled royal enclosure that gradually expanded into a city. The Fatimid rulers also built the Al-Azhar Mosque and its associated university, one of the oldest in the world. There, students studied Islamic law and jurisprudence, Arabic grammar, philosophy, and astronomy. Under the Fatimids, Cairo enjoyed rapid economic growth and became a key stop on the caravan route linking Africa with Europe and Asia. At their height, the Fatimids ruled an empire that stretched from Morocco to Syria and down the Red Sea coast to Yemen. The Fatimids were Shiite Muslims, and their leaders took the title of caliph in deliberate defiance of the Sunni Abbasids in Baghdad. Nevertheless, the Fatimid rulers were mostly tolerant of their Sunni coreligionists, as well as of non-Muslim *dhimmi*s (People of the Book), notably Jews and Christians. They appointed non-Shiites to key government posts, choosing administrators for their ability.

The Fatimid Empire weakened during the 11th century, losing its outlying territories to surrounding powers. In the 12th century, Egypt itself became a battleground between Christian crusaders and the Muslim rulers who had risen to prominence by opposing them. The famed Kurdish warrior Salah ad-Din, known in the West as Saladin, took control of Egypt in 1168, establishing his own Ayubbid Dynasty and reestablishing the land within the Sunni sphere of influence.

This book illustration of warriors fighting on horseback is the work of a Fatimid artist and dates between the 10th century and the 12th century.

THE MAMLUKS

The Mamluks were soldier-slaves originally recruited to serve the Abbasid Empire; their name originates from an Arabic word meaning "owned." Whether bought or captured, the Mamluks were for the most part recruited from Christian families in the Caucasus region of western Asia. Once converted to Islam, they were trained as mounted warriors to serve throughout the empire. They came to play an especially important role in Egypt, where, in 1171, Salah ad-Din (Saladin) established the Ayubbid Dynasty, which paid nominal allegiance to the Abbasid caliphs. On Saladin's death, his sons vied for power, becoming increasingly dependent on the Mamluks, who exerted growing administrative and political influence through their military might.

In 1250, one of the warlords seized power in his own name, establishing a Mamluk regime. His successors repelled the Mongols and scored a number of military victories against the crusaders, culminating in 1291 with the capture of Acre, the last Christian stronghold on the Asian mainland. In the process, they extended their own control over Palestine, Syria, and other parts of the eastern Mediterranean coast.

Mamluk sultans ruled Egypt until 1517, when the land came under the control of the Ottoman Empire. Thereafter, they continued to wield power and influence in the name of the Ottoman rulers, sometimes challenging the authority of their nominal overlords in Istanbul. Mamluk influence finally came to an end in 1811, when the Ottoman-appointed governor of Egypt, Muhammad Ali, massacred nearly 600 leading figures invited to a celebration in his palace; thousands more were killed elsewhere in the city over the following weeks. Although some Mamluks escaped to the Sudan, they posed no further threat to Muhammad Ali's control.

into southern Spain. In the east, Islamic forces moved across Persia toward what is now Pakistan. For the first time, Muslim leaders found themselves ruling a great diversity of peoples, including large numbers of non-Arabs, many of whom had converted to Islam. An Umayyad caliph, Abd al-Malik, was responsible for building the Dome of the Rock in Jerusalem, Islam's third most important shrine. The Dome houses the stone from which, according to Muslim tradition, Muhammad ascended to heaven.

The Umayyad caliphs were better at expanding their empire than at ensuring its internal harmony. Even though Islam insists on the equality of all Muslims, many of the empire's new converts were not treated well. Arabic was the language of administration, and people of Arab descent held most of the positions of authority, marginalizing native communities. The realm also faced continuing challenges from the Byzantine Empire, as well as from the pagan Turkic peoples to the east.

THE ABBASIDS

In 750, discontent with the Umayyads provoked a coup staged by a rival clan, the Abbasids. Most of the Umayyad rulers were killed, although one escaped to Spain, where he set up an Umayyad caliphate. The new rulers moved the capital of the empire to the new city of Baghdad, from where they maintained at least nominal control over the Islamic world until 1258.

By Abbasid times, the days of victorious military expansion were mainly over. The caliphs now focused on the internal development of the empire, notably its legal and administrative systems. Several rulers were interested in scientific advancement, creating great libraries and centers of learning that included Baghdad's famous Bayt al-Hikma (House of Wisdom), a massive library and translation institute that was destroyed during the Mongol invasion in 1258. There, scholars translated Persian and Greek works into Arabic and discussed philosophy, mathematics, medicine, and other sciences. Among their ranks were fugitives from the Byzantine Empire, attracted by the intellectual freedom offered under Abbasid rule. The new dynasty's rulers also showed more enthusiasm than their predecessors for the advancement of non-Arab Muslims.

However, the Abbasids proved unable to retain control over the vast territories conquered by the Umayyads. Within 50 years of the Abbasids' rise to power, northern Africa had fallen to local dynasties that paid little more than nominal allegiance to the caliphs in Baghdad. The Fatimids, the mightiest of the rival dynasties, refused to offer even that courtesy. As Shiites, the Fatimids set up a rival caliphate in their capital, Cairo, from which, at their peak around 1000, they ruled much of northern Africa and the eastern Mediterranean.

In the eastern part of the Abbasid Empire, other territories gained local control, further reducing the reach of the central imperial authority. Meanwhile, in southern Spain, the successors of the Umayyad prince Abd ar-Rahman also laid claim to the caliphate, providing a Sunni challenge to the rulers in Baghdad.

A sign of the Abbasids' diminished effectiveness could be found in the caliphs' increasing reliance on foreign, usually Turkic, soldiers to keep them in power. At first, the Turks had been imported as slave-warriors in the personal service of the ruler, but gradually they

Standing on the site of a preexistent Arab stronghold, the 12th-century Krak des Chevaliers, near Homs in modern Syria, is the greatest of the castles built by the Western Frankish forces during the Crusades.

THE SILK ROAD

Never a single thoroughfare, the Silk Road was a series of interconnected trade routes linking China to the Mediterranean Sea, a distance of around 5,000 miles (about 8,000 km). The paths traversed some of the most rugged parts of Central Asia, including the Gobi and Taklamakan deserts. Although many goods passed along it, the route took its name from the rare Chinese silks that were highly prized in the West.

By the time of the Mongol conquests of the 13th century, traffic along the Silk Road was in decline. However, the westward expansion of Muslim influence under the Il-Khans reinvigorated trade, which flourished under the Pax Mongolica (Mongolian Peace), as long-distance travel became relatively safe for merchants. It was at this time that the Italian adventurer Marco Polo made his celebrated journey to China; in 1325, the Muslim world's best-known geographer, Ibn Battuta, also followed the route.

A number of Chinese technological advances reached the Muslim world along the Silk Road, eventually making their way to Europe. The innovations included gunpowder, printing, and papermaking, as well as the astrolabe and the compass, instruments that helped stimulate the European Age of Exploration. When the Mongol Empire broke up at the end of the 14th century,

Gaochang in China was once an important oasis town on the Silk Road at the edge of the Taklamakan Desert.

the Silk Road once more fell into decline and was eventually replaced by new sea routes to Asia.

Trade by both sea and land was a primary means by which Islam spread beyond its heartland in the Middle East. By the 13th century, Islam was already established as far away as Indonesia, having reached the Indian subcontinent a century earlier.

became powers behind the throne, wielding real authority in the name of their nominal masters. The most important of those groups was the Seljuks, Islamized Turks who took control of Baghdad from an earlier dynasty, the Buyyids, in the 11th century. Like the Buyyids before them, they continued to rule in the name of the Abbasid caliphs, although they were now the true masters of the state.

The Seljuk Turks reunified the empire, but their rule was short-lived. By 1157, their realm had broken up into several smaller states, ruled as independent fiefs by military governors. One such state was established by Nur ad-Din Zangi, who sent a protégé named Salah ad-Din to wage war against the Shiite Fatimids of Egypt. The young man eventually seized power, restored Egypt to Sunni control, and established his own Ayubbid Dynasty. He then turned his attention to the Christians who had established themselves in Palestine during the Crusades. He came to be known in the West as Saladin.

The Crusades had their origins partly in the growing economic and political strength of western Europe, whose predominantly Christian population became increasingly antagonistic to the Muslims' conduct in Jerusalem, a city sacred to both faiths. Tension increased after 1009, when an unbalanced Fatimid caliph ordered the destruction of the Church of the Holy Sepulchre, which, according to tradition, was built on the site where Jesus Christ was crucified and buried. Although the church was later rebuilt with financial aid from the Byzantine Empire, Christian Europe remained concerned, and its fears were intensified by the rise of the Seljuk Turks. The First Crusade was launched in 1095 in response to a request by the Byzantine emperor for military aid against the new Islamic military powers.

The crusaders arrived in the eastern Mediterranean at a time when the Muslim world was fragmented into numerous semiautonomous states. The Europeans, known by the Arabs as the Franks, captured Jerusalem in 1099 and celebrated their victory by massacring not only the city's Muslim inhabitants but also its Jews and Orthodox Christians.

The Franks subsequently established small crusader states along the coast of what is now Lebanon and farther inland, building enormous, European-style castles, some of which are still standing. The most

At 238 feet (72.5 m) in height, the Qutab Minar in Delhi, India, is the world's tallest brick minaret. It was built by the Mughals between 1193 and 1368.

The 17th-century Masjid-i-Shah is the royal mosque in the Safavid capital of Isfahan (a city in present-day Iran).

impressive of those fortresses is Krak des Chevaliers in Syria. The crusaders held Jerusalem until 1187, when the city fell to forces led by Saladin. The Third Crusade was then launched in an attempt to recapture the city. Although it failed in its primary objective, its military leader, the English king Richard I the Lionheart (r. 1189–1199) made a treaty with Saladin that left Jerusalem under Muslim control but guaranteed Christians safe passage on pilgrimages. Subsequently, the tide of war continued to run in the Muslims' favor and, in 1291, the last crusaders were finally driven out.

The Crusades had only a localized and short-term impact on the Muslim world. Their effect on western Europe was much greater, because they brought the continent into contact with the sophisticated urban culture of the Islamic world. Crusaders returned home not only with loot, but also with a wealth of new ideas that would lay the groundwork for the age of European learning known as the Renaissance.

THE MONGOL ADVANCE

A much greater threat to the Islamic world than the crusades arose in the 13th century, this time from the steppes of Central Asia.

THE MUGHAL EMPIRE

Islam came to India in the late 12th century with the foundation of the Delhi sultanate, but the continuing Muslim presence was heavily reinforced under the Mughal rulers 300 years later. In the 1500s Babur, a descendant of Genghis Khan, seized power across much of northwest India. His successors, most notably Akbar the Great (r. 1556–1605), extended Mughal control over all but the southern tip of the Indian subcontinent. The Mughals, whose name reflected their partly Mongol ancestry, spoke Persian at court and introduced many Iranian influences into Indian culture. Akbar himself set great store by religious tolerance, inviting Hindu and Christian theologians to debate with Muslim clerics. When his successor, Aurangzeb, abandoned his open-minded approach in favor of religious persecution, the empire soon showed signs of decline.

At its height in the 16th and 17th centuries, the Mughal Empire covered an area of some 1.3 million square miles (3.4 million sq. km). Its many cultural achievements included great architectural monuments such as the Taj Mahal, which was completed in 1648 as a mausoleum for the favorite wife of Akbar's grandson, Shah Jahan.

The Mughal Empire's decline accelerated after 1725, when it succumbed to both internal discord and pressures from British colonial forces. It finally came to an end in 1857, when the last emperor, who controlled only the area around Delhi, was imprisoned and then exiled by the British as a reprisal for his supposed complicity in the rebellion known to colonial historians as the Indian Mutiny.

The end of Abbasid rule came at the hands of Mongols, who established the largest empire the world had ever seen. At the height of their power, the Mongols ruled an area of more than one million square miles (2.6 million sq. km), 22 percent of the world's land surface, and more than 100 million people.

Under their leader, Genghis Khan, the Mongols operated a uniquely effective war machine. They moved swiftly, traveling and fighting on horseback, aided by the recent innovation of the stirrup. Each Mongol warrior took between two and five horses on campaign. The Mongols used terror as a weapon of war, leaving piled heaps of skulls in the cities they devastated. Although recent research has emphasized the more positive aspects of Mongol rule, the destruction they wrought on the Abbasid Empire can hardly be overestimated.

The Mongols first invaded Muslim territory in the 1220s, occupying the territories of modern Iran and Iraq. Genghis's son, Hulagu Khan, subsequently sought to pacify Islamic lands as far west as Egypt. In 1258, a Mongol army sacked Baghdad, destroying the city that had served as the Abbasid capital for 500 years. The victors then continued westward, seizing Syria and heading south toward Egypt. Their advance was finally halted by Egypt's Mamluk rulers at the Battle of Ain Jalut in Palestine in 1260.

Although the Mongols destroyed the last vestiges of the Abbasid Empire, they were ultimately responsible for a new era of Islamic expansion. Crucially, the Il-Khan Mongol Dynasty that took power in western Asia itself adopted the Muslim faith and set about reconstituting many of the institutions that its Mongol predecessors had destroyed. Although the

Il-Khanate lasted for less than a century, its disintegration prepared the way for the emergence of three major new empires—the Safavids in Persia, the Ottomans in Turkey, and the Mughals in India.

THE SAFAVID EMPIRE

The modern Shiite state of Iran has its roots in the Safavid Empire. The empire emerged in the late 13th century in what is today the northwest of the country. The Safavid dynasty itself had its roots in a religious brotherhood of Sufis, holy warriors who practiced a mystical form of Islam and gradually extended their influence westward into Anatolia (part of present-day Turkey) and Syria. At some point, probably in the 15th century, the Safavids converted from the mainstream Sunni branch of Islam to the minority Shia grouping. In 1494, Ismail, a seven-year-old boy, inherited control of the brotherhood. Under his leadership, the extent of Safavid control increased until it included parts of Iraq, including the old Abbasid capital of Baghdad. During his reign, Ismail imposed the Shiite faith of the Turkish-speaking Turcoman tribesmen (who formed his core supporters) on his largely Persian-speaking subjects; those who opposed the move were persecuted.

The Safavid Empire lasted for more than 300 years and created a permanent presence for Shia Islam in the region. Throughout its existence, its rulers fought continuously with their Ottoman neighbors along the border shared by the two adjoining empires. Control over the frontier lands, located in modern Iraq, alternated between the two powers, creating an area of mixed Sunni and Shia influence that survives to this day, with southern Iraq—the site of the Shia cities of Karbala and Najaf—still firmly Shiite in its religious allegiance.

THE OTTOMAN EMPIRE

For over 500 years, from the 14th century to the early 20th century, the Ottoman realm dominated the western part of the Islamic world. The last of the great Muslim empires, it shaped the development of modern western Asia, and the empire's dissolution after World War I (1914–1918) left a gap that has yet to be satisfactorily filled.

The Ottoman Empire had its roots in the Mongol conquest that put an end to the earlier Abbasid Empire. The Mongols subsequently created *beyliks* (principalities) in Anatolia, with local Turkic governors, known as beys, who swore allegiance to the Mongols and ruled in their name. In 1299, one of the beys, Osman, declared

The Safavid Empire lasted for more than 300 years and created a permanent presence for Shia Islam in the region.

independence from the Mongols. He gained control of some of the surrounding *beyliks* and won military victories against the neighboring Byzantine Empire, further expanding his rule. The English word "Ottoman" is derived from his name.

Ottoman control expanded rapidly over the next century. In 1453, Sultan Mehmet I captured Constantinople, the symbol of Christian power in the east, thereby ending the 1,100-year rule of the Byzantine Empire. The city later became known by its Turkish name, Istanbul.

The Ottomans' westward expansion soon brought the empire into conflict with European powers. In the 14th and 15th centuries, the Ottomans established control over the Balkans and, in 1529, Sultan Suleiman, who became known in the West as Suleiman the Magnificent, almost captured Vienna, a move that worried many European Christian leaders. The confrontation with central Europe's Christian rulers, notably the Habsburg Dynasty that ruled the Austro-Hungarian Empire, continued for more than 300 years.

Baulked at Vienna, the Ottomans continued to expand their realm in other directions, taking Egypt from the Mamluks in 1517 and then extending their influence along the coast of northern Africa as far as the borders of Morocco. On their eastern borders, the sultans contended with their Safavid neighbors for control of the lands that make up present-day Iraq and beyond, establishing bases on the western shores of the Persian Gulf.

Together with the Safavids and the Mughals, the Ottomans formed one of the "gunpowder empires." By the 16th century, mobile artillery units composed of cannon were a vital factor in warfare, and only centralized governments with a high level of administrative efficiency could afford to deploy the vast, mobile armies that made use of them. The Ottomans also benefited from the services of a professional

This oil painting by Louis-François Lejeune (1775–1848) depicts the Battle of the Pyramids (July 21, 1798), in which French forces under Napoleon Bonaparte defeated the Mamluk rulers of Egypt.

army whose elite units were composed of janissaries—slave soldiers recruited in childhood and trained for military service. In time, the empire also built up a strong navy that vied with European fleets for control of the Mediterranean Sea.

OTTOMAN POLITICS AND SOCIETY

The sultans ruled their far-flung empire from Istanbul, which, with a population of 700,000 in the 17th century, was larger than any city in Europe at the time. The Topkapi Palace in which the sultans lived was also the administrative center of their realm. It covered 173 acres (70 hectares) and housed thousands of people in a maze-like complex of courtyards, bathhouses, armories, residential areas, and offices.

Living in sheltered opulence behind the palace walls, the Ottoman rulers exercised absolute power as sultans and caliphs—in other words, as both political and religious leaders. They were hereditary rulers, although succession did not necessarily pass to the eldest son. Instead, a reigning sultan's sons all competed and conspired against each other for the throne.

Ottoman society was highly stratified by class and unusually dependent on slaves. To recruit the janissaries, who served as a main prop of their power, the sultans relied on a system known as the *devshirme* (collection), which brought non-Muslim youths, often Christians from the Balkan provinces, into the service of the empire. The *devshirme* was not voluntary, although the opportunities for advancement that it provided sometimes caused families to seek to have their children selected. The chosen youngsters were taken to the capital and converted to Islam. Those destined to become janissaries swore loyalty to the sultan and were housed in large barracks;

forbidden to marry, they were encouraged to consider each other as family. Other forced recruits were trained to become civil servants. Although technically slaves, nonmilitary enlistees were allowed to marry and sometimes reached high levels within the Ottoman bureaucracy.

Although the military played a key role in the Ottomans' success, the rulers also relied on an efficient administrative system to control their vast realm, which was divided into provinces, mostly ruled by local governors appointed by the sultan. The empire included people of many ethnicities and religions. Ottoman law provided protection for those

Although the military played a key role in the Ottomans' success, the rulers also relied on an efficient administrative system to control their vast realm, which was divided into provinces.

minority communities (known as millets), guaranteeing religious pluralism and thereby reducing potential resistance.

Under the millet system, religious communities were given considerable powers of self-rule. They were able to pass laws in accordance with their religious beliefs and to supervise local tax collection. They operated their own schools, religious buildings, and hospitals. Millet communities in the Ottoman Empire included a variety of groups, among them Greek Orthodox and Armenian Christians as well as Jews. These communities played a major role in the economic life of the Ottoman

Empire. As nationalism increased in Europe, the millets sought greater autonomy.

THE OTTOMAN DECLINE

After the end of the 17th century, the Ottoman Empire made no more territorial gains. Its subsequent decline was caused partly by internal weakness but mainly by growing western European dominance.

As early as the 16th century, European nations, especially Spain, Portugal, and England, became global naval powers. Their colonization of the New World and discovery of shipping routes to the East Indies and the Far East reduced the Ottomans' role as middlemen in East–West trade, depriving the empire of much revenue. European powers, particularly Spain, also established naval predominance in the Mediterranean Sea, severely circumscribing the activities of the Ottoman fleet.

At the same time, the Ottoman Empire lost much of its military superiority on land as Europe modernized its own armed forces. The changing balance of power was vividly illustrated when France's revolutionary leader Napoleon Bonaparte

British general Edmund Allenby leads his troops into Jerusalem in 1917. Britain governed Palestine under a League of Nations mandate from 1920 until 1948.

39

THE ARMENIAN GENOCIDE

Between 1915 and 1917, during World War I, approximately one-half of Turkey's population of two million Armenian Christians died or were deported. Many succumbed to starvation or exhaustion on long forced marches. Armenian schools and churches were closed, and leading Armenian intellectuals were killed.

In 1915, the government of the Young Turks decided to deport the entire Armenian population of Turkey to Syria and Mesopotamia. It regarded the Turkish Armenians—despite pledges of loyalty by many—as a dangerous foreign element bent on conspiring with their Russian coreligionists to upset the Ottoman military campaign in the east. In what would later become notorious as the first genocide of the 20th century, hundreds of thousands of Armenians were driven from their homes and massacred. The death toll of Armenians in Ottoman Turkey has been estimated at between 600,000 and 1,500,000 in the years from 1915 to 1923. Tens of thousands of Armenians emigrated to Russia, Lebanon, Syria, France, and the United States, and the western part of their historical homeland (in eastern Turkey, next to the modern border with Azerbaijan) was ethnically cleansed.

Although most modern historians agree that the Armenians were the victims of genocide, the government of Turkey has strenuously resisted what has become the conventional version of events. Turkish writers and dissidents who have tried to depict the treatment of the Armenians as a crime against humanity have been punished with imprisonment.

invaded Ottoman-controlled Egypt with a military machine that was massively superior to that of his Mamluk opponents. Recurring wars with Russia also took their toll on the Ottoman Empire. In the 19th century, Ottoman sultans borrowed heavily from European banks to finance their war efforts, building up debts whose repayment weighed heavily on the economy and increased the tax burden.

To make matters worse, central authority atrophied under a series of weak rulers. Over a period of 130 years, a succession of minors inherited the throne, leaving real power to be exercised by a succession of advisors and relatives. Reformers tried to establish order with a series of measures collectively known as the Tanzimat (reorganization), which, in 1876, brought the introduction of a written constitution and an elected chamber of deputies. However, the attempts at

modernization came too late for an empire that was already starting to break up.

The first blow was struck in Egypt in the wake of the Napoleonic invasion when the country's Ottoman governor, Muhammad Ali, seized power in his own name. Subsequently, the rising tide of European nationalism energized resistance in the empire's Balkan territories, which began to seek greater autonomy. In 1821, the Greek provinces revolted, winning independence in 1832. Within decades, other European territories, including Serbia, Romania, and Montenegro, had followed their example.

Meanwhile, European powers were making inroads into the Ottoman Empire's heartland. Britain became dominant in the Persian Gulf, taking control of Aden in 1839 and subsequently signing treaties with Bahrain (1880), Muscat (1891), the Trucial Coast (1892), and Kuwait (1899). France focused on northern Africa, capturing Algiers (1830) and Tunisia (1881). Italy acquired Tripoli (part of modern Libya) in 1911.

WORLD WAR I

Through a military alliance of 1914, the Ottoman Empire was drawn into World War I. It joined Germany and Austria-Hungary primarily because Russia, its neighbor and long-term enemy, was a member of the opposing Allied powers, along with Britain, France, Italy, and (from 1917) the United States.

During the conflict itself (1914–1918), Allied troops fought Ottoman forces in Mesopotamia (modern Iraq), the Caucasus, and Palestine, as well as on the Gallipoli Peninsula of Turkey. The Ottomans also faced an Arab revolt, led by Faisal bin al-Hussein, a member of the powerful Hashemite clan in the Hejaz, in alliance with T. E. Lawrence, an eccentric British officer who became known as Lawrence of Arabia. The Arab forces disabled Ottoman supply lines in the region and took the port city of Aqaba. By the end of the war, they controlled much of Palestine and Lebanon, along with parts of Syria, Saudi Arabia, and Transjordan (modern Jordan). Their success fueled Arab nationalism and the desire for independent states.

SHAPING A NEW WESTERN ASIA

On October 30, 1918, the Ottoman Empire signed an armistice with the victorious Allied powers. The surrender marked the end of the dynasty; the last sultan abdicated in 1922. The postwar division of the Ottoman territories laid the foundations of the modern state system in western Asia. By 1919, there was a growing

The Turkish delegation signs the Treaty of Sèvres of August 10, 1920, that brought peace between the Ottoman Empire (which then dissolved) and the World War I Allies.

international awareness of the rights of separate ethnic groups to self-determination. Control of the Ottoman territories was passed to the newly established League of Nations, whose remit was to ensure that future conflicts were resolved by peaceful means.

The League, however, considered the former Ottoman territories unready for self-rule. Instead, it placed them under the temporary stewardship of European colonial powers. Britain was given control of Iraq, Palestine, and Transjordan, while France received Lebanon and Syria. Under the terms of the mandates, the new rulers were supposed to guide their assigned

The architects of peace showed little concern for the aspirations of the indigenous inhabitants. Their decisions had far-reaching consequences for the region that are still being felt today.

territories toward independence. In reality, the mandatory powers had global agendas of their own, and they inevitably prioritized their own interests.

In defining the borders of the mandated territories, the architects of peace showed little concern for the aspirations of the indigenous inhabitants. Their decisions had far-reaching consequences for the region that are still being felt today. Iraq, for example, was created by combining the former Ottoman provinces of Mosul, Baghdad, and Basra into a single state. Although the composite nation thereby created had a Shiite majority, the British colonial authorities chose to put the

minority Sunni community in power under their former ally, King Faisal. The Kurds of northern Iraq, who had hoped for an independent state, were disappointed.

To the west, Britain recognized Transjordan as a separate state in 1923, handing power to the Hashemite dynasty in the person of Faisal's brother, Abdullah I. The rest of the Palestine mandate soon became a problem for the occupying power. Even before the start of World War I, Jews from many parts of the world had begun emigrating to Palestine, drawn by the Zionist goal of creating a national homeland for the Jewish people. Through the 1920s and the 1930s, the increasing influx of Jews caused conflict both with the existing Arab population and with the British authorities. By the eve of World War II (1939–1945), it was clear that the two communities were on a collision course. The problems grew when the Jewish exodus to Palestine increased in the wake of the Nazis' persecution of the Jews of Europe. As tensions mounted, a war-weary Britain announced its intention to surrender the Palestine mandate in May of 1948.

The problem of reconciling the conflicting ambitions of Jews and Arabs then theoretically passed to the League of Nations' successor organization, the new United Nations. However, a Jewish provisional government unilaterally proclaimed the state of Israel on the day the British mandate ended. Neighboring Arab states at once declared war on the fledgling nation, only to be defeated in the ensuing hostilities by the Israeli army. Hundreds of thousands of Arabs fled or were expelled from their homes within the borders of the new state.

LEBANON AND SYRIA

In the French sphere of influence, Syria was already on the way to independence when World War II disrupted the process, although Free French leaders in exile acceded to the principle of nationhood in 1941. Lebanon also proclaimed its independence at this time, although another two years passed before the Free French accepted the declaration. Lebanon was home to a large Christian Maronite population, which, critics claimed, was given preferential treatment by the French administrators, thus laying the foundation for the tensions between the Christian and Muslim populations that led to the Lebanese Civil War (1975–1990).

MODERN TURKEY

The dismemberment of the Ottoman Empire left the Turkish successor government with control over only a small portion of the Anatolian peninsula around the city of Ankara. By the terms of the Treaty of Sèvres in 1920, Greece was given temporary charge of the coastal lands around the port of Smyrna (modern Izmir), while Italy and France were accorded substantial zones of influence in the surrounding area. Istanbul itself was designated an international city and occupied by Allied troops. Although the sultan technically remained on the throne, he was little more than a puppet ruler. The settlement ensured that the Ottomans would never again challenge European hegemony in the region.

The treaty's harsh terms had the unintended consequence of feeding Turkish nationalism, which had first become a force after the Tanzimat reforms. Under the leadership of Mustafa Kemal, who had risen to prominence leading military resistance to the Allies on the Gallipoli Peninsula, a group of Turkish nationalists sought to regain full sovereignty over all territories with a Turkish majority. In 1920, these nationalists formed their own government based in Ankara, electing a national assembly and drafting a constitution. Kemal then launched a military campaign, known in Turkey as the War of Independence, which succeeded in driving the occupying powers out of Turkish territory. On November 1, 1922, a new state, the Republic of Turkey, was declared, ending 623 years of Ottoman rule.

Mustafa Kemal, later known by the honorific title of Atatürk (father of the Turks), became the first president of the new country. He set about enacting a series of measures designed to modernize the nation. His reforms included banning the traditional fez and veil in favor of European styles of dress, reducing the role of religion in education, and replacing Arabic script with the Roman alphabet as a medium for writing the Turkish language. One result of his policies was to orient Turkey westward toward its former European enemies. Another was to establish the nation as an officially secular state—the only one in western Asia. The constitution forbade any role for religion in government and public life; however, religion continued to be important for the population at large.

Today's map of western Asia can be traced directly to the defeat of the Ottoman Empire in World War I, the peace treaties that followed, and the history of the European mandates. Many of the problems of the region were and still are exacerbated by the imposition of borders that reflected the strategic concerns of the victorious Allies rather than those of the region's indigenous inhabitants.

See Also

Life of Muhammad 18–21 ❖ European Colonies and Decolonization in the Islamic World 44–47 ❖ Subdivisions of Islam 128–147 ❖ Mystical Islam 148–149 ❖ Holy Places 174–193 ❖ Philosophy and Science 312–331 ❖

European Colonies and Decolonization in the Islamic World

Although European colonization of Muslim countries is generally thought to have ended in the mid-20th century, some commentators believe that it continues today.

I t is impossible to pinpoint the start of European colonialism in the Islamic world to an exact date. The period may have begun in the mid-18th century with the gradual takeover by Britain of India, several parts of which were predominantly Muslim. However, modern scholars generally agree that the era effectively opened with the occupation of Egypt in 1798 by French forces under Napoleon Bonaparte (1769–1821).

Having gained a foothold in northern Africa, France expanded its territory in the region, invading Algeria in 1830 and establishing a protectorate in Tunisia in 1881. Meanwhile, the French were pushed out of Egypt by the British, who, by 1882, controlled or influenced a range of other Muslim areas, including Sudan, almost all of South Asia, and parts of western Asia and Southeast Asia.

MANDATES

The West gained ground during World War I (1914–1918), when it began to fill the power vacuum created by the disintegration of the Ottoman Empire. In 1916, the Sykes-Picot Agreement (a secret convention named for the chief negotiators, Mark Sykes and François Georges-Picot) paved the way for the division of Turkish-held Iraq, Lebanon, Palestine, and Syria between Britain and France.

At the end of the conflict, these plans were carried out under the auspices of the League of Nations. This newly formed organization, which was intended to guarantee global security, was the brainchild of the

Allies, which had previously declared that the annexation of territory was not one of their war aims. In order to prevent accusations of colonialism, the League awarded the former colonies to the victors in the form of mandates. The crucial difference between a colony and a mandate was that the former was without limit of time, whereas the latter was to be held only until the occupied country was adjudged ready to govern itself. The former Turkish provinces of Iraq and Palestine (including present-day Jordan and Israel) were assigned to Britain, while Syria and Lebanon were administered by France.

Although, in theory, the mandates were technically not the same as colonial control, in practice they shared many similarities. Most of the European powers' resources were devoted to controlling the areas; developing them was a secondary concern.

The mandates ended during and after World War II (1939–1945). France gave independence to Lebanon in 1943 and to Syria in 1946. In 1947, Britain handed Palestine over to the League of Nations' successor, the United Nations (UN). The UN attempted to mediate in the dispute between Jewish settlers and Arabs but was unable to prevent either the declaration of the Jewish state of Israel in 1948 or the ensuing Arab-Israeli war, at

This 19th century illustration depicts Napoleon Bonaparte's decisive victory over Egyptian forces at the Battle of the Pyramids on July 21, 1798.

the end of which Israel controlled 78 percent of the area of historic Palestine (Jordan and Egypt controlled the rest).

In other parts of the Islamic world, Libya became independent in 1951 and Egypt followed suit two years later after a coup. Tunisia and Morocco became free of France in 1956. Elsewhere, the death throes of colonialism were more painful. Algerians endured an eight-year war of independence against the French (1954–1962). In South Yemen, the British were pushed out by civil disorder and uprisings in 1967.

POSTCOLONIAL PROBLEMS

The withdrawal of the colonial powers left the emergent nations with numerous problems, many of which remain unresolved. One of the major difficulties was caused by attempts to maintain frontiers that were drawn by the Europeans arbitrarily, with little or no recognition of historical precedents or demography. The most disastrous effects were those caused by the British withdrawal from South Asia in 1947 and the consequent partition of the subcontinent into two nations with three parts: East Pakistan (modern Bangladesh) and West Pakistan (now Pakistan), which were separated by 1,100 miles (1,800 km) of territory belonging to India. The redrawing of the map of the region provoked hostilities that caused thousands of deaths and the largest mass migration in human history, as millions of Muslims relocated to Pakistani territory and comparable numbers of Hindus, Sikhs, and Christians fled to India.

Among the countries whose borders are mainly no more than artificial "lines in the sand" are Iraq and Jordan. Another continuing cause of dispute is the modern frontier between Afghanistan and Pakistan. This boundary—known as the Durand Line for Henry Mortimer Durand (1850–1924), the British diplomat who drew it in 1893 between Afghanistan and India—made scant recognition of the aspirations of the Pashtuns, who were henceforth divided by a national frontier. Among the legacies of the Durand Line has been the movement for an independent Pashtunistan, a proposed new state for which there is little international support and which is actively opposed by Afghanistan, India, and Pakistan.

Colonialism left other problems for new governments. Foreign powers rarely developed the economies or the polities of the nations they controlled, despite being

Jewish settlers leaving Germany in 1948 to fight for newly founded Israel. Some Muslims view Israel as an extension of European colonialism.

required to do so by the League of Nations' mandates. The postcolonial political elites were often inexperienced or weak. Many business elites were foreigners or held themselves aloof from local economies. In the same way, citizenship rights and property rights were often inadequate because their development had not been a priority of the external powers, which had often sought only to protect their own interests rather than those of the indigenous population. Several national economies had been transformed into overly specialized but underdeveloped systems. A notorious example was Britain's policy in Egypt of maximizing cotton production to the exclusion of much-needed agrarian reform.

RADICAL RESPONSES

The postcolonial response to European domination has varied from country to country, but some trends may be observed. The most important development was that of nationalist or supranational political ideologies and movements of liberation or independence, together with growing senses of national or religious identity. Colonialism was unpopular, but widespread mobilization against the occupying powers was rare because many areas were heavily rural and the intelligentsia and the political classes were relatively small. Where mobilization did occur, it was often in response to specific grievances at the regional or local level; only late in the colonial period did some indigenous leaders amass widespread support. More commonly, indigenous ideologies and movements emerged as an intellectual response to colonialism or used opposition to foreign suzerains to implant and nurture radical politics.

Pan-Arabism emerged as a secular, ethnically based movement of solidarity, partly following the rise of Turkish nationalism in the Ottoman Empire and partly in response to growing European nationalism. Early pan-Arabist thinkers used opposition to foreign interventionism to build support for Arab unity. Nation-state nationalism also emerged shortly afterward, including Palestinian nationalism, which was, in part, a response to Zionism, which, after 1882, encouraged immigration to Palestine.

Crucial also was the wave of Islamic revivalism (and later "political Islamism") that arose in the late 19th century. Jamal al-din al-Afghani (1838–1897) and Muhammad Abduh (1849–1905) developed Islamic concepts of politics and society in the context of a declining Ottoman Empire and growing European penetration into northern Africa and western Asia. In South Asia, Sayyid Abu'l-A'la Mawdudi (1903–1979) was a key Islamist thinker who argued for the gradual creation of an Islamic state.

The postcolonial political elites were often inexperienced or weak. Many business elites were foreigners or held themselves aloof from local economies.

Elsewhere, Islamic revivalism and Islamic reformism were reflected in movements that opposed colonialism or drew on opposition to external intervention. In Russian-controlled Muslim areas, especially in Central Asia, Jadidism emerged as a modernist, internationalizing movement linked to pan-Turkic and pan-Arabist goals and anticolonial ideas. In South Asia, the founder of Pakistan, Muhammad Ali Jinnah (1876–1948), struggled initially toward "home rule," meaning self-government, and, after 1934, worked through the Muslim League for the creation of an independent Muslim nation-state in South Asia. Arguably, the emergence of Pakistan and India was an outcome of political movements that responded to colonialism.

Colonialism inspired widespread suspicion of Western states—whether former colonial powers or later major powers, such as the United States. European powers are still also seen as exploitative, especially in matters relating to oil and gas resources, investment, and globalization. Israel is widely perceived as a Western "implant" in the region, and continued U.S. support for Israel is seen as a form of neocolonialism and interventionism. Likewise, the 1991 and 2003 wars against Iraq are often denounced as attempts by the United States to maintain control over western Asia's oil reserves.

Chapter 3

BELIEFS

Some people claim that Islam is a religion of deeds alone, but nothing could be further from the truth. Beyond the Koran's repeated command to uphold iman *(faith), one sign of the centrality of belief in Muslim consciousness is the development of various schools of theology whose advocates engage in intense and constant debate.*

Muhammad was sitting one day among his companions when an unknown figure suddenly appeared. His hair was unusually black and his clothes were unusually white, and he did not seem to have been journeying. He sat before Muhammad and began to ask the Prophet a series of questions. He first inquired about the message of Islam. Muhammad responded: "Islam is to testify that there is no god but God, and that Muhammad is God's messenger, to perform the prayer, to pay the alms tax, to fast during Ramadan, and to make a pilgrimage to the House [the Kaaba in Mecca] if you are able to." The stranger told Muhammad that he was correct—a remark that surprised the Prophet's companions, given Muhammad's accepted position as a mouthpiece of God.

The stranger then asked about *iman* (faith). Muhammad responded, "It is to believe in God, his angels, his books, his messengers, the Last Day, and to believe in destiny, [regardless of whether it is] good or harmful." Once again, the stranger informed Muhammad that he was correct. He next asked about *ihsan* (excellence). Muhammad responded, "It is to worship

A Muslim washes before prayers at the Jama Masjid, the most important mosque in Delhi, India.

God as if you see Him, and even though you cannot see Him, He certainly sees you." The man then inquired about Judgment Day. Muhammad told him that he knew no more about this matter than did the stranger, although he noted its "signs." The man then departed, satisfied with Muhammad's answers. Muhammad then turned to his companion Umar ibn al-Khattab (c. 586–644 CE), a future successor of the Prophet as one of the four righteous caliphs who guided the Islamic world in the years immediately after his death. Umar ibn al-Khattab told Muhammad that the stranger was in fact the Archangel Gabriel, who came to instruct him.

This account highlights the essentials of Muslim faith by referencing the Five Pillars of Islam and introducing the six pillars (or articles) of faith and the concept of *ihsan*.

THE SIX PILLARS OF FAITH

The Koranic term for faith, *iman*, connotes not just having faith in God but also placing one's trust in Him. The opposite is *kufr*, which signifies not only lack of belief but also an active resistance to the truth. Associated with this concept is *nifaq* (hypocrisy), the condition of declaring oneself a Muslim while secretly adopting a position of *kufr*. The six pillars of faith are one means of distinguishing those who believe from those who do not.

The first pillar of faith is belief in a single God, which entails recognition of God's absolute sovereignty over everything. As such, it would be wrong for anyone having such faith to believe that God shares his powers with any other deities or beings. In fact, *shirk* (associating some other entity with God and his divine attributes) constitutes Islam's cardinal sin. Accordingly, God does not have intermediaries; people can pray to God and ask for His forgiveness directly. No human has the ability to forgive; only God forgives and God hears, sees, and knows all.

The Koran uses the name Allah in referring to God. This is a commonly misunderstood term that is sometimes described as a reference to a moon god or some other Arab pagan deity. In fact, Allah is simply the Arabic word for "God," a point established beyond doubt when one looks beyond Arabic and examines other Semitic languages, such as Aramaic and Hebrew. Those languages use terms similar to Allah in referring to God, such as Elaha (Aramaic) and Eloah (Hebrew). Moreover, it is not uncommon to hear Arab Christians or Jews using the term *Allah* in referring to their own concept of God.

According to Islamic thought, God is ultimately beyond description. For example, one cannot pinpoint God's "location." The Koran asserts that God is simultaneously above us on "the throne" and "closer to us than our own jugular veins." The question of explaining God's relation to time is similarly challenging. Is God outside of time, or does He exist at all times, in the eternal past, the present, and the eternal future? These are questions that Muslims debate.

Nevertheless, the Koran gives God names, or attributes, in order to make sense

Although Islam encourages and generally prefers collective worship, it does not proscribe solitary prayer. Here, an Iranian Muslim prays alone on the veranda of a building.

THE 99 NAMES OF GOD

On the basis of the Koran and the Hadith (sayings) of the Prophet Muhammad, medieval Muslim scholars compiled a list of 99 divine attributes that has since become popular throughout the Muslim world. Today, it is not uncommon to find pendants, posters, and decorative plates that list all the names of Allah, and they are often memorized and even sung. The complete list is as follows:

The Compassionate	The Abaser	The Overseer	The Delayer
The Caring	The Exalter	The Responder	The First
The Sovereign	The Giver of Honor	The Vast	The Last
The Holy	The Humiliator	The Wise	The Apparent
The Source of Peace	The Hearer	The Loving	The Hidden
The Faith-giver	The Seer	The Glorious	The Patron
The Guardian	The Judge	The Resurrector	The Supreme
The Almighty	The Just	The Witness	The Righteous
The Compeller	The Subtle	The Truth (or The Real)	The Guide to Repentance
The Greatest	The All-Aware	The Entrusted	The Avenger
The Creator	The Forbearing	The Strong	The Pardoner
The Rightful	The Magnificent	The Firm	The Clement
The Shaper	The Forgiver	The Guardian	The Owner of All
The Forgiving	The Grateful	The Praiseworthy	The Lord of Majesty and
The Subduer	The Exalted	The Appraiser	Bounty
The Giver	The Great	The Originator	The Equitable
The Provider	The Preserver	The Restorer	The Gatherer
The Opener	The Nourisher	The Life-giver	The Wealthy
The Omniscient	The Accounter	The Life-taker	The One Who Enriches
The Constrictor	The Majestic	The Living	The Preventer
The Expander	The Generous	The Sustainer	The Creator of Harm
		The Finder	The Benefactor
		The Illustrious	The Light
		The One	The Guide
		The Indivisible	The Originator
		The Everlasting	The One Who Remains
		The Able	The Inheritor
		The Determiner	The Righteous Teacher
		The Expediter	The Patient

of the otherwise inconceivable divine essence. For example, it refers to God as "the Compassionate," "the Judge," "the Just," and "the Powerful." The Koran also sometimes refers to God in the first person, using the pronoun "I" and even "We" in an attempt to magnify God without implying that He is more than one entity. Elsewhere, the Koran refers to God as "He," "Your Lord," or, simply, as "Allah." As scholars of Islam have observed, the range of names and pronouns allows readers and listeners to gain a sense of the profundity and complexities of God's being.

When the Koran refers to God in the third person, it uses the masculine pronoun "He." Even so, Muslims generally believe that God is beyond gender, not least because the Koran refers to Him using a wide variety of names that encompass both masculine and feminine qualities. Indeed, the names most commonly associated with the God of Islam are the seemingly feminine al-Rahman (the Compassionate) and al-Rahim (the Caring); preceding almost every sura (chapter) of the Koran is the expression "In the name of God, the Compassionate (al-Rahman), the Caring (al-Rahim)." Both those names are derived from the Arabic word *rahm*, which means, literally, "the mother's womb" and, metaphorically, "the source of compassion." According to the Hadith, God is 99 percent compassion, and in the afterlife His mercy will overcome His wrath; according to the Koran, God's compassion encompasses all entities. His love, however, is reserved for those who earn it, and the ultimate proof of God's love is admission into Paradise.

The Koran also highlights God's role as maker and designer. Even though God creates by simply saying, "Be!," His creation of the universe is described as spanning a period of six stages. Unlike the Judeo-Christian Bible, the Koran describes the creation in relatively general terms. It goes into more detail in describing the creation of humans, highlighting the miracle of life. Humanity originated from clay and water, and each individual is the product of mere fluids, such as semen. While still in the womb, the embryo and then the fetus evolve, and God grants each body the soul that makes people who they are. Humans are born into this world in a state of *fitra*, a natural disposition to purity, and are seen as God's representatives on earth.

Fitra does not mean that people can do whatever they please in their interactions with other earthly species. Even when slaughtering an animal for its meat, for instance, Muslims are expected to take whatever steps are necessary to minimize the animal's suffering. People are also expected to honor plants and trees, as they reflect God's ability to bring life to land that would otherwise be barren. As humans observe the various cycles of life and death, they are reminded that they themselves will be revived after their own demise.

For Muslims, the purpose of human existence is to worship God and to persevere through the many tests that the world presents. The latter include maintaining ethical standards while dealing with a variety of people from a wide range of backgrounds and with radically different ideas. As the Koran notes, however, God created humankind in many nations and tribes so that people might come to know each other. Just as there is only one God, the ultimate goal of believers is to view

Unlike the Judeo-Christian Bible, the Koran describes the creation in relatively general terms. It goes into more detail in describing the creation of humans, highlighting the miracle of life.

themselves as belonging to a single body. That aim explains Muhammad's famous statement, "None of you truly believes until you wish for your brother what you wish for yourself." As the famous Muslim scholar, al-Nawawi (d. 1277), elaborated the point, the Prophet's words were a reference to the brotherhood of humankind, and not simply to Muslims. Although followers of Islam today often

This early 18th-century miniature painting shows the Mughal emperor Farrukhsiyar accompanied by angels. In Islam, angels play an important role as God's loyal messengers.

stress their special connection to their Muslim brothers and sisters by referring to a single Islamic *ummah* (community), it is important to keep in mind that when Muhammad moved to Medina (called Yathrib at the time), the city as a whole, which included Jews and pagans as well as Muslims in its population, was also viewed as a single *ummah*.

Nevertheless, the Koran and Muhammad's teachings do make distinctions between individuals. The categorizations, however, have nothing to do with race, gender, or economic status. In his final sermon, Muhammad declared that whites are not superior to blacks, and Arabs are not superior to non-Arabs. The only quality that makes anyone superior in the eyes of God is piety, and only God knows each person's status in that respect. In His role as judge, God will make this reality known on the Last Day as He differentiates between those who passed and those who failed the test of the Final Judgment.

ANGELS

Beyond the divisions within humankind, God also differentiates between the different types of beings that He created. That leads to the second pillar of faith, angels. Angels are God's loyal servants who rarely, if ever, exhibit free thinking. They have wings and were created from light, which distinguishes them from humans, who were formed from clay, as well as from the invisible forces known as jinns, who are made from smokeless fire and exhibit much the same freedom of thought as is found among humans. Angels play a wide variety of roles, from relaying God's message to chosen individuals to carrying the throne of God, recording the deeds of each individual, and guarding the gates of Hell.

The Koran mentions five angels by name: Gabriel, Michael, Malik, Harut, and Marut. The Hadith literature adds other names, including those of Israfil, Izrail, Nakir, and Munkar. The most prominent is Gabriel, who played a key role in transmitting the Koran to Muhammad, accompanying him on the miraculous night journey to Jerusalem, and guiding him throughout his career. Perhaps the most famous story of Gabriel is that of the first Koranic revelation, when the archangel encountered Muhammad at the cave of Hira, seized him, and then transmitted the first five verses of the Koran's 96th sura.

Despite the differences between the Koran and the Bible, the former asserts that God revealed various books of the latter. That assertion relates to the third pillar of faith, the belief in sacred books.

Gabriel also figures prominently in the Bible. Yet, despite the fact that Koranic descriptions of angels tend to parallel Biblical ones, one significant divergence relates to the figure of Satan. While the Bible portrays Satan as a fallen angel, many Muslims believe, on the basis of certain Koranic passages, that he was never an angel at all but rather one of the jinns, whom they name Iblis. Iblis's first sin—and the original sin of all time—was his refusal to prostrate himself before Adam when God commanded him to do so, thereby displaying pride. The angels all prostrated themselves without question.

That story does not necessarily imply that all jinns are evil, nor does it signify that there is just one Satan. According to the Koran, anyone, whether jinn or human, who motivates others to do evil can qualify as a Satan. Iblis, however, represents the head of all satanic forces. As for the jinns themselves, Muslims disagree on what exactly they are. Many Muslims regard them as forming invisible communities that parallel human ones and that have the ability to interact with the human world from time to time. Other Muslims see them as metaphorical descriptions of the unseen forces within people, for instance the subconscious mind.

THE SACRED TEXTS

Despite the differences between the Koran and the Bible, the former asserts that God revealed various books of the latter. That assertion relates to the third pillar of faith, the belief in sacred books.

The Koran states that the Torah (al-Tawrat) of Moses, the Psalms (al-Zabur) of David, the Gospel (al-Injil) of Jesus, and the Koran of Muhammad itself are all divinely revealed. As a consequence, the Koran refers to Christians and Jews as "People of the Book." Even so, the Koran also states that the previous scriptures were all altered over time. Consequently, for Muslims, the Koran serves as a final text, and the preservation of God's words as they appear in the work is regarded as one of the most important tasks of the Muslim community—a fact that explains why memorization of the Koran is popular throughout the Muslim world. (Those who learn the entire text by heart are given the honorary title of *hafiz*.) It also indicates why most Muslims do not consider translations of the Koran to be the same as the Koran itself. Because some of the content and form is considered to be lost in translation, the original version is

generally preferred in worship, even among Muslims who do not speak Arabic.

The word *Koran* means "recitation" and, unlike the Christian Bible, it is intended primarily to be experienced as an oral text. (In its written form, it is commonly referred to as a *mushaf*, literally, a codex or a collection of sheets.) It is often recited in a manner that is melodic, and those reciting it may pause at certain points in order to prostrate themselves.

The Koran appeals to the intellect by raising questions and leading its listeners to ponder and reflect. How did everything in existence come to be? What is the significance of the existence of day and night or of the sun and the moon? How is it that humans can come into existence from mere fluids?

Some readers of the Koran find the loose structure of the book attractive but, for others, it is a source of frustration. Besides its repetitive nature, most of the Koran does not follow a linear pattern. In that respect it is unlike the Torah, which takes the form of a linear narrative from the creation of the universe to the Israelites' wandering in the Sinai Peninsula. In the Koran, on the other hand, a single sura may briefly refer to several different Biblical and non-Biblical narratives without delving into the specific details of any one of them; instead, each partial story plays a role in elucidating the sura's major theme or themes. The use of repetition and allusion is a common characteristic of texts that are intended to be read aloud, such as sermons, speeches, and poems.

To convey a sense of the Koran's format, a brief outline of the second sura should suffice. The chapter begins with the mysterious letters *alif*, *lam*, and *mim*, which are equivalent to "A," "L," and "M." They are followed by a declaration that there is no doubt about the truth of the Koran and a description of the characteristics of believers, unbelievers, and hypocrites, together with the fate that each can expect. The sura then goes on to recount the story of creation and the roles of Adam, Eve, and Iblis, which in turn leads to a lengthy discussion of the children of Israel in the context of both Moses and Muhammad, and the lessons to be learned from their accomplishments and mistakes. That passage is followed by a brief reference to Abraham and Ishmael building the Kaaba and to the shrine's significance for Muslims. The sura then stipulates various laws for Muhammad's community and eventually returns to the topic of the Kaaba and the importance of freeing it and purifying it. The sura concludes with three verses that summarize what has gone before.

Like the second sura, most Koranic chapters highlight the general themes of monotheism, prophethood, piety, social justice, and life after death. They also refer to events and issues that are specific to Muhammad's own social context. The audience that the Koran addresses is sometimes Muhammad himself, but at other times it may be the Prophet's companions, family, or even opponents, or all Muslims or even all of humankind. The changes in the narrative voice suggest that the Koran was revealed in piecemeal fashion throughout Muhammad's prophetic career, which began on Mecca's Mountain of Light (Jabal al-Nur) in 610 during the Night of Power (Laylat al-Qadr) in the month of Ramadan and continued until his death 22 years later.

The order in which the Koran's 114 chapters are traditionally numbered, however, has virtually nothing to do with the chronology of their revelation to Muhammad. Most Muslim scholars believe that the first to be passed down were the first five verses of the 96th sura, while the last may have been a passage in the fifth sura. While it is often claimed that the present arrangement of chapters is based on length, that assertion, too, is not without its problems. For example, the longest sura is not the first but the second, while the shortest sura is number 108. The theory that the suras are arranged according to their content may be more reliable, with groups of successive chapters sharing certain concepts and expressions.

By looking beyond the Koran and examining reports of Muhammad's life, scholars have been able to determine when most of the suras were revealed. Suras revealed before the *hijra* (emigration) to Medina are categorized as "Meccan." Those chapters, which constitute the majority, tend to be relatively brief, poetic, and general in nature. Suras revealed after the *hijra* are classified as "Medinan." The Medinan suras tend to be longer and more prosaic in tone, sometimes containing detailed legal injunctions. The change in

THE OPENING SURA

The most commonly recited passage of the Koran is the first sura, which is called al-Fatiha (The Opening). A seven-verse invocation that highlights the Koran's major themes, it forms part of every prayer. At the conclusion, most Muslims say "Amin," the Arabic equivalent of the Hebrew "Amen." The sura reads as follows:

"In the name of God, the Compassionate, the Caring. All praise is due to God, Lord of the worlds, the Compassionate, the Caring, Sovereign of the Day of Judgment. It is You we worship and it is Your aid we seek. Guide us to the straight path, the path You have blessed, not of those who are objects of anger, nor those who are astray."

tone reflects the fact that, in Medina, Muhammad was not only a prophet receiving God's message but also a judge and a leader responsible for the well-being of the community as a whole.

MESSENGERS OF GOD

The fourth pillar of Muslim faith concerns the role of divine messengers. As Muhammad's experience as both a prophet and a community leader shows, the messengers' role was not confined to purely spiritual matters. Each messenger was also a prophet, and the Koran indicates that every civilization at some point had been sent a prophet. Even though the Koran mentions fewer than 30 by name, Muhammad is quoted in its pages as saying that there have been a total of 124,000 divine messengers. Among those identified in the Koran are famous Biblical figures (some of them not typically regarded as prophets in the Christian or Jewish view), such as Adam, Noah (Nuh), Abraham (Ibrahim), Lot (Lut), Ishmael (Ismail), Isaac (Ishaq), Jacob (Yaqub), Joseph (Yusuf), Moses (Musa), Aaron (Harun), David (Dawud), Solomon (Sulayman), Elijah (Ilyas), Jonah (Yunus), Job (Ayyub), John the Baptist (Yahya), and Jesus (Isa). They also include non-Biblical prophets such as Hud, Salih, and Shu'ayb, little-known figures who were probably familiar names to Muhammad's contemporary Arab audience.

However, according to most Muslim scholars, not all those prophets counted as messengers. Messengers not only received divine inspiration, as the prophets did, but in addition were given specific missions; they were sent to particular communities in order to warn those who had strayed from God and to give to those who were righteous good news of

God's infinite reward. Messengers also presented their people with divinely inspired texts, which might be written down in sacred books or else passed on orally by recitation. Prominent among those figures were Moses, David, Jesus, and Muhammad.

Most Muslims believe that the individuals whom God selected as prophets were among the very best of humankind. Even so, there is no suggestion that they were not capable of making human mistakes. The 80th sura, for example, is entitled *Abasa*, which means "He frowned," a reference to an episode in which Muhammad frowned when a blind man interrupted an important meeting with one of the leading Meccan pagans. The first 10 verses of the sura criticize Muhammad for his failure of compassion and for not dedicating his attention to the blind man; addressing the Prophet, God states, "You gave no heed to him who came to you with zeal and awe."

Despite such moments of weakness, prophets are generally held to be free of immorality. Most Muslims reject Biblical narratives that cast the prophets in a negative light, such as the Old Testament story of a drunken Lot impregnating his own daughters.

Even though all the prophets and messengers are revered, five of them are given outstanding prominence in the Koran: Noah, Abraham, Moses, Jesus, and Muhammad. The most-cited name in the Koran is, in fact, that of Moses rather than Muhammad; the name Muhammad itself appears only four times. Nevertheless, the holy book often addresses and refers to Muhammad, who occupies a unique position, for the text declares that he is the "seal of the prophets."

THE LAST PROPHET

From early times, Muslims believed that Muhammad's revelation completes and corrects all the revelations that had gone before it. The special position that he occupied inevitably raised the question of how the religious integrity of the Muslim community should be preserved after his death, given that he was the last prophet and could have no comparable successor. Differing answers to that question lay behind Islam's greatest schism, the split between Sunnis and Shiites.

Sunnis, who have traditionally constituted the majority community in the world of Islam, argued that the responsibility for preserving the faith in a post-Muhammadan world fell on the shoulders of the community itself, often understood as meaning the community of scholars. Consequently, the person selected as Muhammad's successor, or caliph, was primarily a political leader, whose duty was to maintain religious law in the land without necessarily himself becoming involved in religious discourse.

For Shiites, on the other hand, the religious integrity of the community depended on a leader, or imam, from Muhammad's own household. The first imam was Ali ibn Abi Talib, Muhammad's cousin, the second and third imams were Ali's sons (and Muhammad's grandchildren) al-Hasan and al-Husayn, respectively. For the largest group of Shiites, a line of infallible imams continued to guide the community until the 12th imam disappeared, going into a state of occultation (hidden from the eyes of everyone but God), an event believed to have occurred in the ninth century. In the imam's absence, elite Shiite scholars functioned as his representatives in a

manner that resembled the majority group's reliance on their Sunni equivalents.

The idea that Muhammad was the final prophet had other consequences, as well. According to the Koran, Muhammad was "sent as a mercy to the worlds," not just to the Arabs. As such, most Muslims consider the Koran itself to have been his main miracle, since it continues to be accessible to people of all races. While Moses overcame the Egyptian magicians and Jesus could raise the dead, Muhammad, who was probably illiterate, introduced a scripture that Muslims generally believe to be more eloquent than anything the pre-Islamic

Even though all the prophets and messengers are revered, five of them are given outstanding prominence in the Koran: Noah, Abraham, Moses, Jesus, and Muhammad.

Arabs were able to produce. It is also, Muslims assert, a book that contains information that a mere mortal—especially one in seventh-century Arabia—could never have known.

However, it should be noted that the Koran was not the only form of revelation that Muhammad transmitted. He also taught his followers through his Sunna (way). Whereas the Koran is the word of God, which Muhammad simply conveyed in his role as messenger, the Sunna represents the Prophet's normative example and understanding of the Koran; it is the real-life manifestation of the Koranic message. Its significance extended to the specific manner in which Muhammad

In this mural, painted in the 16th century in the Harun Velayat Mausoleum in Isfahan, Iran, a prophet figure kneels surrounded by saints.

THEOLOGICAL CONTROVERSIES

Some scriptural portrayals of God have led to intense theological debates at various periods of Islamic history. If God is distinct from humankind, for instance, what are readers to make of the references in the Koran to His "hand" or to the period following creation, when God is said to have "mounted the throne"?

Some Muslim scholars contend that such portrayals should be taken at face value—that the words of the Koran are the literal truth. Other theologians suggest that the passages in question are metaphorical and that readers should not attach literal meanings to anthropomorphism (description of inhuman subjects in human terms) because that literary device is merely a figurative attempt to describe a phenomenon—in this case, God—that is ineffable. After all, the latter group argues, the Koran also refers to humans "lowering their wings" to others as a metaphor for being merciful; obviously such a phrase cannot be taken literally because humans do not have wings. In similar fashion, they claim, references to the hand of God should not be accepted at face value because otherwise they might be taken to imply that the Creator is bound by space and time. Critics of their position ask why God would use terms such as "hand" when He could have simply said "power." Those are just some of the complexities that Muslim scholars have encountered in attempting to understand and interpret the nature of God as depicted in the holy scriptures of Islam.

Perhaps the most controversial of all issues, however, has concerned the status of the Koran itself. If the work is a transcription of God's own words, should it be viewed as a creation of God or as an aspect of the deity? That question acquired more than academic interest during the Abbasid dynasty, when it was asked of Muslim scholars during the most famous of all Islamic inquisitions, the Mihna (literally, "ordeal"), which was established by the seventh Baghdad caliph al-Mamun (r. 813–833). Al-Mamun was a rationalist who aimed to end sectarianism within Islam by establishing a cohesive single creed. He insisted that the Koran had to have been created, otherwise God's speech would have been uncreated and eternal, features that can describe only God Himself. Used as a tool against traditionalist theologians, the Mihna was ultimately a failure and led to a popular countermovement, which was inspired by, among other things, the harsh measures that had been used to punish those who disagreed with the ruler's own position—dissidents were commonly forced to resign from office, imprisoned, and flogged.

In the view of some Western historians, the fact that there was no definitive, written version of the Koran until the ninth century casts doubt over the strength of the link between the Prophet and the book. Islamic scholars, however, maintain that the Koran was transmitted orally throughout the period between Muhammad's death in 632 CE and its first transcription onto paper.

The different versions of the text that were handwritten at various times and in different places throughout the rapidly expanding Muslim world gave rise to a range of interpretations of some of the suras. Those inconsistencies were responsible for a host of theological disputes about their true significance, some of which remain unresolved.

Today, most Muslims regard as unorthodox the view that the Koran was created, in part because God's speech is considered an aspect of God rather than a separate entity. Moreover, it is not uncommon for modern Muslims to cite the Mihna episode as proof that theological debates can sometimes be unhelpful distractions to the practice of Islam and attempts to focus on its Five Pillars.

prayed and to the way in which he understood particular Koranic commands.

Like the Koran itself, the Sunna is considered a form of revelation. Muslims believe that if Muhammad had made a mistake, God would have corrected him (and Islamic sources duly note several instances of God correcting Muhammad's religious pronouncements). As a consequence, the Sunna, in its final form, is considered a divinely approved model for Muslims to follow. The most popular sources for the Sunna are the Hadiths, most of which record Muhammad's statements and actions.

THE LAST DAY

One major topic of the Hadith corpus is the Day of Judgment, the fifth pillar of faith. The precise timing of the Last Day is never mentioned in the Koran, but the text does assert that "The last hour has drawn near." The idea is that human existence on earth will not last forever, and that it is not the only life. A time of judgment will come, and even though we may not see it now, there are consequences for our actions and the beliefs we uphold.

According to the Koran, "whoever has done an atom's weight of good shall see it, and whoever has done an atom's weight of evil shall see it." Accordingly, individuals' earthly lives serve as a test. Those people who pass the test will be granted admission into heaven, while those who fail it will find themselves in hell. It is during the Last Day that those decisions will be made. Even though the time of judgment is described as a "day," it will seem to last for many years for those who are in the wrong. Thus, while it is sometimes claimed that Islam has no notion of salvation in the Christian sense, the notion of heavenly

reward is actually one of the Koran's most important themes.

On what basis, then, is an individual saved? According to the Koran, "humanity is in a state of loss, except those who have faith, do good deeds, urge one another to the truth, and urge one another to patience and perseverance." Nevertheless, the Koran recognizes that people have a predisposition to take the wrong path, even though there is no notion of original sin in Islam. (In the Islamic view, the fault of Adam and Eve is merely representative of human nature as a whole.) In order to be righteous, one has to "swim upstream" against a current that works to pull people under. For example, one does not have to try to feel envious or to feel animosity toward certain people; the sentiment comes naturally. Patience and forgiveness, however, require motivation.

For that reason, Islamic scripture teaches that if an individual commits an evil act, it is recorded as a single evil deed, but if one does a good deed, it is worth at least 10 times as much. Furthermore, simply intending to do good registers as a good deed, as does deciding not to commit evil. Once a believer commits a sin, however, he or she is instructed to seek God's forgiveness. Sincere repentance requires a serious attempt to change. As long as that prerequisite is met, one can expect that God, in His mercy, will indeed forgive. One Hadith states that a person who spent an entire lifetime doing evil was forgiven after turning a corner and feeding a starving animal. However, those who fail to mend their ways can expect to be punished in hell, and they can only finally make their way to paradise once they have rectified themselves.

While some Muslim scholars may have adopted misogynistic attitudes, the Koran makes it clear that salvation has nothing to do with gender. It states: "Indeed, for men and women who submit [to God], believing men and believing women, devout men and devout women, truthful men and truthful women, men and women who patiently persevere, men and women who humble themselves [before God], charitable men and women, men and women who fast, chaste men and women, men and women who remember God often—for them God has prepared forgiveness and a great reward."

As that passage makes clear, the criterion for salvation is not gender, race, or status, but *taqwa* (consciousness of God). The Koran does not portray either sex as being more inclined to sin. In addition, as Muslim feminists are often quick to note, the Koran (unlike the Bible) nowhere states that Eve tempted Adam into committing the first sin; in one passage, in fact, Adam is singled out as culpable.

What does the Koran say about the fate of non-Muslims? That is an issue which Muslims have debated for centuries. While some scholars have maintained that anyone who did not believe that Muhammad was God's messenger would be punished eternally in hell, many have argued that a just and compassionate God would never punish people unless there was sufficient cause. The famous scholar al-Ghazali (d. 1111), for example, argued that God would never cast down his wrath on non-Muslims who either had never heard of Muhammad or had been exposed only to a negative image of the Prophet. As for those who came to know of the "real" Muhammad, so long as they believed in God and the Last Day and were in the process of investigating the Prophet's message when they passed away, then

God's mercy would be upon them. The famous Sufi philosopher Ibn al-Arabi (d. 1240) adopted a similar line of reasoning in maintaining that the basis upon which God will judge individuals is their sincerity. Some Muslim scholars have even argued that God will accept righteous Christians and Jews as they are, regardless of their knowledge of Muhammad. Thus, Muslim perspectives on this issue cannot be said to occupy a single position.

Another Islamic theological controversy concerns the duration of punishment in hell. While most scholars have conceived of the chastisement as being eternal, a significant minority has maintained that hell will one day perish, at which point all its inhabitants will enter heaven. A few scholars have even argued that hell will be

As Muslim feminists are often quick to note, the Koran (unlike the Bible) nowhere states that Eve tempted Adam into committing the first sin; in one passage, in fact, Adam is singled out as culpable.

transformed into a place of joy once its inhabitants have rectified themselves.

As for the nature of hell itself, the Koran refers to it as al-Nar (the Fire). It is a multilevel abode where one encounters extreme heat, boiling fluids, extreme thirst, and hunger pangs. More importantly, those condemned to suffer it exist in a state of being veiled from God, the worst of all punishments.

In between hell and heaven are the "heights," which the Koran portrays as a purgatory of sorts. As for heaven, it is called al-Janna (the Garden), and it is a multilevel abode in which one finds shade, companionship, the best food and drink, luxurious rugs and beds, and flowing rivers of various kinds. According to one Hadith, heaven has what no eye has seen and what no ear has heard. As such, some people believe that these descriptions are merely approximations of what paradise is really like. In any case, the best of all rewards for

This miniature illustration comes from an early-11th-century edition of *Shah-nameh* (Book of kings) by the Persian poet Firdawsi (around 935–1020). It depicts the Golden Age of Earthly Paradise.

heaven's inhabitants will be beholding God and knowing that God is pleased with them, a state that constitutes the realization of the best possible destiny.

DESTINY

The sixth pillar of faith, the belief in destiny, is in many ways related to the first, the belief in God, which is why some Muslim scholars speak of only five pillars of faith. The identification comes about because destiny represents the will and the power of God—in other words, God is in complete control of His creation, which includes time itself. Accordingly, nothing that happens in the universe is purely accidental. As the Koran notes, all calamities on earth, including those that occur among people, are recorded in advance. One Hadith adds, "The pens have been lifted, and the ink is dry." That belief has the practical benefits of discouraging believers from either despairing when difficulties befall them or becoming arrogant when they encounter success. Thus, when speaking of future plans, Arabs habitually add the caveat *Insha'Allah* (If God wills).

The belief that everything is preordained leads inevitably to the classic question of why bad things happen to good people if God is in control of the world. The Koran addresses that problem indirectly in the 18th sura in a brief narrative about Moses. According to the story, Moses seeks the guidance of a wise man, who in certain Hadiths is given the name Khidr (the green one). The wise man states that Moses will be unable to maintain his patience with him, to which Moses responds that he will endure this test "if God wills." They then set off, and the first thing the wise man does—in

accordance with God's command—is to make a hole in a boat. Bewildered, Moses asks him why he would damage someone else's property in that way at the risk of drowning its owners. The wise man reminds Moses of his earlier promise, to which Moses responds that he will indeed be patient. However, soon afterward, the man—again in accordance with God's command—murders a child. Moses is shocked and condemns him for killing an innocent person. The man again reminds Moses of his promise, and so they proceed. Finally, they reach a town whose

The sixth pillar of faith, the belief in destiny, is in many ways related to the first, the belief in God, which is why some Muslim scholars speak of only five pillars of faith.

inhabitants refuse to receive them. Nevertheless, the wise man—still acting on God's instructions—rewards their lack of hospitality by repairing a broken wall in the city.

Unable to contain himself any longer, Moses demands to know why he would not request some form of payment for assisting people who did not deserve his help. Informing the prophet that he has failed the test, the man then proceeds to explain to Moses the wisdom behind each of his actions. By puncturing the boat, he in fact preserved it for its needy owner, who would otherwise have had to surrender it to an approaching king who was forcibly seizing all functioning vessels. The child whom he murdered was fated to become an evil, rebellious individual who

This late-16th-century Persian miniature illustration depicts the expulsion of Adam and Eve from the Garden of Eden.

would otherwise have brought nothing but trouble on his righteous parents. As for the damaged wall, it belonged to two young orphans and there was treasure hidden underneath it. By repairing it at that time, the wise man ensured that its secret would not be discovered until a later date at which the rightful owners would be old enough to ensure that no one would take it from them. In sum, the mysterious wise man makes it clear that all his actions, however inscrutable they may have seemed, were based on God's command rather than on his own will.

Rabia Al-Adawiyya: The Sufi of Love

Perhaps the best known of all the Sufis who devoted themselves to the concept of divine love was a woman named Rabia al-Adawiyya (died 801). Born in the port city of Basra in what is now Iraq, Rabia—the word literally means "fourth"—was so named because she was the family's fourth daughter. Raised in a poor household, Rabia found her life permanently altered when she was captured by robbers while traveling with a caravan and sold as a slave. Her piety, however, so impressed the man who bought her that he freed her, permitting her once more to take up a religious life.

Before long, Rabia's devotion had acquired her a substantial following among men and women alike. She is remembered for her absolute love for God and for her famous prayer: "O God, if I worship You in fear of hellfire, burn me in it. And if I worship You in hope of paradise, exclude me from it. But if I worship You for Your own sake, do not withhold from me Your everlasting beauty."

Today, Rabia remains an influential figure, with mosques named after her throughout the Muslim world and films and books produced about her life.

Thus, the Koran tackles the problem of evil by highlighting humankind's limitations in comprehending the reality of things. Yet the scripture also notes that earthly life was never meant to be easy, making clear that God will test people with "fear, hunger, and loss of wealth, lives, and [life's] fruits."

Some people query why, if the goal of life is to attain the rewards of paradise, God did not simply place humankind in heaven to begin with. The Koran answers the question indirectly in the story of Adam and Eve. In the Garden of Evil, the first were morally responsible for only one task: avoiding eating the fruit of a single tree. Yet they could not even manage that limited duty. In other words, by living in paradise, they were unable to grow morally. The implication is that it is only through the trials of this life that an individual can evolve to reach the point of living a life of serenity in the Garden while maintaining a high moral standard.

Yet that answer, too, raises questions about God's purpose for, had He so wished, He could surely have created humans to be like angels, always doing right. There again, the Koran addresses the issue indirectly. When God informs the angels that He intends to create a representative on earth, the angels themselves ask if He will create a being that spreads corruption and sheds blood, unlike themselves, who simply exist to praise God. God's response is that He knows what they do not know. He then proceeds to teach Adam, the first man, the names, or essences, of things. When God commands the angels in their turn to proclaim these names, they respond by noting that God has not provided them with the necessary knowledge. God next instructs Adam to do the same, and the man succeeds in doing so. God then reminds the angels of His knowledge and wisdom. The moral of the story seems to be that, while humans may have the capacity for sin, they also have a potential for growth that is greater than that of the angels, perhaps because of the human capacity to make moral decisions.

If God controls destiny, do humans have free will? This is another issue that has been widely debated by Muslim theologians and philosophers. While some scholars maintain that individuals have absolute free will, others insist that they have no freedom. The majority of commentators, however, reach a compromise, arguing that, although God is in control of His creation, He has nevertheless granted humankind the freedom to make moral decisions. That line of argument seems to be consonant with the Koran's position, because while some parts of the book indicate that God guides whom He wills and similarly leads astray those whom He chooses, others note that God guides people on the right or wrong path on the basis of their own decisions.

THE PURSUIT OF GOD

The six pillars of faith—in God, the angels, books, messengers, the Last Day, and destiny—represent the beliefs that are required of all Muslims. In a similar vein, the five pillars of Islam—testimony, prayer, the alms tax, fasting, and pilgrimage—are the actions that all must undertake. Even people who do the bare minimum may be considered righteous Muslims and believers. Some, however, go beyond merely seeking salvation to pursue nearness to God, a concept that involves the quest for *ihsan*.

According to the Hadith quoted at the beginning of this chapter, *ihsan* is praying to God as if one sees Him, or, at the very least, recognizes that He sees you. The desire to be aware of God at a higher level of consciousness is a characteristic of prophets and saints, and reflects a mentality that many Muslims associate with the mystical doctrines of Sufism.

SUFISM

Sufis may be either Sunni or Shiite. There is some debate as to the origin of the term *sufi*. One theory is that it comes from the Arabic word *suf* (wool), in reference to the woolen garments worn by ascetic Muslims who renounced the pleasures of the flesh. Today, it is common to translate Sufism as Islamic "mysticism," yet that term encompasses only one of three principal orientations within the Sufi movement, the other two being asceticism and love. The main goal of all three orientations is to achieve self-purification through identification with God.

The ascetic Sufi aims to live as simple a life as possible in order to avoid any distractions that may take him or her away from the path to God. The concept of love, meanwhile, emphasizes unconditional devotion to God above everything else in the universe.

The mystical Sufi seeks union with God. Sufi masters are able to control the ego as they draw closer to God, not through fear of punishment or desire for reward but for the sake of God alone. That state, many Muslims believe, represents the epitome of *ihsan*. Those who attain it find pleasure simply in being in the presence of God's light, a condition best illustrated by the classic "verse of light" passage from the Koran, which states: "God is the light of the heavens and the earth. The parable of his light is like a niche within which is a lamp; the lamp is in glass; the glass is like a shining star; lit from a blessed tree— an olive tree that is neither of the east nor of the west, whose oil virtually illuminates even though no fire touches it—light upon light. God guides to his light whom he wills."

Peoples of the Book

Although the Koran is the holiest book of Islam, Muslims also respect the Bible and claim fellowship with Jews and Christians, whom they call the Peoples of the Book.

Muslims do not view themselves as the only community to have received revelation from God. In many passages, the Koran affirms that what has been revealed to Muhammad is nothing new, but a confirmation of the same divine message of old. The Koran states that every civilization has had prophets who introduced divine books. In addition to the Koran, these include the Torah (*al-Tawrat*) of Moses, the Psalms (*al-Zabur*) of David, and the Gospels (*al-Injil*) of Jesus. However, while Muslims respect the Judeo-Christian Bible, they believe that the Torah, the Psalms, and the Gospels have all been altered in some way, and that only the Koran is the word of God in its purest form.

Nevertheless, because the Bible is not believed to have been completely changed, the Koran honorifically labels Jews and Christians as "Peoples of the Book" and thus Muslims share a special bond with both religions. Jews and Christians are the only groups with which the Koran explicitly permits interfaith marriage. The Koran also declares the food of the Peoples of the Book lawful for Muslims, as long as it does not include items that are explicitly prohibited, such as pork and carrion.

APPROPRIATE RELATIONSHIPS

Beyond this, however, there are disagreements among Muslims over what constitutes an appropriate relationship with the Peoples of the Book. Some Muslims believe that they should never befriend Christians or Jews, but that is a minority view. Nevertheless, Muslims who model their behavior on the example of Muhammad find conflicting evidence about the Prophet's relationship with the Peoples of the Book. For example, when the earliest converts to Islam were persecuted in Mecca, Muhammad instructed many of his followers to emigrate to eastern Africa to seek the protection of the tolerant Christian king of Abyssinia, the Negus. When the Muslims moved to Medina, they made an alliance with the Jewish tribes there, and a rabbi was among those killed fighting for Muhammad at the Battle of Uhud. On the other hand, tensions developed between Muslims and Byzantine Christians, and Muhammad himself accompanied an army that traveled north to the Arabian city of Tabuk to confront a Byzantine army that ultimately never arrived. Back in central Arabia, Muhammad took various courses of action against those Jewish tribes deemed to be a threat.

Muslims who model their behavior on the example of Muhammad find conflicting evidence about the Prophet's relationship with the Peoples of the Book.

As far as beliefs go, recognition of Muhammad as the final prophet and messenger of God is one of the most significant differences between the Muslims and the Peoples of the Book. Apart from that, however, there are many similarities between the three religions. Jews, Christians, and Muslims are monotheists and believe in an afterlife. The Koran acknowledges all of the following Biblical figures as prophets: Adam, Noah (Nuh), Abraham (Ibrahim), Lot (Lut), Ishmael (Ismail), Isaac (Ishaq), Jacob (Yaqub), Joseph (Yusuf), Moses (Musa), Aaron (Harun),

A group of Turkish pilgrims on the hajj look out over the field on which the Battle of Uhud was fought in 625 CE. In this confrontation, the Muslim forces were joined by Jews against the inhabitants of Mecca.

COMPLEX INTERACTIONS

The complexity of the relationship between Islam and Christianity is well illustrated by the Crusades. The first of these attempts by the Christian West to capture Jerusalem was announced in 1095 by Pope Urban II in response to the burning of the Church of the Holy Sepulcher by the Muslim ruler al-Hakim and the maltreatment of Christians by Turkic Muslims called Seljuks. Eastern Christians requested assistance from their Western brethren. The First Crusade was successful in its main aim but thousands of Muslims, Jews, and Christians died during the capture of Jerusalem. Many years later, the Muslims regained the city under the leadership of Salah ad-Din (Saladin). Even though the Crusaders lost Jerusalem, their encounters with Muslims led to increased trade and the exchange of important ideas—ideas that would play a significant role in Europe's Renaissance. Though the Crusades were presented by the Christians as holy wars motivated purely by religious fervor, there were also financial and political incentives for the campaigns, and it was because of those considerations that some crusade battles involved Muslim-Christian alliances confronting other Muslim-Christian alliances.

Relations between Muslims, Christians, and Jews remain complex today, as evidenced by the ongoing tensions between Palestinians and Israelis in the West Bank and the Gaza Strip, the suicide attacks on the United States on September 11, 2001, and the ensuing War on Terror by the United States and its allies. Nevertheless, numerous examples of positive interactions and a recent increase in interfaith work represent a competing trend that highlights the potential for peaceful coexistence.

David (Dawud), Solomon (Sulayman), Elijah (Ilyas), Jonah (Yunus), Job (Ayyub), John the Baptist (Yahya), and Jesus (Isa).

Even so, the Koranic portrayal of these characters differs from the Biblical version. For example, the Koran makes no reference to Eve (Hawa) tempting Adam in the Garden of Eden. Also, the Koran places greater emphasis than the Bible on Ishmael, Abraham's son with Hagar—the Old Testament concentrates on Isaac, Abraham's son with Sarah. Isaac was the ancestor of the Jews, while Ishmael is considered the forefather of the Arabs in general and of Muhammad in particular. Moreover, most Muslims believe that the famous command to Abraham to sacrifice his first son was a reference to Ishmael rather than to Isaac. The Koran also asserts that Abraham and Ishmael were the first to establish the Kaaba in Mecca as a place of worship. As for the Israelites, the Koran praises and criticizes them in almost equal measure. It venerates Moses, who is mentioned by name more than any other person in the book, but condemns his followers for their disobedience.

JESUS IN ISLAM

Another notable difference between the Koran and the New Testament is their treatment of Jesus. The Koran describes Jesus as having been only a prophet and a messenger rather than the Son of God, and thereby rejects the Christian doctrine of the Trinity, which regards God as the Father, the Son, and the Holy Spirit in one person. The Koran also denies that Jesus's mother Mary (Maryam) is divine.

As for salvation, Muslims generally reject the notion that Jesus died for the sins of humanity. According to the Koran, there is no original sin inherited from Adam and Eve, and each individual is responsible only for his or her own deeds. Sins may be erased when believers do good and seek God's forgiveness. The Koran describes Jesus as the Messiah, and many Muslims believe that he will return before the Day of Judgment in order to establish justice in the world.

Like the New Testament, the Koran describes Jesus as a miracle worker and includes some narratives not found in the canonical Christian texts, including stories of Jesus

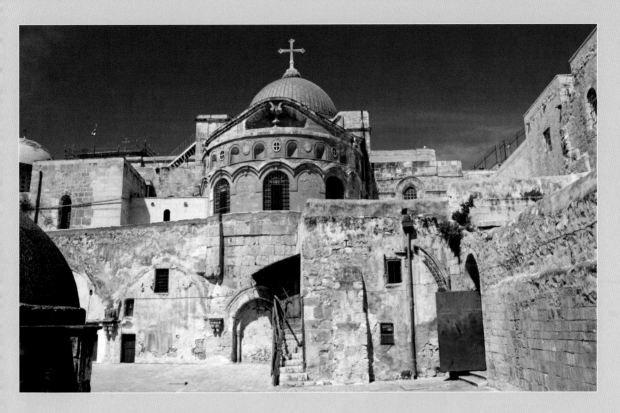

The Church of the Holy Sepulcher stands on the site in Jerusalem where, according to tradition, Jesus was crucified and buried. One of the most sacred Christian shrines, the church was destroyed by the caliph al-Hakim around 1009 but, since its reconstruction in the 12th century, it has always been protected by Muslims when the city has been under Islamic rule.

speaking as an infant and making a bird out of clay. Elsewhere in the Koran, there are references to Jesus's virgin birth. In fact, Mary figures very prominently throughout the work. The 19th sura (chapter) is named after her, and she is mentioned more times in the Koran than in the entire New Testament. Although she is not divine, the Koran describes her as having been chosen by God and elevated over all other women.

It is perhaps because of these commonalities with Christians that the Koran declares them to be the group closest to Muhammad's community. Yet, for centuries after the death of Muhammad, there was much greater conflict between those two religions—as evidenced by the Crusades—than between Islam and Judaism.

INTERFAITH COOPERATION

However, even during the periods of the greatest tension, there were still positive interactions between Islam and Christianity, and also with Judaism. When the second caliph, or successor to Muhammad, Umar ibn al-Khattab, conquered Jerusalem, he allowed Christians to continue their religious practices and permitted many Jewish families to move back into the city (after the Byzantines had expelled them). When a Christian leader asked Umar if he would pray inside one of the city's most significant churches, Umar refused, worrying that later Muslims would desire to transform the church into a mosque. As for the famous Church of the Holy Sepulcher, Umar assigned a Muslim to guard its gates. To this day, individuals believed to be the descendants of that person continue to guard its entrance.

In general, Christians and Jews living under Muslim rule were not forced to convert to Islam. They were classified as *dhimmi*s (non-Muslims within a Muslim state) and were usually protected under the law.

Chapter 4

PRACTICES

While belief lies at the heart of Islam, the faith places a strong emphasis on behavior and, in particular, on the performance of five essential duties known as the Pillars of Islam. This chapter also examines other aspects of Islamic practice, including marriage, divorce, dress, and circumcision rituals.

The scriptural instructions of Islam govern almost every aspect of Muslims' lives. Whether they are greeting friends or neighbors, praying, and even in their business transactions, Muslims try to follow the sacred guidelines. The guidelines are accorded different importance. Some take the form of simple recommendations, while others are obligatory (the latter are known in Arabic as *fard*). Unlike other faiths that divide life into two spheres, religious and secular, Islam provides guidance for a believer's entire existence.

The strict adherence that Islam demands of its followers in everyday life and special rituals has led some observers to categorize the faith, along with Hinduism and Judaism, as an orthopraxy (a religion that emphasizes what one does) rather than an orthodoxy, which stresses doctrine and what people believe. While it would be simplistic to assert that devotion to Islam is measured only by actions adn behavior—Muslim theologians attach comparable significance to what people actually think and believe in their hearts—it is undeniably true that anyone wishing

An Indonesian woman reads the Koran, the sacred book of Islam.

to be regarded as a Muslim must perform various outward forms of worship; those acts are known as *ibada*.

THE SHAHADA

The First Pillar of Islam, on which all the rest depend, is the *shahada*, which must be performed by everyone who wishes to be part of the community of the faith. In Arabic, the word *shahada* means literally "to testify" or "to bear witness." Believers who recite the *shahada* are testifying or bearing witness to two things—first, that there is only one God, Allah (*la ilaha illa Allah*), and second, that Muhammad is the messenger of God (*Muhammadun rasul Allah*). In the ceremony marking an individual's conversion to Islam, the *shahada* is often proclaimed with the words: "I testify that there is no God but Allah and I testify that Muhammad is the Messenger of Allah" (*Ashhadu an la ilaha illa'llah wa ashhadu an Muhammadun rasulu'llah*).

The *shahada* must be spoken in Arabic, which is the first language of Islam and the language of the Koran. It must be said twice in order to authenticate the truth of the belief in Allah as the only God and

Muhammad's role as messenger. Most scholars agree that the pronouncement must be made in the presence of at least one person already of the Muslim faith who can verify the convert's commitment to Islam. Simply mouthing the words is not enough, because uttering the phrase is regarded as genuine only if it is spoken with the proper motivation. The concept of intention (*niyya*) is in fact a major aspect of Islam; in all aspects of the faith, actions, even if carried out correctly, ultimately mean nothing to God if they are not accompanied by proper intent. Every pillar and action that a Muslim performs must have *niyya* if they are to be meaningful in the sight of God.

The *shahada* is simultaneously both an action demonstrating a worshipper's attachment to the religion of Islam and a proclamation of the basic beliefs required of a Muslim. For that reason, most scholars of Islam categorize the *shahada* as both a practice and a belief. The formula is used frequently in daily life as one of the prime statements recited by Muslims during prayers. The *shahada*'s importance is paramount, for even though Muslims are required to follow the four other pillars of Islam, some scholars believe that simply reciting the *shahada* is enough in itself to become a Muslim.

RITUAL PURITY AND CLEANSING

The Second Pillar of Islam is prayer (*salat*). To understand the Islamic attitude to prayer, it is first necessary to understand the importance for Muslims of the concept of purity (*tahara*), which is central not only to prayer but also to the practice of the faith in general. According to one of Muhammad's best known Hadiths (sayings), "Purity is half the faith (*iman*)."

Being in a state of ritual purity is necessary for Muslims to perform prayers and other religious duties. Without *tahara*, all acts of devotion are considered void. The condition requires spiritual and mental preparation, which may involve a range of strategies, such as detaching oneself from worldly desires in order to commune with

Even though Muslims are required to follow the four other pillars of Islam, some scholars believe that simply reciting the shahada is enough in itself to become a Muslim.

God and treating others with kindness and sincerity. However, there is no infallible method of attaining spiritual *tahara*, and the mechanisms for achieving it are not meticulously outlined by Islamic legal scholars—it is left to believers to find their own way.

Physical purity, however, is a different matter. Detailed systems of rules and regulations dictate its requirements, with the exact specifications differing from one Islamic legal school (*madhhab*) to another. Two states of impurity (*hadath*) are recognized—minor (*al-hadath al-asghar*) and major (*al-hadath al-akbar*). Examples of minor impurities include touching blood, urine, or feces; urinating; sleeping (a waste of time); and touching the genitals. For many Muslims, touching the skin of a marriageable individual also counts as a minor impurity. If a Muslim seems unwilling to shake hands with someone of the opposite sex, for example, it is most likely because he or she wishes to avoid

Muslims wash before entering a mosque in Bandar Seri Begawan, Brunei.

skin contact before prayer. Major impurities include the sexual act itself, the emission of semen, and menstruation.

The means of purification needed before carrying out the required prayers and other Islamic rituals are also laid down by tradition. The ablution, or cleansing, that the believer must undergo to remove minor impurities is known as *wudu*. Each school of Islamic law differs on the specifics of *wudu*, but most religious foundations agree that the face, neck, nose, mouth, ears, hands, and arms to the elbows need to be washed, as do the feet and

IMAMS

The word *imam* has many different meanings and functions within the Muslim tradition. In general, an imam is the prayer leader of a mosque. Unlike priests or rabbis, who must be educated and ordained to hold their positions, imams are not always trained for the job. Problems can arise, however, when imams without a proper background in Islamic education attempt to offer their own judgments and legal opinions on religious matters.

Female imams have attracted some Western media attention. The Koran does not forbid women from serving as prayer leaders although, traditionally, Islamic legal scholars have held that a female imam may lead only other women in prayer.

That notion is now being challenged in several countries. In 2005, a Muslim woman led a mixed group of men and women in prayer in New York City. In Morocco and Turkey, women have been given positions as religious educators and consolers by the government, although in Morocco they are still forbidden to lead men in prayer. China and India have women imams functioning as prayer leaders and educators in local mosques, but there, too, they lead only women in prayer.

ankles. Major impurities require more elaborate measures that cleanse the entire body, a ritual known in Arabic as *ghusl*; for believers with access to modern bathroom facilities, *ghusl* usually involves taking a bath.

Many mosques have a place to wash before prayer: There is often a cistern or tank of water by the entrance or in a courtyard. As befits Islam's origins in the arid lands of Saudi Arabia, if water is unavailable, sand and dirt can also be used to clean the body. However, facilities are only provided at the mosque to perform *wudu*; *ghusl* must be performed outside of the mosque.

PRAYER

Once the body, the mind, and the spirit are pure, then a Muslim is ready to pray. Prayer is another essential tenet of the faith—according to another Hadith, if Islam is a tent, then prayer is the center pole holding up the entire structure. Along with *zakat* (charity), prayer is in fact the pillar of Islam that is mentioned most often in the Koran, its importance stressed not only by Muhammad himself but also by other Koranic prophets such as Moses, Abraham, and Jesus Christ.

The *salat* is a strictly defined set of actions and phrases that are performed and recited in a specific order at designated times. Personal prayer (*dua*) is also permitted, but most images of Muslims praying show the *salat*, which is the preferred form of worship.

Muslims observe the following five prayers on a daily basis:
- The Fajr prayer, performed after the break of day but before sunrise.
- The Duhr prayer, performed around the middle of the day.
- The Asr prayer, which must be performed sometime before sunset.
- The Maghrib prayer, performed after sunset but before darkness.
- The Isha prayer, performed after the Maghrib prayer, and which must be completed before dawn.

Muslims must attempt to undertake each prayer at the appropriate time, but if a prayer is missed it is always permissible to perform it later in the day. Believers also say additional prayers for special occasions, and supplementary prayers are added after the normal ones at weddings, religious festivals, and on similar occasions. Only the five daily prayers, however, are regarded as compulsory (*fard*).

Muslim prayer is characterized by the various positions adopted and the phrases uttered throughout the process. The basic sequence starts with the postulants standing and involves bending at the waist, straightening up again, and then going into a sitting position to prostrate themselves with their foreheads touching the ground. After that, postulants perform a second prostration before finally returning to the sitting position. Each motion is accompanied by the recital of a particular quotation from the Koran; for example, at the start of prayer, the worshipper recites the opening chapter (al-Fatiha). Sometimes hand gestures are also involved.

A complete cycle of movements and phrases is known as a rakah. After completing one rakah, the worshipper stands up again to begin a new one. Each of the five obligatory prayers has a certain number of rakahs (usually two) that must be performed.

Also while praying, Muslims must follow certain other prescripts, including a statement of the intention (niyya) to complete a given prayer, which is a necessary first step for the supplication to be acceptable in the sight of God. It is also important to wear appropriate clothing that covers the body. No matter where in the world they may be, all Muslims must face in the direction of Mecca as they pray. Every mosque has a niche known as the mihrab carved in one of the walls that indicates the direction (qibla) in which the congregation should face. The specific geographical focus is, in fact, not so much Mecca itself as the Kaaba, the ancient shrine located in the city's main square, which is supposed to have been constructed by the prophet Abraham himself and his son Ishmael.

THE CALL TO PRAYER

In non-Muslim countries, keeping track of prayer times can sometimes be difficult. Muslims living in predominantly Islamic lands, however, have the benefit of the call to prayer (adhan). In the same way that much of the Christian world traditionally used bells to summon the faithful to church services, so the early Muslim community developed its own method of informing the entire community that the time for prayer had arrived. When the appointed hour for prayer approaches, a muezzin (crier) climbs a minaret (manara) attached to the mosque or some other elevated spot—although technically the adhan can be performed from any location—and announces that the time for prayer has arrived. The actual call to prayer is a melodic proclamation, more of an incantation than an announcement. The adhan follows a basic pattern recognized by Muslims the world over. First comes the announcement that "God is great," followed by the shahada declaration of faith and then the actual call to prayer itself, ending with a repetition of the first line, "God is great." Shia Muslims extend the adhan with additional phrases.

THE MOSQUE

The mosque, or masjid, which literally means "place of prostration," is the preferred location for communal prayer, and, as such, is an institution that plays a central role in the local Muslim community. Historically, the mosque served not only as a place for worship, but also for many Muslims as both a town hall and an educational center. Even today, children travel to the mosques for their studies, and lectures of all sorts can be heard within the building precincts. People meet in mosques to discuss matters of common interest, and the poor look to the mosque to organize the collection of alms.

Ultimately, however, the mosque functions as a central place of worship for the community. Required to pray regularly five times a day, most people would find it difficult if not impossible to travel to the mosque to make each and every prayer daily. Muslims are therefore allowed to pray outside of the mosque, in their homes, at their places of work, outside in the open air, in fact almost anywhere so long as the place in which they perform their acts of worship is not ritually unclean.

COMMUNAL PRAYER

Although praying in solitude is not forbidden in Islam, neither is it actively encouraged; it is generally considered better to pray in the company of at least one other person. At least once a week, however, Muslims are expected to attend communal prayer in a mosque. That

Like the other pillars of Islam, prayer has a multitude of effects on the individual and the community. Its principal role is to demonstrate an individual's relationship to God.

requirement is intended to bring Muslims together and reinforce the social bond of the community. Friday is the Islamic holy day, just as Sunday is for Christians and Saturday for Jews, and all Muslims who can do so are expected to attend the Friday noon prayer (*duhr*). Some legal schools even specify that at least 40 Muslim males must

attend the Friday prayers at the mosque, although others require smaller numbers.

When Muslims gather together in a mosque, the prayers are led by an imam. An imam is not necessarily a religious leader but rather a guide whom the congregants follow through the various prayer cycles in the correct order. Following Friday prayer, the imam or a guest speaker will usually preach a sermon on a topic relevant to Islam. Subjects for the Friday address may range from the basic beliefs of the faith to legal and ethical issues or even political matters. Friday prayers are attended by women as well as men, although the sexes are not permitted to pray together. The women will pray either in a separate room or, if they share the same space as the men, then at the back or in an area separated from the male congregation by a curtain.

THE FUNCTION OF PRAYER

Prayer in Islam is not an act with a single result. Like the other pillars of Islam, prayer has a multitude of effects on both the individual and the community. Its principal role is to demonstrate an individual's relationship to God. Islam is a religion of submission or surrender, and a Muslim is one who submits or surrenders to God. It is in the acts of prayer and prostration that a Muslim demonstrates total submission to God.

In addition to its significance for the individual, prayer is also a communal act that is intended to break down the social divisions created by birth and wealth. Islam stresses not only belief in one God but also the equality of all believers. That is nowhere more evident than in the practice of communal prayer, during which all the faithful, regardless of their status within society, line up shoulder to shoulder. Prayer is not only beneficial to the individual but is an act of cohesion that enriches the whole community.

ALMSGIVING

The Third Pillar of Islam is donations to charity (almsgiving). There are two different types of almsgiving in Muslim tradition: the alms tax (*zakat al-fitr*), which is paid at the end of Ramadan, and the *zakat al-mal*, more commonly referred to simply as the *zakat*.

The Koran frequently refers to the requirement to pay *zakat* in conjunction with the necessity of prayer (*salat*). *Zakat* literally means "growth" or "purity." Muslims believe that wealth can be corrupting, so giving away at least a portion of one's worldly goods can help make the rest of one's wealth pure. To maximize the effect, the Koran encourages people to give as much as possible.

The Koran provides a basic definition of *zakat*, but the details of what alms must be given, when, and to whom have been further elaborated by Muslim legal scholars. Each school of law has its own distinct rulings and opinions, but certain general principles are commonly accepted. First and foremost, *zakat* is incumbent only on Muslims. A second requirement is that *zakat* may be paid only by non-slaves. This requirement may sound outmoded, as freedom is now widely seen as a natural human right but, for much of Islam's history, slavery was a fact of life, and Muslims who were slaves were not required to pay *zakat*. A third condition is that *zakat* becomes payable only if the individual concerned is earning more than

Men worship at a mosque during Friday prayers in Uzbekistan.

ALCOHOL AND ISLAM

Of all Islam's interdictions, the prohibition against alcohol is probably the best known to non-Muslims. The Koran and the Sunna both forbid the use of any substance that can intoxicate. In response, many Muslims avoid alcohol in all forms. They also take steps to avoid restaurants that may cook food in wine or any other variety of alcohol.

Selling alcohol is strictly forbidden in certain Muslim countries, such as Saudi Arabia, but, in others, alcoholic drinks can be purchased in shops and bars. Even in some of the strictest countries, production of alcohol has not ceased. Iran, for example, is well known for its wine regions; the Shiraz grape variety takes its name from the Iranian city.

Most Muslims frown on the consumption of alcohol and despise drunkenness, which in some countries carries severe penalties, such as imprisonment or whipping. Yet the loss of dignity and of respect from their coreligionists is often punishment enough for practicing Muslims caught indulging in alcoholic beverages.

a certain amount (known as the *nisab*), which varies according to the type of income being taxed. That provision arises because of Islam's concern for the welfare of each person and the desire not to burden those who have scarcely enough to support themselves.

A further requirement is that *zakat* can be paid only from money that has been earned legally or from handling permissible products. In other words, stolen funds cannot be used, and illegal earnings cannot be made pure by giving them as alms. Then again, before giving *zakat* to the needy, a Muslim must first pay all of his or her outstanding debts, giving alms only from the sum that remains. Finally, as in the case of prayer, a Muslim must have the proper intention (*niyya*) when giving alms.

Zakat is supposed to be offered in a spirit of charity and purely for the benefit of those in need, not in order to build up one's own status by a public display of generosity.

Zakat is applied to several different categories of income. In the traditional societies in which Islam developed, crops and livestock were the principal sources of wealth. Many of the laws relating to *zakat* focus on assets, such as dates and camels, that were common currency in Arabia during Muhammad's lifetime. Such injunctions may again seem out of place in the modern world but, in fact, many Muslims today still live off the land through agriculture. They continue to apply the *zakat* provisions to their crops and livestock. As a rule, around 10 percent of the yearly yield goes in alms.

In addition to crops and livestock, cash and other assets are also subject to *zakat*. Muslims are expected to put aside 2.5 percent of their annual earnings to this end.

Different customs apply to the collection and distribution of *zakat* depending on where a Muslim lives. In lands where the Islamic community forms a minority, there are generally two payment methods. People can either give their *zakat* directly to worthy recipients or else they can hand it over to their local mosque, which will in turn pass it on to the needy. In countries where Muslims form the majority, too, both of these options generally apply, but there may also be state-run institutions that collect and allocate the tax. Such bodies may be regarded with suspicion if people come to believe that there is an element of corruption in the way in which the money is gathered or handed out.

Zakat serves a twofold purpose—it both provides for those in need and helps to strengthen communal bonds. The Koran identifies the groups that are considered worthy recipients of the tax, and Muslim legal scholars follow the model the holy book lays down with only slight variations.

Among those to whom zakat should be given are the poor, those who collect zakat, converts to Islam who have lost their possessions as a result of their conversion, charitable causes, people in debt, travelers in need, and then anyone else in need (including non-Muslims).

Besides helping individual members of the Muslim ummah (religious community), the tax strengthens the bonds linking the community as a whole. Just as prayer creates a sense of egalitarianism, so too does zakat. Through wealth-sharing, zakat helps create a balance between those with little and those with much.

Zakat is incumbent on all Muslims, but Shiites also pay a second tax known as khums (literally, one-fifth), which requires the donation of 20 percent of earnings to pilgrims, to those in need, or to orphans. The assets that are taxed by khums differ slightly from those under the

The worshippers at this mosque in Jerusalem are all facing south toward Mecca.

zakat. However, in their purpose and intent, the *zakat* and the *khums* are one and the same.

RAMADAN AND FASTING

Fasting (*sawm*) during the month of Ramadan forms the Fourth Pillar of Islam. Ramadan is one of the most active months for Muslims for many reasons. Through

It is difficult to figure out the exact start of Ramadan. The moon must reach a precise crescent shape, as prescribed by Islamic legal scholars, in order for the festival to begin.

sawm and general abstinence, the faithful strive to become more in tune with God, paying extra attention to religious activities such as prayer, paying *zakat*, and reading the Koran. Ramadan is also a time of commemoration, for it was during that month that the first verses of the Koran were revealed to Muhammad.

Ramadan is the ninth month of the Muslim calendar. The calendar follows a lunar cycle and is thus shorter than the Gregorian calendar used in the United States. As a result, Ramadan begins and ends at a different time each year; for example, in 2000, Ramadan was observed in the month of January according to the Gregorian count but, in 2008, the festival was celebrated in September. As Muslims abstain from food each day in Ramadan from sunrise until sunset, the gradual shift in season from year to year has a significant impact on the length of time for which they have to fast because of the changing duration of daylight throughout the year. In the United States, for example, fasting time in January is significantly shorter than in June.

It is difficult to figure out the exact start of Ramadan. The moon must reach a precise crescent shape, as prescribed by Islamic legal scholars, in order for the festival to begin. Technological advances have helped pinpoint the likely start much further in advance than was the case in the past, when each local Muslim judge (*qadi*) determined the beginning of Ramadan within his own jurisdiction. Today, most Muslims follow official rulings on the start of Ramadan as issued by the religious authorities of the countries in which they live. Muslims residing in Europe and North America usually mark the start of the festival at the same time as their coreligionists in Muslim lands, particularly in Saudi Arabia as the country of Mecca and Medina, the two holiest cities of Islam.

For the duration of Ramadan, all Muslims are under an obligation (*fard*) to fast unless they are unable or forbidden to do so. Women who are menstruating or pregnant are not permitted to fast because they are ritually impure. The sick are also exempted if it will endanger their health. Children and the elderly are allowed to participate but, if they are unable to do so, then there is no violation of Islamic law.

Once Ramadan begins, Muslims are expected to abstain from eating food and drinking water in daylight hours. Islamic legal schools differ slightly on what else is forbidden, but most agree that individuals should not become intoxicated, smoke, or engage in sex.

One Ramadan requirement that is often overlooked or taken for granted is the mental discipline that believers are required to display in addition to performing the physical fast. Ramadan is a time to reconnect with God or to become more attuned to one's own spirituality. Physical fasting prepares the soul for that undertaking, but no one can hope to achieve a heightened sense of the divine without correct thought. To keep their minds on God, believers are encouraged to divert their attention from worldly wants and needs; for example, sexual activity and even thoughts of sex have to be avoided. To help people concentrate on the deity, special religious and spiritual activities are prescribed, one of the most important of which is recitation of the Koran. To that end, the holy book is divided into 30 sections, one of which is recited on each night of the month, so that by the end of Ramadan those following the program will have read the whole work.

People who break the rules of the fast risk a variety of sanctions. Anyone who intentionally commits a serious violation is called on by the provisions of Islamic law either to fast for a further 60 days or to feed or provide alms for 60 people. Those who have knowingly perpetrated a minor violation may continue with the fast, adding on extra days at the end for those on which the fast was broken. Accidental violation is less serious, and those who unwittingly break the rules can usually continue the fast without feeling the need to make reparations later.

Most shops and stores in observant Muslim countries remain closed during

This photograph shows Muslims praying at the Islamic Center in Los Angeles, California.

daylight hours in Ramadan. The faithful usually wake up shortly before dawn to allow time for prayer and a snack before the day's fast gets under way at sunrise. The hours until sunset may be spent at home or in the mosque, praying and reciting the Koran, although, in practice, many people spend the time resting in preparation for the night ahead.

With sunset comes the breaking of the fast, usually with a traditional meal such as soup, a glass of water, and a few dates, after which everyone goes to evening prayer (*maghrib*). Once *maghrib* is ended, believers join family and friends to enjoy the main meal of the day. Having eaten, the faithful will then go to the mosque to join in communal prayers, recite the Koran, and perform special devotional acts of remembrance. The most devout will stay until it is nearly time for the sunrise prayer, only sleeping for an hour or so, if at all.

It can be harder for Muslims living in the United States and Western Europe to meet the requirements of Ramadan than it is for their counterparts in Islamic countries, where the pace of life slows for society as a whole. In the West, however, believers have to combine their religious duties with the demands of work and family responsibilities. Mentally, the task is all the more challenging because shops remain open and there are distractions all around that test believers' self-control and make it difficult for them to concentrate their thoughts on God.

Ramadan concludes with two major events, Laylah al-Qadr and Eid al-Fitr. Laylah al-Qadr (literally, "night of power" or "night of destiny") commemorates the time when the first verses of the Koran were revealed to Muhammad through the Archangel Gabriel. There is some dispute as to the exact date of that revelation, but the available evidence suggests that it occurred on an odd day of the month sometime in the last 10 days of Ramadan—namely, on the 21st, 23rd, 25th, 27th, or 29th day. Consensus opts for the 27th, but the significance of the date has faded in recent times, and instead believers tend to concentrate their attention on the last 10 days as a whole, viewing them as the most important time of the entire month, during which all Muslims should redouble their efforts to achieve a state of connectedness with God.

Ramadan ends with Eid al-Fitr, the Feast of the Breaking of the Fast. Eid

GAMBLING AND ISLAM

Gambling *(qimar)* is often mentioned alongside alcohol in the Koran and the Sunna as a forbidden act, yet it has rarely attracted as much attention as the prohibition on intoxicating drinks. Islamic Sharia law defines gambling as occurring any time that goods, money, or services are wagered on an event with an uncertain outcome.

Despite the prohibition, gambling, like alcohol, has managed to survive, both legally and illegally, in Muslim countries. Indonesia once allowed a state-run lottery, but now gambling is officially forbidden, although casinos still continue to function illegally. Other countries, such as Egypt and Malaysia, allow casinos to operate for the tourist trade, and some local Muslims also take advantage of the facilities. Gambling was eliminated in Afghanistan under Taliban rule, but now quail-fighting has returned, with wagers sometimes taken prior to a contest.

Online casinos are a new issue confronting the Muslim world. Many countries, Syria and Jordan among them, have issued laws against the practice of online gaming. However, other nations, including Morocco and the United Arab Emirates, have yet to pass firm laws on the subject.

al-Fitr is one of two major celebrations in the Muslim year, the other being the hajj, or annual pilgrimage. The feast starts with a special communal prayer, after which the rest of the day is spent feasting and giving presents. Part of the gift-giving involves the distribution of *zakat* to the poor.

Although fasting is required during Ramadan, it is by no means limited to that month alone. Fasting is a primary tool that believers employ to atone for transgressions against other people or against God. As such, Muslims may fast at any time except on the appointed feast days of Eid al-Fitr and Eid al-Adha, which takes place at the time of the hajj. Some dates, however, are particularly associated with abstinence. They include the festival of Ashura on the tenth day of the month of al-Muharram, which Shiite Muslims mark with general

On hearing the call from the muezzin at the end of a day's fasting during the month of Ramadan, Muslims in Jerusalem start eating for the first time since dawn.

mourning, while Sunni Muslims fast. In addition, Muslims of both persuasions are encouraged to perform a six-day fast at some point in the course of the month of al-Shawwal, which follows Ramadan in the Islamic calendar.

PILGRIMAGE (HAJJ)

The Fifth Pillar of Islam is pilgrimage (hajj). The hajj provides Muslims with the opportunity to come into direct contact with the faith's preeminent shrine, the place toward which they have been directing their prayers throughout their lives. The pilgrimage takes the form of a reenactment of parts of the experiences of Hagar, Ishmael, and Abraham, who are supposed to be the original builders of the Kaaba in Mecca and so the first people to establish a site of worship to the one God. No other pillar of Islam places a Muslim in such proximity to sacred space.

The hajj is an obligatory (*fard*) act that all Muslims are expected to perform at least once in their lifetime. Yet, unlike the other pillars of Islam, the pilgrimage to Mecca can be difficult to perform, both physically and financially. So the sick and injured are excused from participation in the hajj, especially if taking part would put their lives at risk. In practice, raising money for the trip is often the most daunting obstacle a Muslim will encounter, for travel to Mecca remains expensive. Some Muslims put aside money for a whole lifetime simply in order to pay for the journey. Even then, meeting the expenses of the trip itself is not the only cost, for breadwinners must also be able to cover the expenses incurred by their households while they are away.

The hajj to Mecca is the world's largest annual pilgrimage. At the start of the 1950s, around 100,000 Muslims made the journey each year. By the 1980s, the number of pilgrims had exceeded one million and, in 2007, estimates placed the total at well over twice that figure.

In past times, pilgrims to Mecca faced numerous challenges, including threats of disease, robbery, and even murder at the hands of brigands. The modern age has drastically reduced the risks, thanks to improved travel facilities, but casualties and deaths still regularly occur. In 1990, for instance, 1,426 people were killed in a stampede in a pedestrian tunnel leading from Mecca to the nearby town of Mina. In 2006, at least 346 pilgrims were crushed or trampled to death during a religious ceremony in Mina, a town 3 miles (5 km) outside Mecca in which most of the pilgrims stay on a vast campsite.

The hajj to Mecca is the world's largest annual pilgrimage. At the start of the 1950s, around 100,000 Muslims made the journey each year. By the 1980s, the number of pilgrims had exceeded one million.

The pilgrimage period in Islam begins in Dhu al-Hijja, the fourth month following Ramadan and the last month of the Islamic year. The timing of the hajj, like that of Ramadan, is based on the lunar calendar, so the season in which it falls changes from year to year. In 2007, for instance, the hajj fell in the middle of December in the Western calendar, but in 2008 it began near the start of the same month. The rituals of the hajj take only a few days, but many pilgrims come early

and stay late to perform supplementary rites and rituals during their stay in Mecca.

Mecca and the surrounding sites are sacred for all Muslims. The area as a whole is known as the holy precinct (*haram*). Non-Muslims are prohibited from entering it, although several individuals have found ways of breaching the boundaries in order to observe and record the scenes and rituals of the pilgrimage.

The focus of activities in Mecca itself is the Sacred Mosque (Al-Masjid al-Haram), an open space that houses the Kaaba, Islam's holiest sanctuary. The Kaaba is a hollow cube of granite that stands around 40 feet (12 m) high; the sides actually measure around 35 feet (10.7 m) by 40 feet (12 m). In practice, the stone of which it is constructed is rarely seen because the

outside of the structure is normally covered by a black cloth known as the *kiswa*, embroidered with Koranic verses. Muslims believe that the Kaaba was built by Abraham and Ishmael as the world's first monotheistic shrine. When they turn their faces to pray toward Mecca, they are not just facing the city or the Sacred Mosque but are directing their prayers specifically toward the Kaaba.

The four corners of the Kaaba are roughly aligned with the four points of the compass. A door located on the northeastern side gives access to the interior. Before the coming of Islam, the structure was full of pagan statues, but Muhammad had all the idols removed and rededicated the building to the worship of Allah alone. Near the eastern corner is a

Islamic pilgrims from India prepare to disembark at Jeddah Airport, Saudi Arabia, at the start of the hajj (pilgrimage) to Mecca.

ISLAM AND FOOD

The Koran and Sunna give specific instructions about the foods that are forbidden to Muslims. Pork was strictly prohibited. There were several reasons for this interdiction. First, pork was (and in some countries still is) linked with health problems, such as bacteria, viruses, and intestinal worms that may enter the human body. Second, pork was already a banned food for other religious communities, such as the Jews, and Islam may have chosen to adopt the tradition. Third, pigs were viewed as unclean and lazy.

Avoiding the consumption of pork products may seem a simple matter, but strict Muslims have to be constantly

Shoppers at this bazaar in Afghanistan may assume that everything offered for sale conforms to the stipulations of halal.

on guard against minuscule amounts of pork that may find their way into a variety of products. For example, pork gelatin, produced from the skin of pigs, can be an ingredient in ice cream and yogurt.

Eating the flesh of most carnivores except fish is also prohibited to Muslims, as is the consumption of blood and carrion (the meat of animals found dead). Many of the Islamic prohibitions are also found in Jewish kashruth dietary laws.

black stone known as al-Hajjar al-Aswad, believed to be a meteorite, which, in Muslim tradition, dates back to the time of Adam and Eve. Other places in the immediate vicinity of the Kaaba that have

major significance for Muslims include a low, semicircular building called the *hatim*, which is believed to be the burial place of Hagar and Ishmael, respectively Abraham's second wife and first son.

Before undertaking the actual hajj rituals, Muslims have pre-hajj duties to complete. Before entering the sacred precinct, they must first state their intention (*niyya*) to perform the pilgrimage rites fully and properly. They must then purify their bodies and cut their hair and nails before donning the *ihram*, the accepted dress of pilgrims, which takes the form of two pieces of white cloth. One piece, known as the *izar*, is wrapped around the lower body; the second piece, known as the *rida*, is draped over the shoulders and covers the torso. When wearing the *ihram*, Muslims are considered to be in a state of purity and must avoid sexual thoughts or activities and the use of perfume; in addition, they must not have their hair cut while wearing it. Women, too, wear a white *ihram*-like vestment, which in their case must cover the body to the ankles, wrists, and neck. Women must also cover their hair but are not required to veil their faces. On donning the *ihram*, Muslims chant a sacred phrase known as the *talbiya*, which they continue to utter throughout the pilgrimage. The words state, "I am here, oh my God, I am here."

Following the statement of *niyya*, the ritual purification, and the donning of the *ihram*, pilgrims may enter the sacred precinct through one of the boundary checkpoints, known as the *miqat*. The rituals of the hajj begin in the Sacred Mosque on the eighth day of the month of Dhu'l-Hijja. First comes the *tawaf*, which involves circumambulating the Kaaba in a counterclockwise direction. Pilgrims are required to make seven circuits of the structure. In theory, the first three circuits should be fast and the last four slower but, in practice today, the sheer size of the crowds means that virtually everyone goes slowly. In the course of the circumambulation, pilgrims seek to touch and even kiss the sacred black stone, although most can do no more than reach their hands in its direction. Following the *tawaf*, the pilgrims offer prayers at the Place of Abraham (Maqam Ibrahim), where the patriarch is said to have prayed when building the Kaaba. Once pilgrims have concluded these acts, they have accomplished the *umra* (lesser pilgrimage), an essential step in order to fulfill the entire hajj.

After completing prayer and *tawaf*, pilgrims perform *sai*, which involves proceeding seven times back and forth between the two hills of Safa and Marwah, located near the Kaaba. *Sai* recalls Hagar's desperate search for water when Ishmael was a child, which ended only when Ishmael stamped his foot and the water of the Zamzam Well came gushing from the spot. Pilgrims used to run between the hills, which are around 500 yards (about 450 m) apart, but now the size of the crowds usually reduces the pace to a trot. Originally, *sai* was performed in the open air but, today, the space between the hills is enclosed within a long gallery connected to the rest of the Sacred Mosque by an air-conditioned walkway. Following the *sai*, Muslims retire for the night to the tent city at Mina.

On the morning of the ninth day of the month, the pilgrims travel to Mount Arafat, a 9-mile (14 km) journey. The visit to the holy mountain—actually more of a hill, as it is rises only around 230 feet (70 m)—is one of the high points of the hajj, for it marks the spot where Muhammad gave his last sermon. Pilgrims are required to stand there from noon until sundown in reflection, meditating or praying for forgiveness, a ritual known as the *wuquf* (standing). Failure to perform the *wuquf* is a clear violation of the required hajj rites; without it, the whole pilgrimage is invalid.

When the sun is about to set, most pilgrims set off from the Plain of Arafat fronting the hill to Muzdalifa, a resting area on the road back to Mina. In Muzdalifa, prayers are offered, and pilgrims set about collecting 49 pebbles to use for the stoning ceremony, one of the most interesting rites of the pilgrimage, which takes place on the following day.

Halal Food

Halal food is meat from animals that Muslims are permitted to eat. Muslims are allowed to consume chicken, beef, lamb, most types of fish and shellfish, and birds that are not carnivorous, such as ducks. Many Muslims living in non-Muslim lands feel free to eat in most restaurants as long as they can avoid pork, alcohol, and other forbidden (*haram*) substances.

Not all Muslims, however, are so easy-going in their approach to *halal*. In reality, the dietary rules provide a set of guidelines that instruct Muslims not just as to the animals that may be consumed but also in the manner in which they must be slaughtered. Some restaurants and foodstuffs that many Muslims believe to be *halal* do not, in fact, meet a stringent interpretation of the regulations.

Residence in non-Muslim countries presents great difficulties for Muslims wishing to follow the rules of *halal*, although the situation is now improving. In the past, it was very difficult to keep *halal* because of the lack of suitable outlets, but today finding *halal* food has become much easier. Books and Web sites provide information on places where it can be purchased, whether locally or online, and list *halal* restaurants along with common food brands and products that meet the necessary criteria. Some restaurant chains, including Subway and McDonald's, have responded to the needs of their Muslim clientele by offering *halal* options in selected venues.

After morning prayers on the 10th day of the month, the pilgrims return to Mina for the stoning ritual and for the sacrifices. On arrival, they used to approach three stone pillars, held to symbolize Satan. Using the pebbles collected the previous evening—the total of 49 corresponds with the number of days on which Muhammad was tempted by the devil—they pelted the pillars, aiming to hit each one at least seven times. In 2005, however, following the deaths of several pilgrims during the course of the ceremony, the pillars were replaced by stone walls 85 feet (26 m) long. Even so, the sheer number of people performing the ritual still causes problems, as confirmed by further deaths in the course of the 2005 pilgrimage.

After the stoning of the pillars, pilgrims begin the Feast of Sacrifice (Eid al-Adha), the greater of the two major Muslim festivals. Those pilgrims who can afford to do so slaughter a goat, sheep, cow, or camel in memory of the ram offered up by Abraham in place of his son Ishmael. After the sacrifice, pilgrims usually have their heads shaved or at least some hair removed. Women, too, have an inch or so of hair cut at this time. The sacrifice marks the end of the major rituals of the hajj. The *ihram* may be removed at this point, although sexual intercourse is still forbidden.

The final three days of the pilgrimage are spent in contemplation and prayer and in travel between Mecca and Mina. Pilgrims may repeat many of the rites performed earlier for a second time. Typically, for instance, they will complete another *tawaf* circumambulation of the Kaaba and a second performance of the *sai* ritual, as well as an additional stoning of the Devil at Mina. The 13th day of Dhu'l-

Hijja is considered the last of the pilgrimage, on which devotees will usually again perform a stoning ceremony and a farewell *tawaf*, ending with prayers at the Place of Abraham. Some pilgrims will don the *ihram* again and end the pilgrimage by conducting another *umra*, although doing so is not a requirement.

Following the hajj, many pilgrims follow in Muhammad's footsteps by traveling north to the city of Medina to see the Prophet's resting place and to pray in his mosque. This journey, which retraces the route of the *hijra*, or migration, is known as the *ziyara*.

JIHAD

Many scholars regard the concept of jihad as a sixth pillar of Islam. A verb usually translated as meaning "to strive" or "to struggle," the term has become over-emphasized in recent years in discussions of Islam. It is often taken to be synonymous with holy war, conjuring up in people's minds images of fanatical Muslim preachers calling for violence. It is true that, through the centuries, the word has become connected with the notion that it is Muslims' duty to strive or struggle against people wishing to destroy Islam. This "lesser jihad" has duly captured media headlines, especially in the West, diverting attention from the term's second and more important meaning as the "greater jihad"— the mental and spiritual struggle every Muslim faces in trying to pray five times every day, to fast during Ramadan, to be honest and fair with all people, to forgive, and so on. The greater *jihad* is a true Muslim's daily striving to do what is right.

This photograph shows one of the numerous pilgrim camps on the outskirts of Medina, Saudi Arabia.

FAMILY PRACTICES

The five pillars of Islam clearly demonstrate not just the relationship between the individual and God but also the relationship of the individual Muslim to the rest of the community. Each pillar strives to achieve a sense of equality and fellowship between all believers. The concept of community is paramount in Islam, and the cornerstone of the community is the family. Thus, the roles and duties of family members are as important in Islam as the pillars of worship.

Marriage and procreation are strongly encouraged for male and female Muslims alike. Islam opposes sexual suppression in the name of religion, as practiced by Catholic priests and monks. In contrast, Muslims are encouraged to marry and procreate. In a traditional Muslim marriage, families arrange the match in advance, drawing up a marriage contract (*nikah*) before the ceremony. Before the advent of Islam, no such contracts existed, and wives were treated as their husbands' property. The *nikah*, however, now generally specifies that the dowry should go to the wife herself, not to the male members of her family. Women may also draw up their own contracts for marriage. Within a marriage, a woman's primary role is as the head of the household and the teacher of the children, while men are the providers for the family.

Some Muslim marriage laws may today seem sexist, representing a world of male domination, but in their time they were revolutionary. Before the coming of Islam, men were able to marry and divorce wives at will and without reparation. One of the first constraints the new faith placed on marriage was that a man could only take at the most four wives. Polygyny—the state of having more than one wife—still survives

in Islam, but strict limitations are attached to its practice. The Koran makes it clear that a husband can take additional wives only if he can provide equal love, care, and support for each one of them. In practice, most Muslim men today have only one wife.

Just as Islamic marriage is often misunderstood by non-Muslims, so the Muslim attitude to divorce has been sensationalized beyond the normal understanding and practice. The Koran is clear that Muhammad regarded divorce as an abomination that should never be encouraged. However, divorce remains a legal practice within Islam, as in most other communities.

Just as Islamic marriage is often misunderstood by non-Muslims, so the Muslim attitude to divorce has been sensationalized beyond the normal understanding and practice.

The most common form of divorce in Islam involves a man divorcing his wife by way of the ceremony known as the *talaq* (repudiation). The *talaq* involves two steps. First, the husband must make the pronouncement of divorce, simply repeating the phrase "I divorce you" three times. A waiting period of three months then begins, during which the pronouncement must be restated on a monthly basis. If, at the end of the three months, the husband and wife have not resumed living together or displayed other signs of reconciliation, the divorce becomes final.

Women, too, have the right to divorce their husbands, according to the Koran, but they are not given the option of a simple pronouncement and a three-month waiting period. Instead, they have to present reasons such as insanity, infidelity, or impotence to a religious court in order to win permission to break up a marriage.

CULTURAL PRACTICES

Dress is an important part of Muslim daily life, and the watchword is modesty. According to the Koran, Muslims must not use their apparel as a way of flaunting wealth and privilege, nor should they seek to draw attention to themselves by what they wear. More importantly, they are not permitted to display their flesh, because the sight of it can cause the mind to dwell on carnal thoughts. In order to prevent wandering minds, Muslims believe in covering the body.

Islamic law (Sharia) sets general rules of dress that most Muslims observe. Islamic law specifies that clothing should not be transparent, nor should clothes be too tight or figure-hugging. Muslims are also instructed to avoid clothing that might wrongly identify them as members of a different religion. There are also special provisions made for each sex. Male Muslims are directed to wear clothing that covers the area from the knees up to the navel although, in practice, many of the traditional robes worn in the Islamic lands, such as the djellaba (a long, loose garment

Muslim women shop for wedding dresses at a shopping mall in Tehran, Iran.

MUHAMMAD AS A REFORMER

Most scholars of Islam recognize the Prophet Muhammad not only as the founder of a new religion but also as a social and moral reformer who opened radical new perspectives for the Arab people. In pre-Islamic times, women were treated as property in the Arab lands and had no rights to divorce or to own property. Muhammad recommended monogamy but allowed a man to marry other wives, to a maximum of four, if the additional spouses could be adequately supported. Women were also given the right to divorce their husbands for maltreatment, a completely new privilege at the time. One particularly crucial precedent, established by the Koran, was that women should share in the inheritance left when their husbands died. Previously, all wealth had passed exclusively to male members of the family.

A second group that attracted Muhammad's concern was orphaned children, he himself having been orphaned at an early age. The Prophet sometimes adopted children into his own family.

Muhammad's great desire, which was eventually fulfilled, was to break the tribal hierarchy that dominated Arabia during his lifetime and establish in its place an egalitarian community. His vision was that Islam would dissolve the barriers of wealth and status that had previously set people apart in society. He believed Islam would create equality for all people.

with full sleeves and hood), cover the entire body except the hands, face, and feet. Women's clothing should cover all parts of the body except the hands and the face. Women should also avoid any type of clothing that does not distinguish them from a man.

Muslim rules on women's dress are seen by some Westerners as oppressive, reflecting a male-dominated society. The attire that people usually have in mind in such cases is, in fact, found in only a few, very conservative Muslim countries, notably Afghanistan under the rule of the Taliban, Iran, and Saudi Arabia. The Koran has very little to say about women's attire, other than stressing the need to dress modestly and not be ostentatious. Muslim women around the world wear many different styles of dress. The most conservative of these include the *niqab* (a veil that covers the head and most of the face), the burqa (a full body garment worn over underclothes, often with a *niqab*), and the chador (a body garment that does not cover the face).

The best-known type of Islamic women's dress is the *hijab*, which covers a woman's head and hair but not the face. Of all the types of head and body covering used by women today, only the *hijab* is identified in the Koran, and even there it is mentioned only in reference to the wives of Muhammad, not to all women. In spite of that, the custom of wearing a head covering has become predominant in many Islamic societies. Even so, some Muslims believe that the veil and conservative dress are no longer necessary and have abandoned the *hijab* altogether.

Westerners often associate the *hijab* with repression, yet some Muslim women, particularly those living in the West, have begun using it as a personal statement of their Islamic identity. Some women encounter abuse while wearing the *hijab* but others find that they are treated with respect because of their commitment to their beliefs. Besides being a mark of identity, the *hijab* can also send out a message of liberation, signaling a refusal to blend in with the surrounding society and a desire to express an individual's own culture and beliefs.

CIRCUMCISION

Circumcision (*khitan*)—the removal of part or all of the male foreskin—is a ritual that dates back to at least the time of Abraham. Jews traditionally practice circumcision and Islam has also incorporated the practice into its ritual acts of devotion. It is not required by the Koran, but Muhammad and all the prophets were circumcised.

The Sunna (the recorded actions, sayings, and teachings of Muhammad) recommends that male Muslims should follow this example, and the majority are indeed circumcised. Circumcision today is also recommended for the health benefits that it is sometimes thought to confer.

Female circumcision—the removal of part or all of a woman's clitoris or other

Women in Iran wear the chador in public places; in private, however, they may dress more informally.

external sex organs—is much more controversial than male circumcision. The practice itself is ancient and has been recorded in several different parts of the world, among them ancient Egypt in late pharaonic times. However, in the 1940s and 1950s, it came under scrutiny from both national and international health and government organizations. The practice acquired a new and more recognizable name, female genital mutilation (FGM), which is now the term preferred by experts. Organizations the world over have deemed the practice a violation of basic human rights.

The World Health Organization (WHO), one of the foremost authorities on the procedure, lists four types of FGM occurring throughout the world. The different procedures involved are:

- Type 1: The clitoris is partially or totally removed.
- Type 2: The clitoris is totally removed along with the labia minora, while either all or part of the labia majora are removed as well.
- Type 3: The vagina is narrowed by creating a covering with the labia minora and labia majora. In addition, the clitoris may or may not be removed.
- Type 4: Pricking, scraping, piercing, or incising any parts of the genitals.

Although it is impossible to determine exact numbers, the WHO has estimated that nearly 140 million women living today have experienced some form of FGM, the strongest concentration being found in African countries. Countries with especially high rates of FGM include Djibouti, Egypt, Guinea, Mali, Sierra Leone, Somalia, and Sudan, in all of which more than 90 percent of women between the ages of 15 and 49 are estimated to have

undergone some form of circumcision. However, Africa is not the only continent in which cases of FGM have been recorded. Reports of the practice have also emerged from Middle Eastern countries including Iraq, Israel, the United Arab Emirates, and Yemen, and from Asian countries such as Indonesia and India, as well as from North America and South America and from European countries including England and France; there, however, such incidents generally occur only in isolated communities.

There are many reasons for the survival of FGM in spite of its condemnation by many state governments and international organizations. To begin

The WHO has estimated that nearly 140 million women living today have experienced some form of FGM, the strongest concentration being found in African countries.

with, in most of the societies where FGM is regularly practiced, a patriarchal family structure is still in place, giving many women little or no choice in the matter. Instead, fathers or occasionally brothers decide whether a daughter or sister should be circumcised.

Another reason that FGM continues is that it is seen in many cultures as a mark of identity. In the same way that a Christian child might undergo confirmation or a Jewish boy take part in a bar mitzvah celebration, so genital mutilation is regarded as a rite of passage marking coming of age and the onset of maturity.

Genital mutilation indicates to others in the society that the affected girl has reached womanhood and is therefore eligible to be married. FGM is also sometimes seen as a means of establishing purity, for genital mutilation is regarded as a sign of chastity; women who are not circumcised are suspected of being unchaste, making it extremely difficult for them to find husbands. To avoid such suspicions, women in societies where FGM is the norm are virtually forced to undergo the procedure in order to preserve their honor and dignity.

A final reason that FGM continues to be practiced, and one that connects to all of the preceding ones, is that women in the affected societies believe that their religion commands female circumcision. Whether or not female circumcision is indeed part of Islam is a point that is fiercely debated. The practice is certainly not limited to the Muslim community, for many of the countries with high rates of female circumcision, such as Ethiopia, are home to Christian communities that also perform FGM. Thus, to classify female circumcision as an exclusively Islamic custom is incorrect. Female circumcision is, as previously stated, an ancient practice dating back far before Muhammad and the advent of Islam.

The fact that female circumcision predates Islam and is also known outside of the Muslim world has led some people to claim that the practice is not inherently Islamic and is only a cultural or tribal tradition. However, others argue that, because so many Muslims have accepted the necessity for female circumcision, the practice has become entwined with the religion—in other words,

that female circumcision is Islamic because it is widely performed by Muslims.

Today, there is still no clear consensus on the matter of female circumcision. Muslim legal scholars are divided over its status in Sharia law. Some take the view that it is an obligatory act (*fard*), others maintain that it is not obligatory but not forbidden either, while a third school holds that female circumcision is forbidden (*haram*). The Koran says nothing on the subject.

Scholars who accept the practice as mandatory base their interpretation on one specific reference in the Hadith literature, but many other Muslim scholars claim that the relevant reference is weak *(daif)*. Those who forbid FGM emphasize the negative effects that the practice has on women's health; Islam is always careful to protect individuals, they argue, so any action that can cause harm is forbidden. There are currently no clear statistics available on the respective strengths of the two schools of thought.

Of the four main Muslim schools of Sharia law, the Shafii school is particularly associated with the view that female circumcision is required. Countries with high incidence of FGM, such as Sudan and Somalia, for the most part follow Shafii teachings. Others follow the Maliki school, but its views on the legal status of female circumcision are less clear-cut. In general, most countries with moderate to high rates of FGM, such as Gambia, Mali, and Nigeria, tend to show some degree of intermingling of the Shafii and Maliki traditions. Even within the different legal schools, there is no clear consensus because each group includes scholars who are prepared to argue against the predominant current of thought.

See Also

Defining Islam and Muslims 8–17 ❖ Life of Muhammad 18–21 ❖ Scriptures and Doctrine 102–123 ❖ Subdivisions of Islam 128–147 ❖ Mystical Islam 148–149 ❖

Defining Jihad

Jihad has multiple connotations in the Koran and other Islamic literature, including jihad as interior struggle, jihad as societal reform, and jihad as physical combat.

The modern association of jihad with violence often obscures the complexity of its meanings. The Arabic word literally means "striving" or "struggle." In Islamic tradition, jihad can connote striving against a military enemy or against one's own immoral instincts. It may also mean exerting oneself to achieve social justice or to spread Islam through preaching. While individual Muslims may emphasize one of these meanings over the others, the word itself has a range of possible usages.

THE KORAN AND THE HADITHS

In the Koran, jihad may mean "physical combat," but it may equally refer to a variety of other activities, including the conscientious performance of religious duties, such as prayer and the financial support of the needy. Jihad may also mean a pious seeking of spiritual nearness to God or may refer to the emigration of the early Meccans to Medina. Among other usages, jihad may mean the hard work involved in doing good, in proclaiming God's message, or in raising one's level of self-awareness.

Jihad also has a range of connotations in the Hadiths (collections of the sayings of Muhammad). In the most authoritative of the Hadiths, unlike in the Koran, jihad and physical combat are often synonymous. However, these collections were compiled by men for whom the success of the Arab conquests was proof of the truth of Islam and of God's support for the Muslim conquerors. Such perceptions may account for the emphasis on jihad as physical combat. Nonetheless, the Hadiths also use the word in other contexts, notably as striving nonviolently to promote Islam, to overcome one's own irreligious inclinations, to tell the truth, and to persuade others of the Islamic viewpoint. Pilgrimage is also a form of jihad.

Some Hadiths describe dutiful performance of prayer and serving one's parents as superior to physical combat.

Perhaps it was the success of the Arab conquests that inspired a reconsideration of the meaning of jihad. A movement of ascetics and mystics, eventually known as Sufism, was suspicious of the potential for corruption that frequently accompanies wealth, power, and worldly success. The Sufis attached paramount significance to the sayings of Muhammad that emphasized other aspects of jihad. In particular, they strove against corrupt external influences and made their jihad an internal, moral struggle.

In the Koran, jihad may mean "physical combat," but it may equally refer to a variety of other activities, including the conscientious performance of religious duties, such as prayer and the financial support of the needy.

The two extreme definitions of jihad have sometimes been reconciled by military and legal authorities into a code that, in times of conflict, permits Muslims to fulfill their duties without participation in physical combat.

Although the idea of jihad as an interior struggle is one of the most popular definitions of the term, Muslims

Protesters in Pakistan demonstrate their objections to remarks made in 2006 by Pope Benedict XVI that they construed as insulting to Islam. This photograph reflects the popular Western image of jihad, but the concept is much more complex than a mere desire to wage war against non-Muslims.

MILITANT EXTREMISM

Most Muslims reject the attacks of militant extremist groups, such as al-Qaeda, and the terrorists' efforts to construe such acts as jihad. Moderate Muslim critics observe that no one in al-Qaeda has the political or religious authority to declare a combative jihad. They also note that terrorist attacks violate the limits of legal warfare in Islam. In addition to targeting noncombatants, terrorists often violate the limits of legal warfare by attacking fellow Muslims. This fact illuminates the militant extremist ideology, which perceives even the citizens of many majority Muslim countries as not truly Muslim. These extremists see Islam as being under attack by both domestic and foreign enemies. Their siege mentality leads them to try to justify extreme measures by invoking religious symbols and concepts such as jihad.

It appears that many Muslims are increasingly emphasizing one of the noncombative connotations of jihad, such as personal or social reform. However, all of the connotations of jihad have had varying degrees of appeal in the modern era. Jihad has been a symbol of Muslim identity in response to the encounter with modernity and the global dominance of non-Muslim powers with their foreign cultures and values. For instance, the symbol of jihad was influential in the modern anticolonial movements and continues to be relevant in the postcolonial era, as Western powers have continued to dominate international affairs. From liberal democratic social reformers to militant revolutionaries and extremists, the symbols of jihad—including its many connotations—may be employed to express Islamic authenticity and in an effort to motivate other Muslims to any of a variety of agendas.

have long disagreed about the authenticity of the text on which it is based—the Hadith in which Muhammad tells his followers that "the greater jihad" is "the servant's struggle against his lust." In spite of that reservation, the basic conception of jihad as interior struggle is supported by authoritative passages in the Koran, most notably the verse that states: "Those who exert themselves do so for their own benefit—God does not need His creatures. But we shall be sure to guide to our own ways those who strive hard for our cause: God is with those who do good."

This passage may be taken to support an understanding of the self as the one authentic objective of any jihad and the basic connotation of the term itself as "doing good." Such an interpretation does not necessarily exclude physical combat as a form of jihad; some of the earliest Muslim ascetics who emphasized the interior jihad were themselves involved in combat. Nonetheless, they articulated a comprehensive jihad that emphasized striving to be a better Muslim in every sphere of activity.

JIHAD AS SOCIETAL REFORM

A reported saying of the Prophet Muhammad, which is regarded as highly authentic, states that the highest form of jihad is "a word of truth spoken to a tyrant." For many, this saying illustrates another important connotation of jihad, namely that Muslims should strive to reform society and to promote the Islamic goals of justice, equality, and morality. Thus, activists and social reformers may employ the term to describe their aims. In 2008, a conference at Stanford University, which included prominent scholars such as Khaled Abou el-Fadl, a law professor at the University of California, Los Angeles, described the effort to reform society and define Islam in modern contexts as a form of jihad. Similarly, the Swiss Muslim academic Tariq Ramadan has advocated a reformer's jihad that seeks the elimination of the existing disparities in wealth, welfare, education, and political liberties in the nations of the world. Others, such as the feminist Amina Wadud, describe their efforts to promote the concerns of women as "gender jihad."

JIHAD AS PHYSICAL COMBAT

The Koran and the sayings of Muhammad provide guidance in the conduct of warfare, stating that there is a time for combat and a time for peace. However, all warfare is illegal in Islam unless it meets certain criteria.

Many passages of both texts are open to different interpretations. While some sayings of Muhammad make the inward focus of jihad primary, others seem to advocate an aggressive struggle to spread Islam and Muslim dominion. Thus, Muslims face an interpretive dilemma—they must look to their conscience and their sense of Muhammad's character in order to decide what jihad means. The Koran also has a complex position on combat. Some verses reject the use of force, while others limit its scope; still others advocate it. The best known verse in support of violence is the following:

> Then, when the sacred months have passed, slay the idolaters wherever you find them, and take them [captive], and besiege them, and prepare for them each ambush. But if they repent and establish worship and pay the poor-due, then leave their way free. Lo! God is Forgiving, Merciful.

This passage is sometimes referred to as the "sword verse." It should be noted that the word jihad does not occur in it. The context of the verse is also significant: it is understood to refer to a specific group who presented an obstacle to Muslim worship in Mecca and who violated a peace treaty with the Muslims. Several traditional and contemporary interpreters have viewed this verse as overriding previous verses and sanctioning aggressive combat to spread Islam. However, other Muslims set greater store by another passage in the Koran that approves only defensive combat:

> And fight in God's cause against those who wage war against you, but do not commit aggression—for, verily, God does not love aggressors.

CONFLICT BY THE BOOK

The Koran discusses the legal limits of combat, the circumstances in which violence may be permissible, and the conditions that require a cessation of hostilities—as in the "sword verse" above. Overwhelmingly, Islamic tradition forbids the killing of women, children, and noncombatants. It also outlaws unnecessary destruction of property, especially in residential and agricultural areas. In order to attempt peaceful resolution, either before or after combat has begun, Islamic tradition requires an open declaration of conflict and the conditions under which hostilities may be averted or ended.

Moderate Muslims are eager to emphasize to the English-speaking world that the concept of jihad is neither synonymous with nor can legitimately be used to justify acts of terrorism.

JIHAD: STRIVING FOR PEACE

SCRIPTURES AND DOCTRINE

Muslims believe that the Koran is the revealed speech of God. Muhammad was the Prophet who received the revelation, but Muslims distinguish his speech from the Koran. His sayings and deeds are reported in Hadith literature. Islamic law (Sharia) is derived from the Koran and from Hadiths, as well as from other sources.

Although the Koran and the Hadiths are open to interpretation and are given different emphases, Muslims express their religious commitment largely in terms of their efforts to integrate all three of them into their own lives. Collectively, the Koran and the Hadiths serve as the bases of Islamic doctrines.

The content of the Koran is fairly simple to summarize. The book teaches that there is only one God, entirely unique, an omnipotent creator. God's creatures include not only humans and all the world's life forms, but also angels and other supernatural creatures. In addition, the Koran presents a distinctive balance of God's power and justice and the ultimate accountability of humans to God for their good and bad actions. God will judge His creatures fit for heaven or hell on Judgment Day at the end of time.

The Koran constantly reassures readers of God's mercy, identifying divine guidance as a significant example of such mercy and as a blessing to humanity. Thus, the Koran teaches that God sends prophets with scriptures such as the Jewish Torah, the Christian Gospels, and the Koran itself that warn of the Day of Judgment and help humanity to live righteously. The legal material of the Koran instructs people in that regard, as do its stories of moral role models, such as the prophets.

THE NATURE OF THE KORAN

Muslims do not consider the Koran to be a human record of an encounter with the divine; rather, the sacredness of the volume resides in its revelation of the specific language of God. Believers perceive a unique and miraculous power in the language of the holy book. Most Muslims believe that the Koran is eternal and uncreated and that it provides knowledge that would be impossible to discover without revelation.

Muslims have argued for the miraculous nature of the scripture in other ways as well, pointing in particular to what they perceive as its sublime literary quality. Indeed, the Koran itself challenges others to produce a text like it and asserts that none will be able to do so.

Muslim girls study the Koran at a mosque in Indonesia. The book is the foundation of the Islamic faith.

THE FIRST REVELATION

According to the traditional account, the first revelation of the Koran took the form of an encounter between the Archangel Gabriel and Muhammad during the month of Ramadan in the Prophet's 40th year (610 CE). Muhammad had gone to Mount Hira, near Mecca, for a period of spiritual retreat, as had been his habit. While he slept, Gabriel appeared in the cave. The angel ordered Muhammad to "Recite" or "Read." However, Muhammad replied that he could not read. Gabriel again ordered him to recite. Once more, Muhammad replied that he could not do so. Gabriel told him: "Recite in the name of your Lord who created! He created man from a clot. Recite: for your Lord is most bountiful, He who has taught by the pen, taught man what he knew not." Those were the first words to be revealed to Muhammad and hence became the opening words of the Koran. After a hiatus described as relatively brief and personally troubling, Muhammad continued to receive the revelations of the Koran for the next 23 years.

Mount Hira, just outside Mecca, Saudi Arabia, was the site of the first revelation of the Koran to the Prophet Muhammad by the Archangel Gabriel.

Muslims believe that the language of the Koran cannot be imitated in its content, style, or in any other respect, and hold that this unique quality provides miraculous proof that the work is indeed the language of God. Stories tell of the overwhelming emotional response it received from its earliest audiences and of the way that it inspired spontaneous conversions to the new faith.

Another sense in which the Koran is considered miraculous involves the nature of its reception and transmission. Muslims believe that Muhammad was illiterate and so, they argue, he could not have composed any text, let alone one with the remarkable qualities of the Koran. Rather, as the Prophet himself reported, the text was revealed to him as though it had been engraved on his heart. He then transmitted it by reciting the words to his followers.

The Koran describes itself as a book and, as such, it self-consciously identifies itself with other scriptures. In Arabic, however, the word *qur'an* (Koran) means "recitation," and it is important to bear in mind that, for Muslims, the essential experience of the Koran lies in hearing it aloud. Of course, it may be read like any other text, but expectations that it should present a linear story like other books only obscure the dynamics of its presentation. Rather, the Koran is a collection of sacred recitations, and many of the most productive analyses of the work start from an awareness of that fact.

THE RECITED KORAN

By considering the Koran as, first and foremost, a recitation—and one that Muslims view as miraculous in its nature and full of power as God's own speech— it is easier to understand some of the roles the book plays in Muslim life. Sayings attributed to Muhammad describe the peace of God descending on those who recite the Koran, and Muslims regularly do recite it, both in private and in public, most importantly during their daily prayers. As a result, they are able to recite the short first chapter of the Koran, known as the Fatiha, from memory, along with other passages as well.

In fact, some Muslims succeed in memorizing lengthy portions of the scripture. A person who memorizes the entire work merits the title of *hafiz*

(guardian of the Koran). Internalizing the sacred text in such a manner is also believed to have a transforming effect on the individual. That highly respected accomplishment has long been an important goal for many pious Muslims. Keeping the text fresh in the memory requires constant practice; those who accomplish the task will often recite the work on a wide variety of occasions.

Such recitations are a relatively common occurrence in the Muslim world. As well as at prayer times, the text of the Koran is recited during the month of Ramadan and to commemorate special occasions, such as weddings, funerals, or graduations. Yet the words of the holy book also turn up in everyday contexts. It is not uncommon to hear recorded recitations in offices or in taxis. A major component of some 21st-century Islamic revival movements has been the encouragement of more frequent encounters with the recited Koran—that method of dissemination has become particularly popular in Indonesia, the most populous Muslim country.

Public recitation of the Koran is a skill that is highly developed, and talented reciters can become nationally and internationally famous. Several countries, including Saudi Arabia and Indonesia, hold competitions in Koran recitation. Participants may compete in a variety of styles, and there are separate contests for men, women, and children. Stylistically, recitation may range from sober reading to highly melodic and expressive chanting. The recitation of the Koran is not performed for entertainment and is usually distinguished from singing. In practice, however, reciters may employ elements that draw on the musical traditions of a variety of cultures.

THE ETIQUETTE OF THE KORAN

The awe and reverence that Muslims feel for the recited Koran is extended to the written text. Calligraphic presentations of passages and expressions from the scripture abound in Islamic architecture and in Muslim decorative traditions. Like recitation, this discipline is highly developed and displays a high level of devotion to the book. There are numerous styles of calligraphy, from simple scripts that present the language clearly to elaborate forms that weave the text into complex patterns and images that can be difficult to read. Those various styles may be found written into copies of the Koran,

There are numerous styles of calligraphy, from simple scripts that present the language clearly to elaborate forms that weave the text into complex patterns and images that can be difficult to read.

painted on decorative wall hangings and tiles, or etched into the stonework of buildings.

In the late 20th century, calligraphic quotations also began appearing in a whole new range of contexts, including on T-shirts and computer screen savers. Some of the new media have challenged the traditional etiquette governing written expressions of the scripture. According to the Koran itself, only the pure may touch it—a requirement that has usually been taken to mean that the book should be handled only by individuals who are in a state of ritual purity, attained by the ablutions that precede prayer, which itself,

of course, includes recitations of the Koran. Thus, the basic requirements for approaching the Koran are the same in both its written and recited forms.

However, as in the case of recitation, handling and storing the written text also involve additional rules and conventions. Etiquette dictates that the Koran should always be the topmost volume in any pile of books, preferably set on the highest shelf in a room. Additionally, the text should be stored and recited in a clean place and should always be held in the right hand.

While Muslims vary in their observance of those and other rules, the general principle that written copies of the Koran deserve reverence reflects the fundamental belief that the work represents the word of God. When *Newsweek* reported in 2005 that personnel at the Guantanamo Bay detention camp in Cuba had desecrated printed copies of the Koran, protests erupted in some Muslim nations and there was rioting in Afghanistan. Muslims feel special reverence for their holy scripture, and any perceived mistreatment of it causes deep offense.

THE COLLECTION OF THE KORAN

Muhammad's presumed illiteracy not only contributes to the miraculous aura surrounding the Koran but also has implications for the reception and preservation of the text. Because the Prophet did not himself write down the revelations he received, the task fell to his followers. Sayings attributed to Muhammad's companions provide accounts of the processes by which the work was collected and preserved. However, many of these sayings may be interpreted in a variety of ways.

The conventional account of the collection of the Koran has three essential features. First, it holds that the Koran was transmitted both orally and in written format. The prevalence of illiteracy in the seventh century made oral transmission the primary form. The repeated recitation of the verses encouraged by Muhammad reinforced the memorization and transmission of the Koran. However, other sources suggest that Muhammad, toward the end of his life, employed scribes to create written records of some of the revelations. Most Muslim scholars have traditionally maintained that Muhammad did not collect those records into a single volume during his lifetime, although some accounts have him directing the scribes in the arrangement of substantial parts of the scripture. Either way, the transmission of the Koran in both oral and written form is often seen as a guarantee against corruption of the text.

Another essential feature of the collection process is that it occurred in several phases. According to reports from one of the Prophet's wives, Aisha, Muhammad and the Archangel Gabriel would between them review all the revelations of any given year during the month of Ramadan, ensuring they were correct. In Muhammad's final year of life, Gabriel reportedly reviewed the revelations twice. For believers, that account provides conclusive confirmation of the accuracy of the first phase of the Koranic revelation.

Next, the sources tell us that, following Muhammad's death, a battle claimed the

Muslim children learn passages of the Koran by heart at an elementary school.

THE BASMALAH

The *basmalah* is the phrase, "In the name of God the Merciful, the Compassionate," which begins every sura of the Koran except the ninth. Muslims may recite the *basmalah* at the start of any significant activity, seeking thereby to express their intention to perform the action for the sake of God and to invoke divine blessings. Reciting the *basmalah* is an important step in rendering food halal (permissible for Muslim consumption), and Muslims often begin writings and public speeches with the *basmalah* as an invocation. The phrase is a popular motif in calligraphic art; beautiful renderings of it may be seen on buildings, wall hangings, and amulets.

lives of many of those who had memorized the Koran. Abu Bakr, the first caliph, was thereby encouraged to collect the various revelations so as to prevent them from being lost forever. The material came both from people's memories and from the parchments, leaves, bones, and stones on which the words had been written. The Koran was then inscribed on loose sheets of writing material and kept by Hafsa, another widow of the Prophet. Some of Muhammad's other companions reportedly made collections of their own. Disputes over discrepancies between the various versions led the third caliph, Uthman, to commission and distribute an official collection around 650 CE. According to tradition, the text that Uthman prepared is the basis of the one in circulation today.

If the traditional account is correct, the collection of the Koran was a relatively

rapid process. Only around 18 years passed between Muhammad's death and Uthman's official canon, but the basis of that work was reportedly the collection made by Abu Bakr, who died in 634, only two years after the Prophet.

Even after Uthman's official version appeared, considerable refinement of the Arabic script was still needed and, initially at least, the written text could serve only as a guide for reciting the Koran from memory. For instance, the written Arabic in use at the time failed to distinguish several letters from each other, allowing for variations in the pronunciation and vocalization of the canonical text. Those discrepancies rarely affected the meaning, and several different versions came in time to be regarded as equally orthodox. Nonetheless, one in particular came to dominate. In 1924, that version was adopted for the Egyptian standard edition of the Koran, and with several revisions it has since served as an informal benchmark for other regions, too.

QUESTIONS OF ACCURACY

Some scholars have questioned the accuracy of the conventional account of the collection of the Koran. Secular researchers naturally diverge from Islamic tradition in not seeing the work as a product of divine revelation. In addition, some commentators dispute the historical accuracy of the story. Alternative theories, advanced in the late 20th century, argued for a wide range of possibilities. Some took the view that Muhammad himself assembled the Koran, while others rejected any direct historical connection between the Prophet and specific Koranic passages.

Some of those contentions are thought provoking, but none of them are entirely compelling, and no consensus rejecting the conventional account has emerged. While scholars have asked productive new questions, none of their arguments has been incontrovertible. Generally, those secular scholars who challenge the conventional account focus on non-Muslim sources, on literary or linguistic analyses, and on discrepancies in the sayings of the companions of Muhammad. They have argued that there was more debate in the early Muslim community over the content and arrangement of the Koran than the traditional account allows. In addition, some have extended the date of the work's collection into the eighth century, or have suggested that much of the book's content is influenced by the older Judeo-Christian Bible.

STRUCTURE OF THE KORAN

The smallest organizational unit in the Koran is the verse, or *aya* (plural: *ayat*). *Aya* literally means "sign," and the word is also used in the Koran to refer to signs of God. The holy book regularly discusses such indications of divine intervention, inviting humankind to contemplate them. An *aya* may be an account of God's actions, such as the story of Noah and the Ark, or else a miracle, such as Jesus raising the dead. Yet perhaps the most prominent *ayat* in the Koran are drawn from nature, for the scripture regularly points to the works of creation as indications of the reality and power of their creator. That those signs are synonymous with the word for the Koranic verses says something profound about the Islamic conception of revelation. Nature, history, and scripture are all equated within the term, each conveying messages from God.

At the next level of organization, the 114 chapters of the Koran are known as suras. The Koran does not present its material according to a chronological sequence of events or as a narrative. Rather, the principle of arrangement is

A scholar in Tashkent, Uzbekistan, handles what some consider to be the oldest Koran in the world. This Koran was commissioned by Uthman, the third Rashidun caliph, around 20 years after Muhammad's death. It was brought to Tashkent from Kufa, Iraq, in the 14th century by the Turkic ruler Timur.

roughly according to the length of each sura. The Koran begins with the longer suras and proceeds to the shorter, the brief first chapter being the most obvious exception to that general rule. Because of that arrangement according to length, Muslims usually begin memorizing the Koran with the first sura and then work back from the shorter suras at the end of the scripture. Traditionally, the suras were identified by chapter names; it is a Western convention to represent them by numbers. A few were, in fact, known by more than one appellation, because the titles themselves were not considered part of the revelation. Instead, they were merely tools to aid recitation, study, and discussion.

Other features may also be added to make the Koran easier to use. The possible additions include divisions, indicated in the margins of the text, whose purpose is mostly liturgical in nature. A 30-day division of the text is useful for the common practice of reciting the Koran over the course of the sacred month of Ramadan. A division of the Koran into seven portions enables a complete recitation in the span of a week.

KORANIC CHARMS

Popular lore has long associated the Koran with charms and blessings. For instance, suras 113 and 114 have traditionally been used to ward off evil. Passages from the work, or even miniaturized copies of the complete scripture, may be worn around the neck or placed in homes, offices, and automobiles as amulets. Some people use the Koran as an oracle, opening the book at random and reading divinatory meanings into the passage that presents itself. Folk healers immerse inscriptions from the Koran in water in the belief that the resulting solution has healing powers.

While the work as a whole is not organized on chronological lines, Muslims nevertheless note a rough division between the revelations that were made to the Prophet in Mecca and those that occurred in Medina, and usually label each sura accordingly. That demarcation has significant implications for interpretation and is elaborated in great detail in the Koranic commentaries.

STRUCTURES AND STYLES OF SURAS

It is hard to discuss the structure of the suras without some remarks about their style. The rough chronological division between the Meccan and the Medinan chapters correlates to a large degree with various stylistic and structural features, although the patterns are to some extent obscured by the tendency to analyze them strictly in isolation, rather than within the broader context of the suras as a whole. The fact is that, even though no single, uniform model can be applied to all suras, there are nonetheless motifs that are often shared among subgroups of the chapters.

Besides differentiating between the Meccan and Medinan suras in terms of their structures, styles, and even content, some scholars use essentially the same criteria to further subdivide the Meccan phase into an early, a middle, and a late period. Generally, the early Meccan suras focus on spiritual and moral exhortations. They tend to be the most rhythmic, exhibiting a pronounced and regular rhyme scheme with an evident structure and relatively short verses. Such elements aid memorization and oral performance. Many are introduced with a series of oaths. In contrast, the later ones employ a greater number of narrative elements, a development accompanied by longer, less

rhythmic verses that still, however, often culminate in rhymed phrases. While these endings can seem out of place, because they do not always relate directly to what has gone before, they provide exhortations and reassurances and may also supply a moral commentary that serves to reinforce the discussion while highlighting its revealed nature and the relationship between the audience and God.

The Medinan suras tend to be longer, less rhythmical, and more concerned with law and the regulation of community life than the Meccan suras.

STYLISTIC FEATURES

Much of Muslim belief in the miraculous nature of the Koran is related to its unique style and content. The Koran itself asserts that its like cannot be reproduced, and the view that the Koran cannot be imitated eventually became dogma. That development is crucial for an understanding of the Koran as the epitome of Islamic literary style.

Non-Muslims have sometimes expressed confusion and frustration in their response to the Koran. Such reactions may be exacerbated by their lack of sensitivity to the work's modes of expression and their preconceived notions of the form that a scripture should take. The Koranic style can be challenging for anyone, not only on a first encounter but even after several subsequent readings; it may, however, also be striking and sublime.

Young Indonesian boys read the Koran as part of the lifelong process of studying and memorizing the whole work.

Several distinctive stylistic features help the Koran to hold the attention of its audience. For instance, the work frequently asks open-ended questions of its readers, inviting them to reflect. That rhetorical device brings the audience into the text, encouraging them to take on the queries as their own. The questions also highlight the condition in which believers find themselves; compared to God, they are ignorant, and in seeking answers to their questions they need to be guided by God's superior knowledge through

What can seem repetitious or fragmentary to expectations conditioned by the Judeo-Christian Bible is actually an effective use of narrative in its own terms.

submission to revelation. Similarly, the Koran employs powerful and dramatic imagery and figurative language. In doing so, the holy book engages the imagination of the audience and conveys a sense of God's power in contrast to human limitations.

Another striking stylistic feature of the Koran is its use of pronouns. The scripture presents itself as the speech of God, often employing the first person plural "We" to refer to its narrator. However, it is not uncommon for the text to shift—even in the middle of a passage—from the first person plural to either the third person singular (He) or the third person plural (they). Such alterations of perspective are part of the work's inimitable style, highlighting for Muslims the mysteries of

revelation and the futility of attempts to conceptualize a wholly transcendent God, who defies human comprehension just as He does grammatical categories.

NARRATIVE STYLE OF THE KORAN

The Koran also employs a distinctive narrative style. The work does not begin, like the Hebrew scriptures, with an account of the creation of the universe, nor does it proceed to a relatively linear and detailed history of a people. Similarly, it does not recount the story of Muhammad and the Muslim community in a manner similar to the Gospel accounts of Jesus and the first Christians. Instead, it has its own approach, offering a different conception of what a scripture should be.

Some scholars have complained of repetition and a lack of detail in the Koran. Those traits may indeed frustrate anyone expecting topics to be dealt with once and for all in a single setting. However, what can seem repetitious or fragmentary to expectations conditioned by the Judeo-Christian Bible is actually an effective use of narrative in its own terms. Tales in the Koran are not necessarily told to provide a detailed account of an event. Rather, the work typically employs its brief stories as illustrations of some larger theme, a point that is particularly important to bear in mind with regard to narratives otherwise familiar from the Biblical tradition. In the Koran, those stories are often used to emphasize God's power, guidance, and judgment or the moral example of the prophets. Dispersed throughout multiple suras, they contribute to the continuity of the scripture as a whole by recalling to those who know the Koran each of the various contexts in which they occur.

THE POETRY OF THE KORAN

Islamic tradition usually draws a sharp distinction between the poetic aspects of the Koran and poetry in general. The Koran does not employ the formalized meters and structures of classical Arabic poetry, yet it is equally not simple prose. Instead, it employs a loose type of rhymed prose exhibiting varying degrees of rhythm. Theological tradition regards the difficulty of categorizing the work as further evidence of its miraculous uniqueness.

The Koran's use of rhythm, rhyme, and assonance in a manner that recalls poetry is an obvious stylistic feature. Modern scholars—Muslims and non-Muslims alike—have shown an increasing interest in that aspect of the work because it

contributes a great deal to the Koranic conveyance of mood and meaning relative to content. Those dynamics are largely lost in translations of the scripture.

INTERPRETING THE KORAN

All Muslims have direct access to the Koran in the sense that they recite it frequently and aspire to understand its messages for themselves. However, Muslims have often tended to approach the work through layers of interpretation made by past authorities, in a manner similar to the rabbinic tradition in Judaism. Explications of grammar, of the legal implications of certain passages, and of the historical context of particular verses dominate the interpretative literature, although the commentaries also cover a

A group of girls studying the Koran at a religious school in Tikrit, Iraq. Muslims are encouraged to learn and recite the Koran from a young age.

THE LANGUAGE OF THE KORAN

The desire to recite and understand the Koran has ensured the survival of the classical Arabic in which it is written. Muslims start memorizing parts of the text at a young age and soon learn to interject Arabic expressions into their conversations. Yet most modern Muslims are not native Arabic speakers. Even for those who are conversant with the language, passages of the Koran may be difficult to understand because of the numerous regional variations in the modern colloquial

This Koran is written in a typically ornate and expansive Arabic script. Islam places great emphasis on calligraphy, or the art of beautiful writing.

tongue. The form of Arabic spoken in, for instance, Iraq and other parts of western Asia may be almost incomprehensible to Arabs in Morocco, but the linguistic link between them is maintained through the written Arabic of the Koran.

wide range of other matters including philosophical and mystical readings. Sufism, in particular, allows room for symbolic and allegorical interpretations of the text.

The Shiite tradition holds that the symbolic inner meanings of the Koran require authoritative interpretation by a respected scholar. Some Shiite scholars such as the Iranian Shiite commentator Allamah Tabatabai (1892–1981) emphasized the

importance of interpreting any one verse of the Koran with reference to other verses, a method also approved by Sunnis.

Traditionally, people first looked to the authorities of the past to determine the answer to any question concerning Koranic passages, with interpretations that could be attributed directly to Muhammad obviously being considered the most authoritative. The appeal to precedent was held to limit the risk of individuals manipulating the scripture to suit their own interests. Shiites also held the traditions of the imams to be authoritative.

After Muhammad himself, Sunnis give precedence to the companions of the Prophet, although without considering their views to be infallible, as the Shiites do those of their imams. It is a remarkable feature of the classical commentaries, such as those of at-Tabari (around 839–923) and Fakhr al-Din ar-Razi (1149–1209), that they often preserve conflicting interpretations side by side. Rather than imposing a single interpretation on the text of the Koran, the authors sought to provide a range of possible views, along with supporting documentation. Even today, Muslim scholars hold that interpreters should first evaluate the possibilities transmitted from past authorities, basing their preference for one view over another on a critical scrutiny of the sources.

MODERN INTERPRETATIONS

Traditional scholarship tended to approach the Koran on a verse-by-verse basis and typically failed to develop an integrated analysis of the suras or of the work as a whole. In the 20th century, scholars began to take a more integrated approach, studying the text in terms of its language, styles, themes, and structures.

Beyond a greater emphasis on literary approaches, there have been other significant modern developments in Koranic interpretation. The most dramatic changes have derived from Muslim encounters with science and with European civilization during the colonial occupation of Muslim lands. As a result, the task of modern commentators has been closely linked to the reconciliation of religion with a scientific worldview and the articulation of up-to-date visions of Islamic government in the postcolonial period.

In the late 19th and early 20th centuries, several commentators attempted to reconcile the Koran with science and the values that had emerged from the European Age of Enlightenment and concluded that there was no essential conflict between the three.

A later group of scholars constructed a methodology for isolating timeless principles and messages in the Koran in order to apply them within the changing context of modern times. Those academics were less often commentators on the Koran than scholars of the work in relation to the broader world of Islam as a whole. While those students maintained the belief that God was the author of the Koran, they also argued that the book's language was conditioned by the need to communicate effectively with its original audience in seventh-century Arabia. In their view, modern Muslims need to understand the work in its original context in order to project its true meaning for their own age.

ISLAMIST INTERPRETERS OF KORAN

Some Muslim scholars have argued that the chasm separating today's world from that of seventh-century Arabia has less to do with the lack of a common outlook than with what they perceive as the modern period's lack of faith. According to this interpretation, the Koran's meaning is clear enough for anyone exhibiting the same degree of conviction as the work's original audience. Critics often label that approach as utopian because it evokes the pristine age of the original Muslim *ummah* (religious community) as the only model for modern society and government.

Those who see traditional Islam as providing a comprehensive answer to all questions involving the organization of society can be called Islamists. They look to the Koran for an authentic expression of the faith unsullied by the foreign influences that have made themselves felt since colonial times in Muslim community life, media, and culture.

SUNNA AND HADITHS

Islamists reject some traditional interpretations of the Koran, regarding them as excessively speculative. Instead, they prefer to concentrate exclusively on sayings directly attributed to Muhammad, seeking thereby to enter into the spirit of the early *ummah* through contact with the fundamental sources. Those sayings are the second most important authorities for Muslim belief and practice.

Muhammad's personality and example had a profound effect on those around him in his own lifetime. It was only natural that the Muslim community as a whole should cherish his memory after his death. Although they did not worship the Prophet, Muslims continued to have a special reverence for him, whom many regarded as sinless and protected from error. Indeed, the Koran itself recommended Muhammad as a role model. That, combined with the community's memory of its beloved leader, ensured that Muhammad's sayings and actions were carefully preserved, thereby establishing a defining characteristic of Islamic tradition.

The Sunna (custom) of Muhammad is second in authority only to the Koran in shaping Muslim worldviews and behavior. As a result, the literature recording it, while not technically scripture, functions in much the same way as holy writ.

The Sunna is articulated in the Hadiths, a term that literally means "reports" but is used to mean records of the sayings or deeds of Muhammad. Those reports were carefully preserved and transmitted from one generation to the next, so they are commonly referred to as "traditions." The term *hadith* itself, then, may be defined as the transmitted traditions of the reported sayings and deeds of Muhammad and his companions.

SAYINGS OF GOD

A few Hadiths belong to a special category known as the *hadith qudsi*. Those are Hadiths in which God is the speaker and Muhammad himself is part of the chain of transmitters. They are revelations, but they have been distinguished from the Koran itself and are not an official part of the scripture. Those sayings are usually spiritual in content, as opposed to the more practical focus of the other Hadiths. Their status is often controversial, and not all of them are universally accepted, although Sufis are often fond of them.

A famous example of the *hadith qudsi* is found in the *Sahih* of al-Bukhari: The Prophet said, "God says: 'I am just as My servant thinks I am, and I am with him if he remembers Me. If he remembers Me in himself, I too, remember him in Myself; and if he remembers Me in a group of people, I remember him in a group that is better than they; and if he comes one span nearer to Me, I go one cubit nearer to him; and if he comes one cubit nearer to Me, I go a distance of two outstretched arms nearer to him; and if he comes to Me walking, I go to him running.'"

The following three examples will serve to illustrate the basic structure of the Hadith format:

• Al-Bukhari, a famous collector of Hadiths, reported that Musaddad said that Yahya reported to him, according to Shubah, according to Qatadah, according to Anas, that Muhammad said: "None of you will have faith until he wants for his brother what he wants for himself."

• Qutaybah bin Said said that Abu Awanah said, according to Mansur, according to Abi Wa'il, that Abi Musa al-Ashari said, that Muhammad said: "Give food to the hungry, pay a visit to the sick, and release the one in captivity."

• Asim bin Ali said, that Ibn Abi Dhi'b said, according to Said, according to Abi Shurayh, that Muhammad said: "By God, he does not believe! By God, he does not believe! By God, he does not believe!" It was said, "Who is that, O Messenger of God?" He said, "That person whose neighbor does not feel safe from his evil."

Two important aspects of the Hadith format immediately become apparent from those examples. First, any Hadith should include a record of who initially reported the words or deeds of Muhammad. Those who subsequently passed on the message are also listed in what is known as the *isnad* (chain of transmission). The second part of the Hadith format is known as the *matn* (body), and it is reached only after the names of the transmitters have been listed. Commentators often treat the body as the content of the Hadith because it contains, as it were, Muhammad's message, but the chain of transmission also conveys significant information.

EVALUATING HADITHS

The chain of transmission is particularly important in establishing the authenticity of any statement attributed to Muhammad. Over time, a large number of sayings attributed to the Prophet accumulated, and scholars needed to be able to evaluate the authority of one statement in relation to another. To do so, they began to categorize the Hadiths in a way that made comparative evaluation easier. Determining the authority of any particular Hadith quickly became a complex undertaking.

Ultimately, evaluating the Hadiths required an investigation into the character, talents, personalities, and affiliations of the transmitters. Was a particular source known for his faulty memory or for passing on paraphrased statements? Perhaps a transmitter was renowned for an excellent memory but was also a known partisan of a particular sect. Then again, investigators had to consider the question of historical plausibility. When and where did the transmitters live? With whom did they associate? Could each of the transmitters actually have met each other? The answers to such questions demanded the development of an advanced historical tradition. The discipline that was developed to record the biographies of transmitters and scholars became known as "the science of men."

The theological implications of the body of a Hadith had also to be taken into account in establishing the authenticity of any particular saying. For instance, a statement attributed to Muhammad that obviously contradicted a basic message of the Koran could be considered inauthentic even if the statement otherwise boasted an impeccable chain of transmission. Even so, the main focus of traditional scholarship

WOMEN SCHOLARS OF THE HADITH

Muhammad's 11 or 13 wives (accounts vary) made valuable contributions to the Islamic community's memory of the Prophet through their transmission of his sayings and deeds in Hadiths. One wife, Aisha, is highly regarded among Sunni Muslims for her careful transmission of Hadiths. She remains a role model for women's scholarship, along with Fatima, Muhammad's daughter and the wife of Ali, the first Shiite imam.

Women from diverse locales, backgrounds, and eras continued those women's legacy, making significant contributions to Hadith scholarship. For instance, Karima al-Marwaziyya (d. 1070 CE) was celebrated in her lifetime and afterward as the greatest authority on the Hadith collection of al-Bukhari, one of the most authoritative texts for Sunni Muslims. Biographical sources record the contributions of thousands of women, many of whom used the medium of public lectures to study and teach the Koran. Indeed, women have taught some of the most famous scholars in Islamic history.

Although the freedom of women to participate in public scholarship was sometimes constrained, they continued to study Hadiths. Today, women scholars of Islam reflect contemporary perspectives such as feminism.

was on the chain of transmitters rather than on the body of the Hadiths. In fact, a wide variety of material was conscientiously maintained within the Hadith corpus, even though some of its elements could appear to contradict each other.

That point deserves special attention because it shows that the construction of consistent content in the Hadith canon did not dominate traditional efforts to evaluate the reports. Both activities were motivated by a strong conviction that, after the Koran, the words and deeds of Muhammad provided the surest foundation for right belief and action.

The above observations provide a telling insight into the sophistication of traditional Islamic scholarship. Because the statements of Muhammad were such a valuable resource, it was felt necessary to identify them precisely, not only separating the authentic from the false but also identifying those that were probably authentic along with borderline cases and even those that were probably—but not certainly—false.

That careful taxonomy (classification system) has ensured that nothing of value has been lost, and at the same time helped to guard against the attribution of excessive authority to dubious Hadiths. Generally, then, traditional evaluations exercised caution and presented the authenticity of Muhammad's statements in terms of varying degrees of probability.

CATEGORIES OF HADITHS

Traditional evaluators of Hadiths who sifted through the many various sayings attributed to Muhammad developed several different classification systems. They absolutely rejected some of the reports as false or fabricated and excluded them from the most important collections, although these rejected Hadiths were nonetheless preserved in special works. There was also a category for Hadiths that were considered absolutely authentic beyond reasonable doubt, because their transmission was widely spread among diverse sectarian and theological groups, as well as across geographical locations, making the possibility of a universal conspiracy to accept them incredible. There is still no consensus among scholars about how many Hadiths fall into this category, but there are relatively few.

The bulk of the Hadiths fall into three broad categories of authenticity, being classified as sound, fair, or weak. Entries in the sound category have a very high probability of authenticity and can generally be relied upon. The fair Hadiths are slightly less reliable but may still provide important guidance. That is especially true if a fair Hadith can be corroborated from some other source. The weak Hadiths have an irregularity in the chain of transmission— for instance, an omitted transmitter or one whose reputation is subject to question. Corroboration from a second source may improve their status.

COLLECTIONS OF HADITHS

Islamic tradition remembers the scholars who preserved and transmitted the sayings of Muhammad with admiration and respect. They are described as pious men and women with wonderful memories and intellects keen enough to appreciate subtle distinctions. Many Hadith scholars traveled widely in search of the Prophet's sayings, risking their lives and suffering from lack of food and shelter.

In the Sunni tradition, two of the most famous collectors of Hadiths are Muhammad Ismail al-Bukhari (810–870)

This photograph shows children at a Koran school for boys in Medina, Saudi Arabia.

and Muslim ibn al-Hajjaj (c. 817–875). The two men lived at a time when collecting Hadiths had reached a high level of sophistication. The collections they compiled are classified as *sahih* (sound) because they strove to include only the most reliable traditions according to the most rigorous standards. Their two collections, along with four others, serve as an informal canon of Sunni Hadith literature, although many other works are also consulted by scholars.

Shiites have their own distinct collections of Hadiths. Even when they share the body of a Hadith with Sunnis, the chain of transmission typically differs. In addition to the sayings of Muhammad, the Shia record the sayings of imams such as Ali, Husayn, and Jafar al-Sadiq, which have an even greater authority in Shiite eyes than those of Muhammad's companions have for Sunnis. Because the Shiite Hadith literature includes the sayings of the imams, it tends to be both more extensive than the Sunni equivalent and more detailed in the issues it addresses. For instance, the famous compilation of Muhammad Baqir al-Majlisi (d. 1698) comprised more than 100 volumes.

SECULAR SCHOLARS OF HADITHS

Secular scholarship has also raised some provocative questions concerning the Hadith literature. While both traditional and secular scholars acknowledge that fabrication of Hadiths occurred, the secular fraternity has tended to see the process as more widespread and shows less confidence than the traditionalists in accepting the efficacy of traditional methods for identifying fabricated Hadiths.

Many scholars have presumed that Hadiths that reflected the interests of later

partisans were mostly fabrications. Emphasizing those that were clearly inauthentic, secular scholars have argued that some Muslims deliberately attributed statements to Muhammad in a conscious attempt to bolster their own positions. They therefore regard such Hadiths as valuable source materials for times long after the death of the Prophet.

Islamic legal theorists do not see themselves as making Sharia, because only God can do that; rather, they are attempting to discover God's law by consulting and interpreting various sources.

Toward the end of the 20th century there was a reaction against previously accepted views, and several scholars began to mitigate their criticism of the whole Hadith corpus. They increasingly took the view that individual Hadiths should be evaluated on a case by case basis, and that general presumptions about fabrication should be suspended.

THE DICTATES OF SHARIA

The Koran is the scripture of Islam, the holy writ that takes precedence over all the religion's other authorities. Second in importance is the Hadith literature, which expresses the Sunna and provides the principal channel for interpreting the holy book. In practice, Muslims integrate the Koran and the Hadiths in the articulation of their beliefs and practices, doing so primarily in terms of Islamic law (Sharia), which constitutes their dominant intellectual tradition.

FEMINIST INTERPRETATIONS OF THE KORAN

Many Muslim feminists have discussed the Koran, and authors such as Amina Wadud, Rifaat Hassan, and Asma Barlas have argued that its basic message of human dignity and equality includes gender equality. In their view, men have undermined those values to serve their own interests and maintain the status quo. Those women scholars reclaim the egalitarian values of the Koran, employing disciplines such as linguistics, history, and literary criticism in their reexamination of its meaning, along with their own aspirations and experiences as women. Their approach challenges basic assumptions regarding the status of women in Islam.

Law in the Islamic context should be understood in the broadest sense of the term. Sharia is not just a set of rules explicitly authorized by the Koran and the Hadiths. Rather, it is the total order that God intends, incorporating the general principles that underlie specific instructions given in the sources. The axioms contained in the Koran and Hadiths are not the entire law; there is more to be known about God's intended order. It is therefore impossible that the Koran and Sunna could be irrelevant to any issue, even if they do not appear to address that particular question directly.

Nonetheless, care must be exercised when determining the unstated principles, intentions, and implications revealed in the Koran and the Sunna. As a part of God's revelation, they are too precious to be ignored but are also too powerful to be left to the manipulation of personal inclinations. Muslims have therefore developed sophisticated methods for deriving the law that God reveals and intends. The concept of derivation is very important. Islamic legal theorists do not see themselves as making Sharia, because only God can do that; rather, they are attempting to discover God's law by consulting and interpreting various sources.

The Koran is the first source of law and the most significant legal authority.

It certainly contains legal precepts, particularly from the Medinan period of revelation. However, it is not a detailed legal code and does not provide instruction on many practices that are fundamental to Islam and everyday living. The Sunna of Muhammad, as expressed in the Hadiths, elaborates many of those additional practices and is the second most important source of Sharia.

OTHER SUNNI SOURCES OF THE LAW

There are other important sources that also play a significant role in interpreting and elaborating the Koran and Sunna. Sunni and Shia traditions differ in that respect. Sunnis identify consensus of the community (*ijma*) as a source of law, taking as their authority a famous Hadith in which Muhammad reportedly said: "My people will never agree together upon an error." So, if the community agrees upon the authority of a particular unstated principle, intention, or implication in the Koran or Sunna, then whatever they agree upon has the force of law, in effect being considered infallible. Traditionally, it is then considered a part of what God has revealed concerning His intended order for life.

However, the problem with using *ijma* as a source of law is the difficulty of

The Egyptian parliament is typical of many legislative bodies in the Muslim world that try to reconcile the requirements of the Koran with political necessities.

determining exactly what constitutes consensus. Must there be unanimous agreement across the entire population, or else among scholars, or does a majority opinion suffice? Traditionally, Sunnis have held that an imprecisely defined consensus of scholars is sufficient. Other Muslims limit the definition to the consensus of the early companions of Muhammad. Still others have argued that the basic principle of *ijma* is democratic and that it should reflect the opinion of the community as a whole.

The final source of law for Sunni Muslims is known as *qiyas*, a term that describes an elaboration of the rules in the Koran and Sunna by means of analogy or logic. When a question arises about a particular practice that is not clearly addressed in the primary sources, scholars look for an analogous situation that is so treated and use it to extract a common

principle that can be applied to the previously unaddressed question. The scope of analogy has often been debated in the Islamic legal tradition, and it is now generally agreed that its application must not be arbitrary. For that reason, scholars have attempted to develop precise rules for its use.

THE ROLE OF *IJTIHAD*

A person who seeks to discover the relevance of the Koran and the Hadith literature in relation to issues that are not obviously addressed in the texts exercises *ijtihad*. That term is related to jihad and expresses the same basic meaning—to strive or to struggle. In this context, however, it describes the practice of focusing one's energy and ability to the utmost to determine the unstated principles, intentions, and implications of the divine law in relation to a particular question. Consequently, *ijtihad* is a personal attempt to interpret the sources of law so as to understand how a given point fits into God's order.

Who may exercise *ijtihad*? Historically, Sunnis have tended to reduce progressively the ranks of those permitted to do so. Sunni theologians have increasingly attached a higher value to the precedents set by the interpretative efforts of previous generations of legal scholars than to people's authority to interpret the various sources of law for themselves. Some Islamic scholars have even claimed that the practice of *ijtihad* fell out of use in the medieval period as the authority of precedent increased, although that view appears to be overstated. One of the most interesting developments of the late 20th and early 21st centuries has been the way in which the practice of *ijtihad* has been reinvigorated among Muslim activists, whether conservative or progressive. *Ijtihad* affords such people opportunities to reinterpret the Koran, Sunna, and other aspects of the Islamic tradition in a variety of new ways.

SHIITE SOURCES OF THE LAW

In both Sunni and Shiite tradition, the exercise of *ijtihad* has largely been reserved for scholarly elites. Nonetheless, the concept of *ijtihad* is one of the most distinctive features of the legal tradition of the Shia. While some Shiite scholars have traditionally rejected the practice, the dominant legal school of thought sets great emphasis on *ijtihad*, which is seen as giving scope for the exercise of human reason in determining law, a consideration that has been a consistent part of Shiite tradition. Thus, the exercise of *ijtihad* among Shiites

has not fluctuated in popularity to the same extent as it has in Sunni circles.

The Shiite approach to Sharia law is also distinctive inasmuch as it incorporates into the Sunna the views of the Shiite imams who guided the *ummah* after the death of Muhammad. Typically, Sunni commentators emphasize community consensus, seeing in it an infallible source of law, while Shiites look instead for a sure guide to God's intentions toward imams, the successors to the Prophet.

CONCLUSION

The Koran is the scripture of Islam. For Muslims, it is the speech of God, unique, holy, and eternal. Belief in the Koran and in Muhammad as its messenger has ensured that the work itself and the Sunna have both received minute investigation and careful interpretation. The aim has been to integrate the message of the Koran and the Sunna into the lives and attitudes of believers. Whether recited or read, the Koran as scripture stands separate from the Hadiths, which also provide authoritative guidance, and from Sharia, which further expands the scope of both the Koran and the Sunna in responding to the day-to-day concerns of Muslims.

Those divisions are convenient aids for non-Muslims observing Islam from the outside. For believers, however, such explication is only a dim shadow in comparison to the light of God's guidance as provided in the Koran and the Sunna and by Sharia. Any understanding that takes into account Islam's strength as a system of belief must also allow for the integration of the three within the experience of faith, where they all come together in accordance with the transcendent wisdom of an all-powerful God.

Translating the Koran

Although many Muslims question the desirability—and even the possibility—of translating the Koran from Arabic, the spread of Islam has led to editions in many languages.

Muslims generally call the Koran in any version other than the language in which it was originally written an "interpretation" rather than a translation. They believe that the text was revealed to the Prophet Muhammad in 7th-century Arabia in Arabic and, because of the importance they attach to its original context, it is common for non-Arab Muslims to read the Koran in Arabic even when they do not understand anything of the language apart from the holy book itself. It is not unusual for Muslims to memorize whole suras (chapters) or even the entire Arabic text of the Koran as an act of religious observance. That reverence, however, has not prevented dozens of translators, especially in the 20th and 21st centuries, from rendering the text of the Koran into several languages, especially English, and the majority of these are competent translations.

SPREADING THE WORD

The perceived need to render the Koran into languages other than the original Arabic has increased in line with the growth of Muslim populations whose mother tongue is not Arabic. For non-Arab Muslims, who form around 80 percent of the world's 1.2 billion followers of Islam, solid knowledge of the Koran is essential for common religious practice. One of the most straightforward and practical ways to provide that knowledge is through translations of the religion's most sacred text.

The increased social inclusiveness of religious practices has influenced Islamic scholarship in numerous ways and given rise to some of the first translations of the Koran by women. Among them are *The Noble Koran* (1999) by an Englishwoman, Aisha Bewley, and her husband Abdalhaqq Bewley, and *The Sublime Koran* (2007) by an American, Laleh Bakhtiar. The latter translation has

caused controversy because it renders the Arabic verb "to beat" in a well-known verse on marital relationships as "to withdraw from." In spite of the outrage this linguistic choice caused in some quarters, that definition is well supported by Arabic usage according to *Lisan al-Arab*, a dictionary that was originally compiled in the 13th century and remains widely used today.

Muslims have traditionally been encouraged to spread the message of their faith. It is only natural, therefore, that the religion's seminal text should be available in translation.

Translators have frequently felt the need to address Muslims' ambivalent attitude toward foreign-language versions of the Koran. Islam is a proselytizing religion (a faith that actively seeks converts), and Muslims have traditionally been encouraged to spread the message of their faith. It is only natural, therefore, that the religion's seminal text should be available in translation. In the global culture of the 21st century, Muslim unease with having the Koran in any language other than Arabic has largely given way to practical considerations in which better knowledge of the text seems more important than qualms about departing from the original.

Uncertainties about the legitimacy of translating the Koran at all may also explain the historical dearth of critical studies of foreign-language versions of the work.

This early edition of the Koran in Arabic was produced by calligraphers in Morocco.

MISTRANSLATIONS

The first English translation of the Koran (1649) was by Alexander Ross, who did not know Arabic but translated from a French rendering by André du Ryer that had appeared two years previously. Ross was further handicapped because he did not know French well enough to translate from it, and it appears that his anti-Muslim intention was the key motivation behind his endeavor. His purpose may be judged from the title page, which reads in part as follows: "The Alcoran [Koran] of Mahomet [Muhammad], translated out of Arabic into French. . . and newly Englished, for the satisfaction of all that desire to look into the Turkish vanities."

Ross's work was plagued throughout by gross misunderstandings, countless errors of fact, omissions, additions, and random restructuring of the Koranic text. Subsequent English translations produced before the 20th century suffered from similar faults; among the best known and most inaccurate renditions of the work were those by George Sale (1734), John Rodwell (1861), and Edward Palmer (1880).

This photograph shows a modern English-language translation of the Koran. Most Muslims perform ritual purification before handling the holy book.

Some of these early English translations are now available on the Internet. It is interesting to compare their renderings of the Koran with modern translations, most of which are immensely superior.

The increasing number and variety of translations, however, are currently stimulating an increase in exegetical (explanatory) analysis of a work that plays a major role in contemporary life throughout the Muslim world.

EARLY TRANSLATIONS

The earliest translation of the Koran was a Persian edition that was completed at the end of the 7th century. In the 9th century, the work appeared in Gujurati and Sindhi in parts of India where Islam had been established as the majority religion. The first translation into a European language was a 12th-century Latin version by Robert of Ketton, an English monk. The earliest version of the Koran in

English was produced in the 17th century by Alexander Ross. Ross knew no Arabic and little about Islam but used the work as a forum for discussion of the theological issues that set Muslims apart from Christians. His general purpose was to denigrate Islam.

20TH-CENTURY VERSIONS

Many early translations of the Koran were flawed not only by the intrusion into the text of Christian value judgments and hostile polemics but also by the translators' inadequate knowledge of Arabic and negligible understanding of Islam. However, 20th-century translations have generally exhibited sound scholarship and competent knowledge of the text and its background. The shortage of translations by Muslims motivated Southeast Asian translators to produce more than two dozen different versions, some of which remain in print today. Notable among these are Abdullah Yusuf Ali's *The Holy Qur'an: Translation and Commentary* (1934), Abdul Majid Daryabadi's *The Holy Qur'an: English Translation and Commentary* (1941), and Sayyid Abu'l-A'la Mawdudi's *The Meaning of the Koran* (1967), a multivolume interpretive translation with an extensive commentary. The first scholarly translation of the Koran by a native English speaker was Muhammad Marmaduke Pickthall's *The Meanings of the Glorious Koran* (1935) which earned the approval of many prominent Muslim clerics and is still widely read today.

Two of the most reliable and readable English-language versions are A. J. Arberry's *The Koran Interpreted* (1955) and M. A. S. Abdel-Halim's *The Koran: A New Translation* (2004). Although their titles

might suggest two different approaches—interpretation versus translation—they both succeed in capturing not only the meaning of the text but also much of the grandeur of the original.

A few English translations, however, could not avoid lapsing into Islamic sectarianism. Some have a Shia bias, as was evident in commentaries such as Syed V. Mir Ahmad Ali's *The Holy Koran* (1964) and M. H. Shakir's *The Holy Koran* (1982). Other English-language translations, such as Muhammad Ali's *The Holy Qur'an: English Translation* (1917), were influenced by the beliefs of sects like the Ahmadis and the Qaiyanis, many of whom had migrated to Britain in the early 20th century.

The importance of the Koran to Muslim society is well illustrated in this monumental gateway on the main highway between Jiddah and Mecca in Saudi Arabia, which is designed in the shape of a copy of the holy book on a stand.

Chapter 6

SUBDIVISIONS OF ISLAM

While Islam encourages unity (tawhid), the faith has been divided from early in its history into Sunni and Shia branches. There have also been breakaway movements, including the Druze and the Baha'i, which are now usually classed as distinct religions, while the status of groups such as the Nation of Islam remains contentious.

D escriptions of unity and diversity in Islam tend toward extremes. At one end of the spectrum, Islam is presented as so rife with rivalry that any talk of unity sounds ludicrous. The other extreme minimizes differences and downplays conflict, avoiding discussion of diversity. The challenge is to balance the Muslim commitment to unity with the realities of the Muslim world, particularly relations between the two main divisions of the faith, the Sunni and the Shia.

BASIC DEFINITIONS

The term Sunni derives from the Arabic word *sunna* (the acts of the Prophet Muhammad). Sunnis regard the whole Muslim community as guardian of the Sunna, which, with the Koran, guides their lives. No individual possesses the authority to interpret Islam or its sources or has a unique claim to lead the community. Technically, the leaders of the Sunnis (historically, the caliphs) were chosen on merit, although the caliphate quickly became hereditary in all but name.

The term Shia (literally, "followers") refers to those Muslims who believe that Ali, Muhammad's cousin and son-in-law, and his male descendants through Muhammad's daughter Fatima, possess special authority to lead the community and interpret Islam. Rejecting as illegitimate the first caliphs who governed the Islamic community in succession to the Prophet, they call their leader the "imam." For the majority of Shia, the imam is now in a state of occultation (hidden, it is believed, in heaven), although some Shia follow a "present imam," the Aga Khan (see box).

The word *imam* requires further explanation. The Sunni caliph was the leader of a religious community rather than a religious leader, but the Shiite imam performed both functions. However, Sunnis sometimes called their caliph "imam," while Shia leaders occasionally used the designation "caliph-imam," so those titles can be confusing. *Imam* also means "he who stands first" (in other words, he who leads the prayers) and may be used in the Sunni tradition simply to

This man is an elder of the Druze, a subdivision of Islam that is found mostly in Lebanon.

One of the holiest shrines for Shiite Muslims, this mosque in Najaf, Iraq, contains the tomb of Ali, the fourth caliph and the first imam.

describe a paid teacher and prayer leader in a mosque. The phrase "the Four Imams" refers to the quartet of Sunni scholars after whom the most popular schools of law were named.

DEMOGRAPHICS

Estimates for Islam's share of the total world population range from 20 to 23 percent. Within the Muslim community, the percentage of Sunnis is generally thought to be between 85 and 93.5 percent, with the Shia accounting for 6.6 to 15 percent, although some sources estimate their numbers at 20 percent. A common compromise figure ranks Sunnis at 90 percent and Shias at 10 percent.

Reliable statistics are hard to obtain, as shown by the case of Iraq. According to the *CIA World Fact Book*, the Shia in that country make up between 60 and 65 percent of the population and the Sunni from 32 to 37 percent, with a further 3 to 7 percent listed as "other." Iraq is one of only three nations with a Shia majority, the others being Iran (89 percent) and Azerbaijan (80 percent).

Other nations have substantial Shia minorities. In Pakistan, Shiites make up 20 percent of the population; they counted the Father of the Nation, Muhammad Ali Jinnah (1876–1948), among their number. The equivalent figure in Afghanistan is 19 percent, while Kuwait and Yemen have 36 and 42 percent Shiites, respectively. In Lebanon, Muslims account for approximately 59.7 percent of the population, and more than half (53.35 percent) of them are Shiite.

THE SUNNI-SHIA SCHISM

The split between the Sunnis and the Shiites came about over the question of who should succeed to the leadership of the Muslim community after the death of Muhammad in 622 CE. It is often stated that Muhammad made no provision for the succession, but many Muslims dispute that assertion. Sunnis believe that Muhammad in effect laid down a mechanism for choosing his successor by stating that his community would not agree in error; that statement, they claim, made the community itself responsible for deciding a system of governance by consensus (*ijma*). Sunnis also point to two suras of the Koran that refer to *shura* (consultation) and take the Prophet's revelation that Muslims are those who conduct their affairs by consultation to be a clear instruction on governance.

According to the Sunni view, the community decided after Muhammad's death to appoint a caliph (literally, "successor") as a leader who would be first among equals in the Muslim community. The caliph would be the best person for the task of leadership, but he would also be expected to seek advice from others. His personal opinion would carry weight, given his reputation for piety and knowledge of Islam's sources. However, he would have no exclusive exegetical (interpretative) authority. Exegesis or interpretation would, technically, be the shared responsibility of the whole *ummah* (community).

The first four caliphs were chosen in various ways. Abu Bakr (d. 634), Muhammad's father-in-law, was selected at a gathering in Medina attended by leading Muslims. He nominated the second caliph,

Over time, the idea evolved in Sunni circles that the caliphate was essential for the unity of Islam and that the caliph's primary responsibilities were to protect Islam and uphold Islamic law.

Umar (d. 644), who set up a committee of seven to nominate the third, Uthman (d. 656). The fourth, Ali (d. 661), was chosen by the crowd that gathered in the public square after Uthman's assassination.

The fifth caliph, Muawiyah (d. 680), usurped power from Ali and nominated his own son, Yazid, as the sixth caliph, thereby establishing the dynastic principle. Technically, though, even the succession of dynastic caliphs among the Ummayads (661–750), the Abbasids (750–1517), and the Ottomans (1517–1924) was not automatic but required the approval of the religious and political powerbrokers of the day.

Over time, the idea evolved in Sunni circles that the caliphate was essential for the unity of Islam and that the caliph's primary responsibilities were to protect Islam and uphold Islamic law. References to

DIFFERENCES OF OPINION

One Hadith states, "Differences of opinion among my community are a blessing." A degree of diversity within the Islamic *ummah* has therefore been seen as laudable and even as divinely sanctioned. Some people argue that even the differences between Sunni and Shia are hardly more significant than the differences between the various Sunni legal schools (*madhhib*). The school of the Shiite imam al-Jafar has, in fact, often been regarded as a fifth *madhhab*.

Another tradition predicts that Islam will subdivide 73 times but also states that there is only one right path. Some Muslims, declaring their version of Islam to be the correct one, condemn other Muslims as apostates. Other Muslims interpret the Hadith to mean that each path contains a very small number of wrongdoers, and that no Muslims should be condemned for minor sins, provided that they sincerely believe in Allah and His Messenger.

In Islam, debate is the route to greater understanding of Allah's purpose and meaning. Here, religious scholars discuss Koranic texts at the Grand Mosque in Qom, Iran.

the first four caliphs (in the correct order) can be found in the Hadiths. After Muhammad's death, the first caliphs called themselves *Khalifat Rasul Allah* (caliphs of the Messenger of God, meaning Muhammad), but later leaders changed the title, referring to themselves instead as "deputies of God" and seeking to exercise religious as well as political authority. That move was constantly challenged, for religious authority was, in practice, vested in trained scholars. Furthermore, while the caliphs asserted they were the spiritual and political leaders of all Muslims, no caliphate ever had a significant influence on the large Muslim populations in South Asia, China, and Southeast Asia.

The title of caliph passed to the Ottoman dynasty in the Middle Ages. As the empire fragmented, however, it ceased to carry any political weight and went into abeyance in 1924, two years after the abolition of the sultanate. While some Sunnis have since tried to revive the office, others argue that, by employing the Koran's principles of consensus and consultation, Muslims are free to choose different systems of governance that are better suited to contemporary conditions.

THE MAJOR SUNNI SCHOOLS OF LAW

Most surveys of Sunni Islam identify the major schools of law (*madhhab*) as sub-traditions, although their development was in no sense schismatic. Integral to Sunni Islam, the *madhhab* are primarily concerned with legal matters. However, given Islam's self-definition as a total way of life, it is not easy to maintain a rigid distinction between religion, law, spirituality, and politics. In practice, most Sunnis identify with one particular legal school that influences their outlook on life and their understanding of Islam. On the other hand, Sunnis are not bound by their chosen *madhhab*, and they are free to consult scholars from other legal traditions.

The main schools are named after four eminent jurists sometimes collectively referred to as the Four Imams: Hanafi (d. 767), Maliki (d. 796), Shafi'i (d. 820), and Hanbali (d. 855). The Hanafi school predominates today in Arab western Asia and South Asia; the Maliki school is most influential in northern, central, and western Africa; the Shafii school is found in eastern Africa, southern Arabia, and Southeast Asia; the Hanbali school is almost exclusively followed in Saudi Arabia. Other, smaller schools are the Zahiri and the Ibadi, associated respectively with Dawud al Zahiri (d. 910) and with the Islam of the state of Oman.

The schools differ in many details, most of which do not have an obvious theological aspect. However, minor variations in the prayer ritual and other aspects of observing the Five Pillars of Islam do exist. Hanbalis rely almost entirely on the Koran and Hadith literature, giving little scope to such concepts as analogy (*qiyas*) in their interpretation of the divinely intended order. Hanafis allowed public interest (*maslaha*) as a legal device, and the principle was later accepted by Malikis and by some Hanbalis, but not by Shafis. *Maslaha* allowed early Hanafis to permit non-Arabic-speaking Muslims to pray in other languages, a concession that was not made by other schools.

The dominant view among modern Islamic scholars is that only minor differences exist between the four schools, permitting them all to be accepted within a common Islamic *ummah*. While it is common for the Western media to refer to tolerant or intolerant *madhhab*, many of the policies and customs popularly associated with particular *madhhab*—such as restrictions on non-Muslims in Hanbali Saudi Arabia—are the result of a mixture of political, social, and cultural factors, rather than religious doctrine. These factors influence how the principles of a *madhhab* are implemented, and how closely society follows Islamic traditions. This can be seen in the variation between societies that follow the same school, such as Indonesia and Somalia, which are both predominantly Shafi'i.

THEOLOGICAL SCHOOLS

Besides the *madhhab*, the Sunni community also came to encompass various theological traditions. Usually, those traditions did not take the form of highly organized movements; rather, people chose to identify themselves with a particular school of thought. There were various academies, though, that attracted followers of each school, as well as periods when one or another group enjoyed political patronage.

In the early days of Islam, the Qadarites emphasized free will, believing that people possess power (*qadir*) over their actions, which are not subject to predestination. The Mutazalites emerged in the first decades of the eighth century and were influenced by Greek thought. The first Mutazalite was Wasil ibn Ata (d. 748), who withdrew from the circle of Hasan of Basra (d. 737)—hence the term *mutazali*, meaning "to leave"— over the question of whether Muslims who die having committed a major sin without repenting go to hell. (Wasil took a

AL-ASHARI

Al-Ashari is considered by many to be Sunni Islam's oustanding theologian, acknowledged as the *majaddid* (renewer) of his age (Muslims believe that, in each century, a preeminent reformer emerges to renew the Islamic faith). A descendant of Ali's arbitrator at Siffin, he was born in Basra in what is now Iraq and later inherited wealth that enabled him to devote his life to study, research, and teaching. After studying the Koran and the Hadiths, he entered the academy of the Mutazalite al-Jubbai (died 915) before abandoning his master's position in 912. Al-Ashari's early work, the *Maqalat-al-Islamiyin* (A compendium of different opinions), is nonetheless the source of much of what is now known about the Mutazalites.

Al-Ashari recorded a series of dreams in which Muhammad asked him how he was defending the Koran and the Sunna. When he replied that he had given up rational inquiry as dangerous, the Prophet rebuked him and told him that it was his duty to use reason in defense of Islam. In response, Al-Ashari founded an academy in Baghdad.

compromise view, believing that they did go to hell but suffered lesser punishments there than non-believers.) Often referred to as rationalists, the Mutazalites championed human reason, which, they claimed, was able to deduce right from wrong even without the aid of revelation. Like the Qadarites, they affirmed that people have free will to act as they choose.

The Mutazalites were opposed to those who, like Abu al-Hassan al-Ashari (874–935), taught that God's attributes were revealed as the Koran during Muhammad's lifetime. Al-Ashari did not reject reason but gave it a subordinate status to revelation. Upholding predestination, he argued that God gives people the power to act but that the choice they make has already been determined. Al-Ashari also contributed to the debate about the anthropomorphic verses in the Koran, which describe God as seeing, sitting, or possessing a face, in contrast to other verses that prohibit comparison of God with the human form. To resolve that contradiction, al-Ashari devised the formula *billa kayfa* (without asking how), arguing that Muslims should simply accept that God does not see, sit, or possess a face in the same way as humans.

Similarly, al-Ashari held that the exact nature of God's attributes may be beyond human understanding. God can possess eternal attributes such as speech, mercy, and life without these compromising His oneness, or representing—as the Mutazalites argued—multiple gods. According to al-Ashari, God's attributes were "totally God" but not, individually, the "whole of God." They were also different from each other. Comparison has been made with the Christian understanding of the Trinity, each member of which is wholly God but not the whole of God. The difference, though, is that Christians speak of persons, not attributes, and identify the second person of the Trinity with Jesus, who was flesh and blood.

Although the rationalist Mutazalites are often praised as enlightened, they could be intolerant. Between 833 and 848, the Abbasid caliphs made Mutazalism the state doctrine, and anyone who refused to subscribe to its tenets was jailed under an inquisition known as the Mihna. There are few Mutazalites in the present-day Muslim world, but the principles of Mutazalism continue to have an influence on contemporary Islamic scholars.

Unlike the Mutazalites, the Kharijites believed that sinners who died without repenting went to hell, while the Murjites said that, as long as sinners sincerely believed in God, they would not be eternally punished. The Murjite position discouraged Muslims from rebelling against unjust caliphs, arguing that only God knew their ultimate fate. The Kharijites made several assassination attempts (they assassinated the Caliph Ali in 661) and led various revolts in the early years of Islam.

THE SHIA VIEW

In contrast to the Sunni emphasis on consensus, Shiites contend that Muhammad made provision for the succession by appointing his son-in-law, Ali, as the first imam of the community. When Abu Bakr was selected, Ali took the oath of allegiance because he did not wish to cause a split in the community or to be labeled as ambitious. A group of Muslims may have supported his claim at the time, although he did not press it himself and, indeed, was

Muslims in Istanbul, Turkey, commemorate the anniversary of the Battle of Karbala.

a member of the committee that chose the third caliph, Uthman. Tradition records that Ali was passed over because he stated, when asked, that he would follow his own judgment, while Uthman said he would follow only the Koran and the Sunna. After Uthman's assassination, Ali finally accepted the caliphate on the grounds that only he could unite the Islamic community.

As the fourth Sunni caliph and the first Shia imam, Ali is a respected figure in both main Muslim communities. The split

It was under the sixth Imam, Jafar al-Sadiq, that distinctive Shia beliefs emerged, demarcating more clearly the difference between the Sunni and the Shiite communities.

between the two really began in 657, when a relative of Uthman, Muawiyah, the governor of Syria, refused to step down from office when Ali sought to replace him. Instead, Muawiyah sent troops to confront Ali's army at Siffin, claiming that either Ali was implicated in Uthman's death or, if not, that he had failed to punish those responsible. Ali had already defeated an earlier revolt, led by Aisha, one of Muhammad's widows, at the Battle of the Camel (656).

The confrontation between pro- and anti-Ali factions was the first *fitna* (civil disruption) in Islamic history. Initially, Ali's troops got the upper hand in the engagement at Siffin until Muawiyah's troops placed Korans on the tips of their spears and requested arbitration. The result of the negotiation was inconclusive, but

Muawiyah's supporters acclaimed their man as caliph, and Ali's time of leadership was over in all but name. Muawiyah later extended his influence into Iraq, Egypt, Yemen, and elsewhere, while Ali was confined to Kufa in what is now southern Iraq, where he had transferred his capital from Medina.

The Kharijites ("those who go out") withdrew their support at that stage, declaring that Ali had compromised his leadership by resorting to human mediation when God alone was qualified to decide. They thereby split themselves from the mainstream of the community.

Assassinated by a Kharijite in 661, Ali was succeeded by his son Hasan (identified in Shiite tradition as the second imam). Hasan died in 670; according to Shia sources, he was poisoned. Husayn, identified as the third imam, duly succeeded to the leadership and also claimed authority over the entire community of Muslims, opposing Yazid, who had succeeded his father, Muawiyah, as caliph. Convinced that he had enough support, Husayn marched toward Yazid's capital, Damascus. After several minor skirmishes, he was intercepted by Yazid's army at Karbala, Iraq, where battle was joined in October of 680. Vastly outnumbered (sources say by as many as 4,000 to 130), Husayn was defeated and killed; his head was taken to Damascus and given to the caliph. The dead (numbering 70 or 72) were mutilated, among them Husayn's baby son, Ali Asghar, two older sons, a cousin, and a half brother. Of the family of the Prophet, only Ali ibn Husyan and two sisters survived, with Ali duly succeeding his dead father to become the fourth Shiite imam. That event occurred in the Islamic month of Muharram, during which present-day Shiites still mourn the martyrdoms that took place at Karbala.

THE DEVELOPMENT OF SHIA BELIEFS

It was under the sixth Imam, Jafar al-Sadiq, that distinctive Shia beliefs began to emerge, demarcating more clearly the difference between the Sunni and the Shiite communities. Both share many fundamental beliefs and practices in common, with only apparently minor variations; Shiites, for example, adjust the *shahada* declaration of faith by adding, after "There is no God but God and Muhammad is the messenger of God," the phrase, "Ali is the friend of Allah, the successor of the Messenger of God and his first caliph," thereby acknowledging the imamate. The Shiites also have their own collections of Hadiths, which focus on the role of the family of the Prophet (also known as the People of the House, or Ahlu-al-Bayt) whose members are all revered, especially Ali, Hasan, and Husayn. Most Shia reject the concept of predestination.

Recognized as a legal scholar and as a theologian, Jafar al-Sadiq was admired for his scholarship by Sunnis as well as Shiites. He originated the idea of the imam as infallible, sinless, and divinely inspired. In the view of al-Sadiq, Muhammad was the last prophet, but the imams were preordained to lead the Islamic community, because a just God would not leave His people without a guide. Jafar contended that God always appoints an intermediary between Himself and humanity and, in the absence of the Prophet, the imam mediates His will. A good Muslim therefore owes loyalty and obedience to the imam.

Some Shiites came to venerate Karbala, the scene of Husayn's martyrdom, claiming that the holy site existed even before the world's creation and will be restored on the Day of Judgment to its original paradisiacal state as the dwelling place of Muhammad's family and the prophets.

Muslims in Karachi, Pakistan, celebrate Ashura, the holy day during Ramadan that marks the anniversary of the martyrdom of Ali, the first Shia imam.

THE MAHDI

For most Shiites, the Mahdi is the 12th imam who will one day return from occultation—hiding—to inaugurate an era of righteousness. Some Sunnis also believe in a savior figure linked with apocalyptic happenings, although his identity is less specific than in the Shiite tradition.

Various people have called themselves or been acclaimed as the Mahdi. Al-Mukhtar, who rebelled against the Umayyad caliphate less than 50 years after Muhammad's death in 686, declared that Muhammad ibn al-Hanifiya, a son of the fourth caliph Ali (the first imam of the Shiite tradition), was the Mahdi who would save the Muslims from the injustice of Umayyad rule. Al-Hanifiya was not involved in the rebellion, and no action was taken against him when the Umayyads quashed the revolt. Ibn Tumart (d. 1130), founder of the puritan Almohads, claimed to be the Mahdi, as did the rebel leader Muhammad Ahmad (1844–1885), who was known as the Mahdi of Sudan.

Others say that the imams and their families also preexisted creation, adding faithfulness to the present imam, belief in his authority, and opposition to his enemies to their articles of faith. Often living among Sunnis, Shiites developed the concept of *taqiyah* (concealment), which permitted them to keep their loyalty to the imam secret when threatened with persecution. That principle also served to protect the imam's identity.

Another distinction between the Sunni and Shia communities is that, for Sunnis, the notion of novelty (*bida*) became anathema while, for Shiites, innovation remained possible. The themes of group solidarity, loyalty to the leader, and suffering in the face of injustice are especially prominent in Shia literature. Yazid is demonized and the encounter outside Karbala represented as a battle between good and evil, a view that has not encouraged good relations between the two communities over the centuries. On the other hand, it is wrong to think of the history of Sunni-Shia relations as one of continuous conflict, for the two groups have often lived harmoniously side by side. Between 932 and 1075, the Shia Buyyids ruled more or less as agents of the Sunni Abbasid caliphs, effectively exercising real power authorized by certificates of legitimacy issued in the caliph's name.

There have been ecumenical attempts to bring the two communities together. In 2004, 200 Muslim scholars from 50 countries gathered in Amman, Jordan; among them were Iran's supreme leader, along with such senior Sunnis as the grand imam of Cairo's Al-Azhar University and the grand muftis of Egypt, Syria, and Jordan. Together, they endorsed a statement that became known as the Amman Message, calling for tolerance and unity among all Muslims, Shia and Shiite alike.

TWELVER SHIISM
According to the majority of Shia, known as Twelvers, there were 12 imams. The first 11 were as follows: Ali ibn Abi Talib (c. 600–661); Hasan ibn Ali (624–669);

Husayn ibn Ali (626–680); Ali ibn Husayn (658–713); Muhammad ibn Ali (676–743); Jafar ibn Muhammad (703–765); Musa ibn Jafar (745–799); Ali ibn Musa (765–818); Muhammad ibn Ali (810–835); Ali ibn Muhammad (827–868); and Hasan ibn Ali (846–874).

Shiites believe that the 12th imam, Muhammad ibn Hasan (b. 868), went into occultation, protected by God from danger, while the Shia minority was being persecuted by the Abbasids. At first, he remained in contact with his followers through deputies (a period known as the Minor Occultation) but, on the death of the fourth deputy in the year 941, it was announced that the deputyship would cease. Thereafter, all communication with the imam ceased and the Major Occultation began. Twelver Shiites believe that the 12th imam is the Mahdi (the ultimate savior of humankind), that he is still alive today, although he no longer dwells on earth, and that he will return before the Day of Judgment to establish peace, justice, and righteousness.

Meanwhile, earthly authority within the Shia community devolved in the wake of the Occultation to religious scholars. Constituting a highly organized class, they are often referred to as "clergy." Unlike the imams, however, the religious scholars are not considered to be divinely inspired, although, collectively, they may speak for

Islamic preachers and clergy attend the historic meeting in November 2004 in Amman, Jordan, that called for tolerance throughout the Muslim world.

THE AGA KHANS

The leaders of the Nizari branch of Islam, the Aga Khans are viewed by their followers as infallible. The four holders of the title have been:

- Aga Khan I (1804–1881) (46th Imam)
- Aga Khan II (1830–1885) (47th Imam)
- Aga Khan III (1877–1957) (48th Imam)
- Aga Khan IV (1936–) (49th Imam)

Between them, they have acquired considerable personal wealth. Aga Khan III was a renowned owner of thoroughbred racehorses, a tradition that has been maintained by Aga Khan IV. Aga Khan III was also committed to reforming his religious community, seeking to reposition Nizaris as a school or path (*tariqah*) within Islam and arguing in favor of progress. A philanthropist and humanitarian, Aga Khan III was elected president of the League of Nations in 1937. He passed over his son in favor of his grandson as his successor, convinced that the Nizari community needed a young leader who was in tune with the modern world.

The Aga Khan visits a refugee camp in Jordan in 1990. Note that the Nizari leader does not wear religious clothing.

Aga Khan IV, who has a degree in Islamic studies from Harvard University, has continued to move the Nizari community toward Sunni Islam. (Nizaris have traditionally been flexible in some aspects of Islamic practice, such as observing only three daily prayer times rather than the traditional five.) The founder of the Aga Khan Development Network and many other agencies, Aga Khan IV has expressed some distaste for the word *philanthropy*, preferring to stress the spiritual motivation of his efforts to make the world a more just, sustainable habitat. He has encouraged respect for all faiths and stressed the importance of interfaith cooperation. His uncle, Prince Sadruddin Aga Khan (1933–2003), held important posts at the United Nations, serving as the High Commissioner for Refugees (1966–1978).

the Hidden Imam. Individually, too, the most senior clergy can exercise *ijtihad* (legal decisions or new interpretations of Islam).

To fulfill those senior clerical roles in society, Shia Muslims choose men whose authority they accept in matters of worship and personal affairs (*taqlid*). The scholar with the most support became known as the *marja-al-taqlid al-mutlaq* (literally, "absolute point of reference"). By the end of the 19th century, any scholar considered qualified to exercise independent judgment was given the title of *ayatollah* (literally, "sign of God").

Persia (modern Iran) became officially Shiite with the rise of the Safavid dynasty (founded in 1501). Some scholars speculate that the Safavids chose Shia Islam to distinguish themselves from the neighboring, Arab-dominated Sunni regimes and because the Persian nation had a tradition of investing authority in ancient priestly families that it had inherited from the Zoroastrian past. In contrast, they argue, Arab tribes were traditionally led by chiefs who regularly consulted tribal elders, with the result that leadership was customarily more collegial. Within Iran, there was sometimes tension between the shah (king) and the scholars, but usually the former maintained order and exercised administrative power while the latter had legal authority.

Tension between political and religious authority in Iran peaked in 1979, when the last shah, Mohammad Reza Pahlavi, perceived as a secularizing, Westernizing ruler, was forced into exile. Ayatollah Ruholla Musavi Khomeini became the leader of a new Islamic republic.

Under the Islamist system of government established by Khomeini, Iran has an elected assembly and a president, but all legislation must be approved by a Council of Guardians, composed of Islamic clerics and lawyers, and by the Supreme Leader himself. Twelver Shiism is the dominant tradition in Iran, as also in neighboring Iraq.

SEVENER SHIISM

Splits within Shia Islam have almost always concerned disputes about succession to the imamate. The second largest group of Shia, the Seveners, separated from the majority over the choice of Jafar al-Sadiq's successor. The Twelvers chose Musa, bypassing his elder brother Ismail, whose personal conduct was considered inappropriate. Those who chose Ismail, known as Ismailis, later seized control of Egypt under their 11th imam, who also styled himself caliph. He established the Fatimid Caliphate in Cairo (910–1171) as a rival to the Abbasid regime in Baghdad. The Abbasid dynasty, which had replaced the Umayyads in 750, claimed a family link to Muhammad through his uncle; in the Abbasid view, that overcame the claims of the Fatimids, who were only related to the Prophet through a female line. Initially, the Abbasids enjoyed some Shiite support and may even have hoped for a time to reconcile Sunni and Shia.

After the death of al-Mustansir (the 18th imam in the Sevener tradition and the 8th Fatimid caliph-imam), a split occurred between the Nizaris and the Mustaali, who each recognized a different son as the 19th imam. The Nizaris continue to follow a living or "present" imam, known as the Aga Khan, whose descent can be traced from the Fatimids through the hashashin of Alamut (known in the West as the Assassins). The Mustaali have also subdivided several times and are known today as the Bohras. The Bohras themselves have split between the Dawoodis and the Sulaaimani, each under a succession of *dais* (summoners). Bohras believe that the 21st imam was (like the 12th for Ithna Asharis) hidden by God and that he appointed a *dai* to represent him.

The total number of Seveners across the various sub-traditions is estimated at between 15 million to 30 million. Most Bohras live in India and Pakistan but also in various parts of Africa, Europe, North America, and western Asia. A group of Progressive Dawoodi Bohras under Asghar Ali Engineer claims that the *dai* have exceeded their authority in defining both their religious and spiritual powers.

The Aga Khan has followers in India, Pakistan, Syria, Lebanon, Palestine, Saudi Arabia, Yemen, China, Jordan, Uzbekistan, Tajikistan, Afghanistan, eastern Africa, and South Africa, as well as in Europe, Australia, New Zealand, and North America—a total of 25 countries, according to the imam's official Web page.

Ismaili theology stresses *batin*, the inner aspect of religion and the unknowability of God, who yet reveals enough of Himself to humankind to enable redemption. Perhaps influenced by Gnostic thought, it views the world as possibly the creation of an evil power but believes that good lies hidden within it. Muhammad held the key to knowledge of *zahir* (external truth); Ali held the key to internal truth. *Batin* is also a fundamental component of Sufi theology.

THE FIVER ZAYDIS

Even before the Sevener split, the Shia community had been schismatic. On the death of the fourth imam, a group split away over the succession, rejecting the majority choice, Muhammad al-Baqir, in favor of his brother, Zaid, who was more radical in his opposition to the Sunni Umayyad caliphs. Settling in Yemen, the Fivers established a state under a succession of living imams (later styled kings). The last king-imam went into exile in 1962 after a republican revolution.

Zaydis reject the hereditary principle and do not ascribe any supernatural qualities, such as sinlessness or infallibility, to their imams. The Zaydi imams are said to have "emerged" from among the *sayyid*s (descendants of Muhammad) by attracting the support of their peers.

CONTEMPORARY MUSLIM REVIVALISTS

Some contemporary Muslim movements make headlines in the international media. Those include the Muslim Brotherhood, which is particularly strong in Egypt; Hezbollah, based in Lebanon; and Osama bin Laden's al-Qaeda. While all are involved in politics and have political aims, only al-Qaeda can be described as primarily political; most of them are better categorized as ideological fraternities. Committed to the revival of all aspects of Islam through personal and corporate renewal, they also have social programs. Both the Muslim Brotherhood and Hezbollah support a vast network of

LEGAL SCHOOLS IN TWELVER SHIA

In Twelver Shia, two rival legal schools, the Akhbaris and the Usulis, competed for influence. The former argued against the principle of *ijtihad* (independent interpretation) while the latter supported it. The Usulis won the debate, ensuring a flexible approach to the interpretation of Islamic law that gave certain individuals a greater say in the process. The Akhbaris held that scholars may know more about the tradition but have no exclusive right to interpret that tradition.

A cyclist passes a mosque in a small village in Yemen. Some 42 percent of Yemenis are Shiites, but there are also numerous Nizaris (followers of the Aga Khan).

schools, clinics, youth clubs, and welfare projects, as well as publishing houses and political propaganda machines.

The Muslim Brotherhood (Jammat al-Ikhwan al-Muslimim) was founded by Hasan al-Banna (1906-1949), who became the movement's Supreme Guide. Viewing the West as decadent, immoral, and spiritually bankrupt, he defined Islam as a total way of life in which religion din) and the world (dunya) are two sides of the same coin.

Although less well known, the Jaamati-i-Islam (which functions in India, Pakistan, and Bangladesh) has a similar structure and program. The movement was founded by Sayyid Abu'l-A'la Mawdudi (1903–1979), who lived after 1947 in the newly independent Muslim state of Pakistan, regarding the Jamaat, of which he was the emir (leader), as a government-in-waiting. Critical of Western-style democracy, which in his view replaced God's preeminence with human sovereignty, he coined the term theo-democracy to describe the state he wished to create. He held that the citizens of a modern Islamic state should elect their

leaders, but only from the ranks of pious and qualified Muslims, whose main task would be not so much to make law as to interpret God's will.

In founding the Muslim Brotherhood, Hasan al-Banna was influenced by Salafi Islam. The word salaf refers literally to the earliest generation of Muslims, whose practice and beliefs are held to have mirrored those of Muhammad himself. The practice of taqlid (imitation) of the Salafi developed in the 14th century. It was a response to what some scholars perceived as bida (innovation) in the religious practices of the time. Imitation of the Salafi is mentioned as a religious duty in the work of ibn Taymiyyah (d. 1328), whom Osama bin Laden cites. Salafism was revived in the early 20th century by such thinkers as Rashid Rida (1865–1935), who sought to rid Islam of innovation (including Sufi practices) and return it to the pure, uncorrupted faith of the Prophet's lifetime. Salafism also encompasses the general approach of Muhammad ibn Abd-al-Wahhab (1703–1792), the founder of the version of Islam that enjoys official status in Saudi Arabia. Usually called Wahhabi, Rida's followers refer to themselves as *muwahhidun* (unitarians).

Another group with a Salafist outlook is the Tablighi Jamaat, which has received financial support from Wahhabi-related agencies. Avowedly apolitical, it has not escaped critical scrutiny by Western security agencies following allegations of terrorist links. Founded in the late 1920s by Maulana Muhammad Ilyas Kandhalaw, Tablighi is one of the largest organizations in the Muslim world.

Organizationally, the Tablighi Jamaat resembles both the Muslim Brotherhood and Jamaati-i-Islam. It has an emir at its head and subdivides at grassroots level into

THE ALAWITES

Based principally in Syria, where they make up about 10 percent of the population, the Alawites are a Muslim sect that broke away from Twelver Shiism after the death of the 11th imam. Although they regard themselves as Shia Muslims, Alawite doctrine is regarded as syncretic, or even heretical by some Sunni and Shia Muslims. Alawites do not observe the Islamic

Syrian Druze living under Israeli occupation in the Golan Heights display portraits of the kings Hafez (right) and Bashar al-Assad on Syrian National Day.

prohibition of alcohol, for example, and believe in a form of reincarnation. They currently dominate the government of Syria, whose president, Bashar al-Assad, is Alawite like his father, Hafez, before him. A senior Lebanese scholar formally declared Alawites to be part of the Islamic community in 1974, a move that constitutionally enabled an Assad presidency.

small groups whose members meet regularly for religious instruction, study, and prayer. Like the other two groups, Tablighi Jamaat aims to revive Islam through the inner, spiritual renewal of its members; it also tends to share their negative view of the mystical Sufi tradition. Yet, while members of the Brotherhood, Jamaati, and Hezbollah have all stood for and gained political office with the blessing of their relevant movements, Tablighi forbids its members from taking part in political discussion. In practice, however, the prohibition does not preclude members from taking part in politics under a different affiliation.

A TRADITIONAL MUSLIM MOVEMENT

In Pakistan, between 50 and 70 percent of Sunni Muslims belong to a tradition known as Barelvi Islam, founded by Ahmad Raza Khan (1856–1931). Barelvi devotions are centered on the Prophet and on his knowledge of the unknown, in the belief that Muhammad, although human, possessed a *nur* (light) that predates creation. Barelvis also revere *pirs* (Sufi saints who trace their sanctity through a chain of initiation stretching back to Muhammad).

Barelvis bitterly oppose, and are opposed by, the Deobandis (20 percent of Pakistani Sunnis), who trace their origins to the founding in 1866 of the Deoband Seminary in what is now the Indian state of Uttar Pradesh. Under Wahhabi influence, Deobandis denounce Sufi practices and what they regard as the Barelvi deification of Muhammad. While they teach the unity of religion and politics, Deobandis withdraw from the world in order to concentrate on religious learning. Television, newspapers, and use of the Internet (but not computers) are banned, although the seminary has a home page.

MUSLIM MODERNISTS

Muslims who define themselves as modernist, liberal, or progressive tend to focus on legal and social issues, such as how Muslim societies should be governed and how Islamic law should be interpreted, especially that part of it affecting the rights of women. Although the modernizers have included some distinguished names within their ranks, such as Muhammad Abduh (1849–1905) and Muhammad Iqbal (1877–1938), they did not establish organizations with a structure or influence comparable to those of the Muslim Brotherhood or Jamaati-i-Islam. Abduh served as grand mufti of Egypt and tried to reform the curriculum of Al-Azhar University, Cairo. Iqbal was elected to the Punjab legislature and used poetry to propagate his reformist Islam. He argued that each generation of Muslims should interpret the Koran for itself, guided but not bound by the past.

Iqbal, unlike the Salafis, looked to the future, not to the past, for the ideal Muslim society. He believed that, when humankind assumes full responsibility as God's vice-regent in stewarding and nurturing creation, people will receive fresh illumination from an Infinite Reality. The *ummah* of Muhammad's day was ideal for the Prophet's own time, Iqbal argued, but, as circumstances change, so does the way in which ideals should be practiced. For example, the amputation of hands as a punishment for theft, which was accepted in Muhammad's time, could be replaced in the modern era by severe prison sentences.

THE DRUZE AND THE BAHA'I

With some two million adherents worldwide, the Druze emerged during the Fatimid caliphate as a branch of Sevener

Nation of Islam members attend a street parade in Harlem, New York, in 1996.

The rest practice private prayer but do not participate in religious rituals.

In addition to the messengers honored by all Muslims, the Druze also recognize two ancient Greeks—the philosoher Plato and the mathematician Pythagoras—as lesser prophets. The Druze do not smoke tobacco, eat pork, or drink alcohol, and they slaughter meat according to Muslim rules. Druze men marry one wife, and their highest official, the Shaykh al-Aql, is celibate; if married when chosen for the position, he abstains from marital relations. The Druze were persecuted by the Mamluk dynasty in Egypt (1250–1517) and later by the Ottomans after the Sunni theologian Ibn Taymiyyah declared them the target of a jihad in 1305. When persecuted, the Druze protect their identity by worshipping as Muslims when with Muslims and as Christians when among Christians.

The Baha'i, who number between 5 and 6 million, are also eschatological (believers in a final reckoning at the end of the world). In Shiraz, Iran, Sayyid Ali Muhammad (1819–1850), who called himself the Bab (Gate), predicted in 1844 that the Mahdi would soon return. One of his followers, Baha'ullah (1817–1892), announced 19 years later that he was the anticipated savior and the messenger *(rasul)* of a new religious dispensation.

Baha'is believe in a series of religious dispensations, regard all religions as expressions of universal truth, teach the spiritual unity of humankind, and seek to establish world government. Their Universal House of Justice is in Haifa, Israel.

Baha'is affirm the unity of God, of religions, and of humanity. For Muslims, Baha'ullah's use of the title *rasul* is problematic, given that a fundamental tenet of Islamic faith holds that Muhammad was

Shiism. Some people still regard the Druze as comprising a sub-tradition of Islam, while others consider them to have established a distinct religion. Today, the Druze live mainly in Lebanon, Syria, and Israel.

The Druze regard al-Hakim, the 6th Fatimid caliph and the 16th Sevener imam, as the promised Mahdi. Many people at the time thought al-Hakim insane as a result of his erratic actions, which included destroying the Church of the Holy Sepulcher in Jerusalem, commanding one day that Christians must convert to Islam then rescinding the order the next, and claiming (in the year 1009) to be the earthly incarnation of God.

Hakim disappeared in 1021 on a trip to the Muqattam Hills outside Cairo; there were suspicions at the time that he had been assassinated. The Druze deified him, along with all the previous imams. The imams' teaching, contained in the Book of Wisdom, is restricted information; only around 20 percent of Druze are initiated into study of the text and the faith's esoteric doctrines.

the final messenger. Partly as a result of this perceived heresy, Baha'is have faced persecution, most notably in Iran.

THE NATION OF ISLAM

The Nation of Islam (NOI), founded in 1934 by Elijah Muhammad, developed the Allah Temple of Islam, an organization set up five years earlier by W. D. Fard. Elijah Muhammad viewed Fard, who later disappeared, as a manifestation of God. The NOI also drew inspiration from Marcus Garvey's "Black is beautiful" and "Look to Africa" messages, seeking to instill pride and self-reliance among African Americans.

Elijah Muhammad taught that the white race is evil, that Islam is the authentic faith of black people, and that the United States will be destroyed. He called his movement's places of worship "temples" rather than "mosques" and used the term "minister" in place of "imam." In his preaching, he drew on the Bible as much as on the Koran. One of the principal demands of the NOI was the establishment of a separate nation for African Americans. Members wore distinctive clothes: the women's dresses resembled those of Christian nuns, while the men wore either suits with bow ties or the so-called FOI (Fruit of Islam) military-style uniform.

Elijah Muhammad was succeeded on his death in 1975 by his seventh son, Warith Deen Muhammad, who led the majority of the NOI to a rapprochement with Sunni Islam that involved changing the movement's name several times, latterly to the American Society of Muslims (ASM), switching his own title from supreme minister to imam and renaming the movement's temples as mosques. In 1985, Warith Deen Muhammad decentralized the organization, making each mosque self-governing. While rejecting his father's theology and separatist aims, he retained his father's social ethic, sponsoring welfare and educational initiatives.

In 1981, a minority broke away to join a reconstituted NOI under Louis Farrakhan, who revived the teachings of Elijah Muhammad. The term "Black Islam" is sometimes used to describe both the NOI (which currently has an estimated 50,000 members) and the ASM (claiming at least 1 million members). In 2000, Farrakhan and Muhammad jointly issued a statement of reconciliation in which they rejected any rivalry between their movements. Muhammad stepped down as leader of the ASM in 2003.

AHMADIYYAH: PAKISTANI BREAKAWAY

Around one percent of Pakistanis belong to the Ahmadiyyah Muslim Jamaat, founded in 1889 by Mirza Ghulam Ahmad. Best known for teaching that Jesus is buried in Kashmir, Ahmad saw himself as the modern *mujaddid*, a God-sent reformer identified with the Madhi and the Judeo-Christian Messiah, whose task was to prepare Muslims for the end of the world. Some people regarded Ahmad as a prophet but a breakaway group, the Lahore Ahmadiyyah (founded in 1914), interpreted his teachings metaphorically. In 1974, the government of Pakistan declared followers of the movement to be non-Muslims.

Highly organized and missionary in their aim of winning converts, Ahmadiyyah engaged in debate with their Christian counterparts. In 1912, they established a mosque outside London, England. In the 1920s, they began missionary work in the United States, where their teachings may have influenced the principles of Elijah Muhammad.

See Also
Beliefs 48–67 ❖ Peoples of the Book 68–71 ❖ Practices 72–97 ❖ Scriptures and Doctrine 102–123 ❖ Mystical Islam 148–149 ❖

Mystical Islam

Disapproved by orthodox Muslims but popular with many others, Sufism is a form of Islam that emphasizes direct communication between believers and Allah (God).

T he origin of the word *Sufi* is a topic of much discussion. Among its possible etymological roots are *suffe* ("bench," a reference to where the first Sufis sat to listen to the Prophet Muhammad), *suf* ("wool," the material from which their clothes were made), and *safi* ("purity"). Although it differs from mainstream Islam in some aspects of philosophy and practice, Sufism is not an independent sect. Millions of Muslims identify to some extent with Sufi Islam, which has had a unifying tendency, helping to bridge the gulf between Sunnis and Shiites. Instead, the practices and traditions of Sufism are considered to be an expression of a particular dimension of Islamic belief. Sufis regard the development of *taqwah* (consciousness of God) as one of the principal goals of their spiritual lives.

Unlike orthodox Islam, in which knowledge of God can only come from the scriptures revealed to Muhammad, Sufism stresses inner experience of the presence of Allah. Sufis work to achieve this though solitary prayer, meditation, and chanting. This emphasis on solitary prayer leads Sufis to be perceived by others as neglecting Islam's external rituals, an omission for which they are condemned by some Muslims, particularly Salafis. Many features of Sufism, such as asceticism, meditation, and the negation of the self, can be found in the mystical traditions of other religions, which has led some Muslims to label Sufis as a syncretic sect.

ORIGINS AND DEVELOPMENT

The origins of Sufism can be traced to the time of Muhammad, and, many Sufis believe, to the example of Muhammad himself, who received his first revelation while meditating alone. While the beliefs and practices associated with Sufism have existed since the time of Muhammad, they were not collected into a coherent doctrine until the 11th century, when prominent Islamic scholars such as Al-Ghazali (1058–1111) wrote books that summarized and explained Sufi traditions.

It has been asserted that Sufi practices were once a common part of mainstream Islam rather than expressions of a separate doctrine, and Sufism was not clearly differentiated from orthodox Islam until as late as the 17th century. Indeed, not all Sufis belong to Sufi orders, and many Sunni and Shia Muslims practice Sufi-style devotion.

A WOMAN SUFI SAINT

The earliest Muslims are said to have feared God's wrath. However, a Sufi woman, Rabia al-Adawiyya (717–801), introduced into Islamic mysticism the notion of *hubb*, the love between the "beloved" (Allah) and the "lover." In their devotion to each other, these two become one. Rabia, who never married, is highly regarded among Sufis. When asked why she remained celibate, she replied that she was so wrapped up in the love of Allah that she no longer had any awareness of existing as a "being" separate from God. When the mystic is immersed in the love of God, she said, no duality exists. Since she had no "being," how could she marry? Later, Sufis developed the concept of "the unity of being," interpreting the *shahada* (the First Pillar of Islam) to mean that, if only Allah "is," then everything is divine.

DIFFERENT PATHS

Sufis usually have a master and follow his *tariqa* (path). This is the *murid-murshid* relationship, which is similar to the relationship between the student and the guru in Hinduism. Sufis are spiritual travelers from worldliness to union with the divine. They progress through stages (*maqamat*) that result, by God's grace (*karamat*), in states

Followers of Sufism seek connection with Allah through dance, turning in circles until they enter into a trance.

(*ahwal*) marking their spiritual development. The goal is *farna*, the loss of self-consciousness and of *nafs* (the selfish soul) and their replacement by a permanent consciousness of God. The intermediate stages include *faqr* (renunciation of wealth).

The different *tariqa* include those of the Naqshbandi, the Mevlevi (known in the West as "the Whirling Dervishes"), and the Chishti. The shrines to great Sufi teachers of the past function as pilgrim centers. Selfless service of others diminishes self-centeredness, so humanitarianism has a long history among Sufi orders. They run schools, hospitals, hospices, and clinics (for animals as well as for people). Sufi orders flourish today throughout the Muslim world. An increasing number of non-Muslims identify with Sufi Islam, a development that was encouraged by Hazrat Inayat Khan (1883–1927), the founder of the Sufi Order International. This order emphasizes the essential unity of all faith, which is God's gift to humanity and never a human work. The order builds on traditional, universal aspects of Sufi teaching.

AL-HALLAJ AND AL-GHAZALI

Sufi author Al-Hallaj was executed in 922 for crying out, in ecstasy, that he was the Truth (God). Cited for more than 100 years by orthodox Muslims as a reason for their opposition to Sufism, Al-Hallaj's exclamation was justified by Al-Ghazali (1058–1111), who said that he had merely misspoken—he had experienced intimacy with God but there is a difference between saying that the wine and the wineglass are identical, and saying that we perceive them as identical. Al-Ghazali was a theologian who criticized Islamic falsafah (philosophy) as excessively influenced by Greek Neoplatonism and essentially atheistic, in spite of its references to God. He first encountered Sufis while traveling and became convinced that their way was the true way. He encouraged Sufis to observe the Five Pillars of Islam. This helped to reconcile Sufism with mainstream Sunni Islam.

Chapter 7

MUSLIM CALENDAR, HOLY DAYS, AND FESTIVALS

Islam has its own calendar, called the Hijri calendar. It is based on the phases of the moon and has about 354 days, divided into 12 months. Muslims have various holy days and festivals, such as the Eids. Fasting is prescribed throughout the month of Ramadan, and many Muslims make a pilgrimage to Mecca in the month of Dhu'l-Hijja.

The Muslim calendar is known as the Hijri calendar. The term *Hijri* (from Arabic *hijra*), which is also romanized as Hegira or Hejira, is the name given to the flight of Muhammad and his followers from Mecca to Medina in September 622 to escape religious persecution. This incident—the precise date of Muhammad's journey is not agreed upon—marks the beginning of the Hijri calendar. The abbreviation AH (from Latin *anno Hegirae*, also referring to "After Hijri") is used to denote each year after Muhammad's flight from Mecca. The Hijri year is based on the moon's cycle. There are 12 lunar months, and each month begins with the appearance of the new moon in a crescentlike shape.

HIJRI CALENDAR

Each new day in the Hijri calendar begins at sunset. The Gregorian calendar—used in the United States and most of the world—is a solar calendar with 365 days in a year. The Hijri calendar, which is lunar, has roughly 354 days in its year. Thus, even though the dates of Islamic holy days are the same in every Hijri year, they are celebrated 10 or 11 days earlier in the next Gregorian year. In this way, holy days for Muslims move back in each Gregorian year and therefore, over years, occur in different seasons.

The year 1430 AH began on the evening of December 28, 2008, and ended at sunset on December 17, 2009. This approximate beginning and ending of the Hijri calendar at the same time as a Gregorian year occurs every 30 to 33 Gregorian years.

Islamic holy days, such as the start and end of Ramadan, are always based on the Hijri calendar. The number of days in a lunar month is either 29 or 30, depending on the appearance of a new moon.

People living in Saudi Arabia, Yemen, and the Gulf States have used the moon's cycles as a calendar since long before the advent of Islam—this pre-Islamic era is called *jahilyyiah* by Muslims. Muslim scholars and historians adopted the lunar

More than 100,000 people gather outside the Mosque of the Prophet in Medina, Saudi Arabia, to break their daily fast after sunset in the month of Ramadan. This fast-breaking evening meal is called *iftar*.

The times for daily prayers, in addition to the dates of Christian and Islamic festivals, are given—according to the Gregorian calendar—in this "prayer timetable," which is written in French.

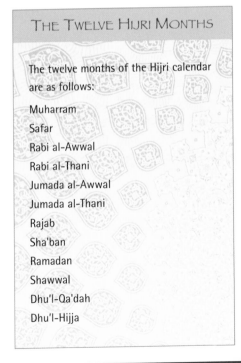

THE TWELVE HIJRI MONTHS

The twelve months of the Hijri calendar are as follows:

Muharram

Safar

Rabi al-Awwal

Rabi al-Thani

Jumada al-Awwal

Jumada al-Thani

Rajab

Sha'ban

Ramadan

Shawwal

Dhu'l-Qa'dah

Dhu'l-Hijja

calculations afterward for their own calendar. Present-day Saudi Arabia officially follows the Hijri calendar, contrary to most of the other Islamic nations, which adopted the more internationally common Gregorian calendar (but still observe holy days according to the Hijri calendar).

ISLAMIC HOLY DAYS

As the day in the Islamic calendar begins at sunset, all days, including holy days, consequently span two days in the Gregorian calendar. The main religious festivals agreed upon and celebrated by Muslims worldwide are the "two Eids": Eid al-Fitr, which means the "feast of breaking the fast" and Eid al-Adha, which means the "feast of sacrifice."

The two Eids are the only holy days that were prescribed by the Prophet Muhammad. Other holy days are recognized as significant events during the history of Islam and may be observed among certain Muslim groups and sects in various areas of the Muslim world, as well as other countries where Muslims have settled and formed communities.

Most Muslims in the world are Sunnis, but a significant minority—between 15 and 20 percent—are Shiites. Differences between Sunnis and Shiites are reflected in which holy days and festivals they celebrate.

Ras al-Aam (1 Muharram). This is the name for the first day of a new year in the Hijri calendar. There are no festivities when Ras al-Aam begins at sunset in the evening, unlike the New Year's Eve celebrations seen in other parts of the world, nor are there any conventional religious rituals after sunrise and during daytime hours. In countries where Muslims are the majority, the first day of the Islamic New Year is a formal holiday.

Ashura (10 Muharram). Sunni Muslims observe this day in commemoration of the Prophet Moses' conversation with God in Sinai, similar to the Jewish Day of Atonement. Particularly devout Sunni Muslims fast on both 9 and 10 Muharram, although it is not obligatory for all Sunnis to fast. Other religious events are also celebrated on Ashura. For example, it is believed that the Prophet Noah left the ark on this day. Some scholars also trace Ashura back to Muhammad's arrival in the city of Medina. In Mecca, the most sacred Islamic site, the Kaaba, is opened for visitors on Ashura.

For Shiite Muslims, Ashura is a day of mourning because it marks the anniversary of the slaying of Imam Husayn (624–680), grandson of Muhammad. Husayn died at the Battle of Karbala. Yazid I (645–683), the second caliph of a region called the Umayyad Caliphate, initiated the battle because he wanted to remove political adversaries so that his own family could rule.

The supporters of Muhammad's descendants—who became the Shiites—considered those descendants to be the only legitimate heirs to the caliphate. The mourning of Imam Husayn's death—and the torture of his family afterward—was established as annual observance in 962 (351 AH) by Caliph al-Mu'izz (932–975). Shiites also view their mourning as an atonement for not having being able to rescue Muhammad's descendants during this time of peril in the early history of Islam.

To best express their sadness and grief, Shiite Muslims observe Ashura by dressing in dark clothes and gathering together to mourn. Some Shiites also express their devotion to Husayn's family by flogging themselves on the chest, arms, and back with sharp-ended metal chains until they bleed. Their rationale for this ritual is that only suffering physical pain can reflect the catastrophic shock to the Muslim world of Husayn's death and subsequent martyrdom. The participants also intend to arouse in observers the utmost pity for Husayn. This ritual flogging is called *ta'ziya*, and it is practiced particularly by Shiites in Iran but also in communities in India, Afghanistan, Iraq, Pakistan, and Lebanon.

Shiites in North America often share their Ashura customs with their non-Muslim friends and acquaintances. This provides an occasion for non-Muslims to become familiar with Islamic traditions.

Even though Sunnis do not mourn the deaths of Husayn and other descendents of Muhammad in the same way as Shiites, they still honor these early martyrs. However, according to Islamic law, mourning is not supposed to last more than three days. In addition, it is seen as a rejection of God's will to grieve for a lengthy period. Although Sunnis respect Muhammad's family, loyalty to its members is not a Sunni condition for piety, unlike for Shiite Muslims.

Mawled (or Milad) an-Nabi (12 Rabi al-Awwal). This day is Muhammad's birthday and is marked by joyful celebrations that vary according to local customs. This anniversary was first observed as a public holiday in Morocco in 1291 (690 AH). The custom was introduced to Egypt by the Mamluk dynasty about a hundred years later.

The countries that were ruled by the Ottoman Turks between the 15th and 20th centuries honor Muhammad's birthday in different ways. In many regions, people gather in a mosque or in a house and chant poems that praise Muhammad.

In Pakistan and India, public gatherings are held to celebrate Muhammad's birthday. In some countries, families exchange traditional sweet dishes. It is against the law in Saudi Arabia, however, to celebrate Mawled an-Nabi because Muhammad himself did not celebrate any birthdays. For this reason, some Muslim scholars do not approve of celebrating this day.

Laylat al-Isra' Wa al-Mi'raj (27 Rajab). Also known as the Night Journey, this holy day celebrates a revelatory journey made by Muhammad. The first stage of the journey is known as al-Isra'a. One night while he was still living in Mecca, Muhammad was sleeping in the Kaaba. The angel Gabriel (Jibril) woke Muhammad and asked him to mount a winged, horselike animal, called al-Buraq. On the back of al-Buraq, Muhammad and Gabriel were flown miraculously to Jerusalem. There, Muhammad met and prayed with prophets, including Abraham (Ibrahim), Moses (Musa), and Jesus (Isa).

The next stage of Muhammad's journey is known as Mi'raj. He ascended to the heavens from the Temple Mount, on which the Dome of the Rock sanctuary now stands in Jerusalem. Muhammad again met with the prophets, each of whom was in his own sphere in the heavens.

Muhammad had been given the command from God that Muslims should perform fifty daily ritual prayers. Moses advised Muhammad to ask God to reduce the number of the prayers. Following Moses' advice, Muhammad went back and forth pleading to God to reduce the number of prescribed prayers. Eventually, God agreed to five daily prayers.

On his return trip from Jerusalem to Mecca, Muhammad saw caravans traveling through the desert. In the morning in Mecca, Muhammad related to others his night's experience, including a description of the caravans he saw in the desert. The nonbelievers laughed at his account and did not take it seriously. Later, the caravans that Muhammad had witnessed in the desert arrived in Mecca and were just as Muhammad had described.

Laylat al-Bara'ah (15 Sha'ban). This date is known as the Night of Forgiveness. In some Muslim communities, the night of 15 Sha'ban is believed to be the time when a person's destiny is decided for the next twelve months. As such, people dedicate a significant part of this night to worship and prayers. Although there is nothing in the Koran or in the Hadith (the words and deeds attributed to Muhammad) indicating the importance of this night, some Muslims fast on 15 Sha'ban and try to be as pious as possible.

Laylat al-Qadr (27 Ramadan). Known as the Night of Power, Muslims commemorate on 27 Ramadan the night in 610 when the first chapters of the Koran

were revealed to Muhammad by the Archangel Gabriel.

The evening of 27 Ramadan is most often presumed to be Laylat al-Qadr. However, the date was not confirmed by Muhammad. Scholars believe that it may in fact have been any of the last odd nights of the month of Ramadan. For that reason, the last ten days and nights of Ramadan are devoted to spiritual cleansing and retreat. During this period, Muslims dedicate time to reciting the Koran and involving themselves in acts of charity. Some devout followers also stay awake during the last ten nights, praying at their mosque or at home.

Eid al-Fitr (1 Shawwal). This day, which means the "feast of fast-breaking," is the beginning of one of the two major religious celebrations observed and looked forward to by all Muslims. This festival, also known as the "minor Eid," lasts three days and marks the end of fasting after the month of Ramadan. Almost all workplaces shut for the festival.

Eid al-Fitr is announced as soon as the new crescent moon is sighted, immediately after the sunset *adhan*, or call to prayer, of 29 or 30 Ramadan. Because a new day in the Hijri calendar starts in the evening, and the month of Ramadan has finished, observers no longer have to perform the *taraweeh* prayer—an extra nightly prayer during Ramadan. It is obligatory for Muslims to stop fasting once the new moon—and therefore the beginning of Shawwal—is sighted. Those Muslims who missed some of their fasting days during Ramadan are not permitted to make up these lost days during Eid. They can select any other days during the next eleven months.

A special congregational Eid prayer is held after sunrise on the first morning of the month of Shawwal. Muslims are required to pay alms, called *zakat*, before the Eid prayers. This prayer serves to remind people of the needy and the less fortunate, even though Ramadan has now come to an end.

Eid is a very exciting occasion for children because they receive gifts, money, and new clothes. Special outdoor areas and parks are decorated with colorful banners and balloons, and amusements such as fairground rides are also set up for young Muslims. Children greet their grandparents and show off their new outfits. This family occasion also reminds the grandparents to hand over the special Eid gift of money. Youngsters are delighted to get money so they can celebrate on their own. They usually hang out together and spend their Eid money without having to answer to their parents. During this time, parents traditionally loosen up their disciplinary rules; for example, they do not impose curfews.

Some Eid customs are gradually disappearing, including that of the night drummer. This was traditionally a man who wandered the streets for the two hours before dawn, chanting and playing his drum to wake up people so that they could eat before sunrise. The drummer and the people who collect the trash knock on everybody's door to get Eid tips. The word for an Eid tip is *iftaryyah*, derived from the original word for breaking a fast: *iftar*.

Eid al-Adha (10 Dhu'l-Hijja). This major Islamic festival is known as the Feast of Sacrifice. It is also called the Greater Eid. This celebration commemorates the Prophet Abraham's obedience to God, who asked him to sacrifice his son. Although the Koran does not specify which son, Muslims believe it was Abraham's elder son, Ishmael (Ismail), son of Hagar (Hajar). In the Hebrew Bible it is Isaac (Ishaq), son of Abraham's wife Sarah. God sent the Archangel Gabriel to Abraham with a ram to sacrifice instead of his son. According to the Islamic tradition, these events occurred in Mina, which is about 3 miles (5 km) outside of Mecca. Pilgrims who visit Mina slaughter an animal, which symbolizes Abraham's resistance to the temptations of the devil. It is optional for Muslims who have not performed the pilgrimage and are celebrating Eid al-Adha to slaughter a nonblemished ram, a camel, a sheep, or a cow; they also have the option not to slaughter an animal.

After sunrise on 10 Dhu'l-Hijja, congregational Eid prayers are performed. Muslims are encouraged—but not obligated—to give charity to the needy, preferably before the Eid prayers, to enable the less fortunate to enjoy the festival. There is no minimum amount for how much someone should donate. The donation may take the form of money, food, or any other commodity.

During the Eid, Muslims make an effort to visit their relatives and exchange greetings, good wishes, and sweets. Without prior appointment, people drop in on their neighbors and make a special effort to see family members whom they seldom visit. New clothes are bought for the occasion, and houses are cleaned in advance for any unexpected guests. Traditions vary among Muslim communities. Some serve meals made from the sacrificed animal. Others offer sweets, juice, and coffee to their guests. Some families meet in the head of their extended family's house for lunch or

dinner, and gifts and money are given to the children, who wear their best clothes.

Like Eid al-Fitr, Eid al-Adha is a joyful time for children, who look forward to it for the whole year. They spend the money given to them by their relatives on snacks, such as candies, cookies, popcorn, and cakes, made especially for Eid and sold by vendors wandering the streets. Again, like Eid al-Fitr, outdoor areas such as parks are decorated and have amusements especially for children.

Inside the mosques, toys and traditional sweets are distributed among the children following the prayers. Children also take part in the service. They approach adults in the congregation with a box, in which the worshipers can drop *zakat*, or charity cash. Although the children have accompanied their parents to the mosque

to have fun and enjoy the Eid, they often like to feel that they can be helpful and therefore take their fund-raising participation very seriously. In Pakistan, Nigeria, and Malaysia, children wear especially bright Eid clothes, which adds to the feeling of celebration.

In some areas, two sets of morning prayers are held in mosques in an attempt to accommodate so many people. In some areas—weather permitting—morning services are held in a large park. After the Eid service, either a feast is prepared or friends and families go to a restaurant for lunch. After the meal, families take their children to the parks so that they can have fun there. Eid al-Adha is usually just a one-day celebration; parents return to work the next day and children go back to school.

Muslims pray outside the Dome of the Rock in Jerusalem. They celebrate the Prophet Muhammad's night journey to the Temple Mount, on which the Dome of the Rock is built.

Eid for Muslims who are a minority in their country is generally more enjoyable when it coincides with a national holiday, such as Christmas or Thanksgiving. When the festivals do coincide, parents get to plan longer and more enjoyable activities for their children.

Eid al-Ghadir (18 Dhu'l-Hijja). Shiite Muslims celebrate the occasion when Muhammad named his cousin and son-in-law, Ali (c. 600–661), as his successor. The festival takes its name from Ghadir-Khumm, an oasis between Mecca and Medina where Muhammad stopped on his return from his Farewell Pilgrimage. There he asked his followers to adopt Ali as their master and obey his orders.

Eid al-Ghadir did not become a festival until Caliph al-Mu'izz made it an official Shiite holiday in 962 (351 AH). Eid al-Ghadir is celebrated in Iran, Iraq, Lebanon, and Pakistan by Shiites. It is a formal holiday only in the countries where Shiites are the majority: Iran and Iraq.

Unlike in other Muslim countries, Iran has no specific dishes that are associated with the Eids, although these holy days are public holidays. This may be partly explained as a result of the Iranian climate varying so widely from season to season. In Iran, the winters are often very cold, while the summers can be very hot. The rotating Eids of the lunar Hijri calendar prevent the preparation of specific festive dishes that are suitable for both seasons.

Fireworks explode above the waterfront to mark the beginning of Eid in Qatar.

Eid al-Ghadir is a major issue of contention between Sunnis and Shiites. Sunnis claim that the Ghadir-Khumm discussion was invented by those who wanted Ali to become their political leader. The Sunnis deny that Muhammad selected any of his companions to be his successor after his death.

Shiite Muslims believe that the Prophet's descendants are infallible by nature and that their authority is absolutely trustworthy as it comes directly from God. Therefore, Shiite Muslims often venerate their religious leaders as saints and perform pilgrimages to their tombs and shrines.

Sunni Muslims, on the other hand, believe that there is no basis in Islam for a hereditary privileged class of spiritual leaders. They refute the Shiite doctrine concerning the veneration of Muhammad's descendants. Sunni Muslims believe that leadership of the community is not a birthright but a public trust that is earned by an individual and may be granted or removed from any leader by the people themselves.

THE MONTH OF RAMADAN

Ramadan is the ninth month of the Hijri calendar, and fasting, or *sawm*, which is the Fourth Pillar of Islam, is prescribed for Muslims during the entire month. Like each new month of the Hijri calendar, Ramadan's first day starts with the sighting of the crescent moon at the end of 29 Sha'ban, the previous month. If the crescent cannot be seen, Ramadan automatically begins the next evening.

Because lunar years are not fixed with the seasons, unlike in the Gregorian solar calendar, Muslims who do not live in equatorial parts of the world will gradually experience this month of fasting in

EID IN NORTH AMERICA

Muslims in the United States and other Western countries generally find it easy to accommodate Eid festivities into their lifestyle. Members of the Muslim communities call their local mosques on the evening of 8 or 9 Dhu'l-Hijja to check for the Eid al-Adha announcement. Families get dressed up and drive to their local mosque or another location that has been set to perform their Eid prayers.

Some Islamic schools in North America begin their Eid al-Fitr holiday on 21 Ramadan. Unlike state schools, Islamic schools do not have a Christmas vacation. Other Islamic schools only have a long Eid break if it coincides with a major U.S. national holiday. Many Muslim communities in non-Muslim countries try to adapt the Hijri calendar to customs of the non-Muslim majority.

different seasons over the years. For example, in 2010 Ramadan falls between August 11 and September 9, which is summer in the United States. However, in each subsequent year, Ramadan moves back 11 days, so 20 years after 2010 it will fall in the middle of winter for several years. Therefore, during a lifetime and depending on where in the world they live, many Muslims experience fasting for Ramadan not only during long, hot days but also during short, cold days.

If Ramadan were based on the Gregorian calendar, people living in certain parts of the world would fast during summer, while in other parts of the world, Ramadan would always coincide with the shorter, cooler winter days. That could cause Muslims living in some parts of the world to feel that they were at a disadvantage throughout their lives.

During the 29 or 30 days of Ramadan, Muslims abstain from eating, drinking, smoking, and sexual intercourse between

It is traditional to buy new clothes for Eid festivals.

sunrise and sunset. Muslims are encouraged to wake up an hour before dawn to have a meal, called *suhur,* in preparation for the upcoming day of fasting. A ceremonial meal, called *iftar,* is made to celebrate breaking the fast at sunset, the time of the fourth daily prayer, which is called *maghreb.*

Before the invention of radio and television, the announcement of *suhur* and *iftar* in Muslim cities used to be made by beating drums or firing cannons. In other towns, certain state employees would knock on people's doors announcing the time for *iftar.* Others would break their fast when hearing the call to prayer, *adhan,* for *maghreb.* Muslims intensify performing good deeds during Ramadan by reciting the Koran and praying.

In some Islamic nations, government offices, schools, and universities close down during the last three days or even the last

week of Ramadan. The break continues until the end of Eid al-Fitr, which immediately follows Ramadan.

Peer pressure is a worldwide phenomenon, and children are particularly susceptible. It is the main motivation for elementary schoolchildren to start fasting.

Children and Fasting

Children younger than 13 years do not have to fast. However, they learn to fast step by step. They start by fasting during the intervals between prayers, which is about three to four hours. Later, they fast for half a day. This build-up is good preparation for when they are 13 years old, so that they can fast the entire day without harm.

Peer pressure is a worldwide phenomenon, and children are particularly susceptible. It is often the main motivation for elementary schoolchildren to start fasting. Those children who fast tend to mock their peers whenever the latter are caught eating or drinking. Children may then ask their parents to allow them to fast, too, often at about the age of seven or eight years. Usually at that young age, it is a struggle for a child to fast for a long time, especially during the later part of the day when they smell the dishes being prepared for *iftar*.

Fasting Exemptions

Adults who are unwell are allowed to postpone fasting until their health has improved. Pregnant and nursing women are also exempted. In addition, people traveling have the option not to fast, but they must make up the missed fasting days later. If someone will not be able to make up the missed days of fasting—for example, an old, very weak person or someone with a chronic disease—he or she has the option to compensate by feeding a poor person one meal for every day he or she missed fasting during Ramadan.

CULTURAL VARIATIONS

Neither the Koran nor the Hadith recommends any specific rules for the types of meals that Muslims should eat before sunrise and after sunset during Ramadan. On the contrary, Muhammad taught a general simplicity of approach, especially when breaking the fast. In spite of this, each of the historically Muslim nations—in Europe, Africa, and Asia—developed its own Ramadan customs.

Ramadan in Egypt

In Egypt, the streets of every town become a festival site every evening immediately after the *maghreb* prayer during Ramadan. Grocery stores and street vendors sell sweets such as *basbusah*, which is a dessert made from semolina and coconut, and *fanoos*, or lanterns, for children. Children carrying colorful lanterns knock on doors and ask for sweets or money. Colorful paper banners hang between buildings, signaling that the greatest month of the Hijri calendar has come again.

In Egypt, the streets of every town become a festival site every evening immediately after the maghreb prayer during Ramadan.

Dried fruits and dates are available everywhere. Children and adults alike enjoy drinking the traditional *qamar eddeen*, which is made from a paste of dried apricots. Bakery shops do well in the evenings, especially with their freshly baked "hair-doughed" *kunafa* and syrup-saturated *qatayif* sweets.

A recent tradition, started in Egypt and gradually embraced by hotels in neighboring Lebanon and the Gulf States, is the "Ramadan tent." This custom was started by wealthy people and movie stars to provide free meals for poor fasting people, as well as those who are running late to reach home for *iftar*. Inside the tent, delicious types of warm food are available. Food is often available in the tents until 2.00 a.m. The tent also provides a good way for people to spend time together, socializing before returning home to sleep.

"Ramadan in Egypt is very much in the streets," according to Norah Hussein, a mother of two who has lived for 25 years in Cairo. "The children are so happy, and people seem so close to one another." The taxi drivers in their old, black-and-white cabs seem cheerful as they zoom around Tahreer Square in the heart of modern Cairo or along the harbor road (corniche) in Alexandria on the Mediterranean coast, looking for customers on their way to restaurants after sunset. "Ramadan in Egypt is different from anywhere else in the world," says Hussein, smiling at the joyful memories it brings her. "I don't know how a place could be more alive than here. Even the pyramids and the Nile River seem to come alive."

In Kuala Lumpur, Malaysia's Islamic Authority performs *rukyah*, the sighting of the new moon, to determine the start of Ramadan.

Ramadan in Malaysia

As in other Muslim countries, Malaysians adapt their lifestyle during Ramadan to devote a few hours each day to reading the Koran, praising God, and spending more time in the mosque. On the last few days of Sha'ban—the month preceding Ramadan—Muslims in Malaysia prepare mosques for more than the usual activities and buy supplies of food. On 29 Sha'ban, observers from the Islamic Authority try to sight the new moon. Once the moon sighting is confirmed, the government announces it on radio and television. Muslims exchange Ramadan greetings, while local authorities sprinkle the streets with water, decorate the parks and public squares, and hang electric lamps in the main streets.

RAMADAN IN THE UNITED STATES

In all of the major cities of the United States, as well as some small towns, Muslims flock to the mosques and Islamic centers for enormous potluck dinners and the *taraweeh* prayer during the month of Ramadan. In the United States, just as in other Western countries, the mosque serves a variety of functions as well as being a place for religious services. In addition to the weekly Friday prayer and sermon, mosques are the cultural centers for the entire Muslim community. They are a meeting point for friends, especially during Ramadan. Therefore, many Muslims socialize at an *iftar* in the mosque rather than dining at home.

Mosques in universities plan their own 30-day program to provide Muslim students on campus with their evening *iftar* meals. Local Muslim families often offer to provide *iftar* for students. Sometimes, restaurants that serve halal food supply the colleges with *iftar* for their Muslim students.

Every Ramadan, Muslim student associations in some universities plan a communal *iftar* for all students on campus. The students invite their non-Muslim classmates, who can also share the experience of fasting. The media often gets involved, too, with local television and radio stations and newspapers covering the activities of the Muslim community.

Muslims in United States are from varied cultural backgrounds: African American, Latin American, Chinese, Pakistani, Malaysian, Turkish, South African, Nigerian, Sudanese, and Middle Eastern. Many mosques in the United States are a melting pot of the rich and colorful Islamic traditions that each culture brings. During the celebrations of Ramadan, Muslims from all different backgrounds enjoy getting together for *iftar*. Many African American Muslims share their *iftar* with non-Muslim relatives, friends, and neighbors, and sometimes with homeless people.

Ramadan in the countryside is celebrated through gatherings at mosques. People also exchange *iftar* meals. Wealthy Malaysians often provide for feasts in the mosques and in the streets for those less fortunate than themselves.

During Ramadan, families try to perform their five daily prayers in their mosque. Throughout Malaysia there are schools that teach the Koran. During Ramadan, the schools intensify their courses, including Islamic law, or Sharia, sciences, Arabic lessons, and Koranic recitation and memorization. Malaysians conclude the month of Ramadan with Koranic recitation in mosques and schools, as well as having services broadcast on radio and television. They then begin their preparations for Eid al-Fitr.

Ramadan in South Africa

When the sun sets on the first day of Ramadan, Muslims of South Africa gather in large groups for an *iftar* feast, dressed in their best clothes. Many enjoy *iftar* outdoors because there is an abundance of halal restaurants in South Africa, especially in Durban, Cape Town, and Johannesburg. Most of the Muslims living in South Africa are of Indian descent. Their ancestors came mainly from Gujarat in western India. They were brought over by British colonists to work as laborers, especially on sugarcane plantations. They have been in South Africa for several generations; their *iftar* is no longer just traditional Indian dishes but a mixture of various types of cuisines, including pasta, curries, and brownies. Other Muslim communities in and around

Cape Town originated from Indonesia and Malaysia. Their traditional spices and dishes have found their way into the mainstream Cape Town cuisine.

Although apartheid—racial segregation—has been abolished since 1994 in South Africa, different communities still tend to keep to themselves. Muslim communities from different backgrounds are no exception. Muslims of Indian, African, and Southeast Asian descent generally do not socialize with one another, even during the holy month of Ramadan.

Ramadan in the Philippines

In the Philippines, Ramadan is a month of coming together and helping one another. Saara Benizamani, a Filipino revert Muslim—someone who abandoned the faith but later returned to it—says that in her city in the province of Pangasinan, Muslims do much more than just the obligatory fasting. They try to make Ramadan a time for reaching out to the non-Muslim community. They visit non-Muslims and explain what Ramadan is and why Muslims mark it by fasting. She believes that it is also a great occasion to remember those less fortunate in the neighborhood. She said this reminds her to be grateful to God and thank Him for the many blessings He has bestowed upon her and others.

During the month of fasting, Muslim women in the Philippines get together during the day to read the Koran, and families go to the mosque at night to perform their *taraweeh* prayer. "Ramadan in the Philippines is very nice because we make it almost obligatory to go to the mosque for *iftar*," Saara says.

"When people finish work at 5:00 p.m., they go to the mosque because they know that it is where the best food will be."

In the mosques, *iftar* often consists of soup with noodles, adobo—a dish made from fish, chicken, or another meat marinated in soy sauce—rice, macaroni, and sweets. "We Filipinos love to eat," Saara says, "which can be a bad thing sometimes!" Because dates are not available in the Philippines, Saara asks one of her Arab friends to ship them to her from their countries. "That way I can break my fast the way the Prophet used to do," says Saara.

ACTIVITIES ENCOURAGED DURING RAMADAN

Acts of charity, such as financial assistance and providing meals to the poor, are required actions for Muslims throughout Ramadan. The month is often called "the month of mercy, blessings, and forgiveness," because God promises these to Muslims who fast and achieve self-mastery over their worldly desires and instincts.

Muslims believe Ramadan is an opportunity for self-improvement and spiritual satisfaction because God's grace is showered on those who obey his commands and fast. Fasting also constitutes a training period of patience and sacrifice during which a person learns to suppress his or her selfishness and feels empathy for the hungry and those in need.

A nonobligatory type of prayer called *taraweeh*, traditionally performed after having completed the night prayer, is encouraged. Apart from gaining blessings and compensating for earlier missed prayers, people enjoy the congregational *taraweeh* in the mosque for social interaction.

Ramadan in Albania

Ramadan traditions vary across the different regions of Albania (as well as in Bulgaria and the states that were formerly part of Yugoslavia, especially Bosnia and Herzegovina). The Balkans region where these countries are located was conquered and ruled by the Turkish Ottomans between the 15th and 17th centuries. Under the Turks, many of the inhabitants converted to Islam, adopting Islamic teachings from their rulers.

During the nights of Ramadan, a *lodra* sounds and stirs people from their sleep. A *lodra* is a double-ended cylindrical drum covered in sheepskin or goatskin. The drummer bangs each end with a different drumstick, producing a two-tone beat.

The food that is eaten for the two meals of Ramadan varies greatly among households. There are many similarities between Albanian and Turkish cuisine. However, Albania also has some unique dishes created from a similar range of basic ingredients. They include *byrek*, a flat flaky pastry pie containing meat, spinach, or curds, which can be eaten hot or cold; pasta in a sauce made from milk, cheese, eggs, and butter; *petulla*, which is fried dough with a savory filling, such as cheese, or a sweet filling, such as jam or cream.

The drummer returns at sunset to announce *iftar*. In Albania, it is not uncommon for Muslims to dine together with Christians during Ramadan. After their meals, many Albanians go to their mosques for their *taraweeh* prayer.

After World War II (1939–1945), Albania was under communist rule until 1992. During that time, all forms of religion were outlawed. Religious practices were punishable, although services—both Muslim and Christian—were carried out in secret. Mosques were forced to shut down, and public Ramadan festivities were banned as well. During this month, devout Muslims

Charity bread is distributed during Ramadan to poor women in Peshawar, Pakistan, to eat as part of their *iftar*.

would try to cover up their fasting and excuse themselves when offered any food or drink.

Ramadan in Mecca, Saudi Arabia

Muslims everywhere on earth turn to face Mecca for their daily prayers. The call to prayer, or *adhan*, echoes through the city. During Ramadan in Mecca, the emphasis is very much on worship and not on food or festivities, as it is in most other Islamic countries.

People may use the Ramadan season as an opportunity for spiritual retreat, so they travel to Mecca to perform their "minor pilgrimage." For them, it is the Ramadan of a lifetime. In Mecca, they are given dates and water for *suhur* and *iftar*. In addition, men with minivans or trucks serving cooked rice and chicken to pilgrims or to the needy are a common sight. During Ramadan, clothes and money are also donated to the poor.

During Ramadan—the holiest of Islamic months—there is much reading of the Koran in the location where it was first revealed to the Prophet Muhammad.

Some Meccans break their fast in the evening at home, surrounded by their families and friends. The meal traditionally begins with soup, followed by traditional *samboosah*, which are fried meat pies, and another main dish. Other residents of the city have their *iftar* in the al-Masjid al-Haram—the Sacred Mosque—where they also perform their *maghreb* prayer with other worshippers.

PILGRIMAGE

The Islamic pilgrimage to Mecca is the Fifth Pillar of Islam and is obligatory for all capable Muslim adults. This spiritual journey commemorates the time when the prophet Abraham brought his son Ishmael and Ishmael's Egyptian mother, Hagar, to Mecca, which at that time was an uninhabited and barren place.

Every male and female Muslim is required to perform the pilgrimage to the most sacred Islamic place, al-Masjid al-Haram, which surrounds the Kaaba, once during his or her lifetime. The pilgrimage is divided into two parts: the obligatory part called hajj—also known as the greater pilgrimage—and an optional part called *umrah*—also known as the minor pilgrimage. In addition, Muslim pilgrims travel to Medina, the burial place of Muhammad. This trip, like the minor pilgrimage, is not obligatory.

Pilgrims have to be financially solvent and physically healthy before undertaking their pilgrimage. They should not have any debts or leave their family or dependents without provisions while they are away. In addition, they must pay for the trip's expenses from their own earnings and not from a loan. Should a Muslim not have enough financial resources or be incapacitated through injury or illness, he or she is then relieved from the hajj obligation.

All male pilgrims wrap their bodies with two untailored white pieces of cotton, signifying the renunciation of pleasures and equality with all believers. This "sacred state" in which the pilgrims begin the hajj is called *ihram*. Female pilgrims do not have to follow a dress code. However, they have to be dressed modestly—which is called *hijab*—covering their body, often in long white robes, and also their hair. Women are not permitted to wear makeup or use scents during the hajj.

Before the hajj begins, each pilgrim performs a ritual ablution and a prayer that indicates his or her response to God's call to perform the hajj: "At Thy service, my God, at Thy service." He or she is then prepared to enter al-Masjid al-Haram.

During Ramadan—the holiest of Islamic months—there is much reading of the Koran in the location where it was first revealed to the Prophet Muhammad.

Minor Pilgrimage—*Umrah*

The *umrah* can be performed either in combination with the hajj or separately from it. If it serves as part of the hajj, it usually occurs on 7 Dhu'l-Hijja. If it is being celebrated on its own, *umrah* can be performed any time during the year.

Accomplishing *umrah* does not relieve a Muslim from the obligation to undergo the greater hajj.

During the minor pilgrimage, a person has to walk around the Kaaba seven times in a counterclockwise direction. On each circuit, the pilgrims traditionally had to kiss the Black Stone, which is kept in a silver frame and embedded in the southeastern corner of the Kaaba. However, due to the vast numbers of people coming to Mecca from all around the world, the pilgrims are permitted just to point in the direction of the stone with their right hand. This ritual of circumambulation is called *tawaf.*

Later that day, the pilgrims perform *sai*, in which they walk rapidly seven times back and forth between two hills, called Safa and Marwa. The route between these hills is now an enclosed long gallery within the grounds of al-Masjid al-Haram.

ORIGINS OF THE KAABA

Traditionally Muslims believe that Adam, the first human being, built a house on the site of the Kaaba with the help of the Archangel Gabriel. The site was chosen because it was the central location of the earth and lay directly below God's celestial throne. The black stone that is embedded in the southeastern corner of the Kaaba is said to have descended with Adam when he left the heavens to begin a new life on earth.

Muslims also believe that after God had spared Ishmael by sending Abraham a ram to sacrifice instead of his son, Abraham and Ishmael built the Kaaba as a place of worship to show their gratitude to God. The Koran also tells that the prophet Abraham was ordered to instruct humankind to make the pilgrimage and walk around the Kaaba. For many years before the advent of Islam, the Kaaba was a place of pilgrimage for many of the tribes living in the Arabian desert.

Over the years, Meccans and the desert tribes had moved away from monotheism—the belief in one God—and filled the Kaaba with more than 300 idols made of wood and stone. After having received the divine revelation that there were no other gods except for one God (Allah, in Arabic), Muhammad confiscated the idols.

Pilgrims may also drink water from the well of Zamzam. The spring of Zamzam is believed to have gushed forth when God heard the thirsty plea of Ishmael when he was abandoned in the desert with Hagar. The well is not open anymore, but its water still flows into underground rooms, where it is poured into containers and given to the pilgrims. Many people take some of the sacred water home with them to share their experience with family and friends who did not go on the pilgrimage.

Greater Pilgrimage—Hajj

The greater pilgrimage—hajj—has to be performed at a specific time of the year. It takes place in Dhu'l-Hijja, the last month of the Hijri year. Only a certain number of Muslims from outside Saudi Arabia get to make the hajj each year. The Saudi government issues a limited number of visas each year to foreign visitors. In recent years, up to about 3 million pilgrims perform the hajj each year.

The first day of the pilgrimage is 8 Dhu'l-Hijja. It is called *yawm at-tarwiyah*, which means the "day of reflection." Pilgrims pass the day in Mina, near Mecca, deep in contemplation. They then spend the night praying.

After the dawn prayer at Mina, the pilgrims—numbering tens of thousands— proceed en masse to the mount of Arafat, which is a hill close to Mecca. This second day of the hajj is called *yawm al-wuquf*, which is Arabic for the "day of standing," or *yawm Arafat,* which means the "day of Arafat."

Facing Mecca, the pilgrims stand on Arafat, contemplating and praying. The most commonly recited prayer is called the *talbiyah*. Muslims consider this day of prayers, contemplation, and reexamination of a one's own behaviors and life as a preparation for and a rehearsal for Judgment Day—when the world ends and God judges humankind.

In spite of its name, people are not required to stand continually throughout this "day of standing." Pilgrims also have the option of spending time eating and talking. However, because it might be only a once-in-a-lifetime journey, most pilgrims try to seize this unique occasion to get closer to their God.

Following sunset, a cannon is fired. This gives the sign that the pilgrims have to head for an open area called Muzdalifa to spend the night. There, people collect pebbles for the following day's rituals. The pilgrims also pray before falling asleep under the stars.

On 10 Dhu'l-Hijja, the pilgrims wake up to perform their dawn prayers and then travel back to Mina to throw seven of their pebbles at the largest of three whitewashed walls—formerly pillars—which symbolize the devil, or Satan (Shaitan). The stoning represents the pilgrims' resistance and struggle against the temptations of evil.

This is a very important day in the Islamic calendar, as it is the first day of Eid al-Adha, or the Feast of Sacrifice. This festival is celebrated by all Muslims around the world and serves as an opportunity for those who are at home to feel part of the pilgrimage, too.

After casting the stones at the devil, pilgrims slaughter an animal. The most commonly sacrificed animals are camels, sheep, goats, and cattle. After the animals are slaughtered, their meat is cooked and eaten by the pilgrims. Any meat that is left over is distributed among the poor. The Saudi State ships some of the meat to Islamic African nations. Some pilgrims choose not to sacrifice an animal. To compensate, they have the option of fasting for three days during their hajj and also for a further seven days once they have returned home.

The pilgrims are now ready to leave the state of *ihram*. To mark this transition, the men have their hair clipped or shaved. Female pilgrims need only cut a lock of their hair. Though pilgrims can now dress in their usual clothes, abstinence must still be observed until they have left Mina.

The pilgrims then return to the al-Masjid al-Haram and circumambulate the Kaaba a final seven times, chanting the *talbiyah*.

On 11, 12, and 13 Dhu'l-Hijja, the pilgrims return to Mina to finish casting stones at each of the three whitewashed walls. Muslims believe that those who perform hajj are promised the fulfillment of their prayers, as well as full forgiveness from God for any of their previous sins.

The pilgrim's ultimate goal in this unique trip is not physical relaxation but spiritual satisfaction through rebuilding bridges with God. The hajj is also a collective form of worship, with Muslims from all over the globe, from all different social backgrounds, all races, all colors, and ages, coming together as equals.

Other Pilgrimages—*Ziyara*

In addition to Mecca's holy places, there are numerous other sites around the world that attract Muslim pilgrims. A pilgrimage to one of these lesser sites is called *ziyara* (Arabic: literally, "visitation"). The *ziyara* is popular throughout the Muslim world, but it is not required or even mentioned anywhere in the Koran. This lack of scriptural approval has led some Muslim scholars to denounce the *ziyara* as idolatry and some have even called for the demolition of pilgrimage sites, including the tomb of Muhammad. These pronouncements have had little effect on the

popularity of the *ziyara*, however, and sites such as the Mosque of the Prophet and the tombs of Sufi saints receive millions of pilgrims each year. *Ziyara* is particularly important for Shiites, who often make pilgrimages to mosques and shrines associated with the Shiite imams or their companions.

AN AMERICAN HAJJI

One of America's most famous Muslim activists, al-Hajj Malik el-Shabazz (1925–1965), better known as Malcolm X, wrote down his feelings about the purpose of the hajj for Muslims in a letter following his return from Mecca:

"During the past 11 days in the Muslim world, I have eaten from the same plate, drunk from the same glass, and slept on the same rug—while praying to the same God—with fellow Muslims, whose eyes were the bluest of blue, whose hair was the blondest of blond, and whose skin was the whitest of white. And in the words and in the actions and in the deeds of the white Muslims, I felt the same sincerity that I felt among the black African Muslims of Nigeria, Sudan, and Ghana. We were truly all the same."

THE TALBIYAH PRAYER

The *talbiyah* is a prayer chanted during the hajj. The Koran attributes it to Abraham.

Here I am at Thy service, O Allah!
Here I am at Thy service.
There is no partner with Thee.
Here I am at Thy service.
All praise and all blessings and favors
   belong to Thee
And all sovereignty is Thine.
Thou hast no partner.

See Also
Brief History of Islam 22–43 ❖
Practices 72–97 ❖
Subdivisions of Islam 128–147 ❖
Holy Places 174–193 ❖

Eid al-Fitr

Eid al-Fitr is one of the two main religious festivals of the
Islamic year; the other is Eid al-Adha. Eid al-Fitr lasts for
three days and marks the end of Ramadan.

Eid al-Fitr is celebrated during the first three days of Shawwal, the 10th month of the Muslim calendar. Shawwal begins as soon as the new crescent moon is sighted after sunset on the 29th or the 30th day of Ramadan, the holy month of fasting. Because Islam follows a lunar calendar, the festival may fall at any time of the year.

The closest equivalent in English to the Arabic word *Eid* is "festival"; *al-Fitr* means "breaking someone's fast."

Eid al-Fitr was first celebrated by Muhammad and his companions in 624 CE, two years after the Prophet's migration from Mecca to Medina. Today, Eid al-Fitr is a full-scale holiday that is observed by all of the world's 1.2 billion Muslims. Although Islamic nations officially close down their offices for all three days of Eid al-Fitr, many shops and service industries remain open for at least a part of the holiday because this is a time for giving and receiving hospitality and presents.

On the morning of the first day of Eid al-Fitr, Muslim men gather together in mosques or in large open areas, such as parks or stadiums, to give thanks to Allah for giving them the discipline and patience to fast throughout Ramadan. The form of words used in this ritual is known as the Eid prayer, which is performed about two hours after sunrise.

In many Muslim countries, women do not traditionally accompany the men to the Eid prayers but stay at home and watch the commemorative public ceremonies on television while preparing for the domestic celebrations that will soon begin.

When the religious rituals are over, the men return home for breakfast with their families. This is no ordinary meal, because it is the first time for a month that they have eaten during the hours of daylight; throughout Ramadan, food and drink may be taken only before dawn and after sunset.

RETAIL INTERLUDE

After breaking the fast, many people go shopping. However, one trip to the souks and malls is seldom sufficient because traditionally everyone in the family has to give or receive a whole new set of clothes to celebrate Eid al-Fitr. As a result, many Muslims start their preparations for the festival much earlier in the year.

A crescent moon rises close to the illuminated minaret of a mosque in Amman, Jordan, on December 16, 2001. Moonrise on that day heralded the end of the holy month of Ramadan and the start of the Eid al-Fitr holiday.

Indian Muslim children greet each other after prayer at Jama Masjid, the principal mosque in Old Delhi, India, at the start of Eid al-Fitr on October 14, 2007.

SEASONAL GREETINGS

During Eid al-Fitr, Muslims typically use a range of five traditional greetings. Regardless of the speakers' native tongues, these phrases are all in Arabic, the original language of Islam. In order of current popularity, these expressions are as follows:

1. **Eid Mubarak:** *literally, "Blessed festival!" but effectively, "I wish you a blessed Eid."*
2. **Kul sana wa anta tayyeb:** *"I hope every year finds you in good health."*
3. **Kul aam wa antum bikhair:** *"I wish that you will always do well."*
4. **Eid Sa'eed:** *"I wish you a happy Eid."*
5. **Taqabbala Allah ta'atakum:** *"May God accept your obedience."*

This stamp was introduced on September 1, 2001, by the U.S. Postal Service to mark the start of that year's Eid al-Fitr.

In many Islamic countries, the traditional Muslim dress code is strictly maintained. Among the nations that most closely adhere to the old customs are Algeria, Bangladesh, India, Indonesia, Morocco, Nigeria, Pakistan, Singapore, and Sudan. During Eid al-Fitr, men from most of these countries wear long, mainly white dresses called djellabas and different types of hats or scarves on their heads. Meanwhile, women wear *abayas*, caftans, *thawbs*, or other long, loose hooded garments.

By contrast, in Turkey and the Islamic countries of the eastern Mediterranean, most Muslims have abandoned traditional Islamic clothing styles, so that when they shop for Eid clothes they buy Western-designed outfits—stylish and colorful clothing that they wear proudly for the occasion.

Among the other festive customs that are maintained in all these countries during Eid al-Fitr is the use of henna to paint brownish or black nonpermanent tattoos on the hands and the feet of girls. In Sudan, this practice is extended to artistic flowerlike drawings on their arms and legs.

SOCIAL FOCUS

Apart from religious observance in the mosque, the most important event on the first day of Eid al-Fitr is a great dinner at which the extended family—parents, children, grandchildren, siblings, and cousins—gather to celebrate the occasion.

The main course is cooked on the day, but much of the rest of the food that is eaten during Eid al-Fitr has to be prepared in advance during Ramadan. Each Muslim country has its own traditional desserts, but one favorite throughout the entire Islamic world is homemade cookies, which take three to four hours of preparation a few days before they are served. Making and baking the Eid cookies is, for many families, a popular group activity in the preparation for Eid al-Fitr. Mothers, fathers, and children join in the process, filling the house with the delicious smell of the crispy pistachio- or pecan-filled cookies.

Throughout the day, while the main meal is being made ready, people travel around their neighborhoods paying brief visits to local friends and acquaintances.

members of the community. This charity is known as Zakat al-Fitr. Donations should reach those who deserve them before the Eid prayer, preferably during the final day of Ramadan. As a consequence, much time is devoted during the final days of Ramadan to preparing the necessary gifts—the women go shopping to stock up on food, sweets, and clothes to give to those who deserve them. Although there is a great annual last-minute shopping rush to get ready for Eid al-Fitr on the eve of the festival, many families begin their preparations around 10 days earlier. In response to this demand, many shops remain open until midnight or later during the second half of Ramadan.

Eid al-Fitr is also a time when Muslims fulfill some of their obligations to share their wealth with other members of the community. This charity is known as Zakat al-Fitr.

The recipients of Zakat al-Fitr gifts are usually relatives or friends but may also be acquaintances or even complete strangers. Within families, the giving is normally reciprocal. The children (who are dressed up in festive clothing) give sweets and small tokens of affection to their elderly relatives, who bless them and give them Eid money in return. The children eagerly collect all the cash they can get and then immediately go off to celebrate on their own. As this is the only time of the year when young people are allowed such luxuries, they look forward to Eid al-Fitr with eager anticipation. They typically go riding with their friends on horses or small motorcycles, or watch children's plays in theaters especially set up for the festival. They may also go to the movies or attend special firework displays. Younger children can buy cotton candies, cakes, and all kinds of junk food that they may not normally be allowed to eat. In the evening, the children return home for the great family meal. After dinner, families typically relax and talk until the end of the evening.

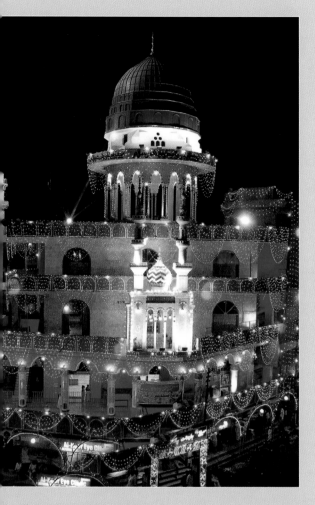

Illuminations such as these, on the exterior of a mosque in Karachi, Pakistan, are typical of the decorations displayed throughout the Muslim world to mark Eid al-Fitr.

At each stop, cookies and coffee are served. People normally make or receive three or four such visits on each of the three days of Eid al-Fitr.

Another popular way of marking Eid al-Fitr is by festively decorating the home. People drape lights on both the exterior and interior of their apartments and houses. Indoors they hang balloons and colorful flags with Arabic legends and Islamic motifs.

A TIME FOR GIVING

Eid al-Fitr is also a time when Muslims fulfill some of their obligations to share their wealth with other

HOLY PLACES

Like most major religions, Islam has three main categories of holy places. One consists of the locations in which the key events are believed to have occurred. Another category is the places of worship— in this case, mosques. The third category consists of the tombs of the most influential people in the history of the faith.

In Christianity, the holiest places are those in which the key religious events are believed to have occurred. Among the foremost of these are Bethlehem, the birthplace of Jesus, and Jerusalem, the site of his Crucifixion. Slightly below these sites in the conventional hierarchy are the main religious centers—these include Vatican City for the Catholic Church and, to a lesser extent, Istanbul for Orthodox Christians. The third stratum is composed of various sites where saints performed miracles—Lourdes in France, for example, where, in 1858, 14-year-old Bernadette Soubirous had numerous visions of the Virgin Mary. A similar three-tiered structure may be applied with reference to the holy places of Islam.

MECCA

The holiest place in Islam is Mecca. Its supreme significance is as the birthplace of the Prophet Muhammad (570–632) and as the location where, in the year 613, he first spoke in public. However, long before the lifetime of the Prophet, this city in the Arabian Peninsula (now part of Saudi Arabia) was already an important religious center, where pagans worshipped tribal gods at the Kaaba (cube), a temple

that housed figurines representing their various deities. The pre-Islamic belief systems of the region were based on the notion that heaven and earth were populated by innumerable gods, headed by the one they called Allah (Arabic for "God").

❖

The pre-Islamic belief systems of the region were based on the notion that heaven and earth were populated by innumerable gods, headed by the one they called Allah (Arabic for "God").

By the 7th century, Mecca had grown into a great caravan city with a richly cosmopolitan atmosphere. Pilgrims flocked to the Kaaba—Muhammad's family was involved professionally in the administration of the shrine—and the city teemed with traders. There was a Jewish neighborhood, and the city's residents also included Christians and merchants from all over the Mediterranean region. As well as being a trading post and a religious site, Mecca was known as a popular center for

Shiite pilgrims reach out to touch the tomb of Imam al-Abbas in the shrine dedicated to him in Karbala, Iraq.

THE GREAT MOSQUE, MECCA

Al-Masjid al-Haram, the Great Mosque, in Mecca, is only slightly smaller than the entire Vatican City in Rome, Italy.

Al-Haram Mosque (The Great Mosque) in Mecca was built on a small open-air site, with the Kaaba at its center, that had previously been used for pagan worship. The start of the area's transformation into the focal point of the new monotheistic religion of Islam was overseen by the second caliph, Umar Ibn al-Khattab (r. 634–644), who ordered the construction of a wall, 5 feet (1.5 m) in height, around the prayer area.

During the 8th century, the wooden columns that held up the roof of the original Muslim building were replaced by marble supports decorated with mosaics. A minaret was also added. The spread of Islam and the consequent increase in the number of pilgrims making their way to Mecca on the hajj necessitated an ambitious expansion program, which included the addition of three further minarets within a greatly expanded land area.

The Great Mosque was radically reconstructed in the 15th century after a devastating fire in 1399 and, again, in the 16th century and the 17th century, when Mecca was a part of the Ottoman Empire. The most recent phase of renovation and new construction began in 1955 under the auspices of the Saudi Arabian monarchy. The Great Mosque now covers 88 acres (36 ha).

The Masjid al-Haram is the only mosque in the world that has no *qiblah* (pointer toward the Kaaba) because the shrine is in plain view.

poetry festivals—tribal clans often fought *zajal* (poetry battles) there as an alternative to armed conflict. In the year 630, Muhammad and the first generation of converts to the new monotheistic religion of Islam conquered Mecca, destroyed the pagan religious idols that surrounded the Kaaba, and converted the temple into a shrine for the worship of a single god, Allah.

This site was later developed into al-Haram Mosque (the Great Mosque), the focal point of modern Mecca. The structure now encompasses both the Kaaba and the sacred well of Zamzam, the underground water source that, Muslims believe, was used to quench the thirst of Abraham's infant son, Ishmael, an event described in the Book of Genesis in the Old Testament of the Bible. The vast building complex of al-Haram Mosque was greatly modernized and extended by the Saudi government in the 1980s and 1990s and now occupies many stories. It is fully air-conditioned and contains an intricate network of pedestrian walkways, escalators, and tunnels. It can accommodate one million worshippers at a time. At certain times of the year, particularly during Dhu'l-Hijja (the Islamic month of holy pilgrimage), even that capacity is insufficient to cope with the flood of visitors, in spite of the fact that only Muslims are permitted to enter Mecca.

AROUND MECCA

Among the most important of the numerous holy places in the immediate vicinity of Mecca are Mount Arafat, Muzdalifah, and Mina, all of which must be visited by pilgrims on the hajj, the ritual journey to Mecca that Muslims are encouraged to undertake at least once in their lifetimes.

Mount Arafat, also known as Jabal ar-Rahmah, is a granite hill, around 230 feet (70 m) in height, 12 miles (19 km) to the east of the city. It was on this outcrop that, Muslims believe, Muhammad delivered his Farewell Sermon to the faithful at the end of his life. Muzdalifah is an open, level area where hajj pilgrims collect one pebble for each of the 49 days that, according to both the Koran and the Book of Genesis, the prophet Abraham was tempted in the wilderness. They take these pebbles with them to Mina, a desert location to the southeast of Mecca, where they throw them away, an act that symbolizes stoning—and therefore rejecting–the Devil.

MEDINA

Around 275 miles (about 440 km) north of Mecca is Medina, the second holiest city in Islam. Originally an oasis settlement, it developed in the pre-Islamic era into the partly Jewish and partly Christian city of Yathrib. Yathrib was conquered by Muhammad after his flight (*hijra*) from Mecca on September 20, 622 (the date that became the first day of the Muslim calendar). Yathrib was later renamed Madinat al-Nabi (City of the

AROUND MEDINA

Among the other important figures buried in and around the city are Hamza, the Prophet's uncle, and his comrades-in-arms who were killed with him at the Battle of Uhud. The bodies of Amr ibn al-As (d. 663), one of the earliest Muslim warriors, who conquered Egypt and Palestine, and of Aaron, the Old Testament patriarch, are traditionally held to occupy tombs at the summit of Mount Uhud on the outskirts of Medina.

Prophet), which became abbreviated to Medina. As with Mecca, only Muslims are allowed to visit the city.

Medina is a city of mosques, the main one of which is Al-Masjid an-Nabawi (The Prophet's Mosque), the first in Islamic history, which Muhammad himself helped to build and in which he experienced a vision of Mecca. It was here that the Prophet was buried, under the famous Green Dome, as, later, were the first two caliphs, Abu Bakr (r. 632–634) and Umar ibn al-Khattab (r. 634–644).

Another important holy place in Medina is Al-Masjid al-Qiblatain (The Mosque of the Two Qiblahs), which was built to commemorate the change of the direction

in which Muslims pray—they originally faced toward Jerusalem but later reorientated toward Mecca. In another part of Medina, a mosque marks the spot—originally on the outskirts of Yathrib—where Muhammad dismounted from his camel to pray before entering the city. Other mosques mark events in the buildup to and the aftermath of the Muslims' defeat by Meccans at the Battle of Uhud (625). These include the place where Muhammad donned his armor, the place where he rested on his way to the battle, the place where he unfurled his banner, and the site of the defensive ditch he dug. Also sacred is the cave on the side of the mountain in which Muhammad hid after the battle.

Minarets dominate the skyline of Medina, Saudi Arabia.

THE DOME OF THE ROCK

The Dome of the Rock is built on land sacred to Christians and Jews as well as Muslims.

Completed in the year 691, the Dome of the Rock is the world's oldest Muslim building, predating the conversion of Al-Haram Mosque (the Great Mosque) in Mecca, Saudi Arabia, to a shrine of Islam.

The Dome of the Rock has an octagonal base, consisting of 24 piers and columns, each 36 feet (11 m) high. On this base is mounted a wooden dome, 60 feet (18 m) in diameter.

The design of the building is a synthesis of established Byzantine architecture and emerging Islamic art forms. Domes were widely used in the 7th century by Eastern Orthodox Christians to house the bones of saints. To this traditional structure—known as a martyrium—was added a characteristically Muslim combination of faience (earthenware decorated with opaque colored glazes), polished marble, and mosaics.

According to the Arab travel writer al-Maqdisi (946–1000), the gold on the dome was obtained by melting down 100,000 dinar coins. In 1998, another 176 pounds (80 kg) of gold were added to the exterior. The cost of this restoration—$8.2 million—was borne personally by King Hussein of Jordan (r. 1953–1999).

The mosaics inside the mosque feature inscriptions from the Koran. Scholars believe that some of these—including a passage which denies that Jesus was the son of God—were deliberately chosen for their explicit opposition to the key beliefs of Christianity.

JERUSALEM

The third holiest city in Islam is Jerusalem, which is known in Arabic as Al-Quds or Baitul-Maqdis (the Noble, Sacred Place). The reasons for Jerusalem's importance are deeply rooted in Islam's origins as a development of Judaism. Although Muslims regard the Koran as the most important religious text, they also acknowledge the Old Testament of the Bible and honor its patriarchs and prophets, such as Abraham, Moses, David, and Solomon. They also revere Jesus as a prophet although, unlike most Christians, they do not regard him as the son of God.

Jerusalem's principal mosque, Al-Aqsa, stands near the Dome of the Rock, a high place in the center of the city from which Muhammad is believed to have made his ascent to heaven.

Jerusalem was Muhammad's destination on the Isra (Night Journey), during which, according to tradition, the Prophet flew from Mecca on Buraq, a mythical winged creature, in the company of the Archangel Gabriel (Jibril). It is also from Jerusalem, on the same night, that Muhammad is reputed to have ascended by ladder into heaven, where he met Abraham, Moses, and Jesus. This miraculous event is known to Muslims as *miraj*.

When Islam was first established, Jerusalem was the Muslims' *qiblah*—the place toward which they turned when they were at prayer. Although superseded as the focus of worship by Mecca only two years after the *hijra*, Jerusalem remained

important in the religion. Jerusalem's principal mosque, Al-Aqsa, stands near the Dome of the Rock, a high place in the center of the city from which Muhammad is believed to have made his ascent to heaven. The Dome of the Rock is also sacred to Jews and Christians as the spot on which, according to the Book of Genesis in the Old Testament of the Bible, Abraham, the first patriarch of the Hebrew people, prepared to sacrifice his son Isaac.

DAMASCUS

The fourth holiest city in Islam is generally agreed to be Damascus, the modern capital of Syria. Damascus emerged as a Muslim capital when Muawiyah (r. 661–680), the first caliph of the Umayyad dynasty (661–750), established his court and a seat of government there at the heart of an empire that expanded over the next century and a half to Spain in the west and the borders of China in the east.

The Great Mosque of Damascus was built during the reign of the sixth caliph, al-Walid (r. 705–715). In spite of having been severely damaged on several occasions, this astonishing building remains one of the outstanding achievements of Islamic architecture. A shrine in the mosque is said to contain the head of John the Baptist, who, in addition to being a Christian saint, is revered as a prophet by Muslims. There is also a tomb that is said to be that of Hud, an early Muslim who evangelized the people of Yemen. In addition, the Great Mosque contains several tombs that are reputed to be those of the Prophet's wives, together with the grave of Muhammad's companion, Bilal, an Ethiopian slave who called the Medina community to prayer.

THE MOSQUE

The interior layout of a mosque is determined by the form of worship—a series of physical movements of bowing, prostrating, and standing while reciting set prayers and at least three chapters from the Koran. This ritual requires an unencumbered space for the worshippers, who line up in rows behind a prayer leader who stands at the front of the concourse. Men are in the front, women behind.

The architectural origin of the mosque is said to be the house of the Prophet in Medina, which was an enclosed open courtyard with shaded areas along the side. There are three main forms of mosque. The first is the Arab hypostyle form, which maintains this open courtyard with surrounding covered areas supported by columns.

The second is the Iranian *iwan* form, which consists of a central courtyard surrounded by four monumental arched gates that contain covered areas for prayer. Third, the Turkish style also includes a courtyard but is primarily a dome-covered area that derives from Byzantine architecture. In all cases, the most striking feature of any mosque is that it is basically just an open space. Unlike a church, it does not use the walls as a medium for imparting any information other than that provided by the *qiblah*, which is mounted on the wall of the mosque that runs perpendicular to the direction of Mecca. Unlike a synagogue, where attention is drawn to

The prayer carpets in most mosques are designed and oriented in such a way that they indicate the direction of Mecca.

the Biblical scrolls, or a church, where the eyes of worshippers are drawn to the altar, there is only the directional orientation.

The main feature of the largely open space of the mosque is the *mihrab*, an apse in the *qiblah* wall, to the right of which is the *minbar* (sermon platform). The origin of the apse is debated. It has the function of magnifying the voice of the prayer leader for those standing behind him. The design suggests a place where a statue might be. The emptiness of the space reinforces the Islamic prohibition of images. It may also recall the Prophet Muhammad, who used to stand before the worshippers and whose physical absence is thus signaled.

The *sajjada* (prayer carpets) that cover the floor of most mosques are not essential furnishings. The earliest Muslims prayed with their faces in direct contact with the ground, and dirt on the nose and forehead was taken as a sign of piety. Later, mats and carpets were allowed. Although there are many designs, all *sajjada* have a directional pointer at the end facing the *qiblah*.

Shiite Muslims have an additional practice of placing a *mohr* (a marker, usually a piece of clay or stone) in front of them to mark the *qiblah*. Sunni Muslims disapprove this practice, which they denounce as idolatry.

The Great Mosque of Damascus was originally a place not only for communal worship but also for religious education, legal proceedings, the treatment of the sick, and the comfort of the poor. The exterior is a synthesis of Arab and Byzantine styles, with a quadrangular perimeter wall measuring almost 1,700 feet (about 514 m) in length. The interior of the mosque is predominantly white and lavishly decorated with mosaics, which are believed to symbolize paradise. One of the mosaics, with an area of more than 43,000 square feet (about 4,000 sq. m), is thought to be the largest artifact of its kind in the world.

Throughout the Muslim world, the focal point of worship—and hence the holiest place in any locale—is the mosque.

The main prayer hall is divided into three aisles, supported and divided by two parallel rows of Corinthian columns. The minaret in the southeast corner of the Great Mosque is called the Minaret of Isa (Jesus) because many Muslims believe that it is here that Christ will appear at the End of the World.

Also of great spiritual significance to Muslim pilgrims to Damascus is the Sayyidah Zaynab Mosque, in which an ornate mausoleum is thought to contain the tomb of Zaynab bint Ali, the daughter of Ali, the first Shia imam, and a granddaughter of the Prophet Muhammad.

The reputation and prestige of Damascus grew throughout the Umayyad period. It became generally accepted among Muslims that the Prophet himself had praised the city, which he is believed to have visited on more than one occasion. According to tradition, Muhammad went there once as a merchant—a small shrine outside the city marks the spot in which he is believed to have rested his camel. The Prophet was also said to have stopped off in Damascus to pray on his way to Jerusalem on the Night Journey.

Mount Qasiyun, to the south of Damascus, is particularly rich in legends. According to one story, it vied with the Dome of the Rock for the accolade of the holiest high place in Islam and yielded to the promontory in Jerusalem only after it was established that Allah would be worshipped in the mosque at the top of Qasiyun for 40 years after the destruction of the world. Qasiyun is also reputed to be the site of several Biblical events. It is thought to be where Cain killed his brother Abel—according to the Book of Genesis, the first murder in human history; a cave shrine near the top of the mountain houses supposed relics of the crime. It is also said to be the birthplace of Abraham. Jesus and Mary are reputed to have taken refuge at the base of the mountain.

BUKHARA

Less easily accessible to foreign pilgrims, because of its remote location in Central Asia, but still vying with Damascus to be regarded as the fourth holiest city in Islam is Bukhara, the second city of Uzbekistan, which has maintained a strongly Muslim atmosphere since it was first captured by Arab warriors in the year 709. Among the outstanding Islamic features of the center of Bukhara are the Ismail Samani Mausoleum, which was completed in the 10th century, the 12th-century Kalan

Mosque, and four historic madrassas—
Ulugh Beg (founded 1417), Mir-e Arab
(1536), Kukeldash (16th century), and
Abd al-Aziz Khan (1652).

MOSQUES

Throughout the Muslim world, the focal
point of worship—and hence the holiest
place in any locale—is the mosque. The
word *mosque* is an English rendition of the
Arabic *masjid*, which, in strict etymological
terms, means any space—enclosed or
in the open air—where believers may pray.
The earliest mosques were modeled on
the courtyard of Muhammad's house in
Medina—open plots that became sacred

because people worshipped on them—but
later buildings became more ambitious in
their scope. However, in spite of numerous
embellishments, the mosque remains
basically an open space, often but not
invariably enclosed beneath an overall
roof. No statues, ritual objects, or pictures
are permitted in a mosque; the only
decorations that are allowed are inscriptions
of verses from the Koran and the names of
Muhammad and his original companions.
The floor of any mosque is normally
covered with mats or carpets for the
comfort of worshippers who rest on their
knees while performing the ritual prayer
(*salat*). The focal point of the concourse

Bukhara, Uzbekistan,
is regarded by some
people as the fourth
holiest city of Islam,
after Mecca, Medina,
and Jerusalem.

ZIYARA

In Islam, the act of *ziyara* involves a visit to any Muslim holy place, especially the tomb of an important *wali* (saint) or theologian and—above all—to the tomb of Muhammad in Medina, Saudi Arabia. Not all Muslim theologians approved of *ziyara*. Some regarded it as dangerously close to a pious reverence that should be reserved for Allah alone. Others—notably followers of the strict Wahhabi branch of Islam—denounced *ziyara* as a form of *bida* (innovation), which deviated from the Koran and the Hadiths and, as such, was strictly forbidden.

In theological terms, the problem with *ziyara* is its implication that Allah may have given over some of his power to human beings. This is contrary to a central tenet of Islam, the one that also prevents Muslims from accepting Jesus as the son of God. However, *ziyara* gradually became so popular with ordinary Muslims that all but the most uncompromising schools of religious thought were persuaded to modify their original strictures in order to accommodate it.

Muslim clerics embraced *ziyara* by means of the following argument. Islam insists that all of humankind should draw nearer to Allah and some people, above all the prophets, obviously achieved that objective. Relying on such people, or invoking them when making a request of Allah, was therefore acceptable.

This new argument further recognized that one of the functions of the prophets would be to intercede with Allah on behalf of their communities on the Day of Judgment. It also addressed the role of the *wali* and the question of their continuing powers after death. The reference in the Koran to "the friends of Allah" became a warrant for the authorization of a second category of human beings—those who were closer to Allah than ordinary mortals but not as close as the prophets. The consequence of drawing nearer to Allah was to acquire *baraka* (blessing), an almost material power that is possessed by every *wali* and that is a source of benefit to those of their followers who can access it. The friends of Allah were capable of performing miracles, but their miracles were of a lower order than those of the prophets. These arguments sanctioned Sufism (Islamic mysticism) and the Shiite doctrines about the importance of the imamate.

The revisionists also tackled the question of the survival of power after death and concluded that, if prophets could posthumously exert an influence on human affairs, the friends of Allah could, too. Part of this argument was based on the idea that any categorical assertion that the saints were dead could be construed as a denial of the reality of resurrection. The Sunni theologian al-Ghazali (1058–1111) asserted that *ziyara* had the double benefit of blessing both the living visitor and the deceased person and that there was therefore nothing wrong with visiting tombs.

One of the first tombs to become established as a place of pilgrimage was the grave of al-Husayn ibn Ali in Karbala, Iraq. Millions of Shiite pilgrims travel to Karbala every year on the day of Ashura—the anniversary of Husayn's death—to visit the tombs of Husayn and his followers.

of the mosque is the *mihrab*, the place from which the imam leads the prayers. The rear of the *mihrab* faces toward Mecca, a direction indicated by a *qibla* (pointer). Beside the *mihrab* is a *minbar*, a raised seat from which the *khatib* (preacher) addresses the congregation. Attached to the main concourse of a mosque is often a minaret (Arabic *madhanah*, "beacon"), from which a muezzin (crier) calls the faithful to prayer, but the minaret is not an essential feature. A mosque may also contain a washroom, which Muslims traditionally use before they pray, but the ablution facilities may be separate from the religious building, although easily accessible from it.

Although the main purpose of mosques is collective worship, many of them also function as educational centers—an outstanding example is Al-Azhar Mosque in Cairo, Egypt, which nurtured the development within its expanding precincts of a school, a university, and a vast library. In addition, mosques originally doubled as courts of Islamic law. Although they no longer fulfill this function, they are still widely used for a range of public events, including political meetings and military parades.

TOMBS

The veneration of tombs is a particularly strong tradition among Shiite Muslims, who have two paramount holy cities— Al-Najaf and Karbala, both of which are in Iraq. The main shrine in Al-Najaf is believed to contain the tomb of Ali ibn Abi Talib (c. 600–661), the cousin and son-in-law of Muhammad. It was the question of Ali's right to the caliphate that caused the great division of Islam into Shiite and Sunni factions. Ali is thus, after the Prophet himself, the figure most venerated by the Shiites, many of whom go on pilgrimages to Al-Najaf. In addition, numerous Iraqi and Iranian Muslims use the city as their starting point on the hajj to Mecca. Ali's shrine (*mashhad*) in the heart of Al-Najaf is housed beneath a great dome, which is gold-plated on the outside and decorated on the inside

This photograph shows a *minbar*—the sermon platform in a mosque from which the *khatib* (preacher) addresses the congregation.

This photograph shows worshippers at the tomb in Al-Najaf, Iraq, of Ali ibn Abi Talib, the cousin and son-in-law of the Prophet Muhammad.

with polished silver, glass, and colored tiles. In the courtyard in front of the dome are two golden minarets. Within the dome, surrounded by walls with barred silver windows and entered through a door with a huge silver lock, is Ali's tomb itself, a highly wrought ironwork structure. Many of the treasures that were originally housed in this building were carried off in the 19th century by Wahhabis, members of a puritanical Sunni Muslim sect that objects to the veneration of saints because of its overtones of polytheism, which they denounce as sacrilege.

Because Shiites believe that to be buried near Ali ibn Abi Talib is almost to guarantee entry into paradise, Al-Najaf contains a disproportionate number of cemeteries for a city of its size (population around 400,000).

Karbala, 55 miles (88 km) southwest of Baghdad, the capital of Iraq, is sacred to Shiites as the location of the Battle of Karbala (680), in which a small band of warriors led by al-Husayn ibn Ali (624–680)—the son of Ali ibn Abi Talib and the grandson of the Prophet Muhammad—was ambushed and massacred by a much larger force sent by the Umayyad caliph Yazid I (r. 680–683). Husayn's shrine in the center of Karbala is surrounded by a boundary wall and entered through wooden gates decorated with glass. The grave of the Shiite martyr is enclosed in a cage beneath a great golden dome. Like the shrine of Ali in Al-Najaf, Husayn's mausoleum was despoiled by Wahhabis in 1801 but was later restored to something approaching its former glory.

Like the shrine of Ali in Al-Najaf, Husayn's mausoleum was despoiled by Wahhabis in 1801 but was later restored to something approaching its former glory.

Also killed at the Battle of Karbala was Husayn's half-brother, al-Abbas ibn Ali, another of Muhammad's grandchildren. His shrine in Karbala is a pear-shaped dome flanked by two tall minarets. The tomb inside is encased in gold and surrounded by an ornate silver trellis.

Al-Kadhimiya Mosque, on the outskirts of Baghdad, is the site of the tombs of Musa al-Kadhim (745–799) and his grandson Muhammad at-Taqi (810–835). These men were, respectively, the seventh and ninth of the 12 imams who were held to be the divinely ordained leaders of Islam

---

SHIITE HOLY PLACES IN DAMASCUS

There are also several Shiite holy sites in Damascus. The head of Imam Husayn (624–680)—which had been sent to the caliph after he was martyred in Karbala—was placed in the Umayyad Mosque. Imam Husayn's daughter, Ruqayya, was buried nearby, and his sister Zaynab is thought to be interred at the southern edge of town. In addition, there are the tombs of numerous important political figures and saints, above all the grave of the Sufi master Ibn Arabi (d. 1240). The importance of Damascus is further increased by the large number of apocalyptic and mystical events that were said to have occurred there.

---

after the death of the Prophet. Shiites who believe in the supreme authority of these historical figures are known as Twelvers—they form the majority among this branch of Islam. Also buried in Al-Kadhimiya Mosque are several distinguished early Muslim scholars and writers, whose tombs are visited by numerous pilgrims.

Another sacred Shiite site in Iraq is Samarra, on the Tigris River. The city contains a shrine to Ali al-Hadi (828–868) and Hasan al-Askari (846–874), the 11th and 12th imams. Originally built in the 9th century, the building was augmented in 1905 by the addition of a great golden dome. Another of Samarra's great religious attractions is al-Malwiyah, a helical minaret that tapers toward its summit. Although its design is thought to be based on that of the ancient ziggurats, it is the only building of its kind in the world.

One of the most important holy places in Afghanistan is Mazar-e Sharif, a town in the north of the country around 35 miles (56 km) south of the border with Uzbekistan. The Arabic *Mazar-e Sharif* means "tomb of the saint," a reference to the variant belief that Ali ibn Abi Talib is buried here, rather than in Al-Najaf. A blue-tiled mosque and a shrine stand on the site of the supposed tomb, which is venerated by all Muslims, especially the Shiites, many of whom make pilgrimages there.

Meshed, in northeastern Iran near the site of the ancient city of Tus, has been an important pilgrim destination since it became the burial place of the fifth caliph, Harun al-Rashid (r. 786–809), and of Ali ar-Rida (c. 768–818), the eighth imam of the Twelver Shiite sect. Although Meshed was devastated by a Mongol attack in 1220, many of the original buildings survived, and they were later adorned by the Persian Shah Rokh (r. 1405–1447) and his wife, who together oversaw the construction of one of the world's greatest mosques.

Another of Iran's Shiite centers is the city of Qom, where Fatimah, the sister of Imam Ali ar-Rida, died and was buried in 818. In the 17th century, Fatimah's grave was adorned with a beautiful golden dome,

The sacred hill of Takht-i-Suleyman overlooks the city of Osh in Kyrgyzstan.

and Qom thereafter became a place of pilgrimage for Shiites from all over the Muslim world. It is now the burial place of 10 Persian kings, including Shah Abbas II (r. 1642–1666), whose remains are interred in an ornate mausoleum, and of more than 400 Islamic saints. On the southern outskirts of Qom is a group of five mausoleums (mostly 14th century) adorned with multicolored plasterwork.

The holiest place in the city of Esfahan, Iran, is the Masjid-e Jame (Universal Mosque). Founded in the 11th century, it has since been improved and expanded almost continually. It is surrounded by a square courtyard, each wall of which contains a gate oriented toward a cardinal point of the compass—north, south, east, and west. At the heart of the complex is a large brick dome, within which is a smaller, domed chamber; both structures date from the 11th century. At the northern end of the courtyard, mounted on a series of arches, is another dome, beneath which is a small chamber made

of gray bricks. The Masjed-e Jame complex also contains a school, a library, and various private chapels.

Another long-established destination for Muslim pilgrims is Osh in Kyrgyzstan. Takht-i-Suleyman (Solomon's Throne), a hill in the western part of the city, is thought by some to be the site of Solomon's tomb. At the summit of the rocky promontory is a small mosque, which dates from 1510. The sloping paths to the top are marked out by prayer flags, small pieces of cloth.

SUFI SHRINES

The worship of anything or anyone other than Allah (God) is contrary to the spirit of Islam, which has been opposed to the veneration of images and individuals since its foundation. Nevertheless, the achievements and virtues of outstanding people have always held great mass appeal to ordinary Muslims, whose predilections have been encouraged by Sufis (Islamic mystics). Although strictly orthodox Muslims—notably the Wahhabis— vigorously resist hero-worship and idolatry, there are cults of personality throughout the world of Islam. Of particular attraction to Sufis are men and women who have somehow interceded between the seemingly distant deity and the human race—those held to have charismatic powers (*karamat*) that enabled them to transport themselves miraculously from place to place, to control animals, inanimate objects, and natural phenomena, such as the weather, and to display evidence of having come from or gone to the afterlife. Thus, although the notion of sainthood, as widely understood and practiced in the Christian church, was explicitly forbidden by Muhammad, many Muslims nevertheless

make pilgrimages to, and perform acts of worship at, the graves and shrines of distinguished people.

There is a hierarchy of living Sufi saints. At the top of the list are 40 *abdal* (substitutes), who are immediately replaced when they die. The following are some of the best-known Sufi saints in history.

There is a hierarchy of living Sufi saints. At the top of the list are 40 abdal (substitutes), who are immediately replaced when they die.

Al-Ghazali (1058–1111) was a Muslim theologian and mystic whose greatest work, *Ihya ulum ad-din* (The revival of the religious sciences), helped to make Sufism an acceptable part of orthodox Islam. Al-Ghazali was born and died in Tus, Iran, and although the exact location of his remains are unknown, many people believe that they lie within the city's Haruniyeh Dome, which has

The Green Dome in Konya, Turkey, is the mausoleum of the Sufi poet Rumi.

consequently become a holy place to which people from all over the Islamic world make pilgrimages.

The city of Uch, in the Punjab Province of Pakistan, is the burial place of several Sufi mystics, most notably Syed Jalaluddin Bukhari (1192–1291) and his family, whose tombs, originally separate, were brought together from the 14th century beneath a series of domes. Bukhari is venerated for his work in persuading numerous Asian tribes to convert to Islam. However, not all of Bukhari's missionary

work was successful—according to one legend, he attempted to convert Genghis Khan to Islam, but the Mongol emperor ordered him to be put to death. Bukhari was saved only by divine intervention.

Jalal al-Din ar-Rumi (1207–1273) was the greatest Sufi mystic and poet in the Persian language. Rumi was born in Balkh (a city in present-day Afghanistan) and moved in his twenties to Konya, Turkey, where he taught in a madrassa (Islamic school). His work influenced mystical thought and literature throughout the

Muslim world. After his death, his disciples formed the Mevlevi, a Sufi order that is still active today. Because of the Mevlevi's distinctive ritual dance, members of the order have become known in the West as Whirling Dervishes. Rumi's mausoleum in Konya, the Green Dome, is now a museum and a popular place of pilgrimage for (mainly Turkish) Muslims.

A direct descendant of the Prophet Muhammad, Ashraf Jahangir Semnani (1308–1405) was born in Semnan, Iran. He expanded Sufism and founded a new Sufi order, which was named Ashrafia for him. He became a Sufi saint, and there is a shrine to his memory at Kicchocha Sharif in Uttar Pradesh, India.

Otman Baba (1378–1478) was a Sufi dervish who traveled throughout the Ottoman Empire and attracted a following among Muslims of all kinds. When he died, aged 100 years, he was buried in Teketo, a village in modern Bulgaria. A posthumous biography ascribed miracles to Otman Baba; his tomb then became a shrine that is still visited by pilgrims from many parts of the Balkans and Turkey.

Shah Hussain (1538–1599) was a Sufi poet who pioneered *kafi*, a distinctive verse form that became popular with his coreligionists in the Punjab region of India and Pakistan. Hussain is buried with Madho, a Brahmin boy whom he loved, on the outskirts of his native city, Lahore. On the anniversary of Hussain's death, memorial celebrations are held at his shrine.

The author of more than 40 prose works and collections of poetry on Sufism, general mysticism, and related topics, Sultan Bahu (1628–1691) founded the Sarwari Qadiri order. The study of

his life and work remains popular in the 21st century; his mausoleum, at Garh Maharaja, near Jhang in the Punjab, Pakistan, is a Sufi shrine that receives many thousands of pilgrims every year.

Rahman Baba (1653–1711) was a distinguished Pashto Sufi poet. His one extant work, *The Diwan of Rahman Baba*, is widely regarded as the most important literary landmark in the Pashtun language. Rahman Baba's shrine in his native Peshawar, Pakistan, was badly damaged in March of 2009 by Taliban militants who reportedly objected to its being visited by female pilgrims.

Rumi's mausoleum in Konya, the Green Dome, is now a museum and a popular place of pilgrimage for (mainly Turkish) Muslims.

Riaz Ahmed Gohar Shahi (1941–2001) was an author who founded one of the most recent new adjuncts of Sufism. At age 20, Shahi abandoned a successful career in industry to pursue his spiritual quest. He gathered many acolytes, but his popularity with Sufis alienated orthodox Muslims, and he was frequently subjected to fierce criticism and physical attacks. Forced into exile, Shahi died in Manchester, England. His body was returned to his native Pakistan and buried near Rawalpindi at the headquarters of the Sufi movement he created, Anjuman Serfaroshan-e-Islam. The shrine constructed there to his memory is regularly visited by pilgrims from all over the world. Many of Shahi's followers believe that their leader

MULTAN

The Mausoleum of Hazrat Baha-ud-Din Zakariya is one of many Sufi shrines in Multan, Pakistan.

Multan, in the Punjab Province of Pakistan, has 14 mosques and innumerable Sufi shrines, which make the city a popular pilgrimage destination for more than 100,000 Muslims from all over the world every year.

One of Multan's most famous landmarks is the Mausoleum of Hazrat Baha-ud-din Zakariya (1170–1267), who was born near the city and educated at a madrassa (Muslim religious school) in Baghdad. As an adult, he went on the hajj to Mecca and also visited several other cities, including Jerusalem and Damascus. After he returned to Multan in 1222, he became a preacher and over the next 15 years converted

thousands of people to Islam. When he died, he was sanctified by the Sufis, many of whom came to pray at his grave.

The tomb in which Hazrat Baha-ud-din Zakariya's body was interred—and which he is said to have designed himself—is 51 feet 9 inches (15.8 m) square internally. Above it stands an octagonal structure surmounted by a great dome. The Mausoleum also contains the bodies of several of Hazrat Baha-ud-din Zakariya's descendants, including his son Sadr-ud-Din, who, according to tradition, gave all his father's vast wealth away to the poor.

is not dead but that he has merely undergone an occultation (a temporary disappearance from human view) and will reappear on earth when the time is right.

SUFI SHRINES IN THE UNITED STATES

Although most Sufi shrines are in Central Asia and South Asia, their numbers are increasing in the Western Hemisphere, particularly in the United States.

The story of one of the most prominent U.S. Sufi shrines began in 1971, when Bawa Muhaiyaddeen came from his native Sri Lanka to the United States at the invitation of a group of university students. He settled in Philadelphia, where he created an influential movement that now has branches throughout the United States

Although most Sufi shrines are in Central Asia and South Asia, their numbers are increasing in the Western Hemisphere, particularly in the United States.

and Canada. Muhaiyaddeen was a Sufi mystic painter and the author of several books, which he dictated to English-speaking acolytes—Muhaiyaddeen's own first language was Tamil—who spoke better English than he did himself. Muhaiyaddeen became well known for his efforts to mediate during the Iran hostage crisis (1979–1981). In 1984, the Bawa Muhaiyaddeen Fellowship opened a mosque in East Fallowfield, Philadephia, Pennsylvania. When the founder died in 1986, he was buried in a mausoleum on a nearby farm where his followers grew

fruits and vegetables—his form of Sufism rejected meat-eating. Muhaiyaddeen's tomb quickly became an important destination for pilgrims from all over the world who wish to pay their respects to this remarkable Sufi teacher.

Several other Sufi graves in the United States have become destinations for pilgrims. Among them is the tomb in Novato, California, of Hazrat Shah Maghsoud Sadegh Angha (1916–1980), the 41st master of the Oveyssi Sufi Order. There are other sacred Sufi shrines in Adelanto and Santa Clara (California) and in Questa (New Mexico).

CONCLUSION

The varied nature and extensive geographical distribution of the holy places of Islam are an indicative reflection of the variety and adaptability of the religion as a whole. The paramount focal points are Mecca and Medina, in which the Prophet lived, worked, and died, and it is to these cities that Muslim pilgrims make the traditional hajj. However, shrines have proliferated throughout the Muslim world, partly because it is not always practically possible for believers who are poor or who live in faraway lands to make the costly and physically demanding journey to Saudi Arabia. Another important reason for the large number of Muslim holy places in almost all parts of the world is the popularity of Sufism. This unorthodox variant of Islam, although not universally approved by Muslim traditionalists, has enormous appeal to ordinary believers because—in spite of its inherent mysticism—it demystifies the theology by acknowledging the possibility that Allah can work through humans, who are thus capable of supernatural feats.

See Also

Brief History of Islam 22–43 ❖ **Muslim Calendar, Holy Days, and Festivals** 150–169 ❖ **Jerusalem** 194–197 ❖ **Visual Arts** 198–219 ❖ **Architecture** 222–245 ❖

Jerusalem

Muslims have had a presence in Jerusalem since they first conquered the city in 638 CE. It contains sacred Islamic sites, including the rock from which Muhammad is believed to have ascended to heaven on his miraculous Night Journey.

I n Muslim eyes, Jerusalem, in Israel, is the third holiest city in the world (after Mecca and Medina, both in Saudi Arabia). The city contains sites sacred to Muslims—as well as to Jews and Christians. The intensity of Muslim emotion about Jerusalem has been heightened in the last half century as a result of the conflict between Israelis and Palestinians.

Three key events in the history of Jerusalem have shaped Islam's view of the city as a sacred place: its conquest by Muslims in 638 CE, just a few years after the death of Prophet Muhammad (c. 570–632); the recapture of the city by Saladin (1138–1193) from the Christian crusaders in 1187; and the capture of East Jerusalem by Israeli forces after the Six Day War in 1967. (The city had been divided after the Arab–Israeli War in 1948. West Jerusalem became part of the newly formed state of Israel, and East Jerusalem, including the old city, was annexed by Israel's neighbor, Jordan.)

SACRED CITY

The Koran does not mention Jerusalem explicitly, though it is connected to Muhammad's Night Journey, in which he traveled miraculously from Mecca with the Archangel Gabriel (Jibril) on a horselike creature called Buraq to a place now considered by Muslims to be Jerusalem, from where he later ascended to the heavens to receive divine guidance.

Jerusalem's status as a holy city was somewhat reduced when Muhammad changed the direction of prayer from Jerusalem to Mecca in 623–624. In addition, Muslim commentators often debate whether Muhammad actually prayed in Jerusalem or just passed through it. If he did pray there, the sacredness of the city for Muslims would increase. In Islam, Jerusalem has also come to be viewed as the location of the apocalypse (Judgment Day), and one legend indicates that at that time the Kaaba will travel from Mecca to pay homage to Jerusalem.

The conquest of Jerusalem by Muslims in 638 is not presented as a particularly special or culminating event in the Muslim sources. Its conquest was just part of a larger process of expansion. However, there seems clearly to have been a special fascination with the city.

Caliph Umar (c. 586–644) is believed to have been given a tour of the city by the Christian patriarch Sophronius (560–638) when he wanted to find a location suitable for Muslim prayer. This tour culminated in Umar choosing Haram al-Sharif, or the Temple Mount, on which two Jewish temples had previously been built. This area was a prominent empty space in the city. The previous Christian rulers had used the area as a dump to reinforce the permanence of the destruction of the Second Temple, as predicted by Jesus.

Umar's decision to clean the area and build a structure where Muslims could pray followed a pattern used in other conquered cities. However, in Jerusalem it carried extra meaning because of the varied spiritual resonances of the city. By the end of the seventh century, two buildings had been erected proclaiming Muslim identity in the city: a mosque, the Masjid al-Aqsa, named

The golden roof of the Dome of the Rock—an Islamic shrine—dominates Jerusalem's skyline. In the foreground, Jews come to pray at the Western, or Wailing, Wall—remnants of the Second Temple, which was destroyed by Romans in 70 CE.

in reference to the point of Muhammad's ascension to heaven on his Night Journey, and the Dome of the Rock, a magnificent shrine and the oldest surviving Islamic building in the world (finished in 691).

The Dome of the Rock is not a mosque. Its octagonal shape and two ambulatories, or cloisters, indicate it was meant as a commemorative structure according to a Byzantine model for similar structures. Inside, at the center of this shrine, is a huge rock, and the logic of the building is to invite visitors to walk around the rock in a similar manner as pilgrims encircle the Kaaba in Mecca.

There are three major interpretations for the purpose of the building. The first—now largely dismissed—is that Caliph Abd al-Malik (646–705) built it to replace the Kaaba in Mecca as a pilgrimage site because Mecca was at that time under the control of a rival caliph. The second explanation is that the building was erected to commemorate Muhammad's ascension to heaven from

Jerusalem emerged again on the world stage in 1099, when it was captured by the crusaders.

the rock. The problem with this interpretation is that another rock on the Temple Mount is said to have been the ascension point. More important, the connection of the Dome with the legend seems to have developed only gradually. The third interpretation arises from a reading of the inscriptions in the monument, especially the Koranic quotations that have a strong anti-Christian message—that God (Allah) did not have a son. These quotations served to proclaim a new Muslim presence and rulership in Jerusalem, as well as a rejection of the theological claims of the Christians about Jesus being the son of God.

Many Jews believe that the Rock is Mount Moriah, where Abraham (Ibrahim) was asked to sacrifice his son as a test from God. Because Abraham has a special place in Islam, honoring the rock is especially appropriate. However, Muslims now believe that Abraham's test took place in the valley of Mina, outside Mecca. Therefore,

this connection to Jerusalem is now invalid for Muslims.

The relationship between the Dome of the Rock and the mosque on the Temple Mount is similar to that of the Christian Church of the Holy Sepulcher, which contains a space for prayer as well as sacred momuments—in this case, Golgotha, the site where Jesus was believed to have been crucified, and his tomb (sepulcher). The Islamic Temple Mount complex may have been built to rival or surpass the church. In addition, the rebuilding on the Temple Mount had apocalyptic resonances at least for the Christian of Jerusalem, who believed that the restoration of the Jewish temple was a sign of the return of Jesus. It is not inconceivable that the Muslim rulers of the city played on stirring up the Christians' apocalyptic expectations.

These Muslim monuments were built under the Umayyad dynasty, which was in power from 661 to 750. The capital of the Umayyad caliphate was Damascus in Syria. Both Jerusalem and Medina—which had previously been the center of the Muslim world—were now relegated to the periphery. Having Damascus as the capital helped better control the center of the empire, which at that time was in Iraq.

Jerusalem was therefore a backwater in the Muslim world. Even its regional political importance was eclipsed when Ramla—in what is now central Israel—was founded by the Caliph Sulayman (674–717) as the Muslim political capital of the region (Palestine). Jerusalem also tended to have to share importance with Hebron, about 19 miles (30 km) from Jerusalem and the burial place of the Jewish patriarchs, including Abraham and Isaac (Ishaq).

SALADIN'S RECONQUEST

Jerusalem emerged again on the world stage in 1099, when it was captured by the crusaders. The slow Muslim response to the conquest may indicate that at that time the area was not seen as of obvious strategic or symbolic importance. However, its importance grew, and Saladin's reconquest in 1187. was his crowning achievement—especially as the tolerance he displayed toward the reconstruction of a multiconfessional city was in stark contrast with the actions of the crusaders. Rather than

Israeli soldiers cheer in front of the Dome of the Rock after capturing Old Jerusalem from the Jordanians in 1967. Since 1967 the Temple Mount has been managed by a Muslim organization but ultimately remains under Israeli control. Israel enforces a ban on non-Muslim prayer at the site and discourages visits by practicing Jews.

try to resettle the city with Muslims, Saladin allowed the return of the various communities that had lived in Jerusalem before the crusaders arrived, including a significant non-Muslim population. Nevertheless, a deliberate policy of Islamization of the city and the land followed. Churches were turned into mosques and the monuments on the Temple Mount, and throughout the region, were refurbished during the Mamluk dynasty (1250–1517).

REUNIFICATION

The 1967 Six Day War reunified Jerusalem, which had been divided in 1948. Israelis now controlled all of Jerusalem, and the Western Wall at the base of the Temple Mount was restored to them. The wall had long been an object of devotion for Jews—a place where they annually mourned the destruction of the Temple that had once stood there. The new Israeli rulers allowed Muslims to remain as administrators of the Temple Mount. To respect and affirm the Muslim identity of the Temple Mount, the Israeli government banned prayer on the site by non-Muslims. In addition, the Rabbinate—the Jewish

religious governing body of Israel—issued a strict prohibition on Jews entering any portion of the Temple Mount, a decision reconfirmed in January 2005.

Present-day Jerusalem is the largest city in Israel. It has a population of about 750,000, split about 64 percent Jewish, 32 percent Muslim, and 2 percent Christian. The Temple Mount continues to be a flash point and source of controversy and occasional confrontation as the religious positions and political interests of Muslims and Jewish Israelis interact and clash. Both sides acknowledge that solving the problem of Jerusalem will have to be the final stage of any peace process because the issues concerning sovereignty over the city are so historically complicated and fraught. The most difficult part of that issue is the Temple Mount.

In the city of Jerusalem itself, there have been many centuries of Muslims, Jews, and Christians living side by side—always with tensions, controversies, and confrontations, but nevertheless largely peacefully. This example may very well offer a glimmer of hope for finding a solution to the conflict between Muslims and Jews in Israel and the Middle East.

Chapter 9

VISUAL ARTS

Islamic art has a long and illustrious history. Emphasizing what in the West would be called the decorative tradition, it has a distinctive concern with beautifying the objects of everyday life. Calligraphy plays an important role, while figurative representation is limited, reflecting the strictures of conservative interpreters of the scriptures. The heritage is very much alive today as the present generation of artists seeks to come to terms with new, global influences.

This illustration from a 16th-century *falnama* (book of omens) shows the ascent to heaven of the Prophet Muhammad on the back of Buraq, a mythical horselike creature. Visual representations of Muhammad ordinarily exclude depiction of his face.

Art in the Muslim world may be defined in a number of ways. Here it is defined as comprising aesthetically pleasing objects that have been created for both secular and religious purposes, either in lands under Islamic rule or in lands in which a large and influential percentage of the population was or is Muslim. In this definition, such objects do not necessarily need to have been made by Muslims for Muslims, but they must come from within the context of Muslim culture. Although Islamic visual art is too versatile and too widespread—both geographically and in form—for useful generalization, it is safe to assert that it is characterized—and often instantly identifiable—by a brilliant use of color and a remarkably deft balance between design and form.

The history and development of Islamic visual art may be divided chronologically into four main periods. Early Islamic art coincides roughly with the foundation of the religion in the 7th century and extends to the 10th century, by the end of which it gives way to the medieval period, which lasts until the end of the 15th century.

During those 500 years, various regional powers emerged throughout the Muslim world. Each of these regions developed its own characteristic indigenous forms of artistic expression—from then onward, in any discussion of Islamic art, divisions may be made by region as well as by time. The late Islamic period—from the beginning of the 16th century to the end of the 19th century—was characterized by art produced under the patronage of powerful dynastic rulers. Modern Islamic art—from the beginning of the 20th century to the early years of the 21st century—has addressed, adapted, and assimilated the influence of numerous non-Muslim styles. The resulting synthesis of artistic influences contains recognizably exotic elements but remains distinctively Islamic.

CALLIGRAPHY

If Islamic visual art has a single, overriding, pervasive feature, that element is calligraphy (beautiful writing). In the Islamic world, calligraphy is incorporated into almost every form of creativity—not just painting but also glassware, masonry, metalwork,

A calligrapher at the King Fahd Complex for Printing in Medina, Saudi Arabia, transcribes part of the Koran.

pottery, textiles, and wood carvings. The widespread use of calligraphy is derived in significant part from the veneration of the Koran, the Muslim holy book, which is written in Arabic, a script with great potential for artistic expression. Muslims regard the written word as sacred, and Muslim artistic tradition does not generally embrace the widespread Western idea that images and writing are discrete and mutually exclusive modes of expression. When the Persian, Turkish, and Urdu languages adopted Arabic script, and with it the Arab predilection for ornate writing, calligraphy became standard practice throughout the widening Islamic world. It eventually spread across northern Africa and central Asia in a broad band that extended from Morocco to Malaysia.

Calligraphy is often combined with geometrical patterning and stylized vegetal forms, two other elements that have been integral to Islamic art from its earliest known manifestations and which remain important today. These three visual elements are all seen as mirroring and inviting contemplation of the unity and beauty of God's creation, even when they occur in art not made for expressly religious purposes. They are incorporated into both traditional and new forms. Today they might appear in large-scale paintings on canvas; in photographs and other graphic images on paper; in digital, video, and film works; on functional wares in clay, glass, and metal, and in nonfunctional sculpture in those and other materials; in immense architectural murals; and in exquisite pieces of jewelry and textiles of all sorts.

The use of calligraphy and patterning is, to some extent, a response to the

Islamic tradition of nonrepresentational art. There is no figurative imagery in Muslim religious art because imitations of God's creation—which, for the purposes of art, is usually defined as humans, animals, and some manufactured objects—are regarded as idolatrous based on various injuctions in the Hadith. However, in Muslim secular art, portraits and other representations of the human form have been strong elements since at least the eighth century, although the methods of depiction are less realistic than in the West and are generally more metaphorical than literal. Therefore, even though the most important media of artistic expression in the West have traditionally been painting and sculpture, in the Islamic world the decorative arts predominate.

THE EARLY CENTURIES

The first stage of development in Islamic art began in the seventh century and lasted until the ninth century. During that period, Islam spread rapidly from its cradle in Arabia as far west as the Iberian Peninsula in Europe, and north and east across Asia into the areas that are now the states of Azerbaijan and Pakistan. Although little is known about the artistic traditions that predated Islam in Arabia, it is clear that, as the Arabs expanded their sphere of influence, their artists adopted some of the styles and techniques that were already established in the regions into which they expanded. In Persia, for example, Islamic art was clearly influenced from the outset by preexisting Sassanian traditions; in northern Africa, the influence of Rome (which had colonized and influenced extensive stretches of the continent's Mediterranean coast) was soon noticeable in the Islamic visual arts, particularly in glassware.

One of the earliest and most glorious examples of Muslim art—the Dome of the Rock, built between 685 and 691 by the Umayyad caliph Abd al-Malik on the Temple Mount in Jerusalem to mark the spot from where Muhammad ascended to Heaven on his Night Journey—is a major example of cross-cultural stylistic synthesis. Its external design is plainly based on Byzantine Christian models, and the craftspeople who decorated it were almost certainly Byzantine Christians. Yet the embellishment of the shrine is definitively Muslim. The lower parts of the interior walls beneath its dome are covered with geometrically shaped marble plaques and panels in which the veined stone has been placed in symmetrically oriented pairs. The walls' uppermost sections and the interior of the dome are encrusted with glittering glass mosaics that depict stylized plant forms and other motifs inspired by late antique and Byzantine mosaics. Situated between the bottom of the dome and the base on which it rests is a broad, intricately articulated band of calligraphy that communicates Koranic refutations of certain tenets of the Christian faith and proclaims Islam as the successor to both Christianity and Judaism.

It is noteworthy, also, that the structure does not include any of the representations of the human figure that would have been included in a typical Byzantine building. Instead, the mosaic decorations in the Dome of the Rock feature what, in a Byzantine mural, would have been strictly background elements—stylized plant forms, for example. It is the adaptation of existing visual forms—including Arabic calligraphy, which predated the divine revelations to Muhammad—to Muslim religious or secular ends that makes the Dome of the Rock a distinctively Islamic work of art.

Another example of calligraphic inscription in the earliest Muslim art is the *tiraz* band (*tiraz* is the Persian word for "embroidery"). *Tiraz* bands are narrowly woven strips of embroidered cloth that were made in Persia in the late ninth century for the Abbasid caliph al-Mutadid. These arm bands were awarded by the caliph as signs of honor and favor. The cloth is *mulham*, a blend of cotton and silk, which has been dyed vibrant yellow; the embroidered inscription is in silk. The origins of this textile and others like it predate Islam and involved the giving of a garment or cloth as a token of honor. It

was recorded, for example, that the Prophet himself had given his robe to a follower.

At that time, textiles were much commonly available than they a Consequently, the idea of a spec oven and embroidered piece ried with it all kinds of symb portance. The fusion of Arabic calligraphy with preexisting customs adaptable to Muslim culture resulted in an object that challenges Western models of art as a painting in a frame, hanging on a wall. The Islamic conception of art may perhaps be better understood by bearing in mind that, in the Muslim world, art has traditionally been

This photograph shows the exterior of the Dome of the Rock in Jerusalem.

integrated into daily life and activities with the aim of beautifying everyday experience rather than as a type of holy sacrament. Most artifacts were made for ordinary people rather than, as often in the West, for an elite class of art patrons, and that remains the case in the 21st century.

THE MEDIEVAL PERIOD

By the mid-ninth century, the original Islamic dynasty, the Abbasids, had begun to fragment. By the year 900, their previously wide-ranging power was effectively restricted to Iraq. Meanwhile, numerous self-determining Muslim dynasties had established themselves in regions from the Iberian Peninsula through northern Africa to Persia, and each new power center fostered the development of indigenous styles of Islamic art.

Between the beginning of the 10th century and the end of the 15th century, the caliphates or ruling dynasties of the first period of Muslim history broke up into smaller, regional ruling families that included, among others, the Umayyads in Spain and Portugal, the Fatimids in Egypt and other parts of northern Africa, and the Seljuks in Turkey. Although Spain and Portugal were lost to the Muslims after the Christian Reconquista in the late 15th century, Islam expanded in this period in

This photograph shows some of the detail of the decor within the Dome of the Rock in Jerusalem. Note the typically Islamic geometrical and vegetal patterns.

other directions—not only northward through Turkey and north of the Caspian and Black seas, but also farther south in Africa and east across the South Asian subcontinent. Fragmentation was not only political and ethnic but also increasingly religious, as mainstream Sunni domination faced a number of challenges, including an increase in the Shiite population and the rise of Sufi mysticism and conservative Sunni reformers in northern Africa.

Fragmentation brought greater regional diversity in art, yet certain forms and motifs remained and became pervasive throughout the Muslim lands. Calligraphic inscriptions were still important, being incorporated into the decoration of metalware, ceramics, textiles, and books in cultures throughout the Islamic world. Human and animal figures decorated functional wares and were used to illustrate two great literary works: the witty *Maqamat*—a collection of rhymed stories by al-Hariri (1054–1122), a Seljuk official in Basra—and the *Shah-nameh*, Persia's national epic composed by the poet Firdawsi in the early 11th century.

By the end of the period, the arabesque—a style of rendering and arranging sinuous, stylized vegetal motifs according to intricate geometrical patterns—had come to dominate decorative schemes in all artistic media throughout the Muslim world.

All those elements—varied uses of calligraphy and figuration as well as the increasing use of the arabesque—can be followed in ceramic wares, an area of great innovation during this period. Lusterware, which was developed by ceramists in Iraq during the ninth century, rapidly became popular throughout the Muslim world. It spread to Egypt and Syria under the Fatimids. By the second half of the 12th century, it had reached Iran, where it was developed to its highest level of artistic proficiency in the city of Kashan.

Manufactured according to a secret formula that was closely guarded by a few families of potters, Kashan lusterware was typically decorated with intricate spiral patterns or with images of birds and animals. It was a characteristic of Kashan that, for reasons that no-one today fully understands, animals were almost always depicted with spots, regardless of their species.

The technique of *sgraffito* (Italian for "scratched") was another development of Muslim ceramists; it allowed artists to draw fluidly through a thin layer of clay to reveal a contrasting ground beneath.

Another innovation in Islamic ceramics was *cuerda seca* (Spanish for "dry cord"), a technique in which rope is used to outline and contain the glazes applied to tiles; the rope burns away during the firing process. By the early 15th century, *cuerda seca* had become widespread throughout the Islamic world, from the Iberian Peninsula to Persia. In an effort to reproduce the quality of Chinese porcelain, which had been introduced to the Islamic world by the Mongols, who conquered vast expanses of Asia from the 12th century, Iranian ceramists developed a mixture of ground quartz, ground glaze, and white clay. This mixture allowed pigments, including cobalt (a rich blue mineral that was mined in Iran), to be applied to the clay bodies without fear of them running during a first firing in the kiln. After a clear glaze was applied, the pieces were fired a second time. The process of underglaze painting, followed by a clear glaze, had a profound impact on ceramic production, not only throughout the Muslim world but also in China.

There were also significant advances in metalworking techniques. The inlaying of brass or bronze with precious gemstones and metals had previously been practiced on a small scale but, during the medieval period, it became widespread and led to the creation of a wide variety of highly worked drinking vessels and ornaments, such as candlesticks, inkwells, and penholders. In keeping with long-established Islamic tradition, most of these artifacts were adorned with calligraphic inscriptions in Arabic.

Late Islamic Visual Art

The third stage of artistic development took place between the start of the 16th century and the end of the 19th century.

The tiling in the domed ceiling of this mosque in Shiraz, Iran, shows the colorful use of arabesques and geometrical mosaic work that typified Islamic visual art in the medieval period.

BLUE-AND-WHITE CERAMIC WARE

Blue-and-white ware—the name given to white porcelain that is decorated with blue slips under the glaze—probably originated in western Asia. It was introduced in the 13th century to China, where it developed into a distinctive and highly prized style during the Ming dynasty (1368-1644). When some of the earliest Chinese creations of this period found their way back into the Islamic world through Mongol expansion and peacetime trade across Asia, they created a high level of interest and inspired imitations that soon acquired original Muslim stylistic traits.

In the early 17th century, Shah Abbas the Great (r. 1588-1629) built a great collection of Chinese porcelain, which he displayed at his ancestral shrine at Ardabil in northwestern Iran. The beauty of these works increased the popularity of blue-and-white ware throughout the Islamic world, and from there its influence spread throughout Christian Europe.

The period saw relatively little territorial expansion in the Islamic world but did bring a consolidation of various Muslim empires that included the Ottomans (centered in Turkey), the Sharifs (Morocco), the Safavids (Persia), and the Mughals (India). The last of the great Muslim empires to emerge was that of the Ottoman Turks, which had its beginnings in the 13th century and came to an end in the aftermath of World War I in 1918.

The Ottomans' golden age spanned the 15th century through the 17th century. The period saw intense artistic activity, particularly after Ottoman expansion into Iran led to the dissemination of Persian artists and artistic ideas throughout the growing empire. Muslim artists migrated farther east, from Iran to India, where they brought a lasting influence to bear on the creativity of the Mughal Empire.

The Ottomans and the Safavids maintained their long-standing interest in porcelain, and their rulers assembled great collections of Chinese blue-and-white porcelain that influenced the indigenous styles of both empires. The Ottomans, in particular, were inspired to develop a style of pottery known as Iznik ware for the city in northern Anatolia that became the center of production. Iznik ware was typically soft, with a sandy appearance created by the combination of the grayish-white clay that was abundant in the region with slips (thin, white mixtures of clay and water). Most Iznik ware took the form of flat dishes, but there were also significant numbers of bowls, jugs, and vases. They were usually painted in the classic Islamic style, with linear geometrical and symmetrical vegetal motifs, but numerous examples were also decorated with designs inspired by the animal kingdom. Early Iznik ware was blue and white, in homage to its Chinese inspiration but, by the mid-16th century, the color scheme had diversified. It eventually incorporated black, green, purple, turquoise, and red. Iznik ware peaked around 1600 and then went into an irreversible decline; production ceased at the end of the 18th century.

Woodworking also thrived under the Ottomans and, as the empire's wealth grew, the degree of ornamentation became increasingly opulent. At the height of imperial power, the finest wooden artifacts were regularly inlaid with mother of pearl and tortoiseshell and, in the finest pieces, precious metals and gemstones.

After around 1800, Western observers began to perceive and report Ottoman culture as declining and, ultimately, as dysfunctional. That perception has sometimes been used to characterize Muslim civilizations in general, in contrast, for example, with the dynamism of modern Western culture, which was ignited by the Renaissance and reenergized during the Enlightenment. From a European and North American point of view, modernization (particularly in respect to science and politics) is a positive development. This mind-set has allowed some Western critics to perceive many Islamic cultures, which have not entirely embraced modernity, as stagnant or backward.

Yet such a perception of the Muslim world and its diverse cultures reveals as much about the views of Western historians as it does about the subjects they address. A perception of stagnation is particularly unhelpful in respect to Muslim art, which continued throughout the 18th and 19th centuries to assimilate techniques, genres, and media from the non-Muslim world at the same time as it was in turn influencing many European artists with its "exoticism," from Eugène Delacroix (1798–1863) to Henri Matisse (1869–1954). At the same time, Muslim artists reacted to existing Islamic traditions, reinventing, refining, and sometimes even rejecting them. The period was, overall, one of great artistic complexity and ferment in both the Muslim and the Christian worlds.

One area in which European influence quickly became apparent was in the adoption of oil painting by Islamic artists. At the same time, Muslim painters also adopted the large-scale imagery and themes long associated with oil on canvas, including naturalistic still lifes, landscape paintings, and life-size portraiture. In the early 21st century, many commentators

WAR RUGS

From tales of flying carpets to items sold at online auction, the form of Muslim art that is best known but also perhaps least understood in the West is the oriental rug. Rugs and carpets have symbolized the exotic East for centuries. At the same time, they have become a common fixture in homes from Fort William, Scotland, to Fort Worth, Texas.

In the 1980s, a new kind of rug began to appear. These rugs were made in Iran and Pakistan by refugees from the Soviet invasion of Afghanistan. Some looked very much like traditional tribal rugs except that, on closer inspection, the curling, leaf-shaped motifs known as botehs turned out to be hand grenades or helicopters;

the medallion-like shapes called guls took the form of stylized tanks. Other rugs had more explicit details, with M-16 and AK-47 assault rifles easily distinguishable.

As international awareness of "war rugs" increased, some were acquired for museum collections. They became subjects of academic study, and debate about what constitutes a war rug stimulated the creation of Web sites, such as warrug.com. Today, many collectors embrace war rugs as a new form of folk art, and enthusiasts marvel at how almost identical rugs feature small differences that reflect the individuals who wove and knotted them. Most connoisseurs of traditional Muslim textiles, however, dismiss them as commercial gimmicks.

The practice of dyeing the body with henna is widely associated with Hinduism, but it is widely practiced—and may even have originated—in the Islamic world.

from both cultures highlighted the contrasts between the cultural values of the Islamic and Western worlds; some Muslims criticized modern Western art as decadent and immoral, for example. It is fascinating, then, to consider the ways in which the Muslim art of the 18th century through the early 20th century reflected a creative mediation between traditional Islamic ways and Western values.

The enduring importance of calligraphy is reflected in 19th-century Ottoman culture, which some scholars consider to have marked the apogee of that art form. However, while pen on paper is the medium most frequently associated with the art of calligraphy and the recording of God's word, the importance of beautiful writing is also seen in countless other works of art from this period.

Also during the late Ottoman period, *mehndi*—the temporary "tattooing" of hands (and often feet) with henna dye, a practice traditionally associated with preparing women for special occasions such as marriage—became an integral form of Islamic art, even though its cultural origins may be debated. Did it begin in Morocco and spread eastward after Muslim Arabs conquered northern Africa in the eighth century? Was it carried west from India, where it has a cultural rather than a religious significance, being common among both Muslims and Hindus? Regardless of the direction and circumstances of its diffusion, Islamic *mehndi* adds calligraphic quotations from the Koran to the rich mix of decorations contributed by other indigenous traditions.

The Islamic craft that is best known in the West is carpet weaving. Although the practice is at least as old as the Islamic religion, the oldest surviving carpets date from the medieval period. Earlier creations have either been destroyed or disintegrated because of the relative fragility of the material from which they were made.

Carpets from Asia Minor and the Caucasus are made of coarse material and are decorated with colorful stars, polygonal shapes, and stylized Kufic script (the earliest existing Islamic style of handwritten alphabet, which was used by early Muslims to record the Koran). Highly stylized animal forms were also woven. In addition to real-life creatures, some carpets depicted the ancient legend of the mortal combat between a dragon and a phoenix.

MODERN ISLAMIC ART

Muslim art of the 20th and 21st centuries is more complex than Islamic art because, while it continues to include the traditional forms of historic Islam, it has increasingly used painting and sculpture, video and photography, and many hybrid contemporary art forms. At the same time, Islamic art reflects the challenges that come with the continuing adaptations that Muslim artists have made and are making in the face of globalization. For example, as works by various Islamic artists—some of whom have studied in the West—are increasingly sought

by international art institutions, sellers, and buyers, questions are posed about how "Muslim" they and their art really are.

The influence of Western cultural values and artistic techniques began in earnest after the dissolution of the Ottoman Empire at the end of World War I (1914–1918), when European nations, notably Britain and France, attempted to occupy the power vacuum left by the Ottoman collapse in western Asia and southeastern Europe. The level of cross-fertilization was raised later in the 20th century by the spread and growing accessibility of radio and television.

Yet, in spite of a consequent blurring of boundaries between the Muslim and the

The influence of Western cultural values and artistic techniques began in earnest after the dissolution of the Ottoman Empire at the end of World War I (1914–1918).

non-Muslim worlds, there are still several reliable ways of identifying an ongoing Islamic tradition. Muslim art today generally continues to focus on daily life, highlighting its beauty and worth as an integral part of God's creation. Admittedly, the truth of that generalization is not always immediately apparent in the works themselves. For example, a colorful abstract painting by a Muslim artist may not appear at first viewing to differ greatly from a similar canvas created by a Western artist. Yet, for the Muslim artist, the work will almost certainly convey faith-based values, whereas, for the Western artist, it will more likely be an exercise in color and texture.

BOOKMAKING

The establishment of Islam in the seventh century was followed in the eighth century by the introduction to the religion's heartland in Arabia of papermaking techniques developed in China. Muslims have always attached great importance to the written word, not only to its meaning but also to its physical manifestation. As a consequence, they have always made great efforts to ensure that books, the paper they contain, and the script in which they are written are all beautiful as artifacts. By contrast, in the West, such traditions, while by no means unknown, are by and large less strictly observed. In Christendom, bookmaking and calligraphy are, in all but a few cases, classified as handicrafts; in the Muslim world, they are traditionally art forms.

The work to which the greatest artistic labors were devoted was, and continues to be, the Koran. Many of the earliest calligraphers of the holy book of Islam left no record of their identity, but a few are known by name. Among them was Ibn Muqla (d. 940), vizier in Abbasid Baghdad, who introduced a new method of Arabic orthography that was later adopted throughout the Islamic world. Ibn Muqla influenced perhaps the most famous calligrapher of all, Ali Ibn Hilal, better known as Ibn al-Bawwab (d. 1022), also of Baghdad, who is believed to have produced 64 copies of the Koran by hand, one of which is now displayed in the Laleli Mosque in Istanbul, Turkey.

Another great early master of calligraphy was Yaqut al-Mustasimi (d. 1298), a eunuch slave who served the last Abbasid caliph and survived the sack of Baghdad by the Mongols in 1258. The creator of 364 *mushafs* (manuscripts), al-Mustasimi spawned a school of seven students who elaborated his stylistic innovations and spread his techniques throughout the Muslim world.

During the medieval period, millions of manuscripts were written and meticulously illuminated by scribes and artists. In addition to the Koran, a host of literary works were produced, together with books on jurisprudence, music, philosophy, and science. In addition to being beautiful artifacts, these books were major contributions to human thought; some of them became just as influential in the West as in the lands of their creation.

Medieval Arabic manuscripts were preconceived in great detail before scribes first put pen to paper. The number of lines per page, the number and position of all the illustrations, and where the chapter divisions would fall were all determined at the outset, in much the same way as modern publishers of printed books normally work from flat plans. The next phase of preparation was the ruling of lines across all the sheets of paper. After that, the calligraphers set to work, leaving clearly marked spaces for the subsequent insertion of illustrations and diagrams. The writing materials were reed pens and ink made from a mixture of soot, water, and various kinds of gum or resin from trees as a binding medium.

After the entire text had been transcribed, the book was handed over to designers, who embellished all or parts of the work with symmetrical designs that were either geometrical or resembled vegetation. This phase of production began with a faint outline or underdrawing, which was then fleshed out with fine paintbrushes made from cats' fur. The paint was made from minerals that were pulverized with pestles in mortars and then mixed with water. The color blue was derived from lapis lazuli, red from cinnabar, and green from malachite; gold and silver were inimitable, so the real precious metals were used for both those colors, which were used in the representation of, respectively, sky and water.

The final phase of the bookmaking process was the binding. The pages of the finished manuscript were sewn together between leather covers, which were embossed with stamping machines and decorated with gilt.

In other respects, the essentially Muslim quality of a work of art may exist as much in the eyes of the beholder as in the artist's original intention. For instance, a modern Muslim artist's installation addressing popular culture's impact on traditional family life can be perceived either as a statement of youthful rebellion or as a sad admission of loss.

Another important point to remember is that today, as in past centuries, the best artists consider and adapt external practices and trends that can be used in ways that relate to Muslim tradition. Today, that may mean making use of Western abstraction or the medium of film. However, as in the past, there are exceptions. Artists who have developed their aesthetics and techniques in relative isolation, without

undue pressure from foreign cultures, may not make many or any conscious decisions about how to proceed with their art. However, most serious artists look at what other artists, in other places and in different cultures, are doing. With that awareness comes the need to choose how to respond with their own art—and sometimes that response takes the form of a reaction against conventions that are rooted in Islam.

Such decisions have been particularly difficult since the first half of the 20th century, when Pablo Picasso (1881–1973), Henri Matisse (1869–1954), and other European modernists exerted an irresistible influence on art. This was also a time when many Muslim peoples were grappling with postcolonial independence and trying

This late-20th century bookstore display in Morocco contrasts sharply with its contemporary Western equivalents. The large upright volumes include copies of the Koran; the other book covers are adorned with calligraphy and geometrical shapes and patterns, but images of living creatures are conspicuous by their absence.

to reconcile cultural traditions with new national identities. With globalization, artists' options have become even more complicated.

Instead of being divided into chronological periods, the contemporary phase of Islamic artistic history is more usefully divided according to forms and media: traditional ones, such as ceramics, weaving, and the art of the book; and more recent developments, including installation art, video, and freestanding sculpture. These

Among the traditions that have remained unbroken is calligraphy, which is practiced by Islamic artists today with the same devotion and felicity as it was during the lifetime of the Prophet Muhammad.

categories are not comprehensive—there are, in addition, numerous hybrid forms— and the range of areas demonstrates clearly that art in the Muslim world overall is not created in ignorance of all the potential options but rather out of a conscious choice between them. Among the traditions that have remained unbroken is calligraphy, which is practiced by Islamic artists today with the same devotion and felicity as it was during the lifetime of the Prophet Muhammad.

One of the most striking innovations of the modern period is the development of a stratum of service industries—art institutions and art dealerships, for example—that, in the West, would be called "the art world." Before the 20th century, such businesses were largely unknown in the Muslim world, where there was little

concept of individual authorship of works of art and, as a consequence, of their commercial potential.

BOOK ART

With its roots in the Koran, with pages and covers made from carefully chosen materials, with verses and illustrations in inks and paints compounded from myriad substances and inscribed by rigorously disciplined artists, and with content inspired by great events and poetic and spiritual works of the past and present, the hand-made book is the quintessential work of art in the Muslim world. It has been an especially important form in Iraqi art, and several of Iraq's best modern artists produce a wide range of handmade books, some of them unique, others in limited editions. The genre includes rough sketchbooks and polished, finished products; books that verge on being paintings or fold-out sculptures; books bound traditionally in leather, loose-leaf books, books in boxes, books that are collages of bits of salvaged scraps. Many or most of them feature calligraphy—drawn by hand or produced by digital printers, sometimes blended with words and phrases written in the Roman letters of the West.

PAINTING

Perhaps the best way of demonstrating the tremendous breadth of painting in the modern Islamic world is by reference to two artists whose works stand at opposite ends of a continuum in respect to sophistication and approaches to tradition and contemporary values. One is Chaibia Tallal (1929–2004) from Morocco, an unschooled artist widely known simply as Chaibia. The other is the Iranian Farhad Moshiri (b. 1955), who was born in Shiraz and lives and works in Tehran, after receiving his formal education at the California Institute of Arts (CalArts) in Valencia, California.

Chaibia was born and raised in the outskirts of Casablanca. She demonstrated her creative impulses as a child but she was not sent to art school to study. Even so, she began painting pictures of the Moroccan landscape and peoples, and she eventually came to the attention of Pierre Gaudibert, director of the Modern Art Museum in Grenoble, France, who helped launch her career. Chaibia's paintings have been compared to the works of Matisse, who spent time in Morocco and was influenced by his experiences there. Chaibia's pictures feature broadly painted, intense patches of color and outline that coalesce into faces and figures. Her pictures have a celebratory feeling that appeals to a broad range of people. In Europe, her work is often categorized as *art brut*—raw, innocent, and untainted by formal training. Her paintings are widely displayed in galleries and museums in the United States, France, Syria, Spain, Switzerland, and Morocco.

In contrast to Chaibia, Moshiri's training exposed him to one of the more sophisticated programs for cutting-edge art in the United States. CalArts graduates are typically more concerned with ideas about contemporary culture than they are with any particular medium. Moshiri has worked in video and installation art as well as in painting, and many of his paintings might better be described as mixed-media works. The works for which he is best known are his images of traditional storage jars overlaid with calligraphy.

People who buy Moshiri's paintings include Muslims and non-Muslims who appreciate the way he conveys the complexity of being a Muslim in today's

world. Moshiri is the first western Asian artist whose work has sold for more than $1 million at auction. The painting in question, *Faghat Eshgh* (Only love), features the Farsi words calligraphically rendered in Swarovski crystals and glitter on a black-painted canvas. It was sold at the Dubai

This ornately lettered and illuminated page is from a 14th-century Koran. The hand-made book is still a popular art form in the Muslim world.

branch of the British auction house Bonhams to a western Asian bidder.

SCULPTURE AND CERAMICS

Traditionally, sculpture has played only a minor role in Islamic art, and even today it is not a major art form. Yet artists in the Muslim world have come to prominence for their sculptural works, among them Abdulmari Asia Imao (b. 1936) of the

Philippines, Ataev Nurmuhammet (b. 1943), and Madatov Edi (b. 1930), both from Turkmenistan.

Muslims comprise a minority in the Philippines, and there is tension between them and the Catholic majority. In spite, or perhaps because, of his devotion to Islam, in 2006, Imao was recognized as the National Artist of the Philippines—the first Muslim to receive that honor. In his

This statue of Saparmurat Niyazov ("Turkmenbashi"), president of Turkmenistan is one of hundreds that Niyazov commissioned during his 15-year rule.

citation, the award organizers praised Imao's popularization of traditional Filipino Muslim motifs (incorporating Hindu and native elements) in ways that also relate to Christian folk art. In the international Muslim community, Imao is admired for sculptures composed of calligraphic elements representing the 99 names of Allah. Imao is active in his homeland as a teacher and consultant, and he is also renowned abroad for his expertise in casting brass. His work is exhibited and collected by institutions in the United States and in Asia.

Traditionally, sculpture has played only a minor role in Islamic art, and even today it is not a major art form. Yet artists in the Muslim world have come to prominence for their sculptural works

Public sculpture is common in Muslim nations whose leaders (like their Western counterparts) encourage patriotism through the erection of monuments that combine elements of architectural abstraction and figural representation. In the Muslim world such projects are often associated with the cults of personality fostered by dictators like Saddam Hussein (r. 1979–2003) of Iraq and Saparmurat Niyazov (r. 1990–2006) of Turkmenistan. Niyazov, in particular, was known for commissioning hundreds of statues as part of his effort to style himself as the *Turkmenbashi*, or "father of the Turks." As a result of this patronage, sculpture is a more prominent art form in Turkmenistan than it is elsewhere in the Muslim world.

Ataev Nurmuhammet is a veteran in the realm of public monuments in Turkmenistan. While Nurmuhammet has sculpted several portraits of Turkmen heroes such as the composer Nury Halmammet, his favorite subject is the horse. Nurmuhammet represents horses as the heroic beasts that they are in Turkmenistan, where the national emblem is the Akhal Teke—an ancient and spirited breed renowned for its strength, speed, stamina, and courage. Nurmuhammet has also created several statues of the mythological winged horse from Greek mythology, Pegasus, one in the form of a monument entitled *Sentinel*.

In contrast, Madatov Edi's work is rooted in regional folk art, even though he was formally trained at the Art Institute in Tashkent, Uzbekistan. Edi primarily carves in wood, which is usually associated with primitive art but was valued by such artists as the Frenchman Paul Gauguin (1848–1903) and the Romanian Constantin Brancusi (1876–1957) for that very reason. Indeed, there is a hint of Brancusi in Edi's sculptures, whose tall, narrow forms link them to the tree trunks from which they were carved. Edi focuses on the human figure, frequently using combinations of rough and smooth carving to create surfaces of bodies and clothing. Often, Edi paints his works with bright colors or in black and white, forming a contrast with the pale tones of the unstained wood.

In the medium of ceramics, modern artists' emphasis is on utilitarian objects that enhance daily life as well as on small, decorative sculptural pieces, but there are also individuals who use clay to make sculpture on a scale that could be called architectural. One such is Zeinab Salem. Born in 1945, Salem is best known for her hollow clay works whose form mimics that

This 21st-century Moroccan mosaic shows that the use of Arabic script remains a major component of modern Islamic art.

of the palm tree—an element of daily life in her native Egypt. Often, she makes ensembles of columns of varying heights, with some upright and others leaning or resting horizontally, as though in a state of ruin. Although it is possible to see references to historic Muslim architecture in Salem's work, her rough surfaces, which bristle with random root growths and husks, are much more naturalistic than the traditional use of vegetal motifs in Muslim art and architecture. Salem has twice won the Grand Prize in the International Cairo Biennial, and her work is found in public and private collections in Egypt, France, Germany, Italy, Morocco, the Netherlands, and the United States, where it has been exhibited at the National Museum of Women in the Arts in Washington, D.C.

WEAVING

Weaving in the Muslim world is usually thought of in terms of the woolen rugs, bags, and other items associated with cultures in western and central Asia. Production weavers in Afghanistan, Iran, Turkey, Turkmenistan, and other historic carpet centers continue to produce beautiful works in both traditional and experimental designs, both on commission and for the open market.

Yet wool is not the only material employed by weavers in Islamic cultures, and textiles are produced in other parts of the Muslim world. Silk, cotton, and less common plant fibers such as rice straw, pandanus, banana bark, ramie, and cassia fruit skin are used in places where sheep's wool is not the only option or is not an option at all. In the Muslim village of Oring-oring on the Philippine island of Palawan, for example, women weave pandanus mats whose decorative patterns are built into the criss-cross layering of fibers. The geometry of these patterns contrasts with the vivid, figural pandanus weavings that are traditional to the Philippines' Catholic majority. Islam was introduced to the Philippines at least 200 years before the Spanish imposed Catholicism in the 16th century; since that time, Muslims have resented foreign rule and influence. Since the 1970s, Muslim attempts to achieve autonomy for the islands that they inhabit have frequently been violent. The weaving of abstractly patterned pandanus mats is a statement of their independent identity.

Weavers in Muslim cultures from Indonesia to Uzbekistan use the ikat dyeing process to create dazzling garments, bags, draperies, and other items in cotton. Ikat is a method of tying threads into tight bundles before they are dyed so that carefully calculated segments of each thread are left untouched by the color. The threads are tied onto the loom vertically to create the fabric's warp; when the horizontal weft is interwoven, the resulting fabric has a pattern of dyed and undyed areas built into its structure. The term *double ikat* describes fabrics woven from both warp and weft threads dyed according to this process.

Whereas Muslims probably invented the ikat technique in central Asia, weavers in southeastern Asia adopted and adapted the process to create abstractly patterned textiles that are in striking contrast to the often figural ikats made by Hindu and Christian weavers. Another motif of contemporary Muslim ikat is verbal inscriptions, including calligraphic phrases in Arabic that invoke God's protection for the wearer.

GRAPHIC ART

The term *graphic art* covers a constantly expanding and shifting mix of genres and processes that include writing, drawing, printing, and photography, among others. Calligraphy is the most important form of Islamic graphic art, but cartooning, poster design, typography, film-based and digital photography, and the fine-art processes of etching and lithography, and others, all have their place in modern Islamic visual arts.

Shirin Aliabadi (b. 1973) is a Tehran-based artist who works in various media but has become known internationally for her ironic photographic portraits of fashionably groomed young women. Aliabadi's subjects wear blue or green contact lenses, and their bleached-blonde hair pushes out from beneath skimpy veils. Their aspirations to foreign standards of beauty can be

Cartooning takes many forms in the Muslim world, including caricature, editorial cartoons, and comics as well as illustrations for posters, books, and other mass-media items.

interpreted in many ways, including as a form of rebellion against Iranian cultural norms. Aliabadi has collaborated with Farhad Moshiri to create other works that comment on the lifestyles of young Iranians. Like Moshiri's art, Aliabadi's work appeals to affluent and sophisticated collectors, Muslim and non-Muslim alike.

Cartooning takes many forms in the Muslim world, including caricature, editorial cartoons, and comics as well as illustrations for posters, books, and other mass-media items. It is also the primary medium for representing people, animals, and other elements of the physical world, as well as a medium in which artists sharply express their points of view. One such artist is the Syrian Sahar Burhan (b. 1967). Her simple line drawings have been published in newsprint and the Internet and are analyzed on Muslim blogs and message boards. Another such artist is Shahid Atiqullah (b. 1955), the most widely published editorial cartoonist in Afghanistan, whose spare drawings are also exhibited in art galleries and cartoon expos in both Muslim and Western nations.

Seyran Caferli's deceptively delicate, watercolor cartoons received second prize in the 2008 Tehran International Cartoon Biennial. Caferli (b. 1966) is typical of Muslim artists in many media, in that he is active in artists' organizations in his own country of Azerbaijan as well as participating in activities on an international level.

The uses and displays of calligraphy as a graphic medium in the Muslim world defy any summary, but four examples may serve to communicate the possibilities that currently exist. One of the pioneers of calligraphy in contemporary art was Shakir Hassan al-Said, of Iraq, for whom the drawing of letter forms, as well as non-alphabetical calligraphy, became a form of mystical meditation. Al Said (1925–2004) was one of the first Iraqi artists to merge modern Western ideas of art with traditional western Asian forms.

Haji Noor Deen Mi Guang Jiang (b. 1963) is a Chinese Muslim calligrapher whose fusion of Arabic letter forms and Chinese techniques has resulted in a

This photograph shows *Kuba*, a video art installation by Kutlug Ataman that was displayed in 2005 in a warehouse in London.

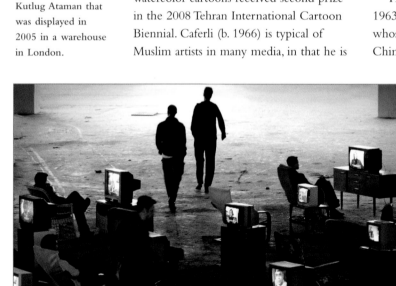

unique new approach to Islamic graphic art forms. Noor Deen has come to world attention for his achievements and has conducted workshops at Harvard, Cambridge (England), and the Massachusetts Institute of Technology (MIT), among other renowned universities. A 2008 calendar featuring 12 examples of Noor Deen's work reflects the Islamic blessing of everyday life.

Another graphic artist is Ali Omar Ermes (b. 1945), who was born in Libya but has lived in London since the early 1980s. Ermes usually focuses on the shape of single letters. Because he uses a brush and because his technique departs from the strict conventions of calligraphy, many of Ermes's works are more accurately classified as paintings. Yet *The Letter "Kaf"* (1991) is very stark and graphic—and, indeed, it is a serigraph, a form of limited edition printing. In this work, Ermes uses the blocky Maghribi script of northern Africa to create a shape that has a disciplined, monumental presence.

Finally, because calligraphy is so fluid, translating it into the fixed medium of type is a particular challenge. Mamoun Sakkal, a Syrian-born architect and graphic designer based in Washington State, has created a collection of greeting cards and translated Arabic script into fonts that can be used on computers. Among his digital fonts is a version of the weighty, angular Kufi script, which was favored during the early Islamic era and was often used in architectural inscription; Sakkal's font can be adapted to varied typographical weights. Sakkal also invented a font in Naskh for Microsoft Word. Naskh (a variant form of Arabic) is another old script that has been extensively used for copying the Koran and the Hadiths.

INSTALLATION ART

Installation art is about creating a whole from materials and objects and the space they occupy. An installation can incorporate everything from food to stacks of newspapers to immense video screens; all have been exhibited as part of the form. Given their multimedia nature, installations are often the work of multimedia artists whose other projects may involve film or still photography.

One of the most important and productive contemporary installation and film artists is Kutlug Ataman (b. 1961), who divides his time between Istanbul (Turkey), London (England), and California. Ataman came to the United States as a young man after being arrested in his native Turkey for alleged left-wing political activities. He received his BA and MFA from the University of California, Los Angeles. Ataman's work does not exist solely within the Muslim world but bridges the Muslim and Western worlds.

One of Ataman's most important works is his video installation *Paradise*, which debuted in 2007 at the Orange County Museum of Art in California. The title refers to an ideal place that lies at the heart of Islamic and Christian beliefs alike. In Ataman's art, Orange County is treated as Paradise; the installation features real people talking about their lives there. Another of Ataman's noted works is *Twelve*, which was shortlisted for Britain's Turner Prize in 2004. In this installation, 12 Syrian men and women tell their stories of reincarnation; each narrative is presented on its own screen, and stools are provided for the audience to sit on. Ataman's art focuses on the dignity and beauty of people and their lives in ways that can be perceived as intrinsically Muslim.

See Also

Scripture and Doctrine 102–123 ❖ Arts Festivals 220–221 ❖ Architecture 222–245 ❖ Literature 248–267 ❖ Performing Arts 270–289 ❖

Arts Festivals

Arts festivals allow Muslim communities to improve public understanding of their culture, preserve traditional forms of cultural expression, and foster the development of new forms.

The societies of the Muslim world have a long history of rich and diverse cultural expression. In each of the regions to which Islam has spread, the visual language of Islamic art and design interact with local traditions to create new and different forms of cultural expression. In Western countries like the United States, in which Muslims represent a minority of the population, the Muslim communities of many colleges and cities have begun to organize arts festivals and events to raise the profile of Muslim art and dispel myths about the culture of the Muslim world. Similar, larger-scale events have been held in some parts of the Muslim world in recent years with the aim of raising the profile of Muslim culture on a global scale.

THE PURPOSE OF ARTS FESTIVALS

In the aftermath of the terrorist attacks on the United States on September 11, 2001, many Muslim organizations and communities felt that it was important that the general public was provided with a range of perspectives on Islam and Muslims, beyond the fundamentalist ideologies that were the focus of media attention at the time. Muslim arts festivals in the United States are often eager to stress the broad and varied range of cultural and spiritual traditions within the Muslim world, as well as the ways in which these cultural traditions have been integrated into the culture of the United States. In addition to exhibitions of the traditional art, dance, crafts, and literature of the Muslim world, arts festivals feature the work of American Muslim artists, writers, musicians, and comedians.

On university campuses, Muslim students celebrate their Islamic cultures by designating a week, known as "Islam Awareness Week" for educational events, public performances, and demonstrations of traditional crafts. During this week, every campus has its own program of celebration under the auspices of the MSA (Muslim Students Association). The purpose of these events is to promote positive images of Islam and Muslims and also to correct established stereotypes about Muslim beliefs and culture. Islam Awareness Week, among other activities, includes an array of artistic events, such as exhibitions, theatrical performances, cooking classes, and fashion shows.

A typical example of this type of Muslim arts festival is the Indiana University "Middle Eastern Arts Festival." This festival encompasses all the religions and cultures of the Middle East, as well as the cultures of Muslim nations around the world. The program features music and dance from the Middle East, art exhibitions, museum events,

The purpose of these events is to promote positive images of Islam and Muslims and also to correct established stereotypes about Muslim beliefs and culture.

and presentations by artists and scholars. Exhibits of calligraphic manuscripts in Arabic are hosted in the university library and there are performances by dancers from Egypt, Saudi Arabia, Lebanon, and Turkey.

OLD AND NEW CULTURAL FORMS

For many Islamic arts festivals, the most important attraction is an exhibition of art from the Muslim world, usually loaned to a local museum from private collections or from the collections of other museums around the

Dancers dressed in traditional Persian costumes dance along Madison Avenue, New York, during the first annual Persian Parade held in 2004 on the Persian New Year. The parade celebrates the culture of the city's large Iranian American population.

world. These exhibitions celebrate the art and culture of the Muslim world, from ancient Mesopotamian statues to the work of contemporary Muslim artists. In the months after the events of September 11th, 2001, for example, many small exhibitions and cultural events were arranged in New York to coincide with major exhibitions of art from the Muslim world at Metropolitan Museum of Art.

There is more to these cultural festivals than just demonstrations of traditional cultural expression, however. Muslim culture in the United States, like Muslim culture in other countries, has changed and adapted, incorporating aspects of local culture and thought into traditional forms of cultural expression. Since the terrorist attacks on the United States on September 11, 2001, many comedians with Muslim ethnic backgrounds began to use material based on their cultural background and their personal experiences of current attitudes toward Muslims in the United States. In 2003, building on the success of comedy shows like the *Axis of Evil Comedy Tour*, a group of Arab-American comedians founded the "New York Arab-American Comedy Festival," a yearly event that has

since expanded to showcase the work of Arab-American musicians, actors, and playwrights, as well as popular comedians such as Negin Farsad, Ahmed Ahmed, and Dean Obeidallah.

Celebrations of Islamic art and performance are not limited to large urban areas and college towns, however. Islamic art exhibitions and small community festivals are now held across the United States. Small galleries around the country have exhibited the work of Muslim artists such as Asma Ahmed Shikoh, whose paintings and installations examine the relationship between Islam and Western culture, especially in relation to Muslim women; Salma Arastu, whose abstract paintings incorporate elements of both Western and Islamic artistic tradition; and Mohamed Zakariya, whose traditional Islamic calligraphy has won numerous awards in the Islamic world.

Chapter 10

ARCHITECTURE

Islamic architecture had its origins in seventh-century Arabia. It then spread to Egypt, Syria, Mesopotamia, India, northern Africa, and the Iberian Peninsula in the wake of the Muslim conquest of those vast and varied regions, from which it in turn absorbed many architectural elements. It is now found throughout the world.

Of all the forms of Islamic art, architecture is the most readily accessible. Wealthy and powerful patrons commissioned architects to express the patron's piety and might through monumental mosques, tombs, palaces, and other buildings. Because many of the original building materials were delicate and fragile, the ravages of climate and time have wiped away many of the earliest structures, but enough of them have survived—either in the form of buildings that are still standing or as records in books, paintings, and plans—to give historians a fairly clear sense of the origins and development of architecture in the Muslim world.

The growth of Muslim architecture may be split chronologically into medieval, early modern, colonial, and contemporary phases. In turn, the chronological periods can be subdivided by geography. Different traditions link the Arab lands, comprising the Arabian Peninsula, Mesopotamia, Syria, and Egypt; a Eurasian region composed of Anatolia (modern Turkey) and the Balkans; and northern Africa, including not only Algeria, Morocco, and Tunisia but also, by

Aleppo, Syria, is architecturally typical of cities in the modern Muslim world.

extension, the Iberian Peninsula, which came under Muslim rule in medieval times. Other important stylistic sectors include Central Asia, a region comprising modern Afghanistan, Iran, Kazakhstan, Kyrgyzstan, Tajikistan, Turkmenistan, and Uzbekistan; the South Asian subcontinent, incorporating Bangladesh, India, and Pakistan; and finally, Islamic Southeast Asia, including Brunei, Indonesia, and Malaysia. Parts of China, the Philippines, and Thailand also have significant Muslim populations and notable examples of Islamic architecture.

With the migration of Muslims to western Europe and North America from the 20th century on, a new tradition of mosque design has emerged as the latest addition to this architectural mosaic. The same holds true to a lesser extent in certain Latin American countries. Muslim architecture in the 21st century is found virtually throughout the world.

Architects working in the Muslim tradition have used local building materials, whether stone, brick, or wood, and have learned from the other cultures with which they come into contact. They have also employed a variety of different techniques. Typically, surfaces may be decorated with geometric, floral, vegetal, and calligraphic patterns, in stone, brick, stucco, wood or glazed, patterned tiles.

ARCHITECTS IN THE MUSLIM WORLD

The builders of the earliest mosques, forts, palaces, bazaars, baths, caravansaries, tombs, and other structures were for the most part anonymous craftspeople who used techniques that had first been employed

IBN TULUN MOSQUE

Built by Ahmad ibn Tulun in 879 and in a remarkable state of preservation, the Ibn Tulun Mosque in Cairo, Egypt, provides a striking example of the structural techniques and decoration of the earliest period of mosque design. Its large central court is enclosed by colonnades five aisles deep on one side and two aisles deep on the other three sides. Brick piers with engaged columns, also molded in brick, support stilted, pointed arches. All the surfaces are coated with fine, hard stucco into which ornamental bands, soffits (overhangs), capitals (the tops of columns), and bases

are cut. The openwork windows are of alabaster. The minaret has an exterior open stair that winds in ziggurat fashion from the two square lower rounds around the circular upper extension to reach an octagonal kiosk. Architectural historians believe that the mosque might have imitated, on a smaller scale, the vast Friday Mosque, built 30 years earlier in the Abbasid capital of Samarra and long since destroyed.

This photograph shows the minaret of the Ibn Tulun mosque in Cairo, Egypt.

many centuries before the rise of Islam; some of their working methods are still in use today. The architects of the Muslim world included specialists who were highly trained in calculation and design and were capable of imaginative, innovative, spatial ideas and brilliant craftspeople who performed the dual roles of designer and builder. Unsurprisingly, given the concentration of patronage, whether imperial or mercantile, in urban areas, most of the builders found employment in cities. Many traveled long distances to undertake commissions wherever their skills were required.

Some individuals in the western Islamic countries are known to have received formal architectural training from the late 18th century on. However, little is known about the practitioners of earlier times. With the exception of a few famous names, most of them worked anonymously until the modern era, in part because the profession was often practiced in families, with skills being handed down across the generations.

PLACES OF WORSHIP

The foremost Muslim contribution to world architecture is the mosque, which is designed as a place for congregational worship. The Arabic word for mosque, *masjid*, literally means "the place where one prostrates oneself in veneration." The Koran specifies in separate suras that a place of worship should be set aside as a sanctuary and that the direction of prayer should be indicated in some way: "And now verily We shall make you turn (in prayer) toward a *qibla* (direction of prayer) that is dear to you. So turn your face toward the *masjid al-haram* (Mecca) and, wheresoever you may be, turn your faces (when you pray) toward it."

The quotation makes no mention of a building, only of a place to pray. The specific call is to prayer because every adult Muslim, male or female, is bound to observe the five *salat*s (daily prayers) at dawn, midday, in the afternoon, at sunset, and in the late evening. In addition, Friday is the weekly day of communal worship, when all adult male Muslims are expected to come together for prayers at midday. Finally, *salat*s are performed annually on the two Eids (festivals), one at the end of Ramadan, the other after the hajj.

The very first mosque was Muhammad's own house in Medina. It took the form of a simple rectangular enclosure, containing rooms for the Prophet and his wives along with a shaded area on the south side of the courtyard that could be used to pray in the direction of Mecca. That building became the model for subsequent mosques, which retained the same basic courtyard layout, with an area for prayer provided against the *qibla* wall. An early development of that basic plan was the provision of shade on the other three sides of the courtyard. The roofs of those colonnaded areas were supported by wooden columns.

Several features that were later to become standard elements of mosque design were introduced at an early stage. The first was the *minbar* (pulpit), which was used by Muhammad to deliver sermons. Then there was the *mihrab* (prayer niche), which was always located in the *qibla* wall. The minaret—a towerlike structure that is the most conspicuous feature of mosques in many Muslim societies—has the least liturgical significance of all these basic elements. Its purpose of providing a platform from which to call the faithful to prayer has largely been made redundant by the advent of electronic public address systems in modern times. Like minarets, the domed mosque was also a later innovation. To this day, the primary feature of mosque design is a *qibla* wall facing Mecca, with a niche in the center where the imam stands to lead the congregation in prayer.

PALACES AND ROYAL DWELLINGS

Architects designed palaces from the early days of the Islamic era, but most of the early complexes have vanished. They were often built of relatively fragile materials such as wood or mud bricks that failed to withstand the ravages of time. Varying in plan and size, Muslim palaces were often agglomerations of units arranged around interior courts. They were often set in extensive gardens or had gardens within them, and those green oases provided shade and cooling in the hot, dry climates of much of the Muslim world.

By far the best-known surviving Islamic palace is the Alhambra, built for the Moorish rulers of the kingdom of Granada in southern Spain. The Alhambra dates from the 14th and 15th centuries and the complex actually comprises several palaces built for a succession of kings.

The Alhambra contains numerous patios, or terraces. The most famous are the Court of the Lions and the Myrtle Court, each of which have chambers of officials adjoining them. Those courts are richly decorated with tiles of many shapes and colors and with polychrome stuccos carved in rich patterns. The vaults and domes of the Alhambra are decorated with *muqarna*s (a kind of decoration that resembles stalactites adorning the wooden ceilings). Around the courts are arcades, which have unusually slender columns that support multicolored filigree stucco arches.

The Alhambra stands on a rocky outcrop above the city of Granada, Spain. Visible in the background is the Sierra Nevada mountain range.

Historians of Muslim art generally regard the Alhambra as the highpoint of palace architecture in the Islamic world.

HOUSES AND HOMES

Although Islam has given social coherence to vernacular buildings throughout the Muslim world, it is often difficult to distinguish domestic architecture by religion alone. Traditionally, the predominant house layout throughout the Islamic world has been the courtyard plan, which offers both physical and social advantages to residents. The protection offered by the compound wall is psychologically and practically important in both rural and urban areas; in towns, the compound walls also serve as divisions between dwellings. The courtyard offers privacy, albeit at the expense of outward views other than onto the street itself. The system allows a high density of site usage. This was an important consideration in historic times, when settlements were limited by the size of their city walls and by the necessity of carrying water from wells and fountains.

The courtyard is also very effective in moderating climatic conditions in desert or tropical regions. With minimal ground exposure, a complex of courtyard housing has the advantage of providing a high level of protection against harsh sunlight. The lower levels of habitation are well shaded, as are the narrow streets.

The functional and climatic advantages of such an arrangement are the principal causes of its resilience. In places where dwellings were built so close together and rooftops were used as sleeping areas, it became unacceptable for one structure to be higher than another. Overlooking a neighboring roof was considered an invasion of privacy. As a consequence, common law emerged that effectively controlled the height of buildings, limiting them to the same level. This characteristic urban form was found throughout western Asia and to some extent also in Central and South Asia, except in hilly areas.

The height and orientation of buildings have traditionally been determined by considerations such as the prevailing wind direction. Towers reach up to catch cool breezes in Afghanistan, Iran, Pakistan, and the states of the Persian Gulf, as well as in

Urban society is drawn into closely knit groups, of which the most important focuses on the mosque, attended daily by the local male population.

parts of northern India. In the Iraqi cities of Karbala, Mosul, and Baghdad, wind scoops project above the walls to catch the summer northwesterlies, deflecting the dry air into cool, damp basements. Each different type of building gives the areas in which it is located a distinct local character.

In response to social and practical needs, builders in the Muslim world created a structural matrix in which individual buildings dissolved into the larger urban conglomeration for the good of the community as a whole. To this day, many substantial houses in Aleppo, Baghdad, Cairo, Damascus, Isfahan, and Lahore have only a single door providing access to the street. Such buildings have no external elevation or view whatsoever. A fundamental cause of this feature of Islamic architecture is the philosophical

This photograph shows typical houses on stilts in Sulawesi, Indonesia.

background of Islam, which emphasizes social cohesion. Urban society is drawn into closely knit groups, of which the most important focuses on the mosque, attended daily by the local male population. The geographically determined orientation of the mosque itself may set the alignment for the housing that surrounds it. That orientation is in turn often reinforced by the prayer focus within the home and the perception that some directions are more propitious than others. In other words, the cohesion of the Muslim city can be seen as a product of the prevailing social ethos and the influence of faith, as well as of long tradition, available materials, and the effects of climate.

There are many regional variations on the courtyard house pattern. In the Hijaz region of Saudi Arabia, the upland cities of Mecca and Medina have buildings made of stone. Although earlier domestic buildings have virtually been obliterated by the regeneration that accompanies wealth,

there was at one time an impressive tradition of multistory building, with street façades up to four stories high fronting complexes of courtyard structures. The clustered, multistory houses of the Saudi port city of Jidda produced towered streets, patterned and pulsating with visual energy. In Abha—the capital of Saudi Arabia's Asir province, a highland region of greater rainfall—there was a strong tradition of banded rubble walling laced with timber.

In the high, green lands of Yemen, battered walls and small openings have been combined to produce a semifortified aspect to homes. There, the courtyard tradition was abandoned in favor of high-rise developments. In the region around the capital, Sanaa, many walls are ornately adorned with whitened brick in intricate patterns. Heights vary and the buildings cluster, as they also do at stone-built Hajjara in the mountains and at Mukalla in the Hadramawt region on the Gulf of Aden. Inland, the cities of the Hadramawt rise eight or nine floors high. These are the "skyscrapers" of vernacular tradition: earth-rendered, many-windowed, and built of mud and stone. Shibam is the most famous of these once-remote towns of tightly planned houses, towering above the date palms of their fertile wadis, the upper rooms airy and private, with increasing numbers of windows as the buildings rise.

In Istanbul, Turkey, houses of similar floor plan rise five and six stories above the sparkling waters of the Bosphorus, which separates the European and Asian landmasses. Waterside timber façades have traditionally lined the shores of the waterway from Istanbul to the village of Emirgan. Leaning gently as decay has bitten into their lower levels, they, too, reflect the patterns and philosophies that pervade the region. Beneath them, in favored positions on the shore, stand single-story or balconied pleasure houses, built to centralized plans that are effectively those of the courtyard houses found across a region that stretches from northern Africa to northern and central India.

In Southeast Asia, domestic architecture traditionally responded directly to the environmental conditions of the region and to the available building materials. Until modern times, traditional homes were not designed by professional architects; instead, they were the work of skilled villagers, led by carpenters and masons. Across much of Indonesia, the region's wet, monsoonal climate required that traditional homes were built on stilts to avoid flooding. The raised floors served a variety of purposes; they allowed breezes to moderate the hot tropical temperatures, elevated the dwelling above the level of storm water runoff and mud, allowed houses to be built on rivers and wetland margins, kept people, goods, and food from dampness and moisture, and raised living quarters above the range of malaria-carrying mosquitoes.

Many forms of traditional Islamic architecture—the so-called *rumah adat*—have walls that are dwarfed by a large roof, often saddle-shaped, that is supported independently by sturdy piles. In general, traditional styles of roofing are sharply inclined to allow tropical downpours to drain off quickly and feature large, overhanging eaves, designed to keep water out of the house and to provide shade on sunny days. In particular, the houses of the Batak people in Sumatra and the Toraja people in Sulawesi are noted for their stilted shapes with great, upsweeping ridge ends that recall the shape of boats. In hot and humid low-lying coastal regions,

homes can have many windows to provide good cross-ventilation, whereas in the cooler, mountainous interior, homes often have vast roofs and few windows. The traditional Malay house is a wooden building with tall, thatched roofs in three or more tiers.

FUNERARY BUILDINGS

Another widespread feature of Islamic architecture is the monumental tomb. The Prophet Muhammad disapproved of excessively ostentatious graves, and some interpretations of Islamic tradition have also frowned on them. Despite this, a strong tradition of funerary architecture developed in many parts of the Muslim world.

The Taj Mahal is the most famous mausoleum in the Islamic world. It forms one of a series of imperial Mughal tombs, and its design is considered the high point of Muslim funerary architecture. Built to house the body of Mumtaz Mahal (1593–1631), the principal wife of Emperor Shah Jahan, who was eventually also buried within its walls, it is located on a terrace on the banks of the Jumna River overlooking the imperial palace in Agra, which at the time was the capital of the Mughal Empire. Fronted by walled gardens adorned with a famous reflecting pool, the Taj Mahal is the centerpiece of an architectural complex that took around 20 years to build.

The Taj Mahal is said to have been conceived as a vast allegory of the Day of Resurrection, when the dead will rise to be judged under the divine throne. Specifically, the complex was designed to represent paradise, the hoped-for destination of those buried within its walls. Its garden is entered through a magnificent sandstone gateway, and features four water

The gardens of the Taj Mahal are intended to represent those of Paradise.

channels that replicate the four rivers of paradise. The raised marble tank at the intersection of the channels recalls the celestial tank of abundance. The tomb itself stands for the seat from which Allah will dispense justice, its four minarets representing the four supports of the divine throne of medieval cosmology.

The allegory is spelled out by Koranic calligraphy, which appears on the surface of the main gateway and also on the tomb's arches; in particular, sura 89 of the Koran, quoted on the gateway to the complex, reminds believers of the dread Day of Judgment as well as of God's mercy. The principal architect of the Taj Mahal is thought to have been Ustad Ahmad of Lahore; the calligrapher was Amanat Khan of Shiraz in Iran.

MODERN MUSLIM ARCHITECTURE

The interaction of Islamic architecture with the building design traditions of the Western world started in the 19th century and intensified in the 20th century, when the traditional architectural vocabularies that had distinguished one region from another were increasingly subsumed in a common international style. Such major cities of the Muslim world as Aleppo, Baghdad, Bukhara, Cairo, Damascus, Delhi, Isfahan, Istanbul, Lahore, Rabat, Tehran, and Tunis were transformed by the introduction of wide, straight thoroughfares that cut through the existing, mazelike fabric of narrow, winding lanes and cul-de-sacs and set the patterns of future urban growth. The street, which had previously been merely an artery of communication, became a distinct component of the urban conglomeration in its own right.

Traditional Islamic architectural elements and planning concepts were gradually abandoned in favor of Western ones. Such features as wooden latticework and complicated entry sequences separating the interior of a structure from the street were abandoned, while new features, such as concepts of overall symmetry and frontal axiality and the use of classical orders, became fashionable. Western building types gradually replaced traditional ones; the primary and secondary school, the polytechnic, and the university were substituted for the madrassa (the old-style Islamic school), and the villa or apartment unit replaced the courtyard house. At the same time, new construction methods and materials were introduced: steel and, more importantly, reinforced concrete became widespread. Western-trained architects and engineers acquired overwhelming influence. Some came from Europe and North America, but others were local people who had trained either in the West or in new local schools established on European models. Professional organizations and, to a lesser extent, labor unions replaced the traditional guilds.

CONTEMPORARY TRENDS

As architecture in the Islamic world became increasingly integrated into the international style, only one type of building retained a clear and autonomous Islamic identity: the mosque. The Islamic revival, itself a Western design methodology, appeared in the 1860s and influenced a return to the heritage of the Islamic world. Revivalism played a dominant role in mosque architecture of the first half of the 20th century.

ALHAMRA ARTS COUNCIL, LAHORE, PAKISTAN

Pakistan's cultural life received a major boost when the Alhamra Arts Council decided to construct a permanent building for its activities. As a first step, architect Nayyar Ali Dada designed a 1,000-seat multipurpose auditorium that was opened in 1979. Additional buildings followed, and the complex was completed in 1992. Throughout its construction, the same basic concepts were preserved, centering on various combinations of polygonal shapes designed to meet the acoustic requirements of the performing arts. Those forms were ingeniously placed in a setting of semi-enclosed courtyards and green spaces. Another basic idea was the use of handmade red bricks with traditional local mortar as a veneer covering the cast-in-place concrete walls. Red brick is the main building material of the Lahore Fort and Badshahi Mosque, the two most important historic buildings in the city. It was also the material most widely used by the British in colonial times, and additionally recalls the red sandstone architecture of Mughal Lahore. Through the skillful use of local materials and traditional forms, Dada evoked the memory of the Mughal forts. The Alhamra Arts Council complex appropriately provides a sense of continuous identity, linking the young nation of Pakistan to the ancient heritage of the South Asian subcontinent.

This mosque in the United Arab Emirates is a synthesis of modern architecture and traditional Muslim religious values.

However, revivalism and historicism proved to be no substitute for innovation and creativity, and it was not long before architects began to question the received wisdom. The projects of the Egyptian architect Hassan Fathy (1900–1989) provided early examples of a different approach. Fathy's chief interest lay in housing the poor in a healthy environment at minimal cost. He successfully applied time-honored design methods and trained rural Egyptians to make their own building materials.

In his design for the village of New Qurna near Luxor, Fathy sought inspiration in the architecture of his native Egyptian countryside, using vernacular forms for the various structures, including the mosque, along with local materials and construction techniques. The buildings, erected by the villagers themselves, have bearing walls and vaults of mud brick, not reinforced concrete, built thick to keep the houses cool in hot weather. Fathy's work was largely unremarked at first but, by the 1970s, it had begun to influence architects in many developing countries.

From the late 1940s to the 1960s, such architects as Sedad Hakki Eldem of Turkey, Rifat Chadirji of Iraq, and Kamil Khan Mumtaz of Pakistan began to reject direct revivalism and to advocate in its place a more sparse use of surface ornament for most types of buildings. The mosque, however, was problematical, because providing a sense of visual continuity with the past was difficult to reconcile with the conflicting need to incorporate the essentially ahistorical architectural developments of recent times. One solution was to adhere to historicism and ignore modern developments; that was the approach adopted in the Uthman Mosque in Damascus, which was designed by Muhammad Farra in 1961 and completed in 1974. Another solution attempted to synthesize the two requirements by preserving traditional elements, usually the minaret and the dome, but abstracting them into a more contemporary arrangement that maintained a visual link with the past. Early examples of that synthesis include Eriche Baharuddin's Negara Mosque in Kuala Lumpur (started in 1956, completed in 1967) and Walter Gropius's project for the mosque at Baghdad University (completed in 1958), which included a large, bulbous dome touching the ground at three points and placed within a circular reflecting pool.

A third solution to the clash of styles rejected revivalism altogether. Mosques inspired by that approach, such as that built for the Etimesgüt Armed Units in Ankara, Turkey (designed in 1965 by Cengiz Bektas), the Sharafuddin White Mosque in Visoko, Bosnia (designed in 1967 by Zlatko Ugljen, completed in 1980), and the Aisha

Bakkar Mosque in Beirut (designed in 1970 by Jaafar Tuqan), reflect the influence of 20th-century European modernist architects, such as Le Corbusier and Alvar Aalto. In all three mosques, visual connections with the past are almost nonexistent. The dome is absent, while minarets are transformed into highly abstracted vertical elements. Despite their architectural merit, these ahistorical mosques have not achieved much popularity and remain few in number.

In the 1970s, mosque construction accelerated due to a rise in religious sentiment. That quantitative change was accompanied by more varied approaches to design. Earlier efforts to combine the traditional with the contemporary continued. More conservative combinations marked the works of such architects as Muhammad Makiya. In his religious buildings, most notably the State Mosque in Kuwait (1976–1984), traditional elements are emphasized over

Qurna in Egypt is a modern development that has maintained traditional Islamic architectural principles.

contemporary ones. The courtyard of the
mosque is surrounded by porticos, which
are made of exposed concrete and have flat
lintels instead of arches.

Mosques showing a higher level of
experimentation have proved quite
popular. Like Gropius's design for the
mosque at Baghdad University, these
structures are often highly expressionist,
even flamboyant. One example is the King
Faisal Mosque in Islamabad, Pakistan
(designed in 1970 by Vedat Dalokay and
completed in 1984), which takes its
inspiration from the imperial mosques of
the Ottoman period.

Several architects have modified the
ideas expressed by Hassan Fathy in his

Modern architects are making
sure that the new architecture
gives a sense of place by
the incorporation of, and reference
to, local icons.

design for New Qurna. In a series of
mosques designed in Jidda and Medina
during the 1980s, Abdulwahid Alwakil
maintained some of Fathy's vernacularly
inspired forms and his use of traditional
materials and construction techniques,
combining those characteristics with direct
revivalist elements, mostly borrowed from
Egypt's Mamluk and Ottoman architectural
heritage. In the Great Mosque in Riyadh,
Saudi Arabia (completed in 1985), the
Jordanian architect Rasem Badran used
contemporary technology but sought to
relate the design to the vernacular
architecture of the Najd, the region in
which the mosque is located.

MODERN SECULAR ARCHITECTURE

Beyond the sacred architecture of mosques,
architects working in the Muslim world
since the mid-20th century have had
to respond to the challenges of new
technology, expanding populations,
changing economic conditions, and
renewed national aspirations.

Architects now pay attention to a call to
design projects that are labor-intensive,
helping address the problem of widespread
unemployment. They are highly conscious
of environmental conditions and the
specific demands of the site. They are
careful to use local building materials and
techniques but seek to use modern
technology where appropriate while at the
same time integrating old techniques into
contemporary applications. They also
commonly seek to involve local
populations in decision making in large-
scale projects. Finally, modern architects are
making sure that the new architecture gives
a sense of place by the incorporation of,
and reference to, local icons.

For many countries, retaining and
perpetuating a sense of national identity
is an important function of architecture.
Changing social norms and gender
relations are also beginning to influence
the way in which buildings are designed
and built.

Some representative examples from
different parts of the Muslim world
can help suggest the variety of the
new architectural environment. One major
structure, undertaken in Egypt in the final
years of the 20th century, shows a clear
sense of continuity with the historic past.
Built close to where the great library of
Alexandria stood in late Classical times,
the new Bibliotheca Alexandrina is an
architectural landmark intended to revive

the spirit of its celebrated predecessor in the contemporary world.

The building's main feature is a slanted, disk-shaped roof emerging from the ground. The structure is divided into cells, designed in the abstracted shape of human eyes and eyelids, to allow natural light to filter into the grand reading hall below. The hall itself, divided into seven terraced levels following the inclination of the roof above, enjoys excellent light, providing a comfortable and pleasing environment for study. The size of the building—11 stories high and 525 feet (160 m) in diameter— might seem overwhelming, but the fact that four stories are below ground level reduces the apparent height. With deceptively simple façades and a wide piazza, as well as a gently inclined roof, the building is light, open, and inviting.

OPULENCE IN THE GULF STATES

Until the oil boom of the 1970s, Dubai was a small fishing and trading port, but since then it has prospered enormously. In 2008, the city-state on the Persian Gulf had a population of 1.6 million people and a $37 billion economy based largely on trade, manufacturing, and financial services. Although the economy was badly hit by the economic downturn of 2008–2009, Dubai's wealth had already changed the face of the city with ambitious architectural projects. With a focus on business and tourism, the city saw construction on an unprecedented level—in 2008, it was reported that it contained one-quarter of all the world's building cranes.

One of the centerpieces of the Dubai construction boom is the Burj al-Arab (Tower of the Arabs), a luxury hotel

KAMPUNG KALI CHO-DE

Kampung Kali Cho-De is an urban village settlement built on government-owned land on the banks of the Cho-De River in Yogyakarta, Indonesia. The site was previously used as a refuse dump. The inhabitants comprised 30 or 40 families whose members provided menial labor for the city market nearby. All the squatter dwellings originally consisted of cardboard cartons covered in plastic sheeting, which disintegrated, along with the site itself, in every heavy rainstorm.

In 1983, the Yogyakarta municipal authorities were on the point of demolishing the settlement when they were persuaded by a community leader, Willi Prasetya, and a self-taught local architect, Yusuf B. Mangunwijaya, to maintain the site and upgrade it. Work began that year and was completed by 1985.

The design process required few drawings. The narrow, steeply sloping site was shored up by a series of stone retaining walls. The refuse had been compacted over many years into a foundation firm enough to permit lightweight construction, and it proved able to support traditional wooden A-frame stilt houses built on simple conical concrete footings. Bamboo posts were used for joists, and plaited bamboo for walls and floor covering. The roofs were made of tiling or corrugated iron. Three carpenters and two masons from rural villages provided the only hired labor; the rest of the workforce consisted of the tenants and volunteers. In consultation with local art students, the tenants painted the exteriors of their houses with traditional animal, plant, and monster motifs. This small-scale village project is a good prototype for others in Indonesia and beyond.

This photograph shows the Burj al-Arab hotel in Dubai. Note its resemblance to the sails of an Arab dhow (sailing ship).

designed by British architect Tom Wright and completed in 1999. Standing 1,053 feet (321 m) high, it is the world's tallest building to be used exclusively as a hotel. The skyscraper stands on an artificial island, connected to the mainland by a curving bridge. It is an iconic structure, designed to symbolize Dubai's urban transformation and to mimic the sail of a traditional Arab boat.

While the exterior of the Burj al-Arab manifests an ultramodern sculptural design, the interior guest space is a compilation of lavish architectural styles employing motifs from East and West. Some critics see the building as a monument to the triumph of money over practicality. One journalist described it in the following terms: "Fabulous, hideous, and the very pinnacle of tackiness—like Vegas after a serious, no-expense-spared, sheik-over."

In another Gulf state, Kuwait, there has been a noteworthy attempt to combine luxury leisure development with utilitarian practicality. Kuwait's water towers, now icons of that small country, are the most visible aspect of a supply and distribution network connected to two existing seawater desalination plants.

Built in 1976 by a Swedish firm, the main tower is a hollow concrete column approximately 600 feet (about 185 m) high that supports two spheres. The larger sphere, 245 feet (75 m) across, contains a restaurant, banquet hall, cafeteria, and indoor garden, all set above a reservoir contained in the lower half of the sphere with a water capacity of about 160,000 cubic feet (about 4,500 cu. m). The smaller sphere above it is approximately 400 feet (about 120 m) tall and houses a revolving observatory with a café. The second tower of the group, which is not accessible to the public, supports a spherical water tank. Except for glazed areas, the spheres of both towers are surfaced in steel plates enameled in bright colors, serving as sun reflectors and inspired by mosaic-surfaced Islamic domes. A third structure, a concrete needle equipped with floodlights, illuminates the other two towers. All the other towers in the system are mushroom-shaped and painted in varied patterns and colors.

MARRYING STYLE AND FUNCTION

The desire to combine striking visual appeal with practical efficiency also informs the Hajj Terminal at Jidda Airport, Saudi Arabia. Designed by the U.S. firm of Smith, Owing, and Merrill, this structure is the gateway to Mecca for most of the million or more pilgrims who fly to the holy city each year. The Hajj Terminal is designed to accommodate a maximum of 50,000 people for up to 18 hours in its arrival hall, while the departure facilities can accommodate 80,000 people for periods of up to 36 hours.

Roofed by a fabric tension structure that covers a greater area (100 acres, or 40.5 hectares) than any other roof in the world, the terminal provides benches, banks, shops, and restrooms for pilgrims. The terminal comprises 10 modules, grouped into two lots of five separated by a landscaped mall. Each of the modules consists of 21 tent units 150 feet (46 m) square, giving the two large terminal units a total of 210 tents between them. The tents are hooked to steel rings hung from suspension cables that are draped from single pylons in the interior of the module, from ladderlike double pylons at the module edges and from four-pylon towers at the corners. The air-conditioned arrival buildings are located under the tents along the outside edge of the terminal units, parallel to the aircraft aprons. The imaginative design of the roofing system is both elegant and functional, making it an icon of the new architecture of Saudi Arabia.

The problems posed by the construction of a new Social Security Complex in Istanbul, Turkey, were of a very different order but were well addressed by a local architect, Sedad Hakki Eldem. In the 1960s, when the project was designed, and during its construction stages, Turkish architects were engaged in a reassessment of the tenets of the modern movement, leading them to seek a "new regionalism" as an answer to the dominance of the International Style. Eldem's office complex reconciles elements of both theoretical positions. The plan is as disciplined and rational as the modernist canon requires, yet also responds to its regional context, remaining sensitive to its site, which is a steeply sloping plot at the corner of a major intersection, and respecting the historic landmarks nearby. At the time of its design, its architect would normally have been expected to assemble the space into a high-rise slab that dominated its setting. However, Eldem's low, cascading structure links a dense old quarter of wooden houses at the top of the hill with the contemporary buildings that line the modern boulevard below. Architectural critics around the globe consider the building to be one of the earliest and most refined examples of contextual architecture in the international modern movement.

An Agricultural School in Africa

In Guinea, on the Atlantic coast of Africa, the design of the Kahere Eila Poultry Farming School has resonated throughout the developing world as an example of architecture that is democratic and accessible in both form and function.

The school's remarkable story began in the early 1980s when Alpha Diallo, an agronomist, and his uncle Bachir, a veterinarian, formed the idea of setting up a poultry farm to help improve the diet of Guineans. Both men won scholarships to study in Europe. Alpha went to Hungary, where he developed an interest in the Finnish language (which is related to Hungarian) that led him to translate the *Kalevala*, Finland's national epic, into his native language, Fulani. On a visit to Finland, he met Eila Kivekäs, a local anthropologist. When Alpha died suddenly in Finland in 1984, Kivekäs arranged for his body to be returned home.

Soon afterward, Bachir, then in Canada, received a phone call from Kivekäs, who proposed that he return to Guinea and work with her on the poultry project, which Alpha had discussed with her. The two started work in 1986 at Koliagbe, near Kindia, a town 75 miles (120 km) from the coast. Three years later, Kivekäs founded a development association named Indigo, which went into partnership with the farm.

From its inception, education was one of the project's primary missions. In 1997, when the facilities could no longer accommodate the number of students and trainees, Kivekäs proposed to Bachir that school facilities be provided near the main part of the farm. To build the school, she commissioned a Finnish firm of architects, Heikkinen-Komonen, which had worked on earlier Indigo projects, translating Finnish structural ideas to local craft conditions.

In the region around Kindia, the traditional form of dwelling is a round structure with a conical, thatched roof. Three variants on this type, each with a distinct function, are grouped around an open space, usually with a large tree in the center, which is the site for household activities, such as food preparation and laundry. The walls are usually made of clay bricks, fired in local kilns. The quality of the bricks is poor, and a considerable amount of wood is required for the firing.

For the new complex, three main areas were required: a classroom, student quarters for up to 12 people, and teachers' accommodation. Following local tradition, the architects organized those areas around a courtyard centered on a tree. They based their plan on a 4-foot (1.2 m) grid, imparting a simple but formal elegance to the architecture. For the construction, they employed wood-frame technology in combination with load-bearing walls made from double layers of specially developed, stabilized earth blocks. The blocks do not need firing, thereby helping to conserve resources. They also act as heat collectors, moderating room temperature, and their hard, smooth finish does not require rendering. The wider span of the classroom is covered with the aid of simple metal trusses combined with the wooden beams. The tallest columns, those of the classroom porch, are made of four posts fastened by intermediate wooden blocks and steel bolts, an economical way of overcoming a shortage of long pieces of hardwood. All the primary materials were sourced locally.

The significance of introducing new building techniques to the region is well illustrated by the example of the school's head mason. After training in the stabilized earth-block technique, he went on to use the blocks in private houses, small industrial installations, and even a mosque, which has greatly helped to boost local production of the blocks.

The Kahere Eila Poultry Farming School provides a rare example of architecture that successfully bridges cultures and building methods while also maintaining the local characteristics of its context. The elegant design combines the timber structures typical of Finland's native architecture with local African materials, improved by simple technological advances.

POST-INDEPENDENCE SOUTH ASIA

On gaining independence in 1947, Pakistan inherited the twin heritage of the Mughal emperors and the British Raj. Thereafter, Pakistani architecture developed under the influence of modernism, which reached a peak in the city of Islamabad, which was purpose-built in the 1960s to replace Karachi as the national capital. Although the city took its name from Islam, the original master plan ironically lacked a mosque, a gap that was rectified only in 1984 when the King Faisal Mosque was completed.

Initially part of Pakistan, Bangladesh achieved independence after a bitter civil war in 1971. At that time, a new parliament building was already under construction, having initially been authorized by the Pakistan government in 1961 as a home for the national legislature. The design was by the Estonian-born American architect Louis Kahn (1901–1974). Through a thoughtful and intelligent exploration of form, Kahn clarified an approach to architectural design that drew on local architectural traditions without merely copying them. Instead, Kahn reinterpreted and transformed the tradition through a process that applied concepts of construction technology to conditions specific to the designated capital of Bangladesh, Dhaka.

The result is a building that is universal in its architectural sources yet could have been constructed nowhere else. The National Assembly Building is divided into three zones, the central one of which houses the assembly itself, which takes the form of a 300-seat amphitheater. Around it

This photograph shows the lobby of the Datai Hotel on Langkawi Island, Malaysia.

lies an intermediate zone that connects to the public and press galleries, and which is surrounded in turn by an outer zone providing space for offices.

PRESTIGE PROJECTS IN MALAYSIA

Until the 1950s, Muslim architecture in what was then Malaya was a healthy mix of Indian Islamic and colonial styles, locally known as Moorish architecture. In the post-colonial 1960s, architects sought inspiration for a national style in traditional Malay houses—wooden buildings with tall thatched roofs in three or more tiers.

Since the 1980s, there has been an attempt to move toward forms that are identifiably more Islamic. Mosque architecture has produced an eclectic blend of Indian Islamic and Mughal influences, with a taste for domes, minarets, and traditional color schemes borrowed from the Egyptian Mamluk or Safavid Persian traditions. Some Malaysian postcolonial secular architecture continues to be inspired by local models, one example being the National Museum in Kuala Lumpur, whose roof takes the traditional form. In addition, however, a new generation of architects is going beyond familiar styles to experiment and innovate.

The Datai, a five-star hotel on a popular resort island in northern Malaysia, provides an example of how developers and architects can cooperate to achieve a synthesis of terrain and built form, blending vernacular styles and modernism along the way. The Australian architect Kerry Hill was involved in selecting the 1,850-acre (about 750 hectare) site, which includes a beach, an untouched rain forest, and a sensitive ecosystem of swamps, streams, and wildlife. The hotel contains 84 rooms divided between four blocks, linked by open walkways and arranged around a swimming pool. There are also 40 detached villas, which are located on the lower slopes of the site between the ridge and the beach. Communal areas, such as restaurants, a spa, and a beach house, are distributed around the site in pavilions, a form drawn from the local building vernacular.

The various elements of the complex also follow local traditions in being built on either stilts or heavy stone bases to protect them from ground dampness, and in the use of generous overhangs to provide shelter from heavy rainstorms. Local building materials, notably timber harvested from the forest, are used extensively throughout. The construction is an elegant synthesis of traditional and contemporary building methods. Alignments, finishing, joinery, and materials coalesce to create a sophisticated structural vocabulary. The

level of finish achieved has set a new regional standard.

Though finely wrought, the complex has been designed to weather naturally. A pleasing patina is already evident on railings and exposed wooden beams, which are not painted or polished but allowed to age naturally. Creepers grow over the stone bases of buildings, which are resistant to dampness. The open pavilions and walkways admit cooling breezes and generous shafts of light while enhancing a sense of interaction with nature. Since the local varieties of wood used for the interiors are also the predominant building material, the hotel offers a seamless integration of interior and exterior. The hotel's popularity is a testament to the architect, whose responsible and sensitive approach has provided a luxurious and sophisticated ambience while respecting a remote and fragile natural environment.

THE PETRONAS TOWERS

The challenges facing the builders of the Petronas Towers, located in the heart of the Malaysian capital, Kuala Lumpur, were of a very different order. The skyscrapers

ZAHA HADID

Born in Baghdad in 1950 and later based in London, by the start of the 21st century Zaha Hadid was among the most famous contemporary Muslim architects. Many of her most important projects have been built in Europe and the United States. In 2004, she became the first woman to to win the prestigious Pritzker Prize for Architecture. Her two most famous projects are the Rosenthal Center for Contemporary Arts in Cincinnati, Ohio, completed in 2003, and Serpentine Gallery Pavilion in London, England (a temporary structure completed in 2000). Hadid rejects the conventional rules of space: walls, ceilings, front and rear. Instead, she reassembles them in what she calls "a new fluid kind of spatiality" of multiple perspective points and fragmented geometry, designed to reflect the chaotic fluidity of modern life. Hadid's passion for shadow and ambiguity is deeply rooted in Muslim architectural tradition, while its fluid, open nature is a politically charged response to the highly fortified urban landscape of modern western Asia.

provided the centerpiece of the mixed-use Kuala Lumpur City Center (KLCC) complex, set in the midst of a thriving commercial district. Rising to a height of almost 1,500 feet (452 m), the towers were the world's tallest buildings at the time of their completion in 1998.

The Petronas complex is at the forefront of modern construction technology, while adopting a form derived from a traditional Islamic pattern and also making extensive use of local materials. The towers have become popular exemplars of contemporary architecture in Malaysia, and their elegant form makes them the country's most significant urban landmark.

The story of the Petronas Towers began in 1981, when the government of Malaysia undertook the development of a 100-acre (40 hectare) site in the heart of Kuala Lumpur's emerging business district, the Golden Triangle. A competition was held that was won by the U.S. firm Cesar Pelli & Associates. The project design that they presented took the form of two squares interlocking to create an eight-pointed star, modified by placing eight semicircles in the angles of the corners to create more floor space. Each tower rises 88 stories high and provides over 2.3 million square feet (213,700 sq. m) of floor space, including an additional circular "bustle" or annex 44 stories high. The towers taper at six separate points, with the walls of the upper levels sloping inward. Both towers are topped by a conical spire and a pinnacle 240 feet (73 m) high.

The structure supporting both towers comprises a ring of 16 cylindrical columns of high-strength reinforced concrete, placed on the inner corners of the star-shaped plan to form a soft tube, with the columns linked by arched ring beams, also made of structural concrete. The columns are nearly 8 feet (2.4 m) in diameter at the base, but taper as they rise through the floors, as well as sloping toward the center of the towers. At the center of each tower is a square core, which contains elevators, mechanical shafts, and other services, with beams extending out to the perimeter columns. The core occupies 23 percent of the floor plan— a relatively low ratio in comparison to other skyscrapers.

The towers' foundations consist of a piled raft just under 15 feet (4.5 m) thick, supported on rectangular friction piles varying in depth from 130 to 345 feet (40–105 m). The towers are connected at the 41st and 42nd levels, 550 feet (about 170 m) above street level, by a sky bridge.

Each tower rises 88 stories high and provides over 2.3 million square feet (213,700 sq. m) of floor space, including an additional circular "bustle" or annex 44 stories high.

Designing the bridge proved a complex task, since the structure had to accommodate the movements of each tower. The towers are also joined at their base to form a six-level retail and entertainment complex with a central atrium. From the atrium, two "streets," lined with over 300 shops, cafés, and restaurants, extend along opposing axes. In addition, the complex includes an 880-seat concert hall, an art gallery, a library, and an interactive science discovery center, as well as a four-story underground parking garage.

This view of the Petronas Towers in Kuala Lumpur, Malaysia, shows the walkway that connects the two skyscrapers.

Throughout the Petronas complex, automatic controls and advanced communication systems reduce energy consumption and promote convenience of use. One such system controls vertical transportation, which is provided by double-decker elevators capable of carrying 26 people per deck. The integrated energy-conservation concept of the towers is based on an innovative "cool-recovery" system, which uses heat from exhaust air to power the cooling of outside air as it enters the building. The system reduces by 50 percent the amount of energy used in the building's air-conditioning system.

The Petronas Towers complex combines modern technology with a sense of cultural identity. It has also introduced new architectural standards to Malaysia in terms of both construction and design.

BEYOND THE MUSLIM WORLD

Islamic architecture has influenced design in the West for many centuries, notably exporting the pointed arch and cuspings in the medieval era. In the 18th and 19th centuries, Moorish architectural elements formed part of the European attachment to Eastern exotica. Buildings in England showing an Islamic influence included the work of William Chambers at Kew Gardens in London, and the Arab hall in the house built by George Aitchison for the painter Frederick Leighton in the Kensington district of the capital. The

most famous of all, however, was the eclectic Royal Pavilion in Brighton, whose exterior resembles a late Mughal palace complete with bulbous domes, *chhaja*s (projecting eaves), and *chhatri*s (domed kiosks), while its interior is decorated with Chinese themes. In Germany, Friedrich Ludwig Persius's steam-engine house in Potsdam took the form of an Egyptian Mamluk mosque while, in Dresden, a tobacco factory was built with chimneys resembling minarets.

Such exoticism predated the arrival of large numbers of Muslim immigrants in Europe. In more recent times, a new architecture directly associated with people of the Islamic faith has emerged in many European cities.

One striking example is the Institute of the Arab World in Paris. The Arab cultural center occupies a beautiful site on the left bank of the Seine River. It is a rectangular glass building built over a steel

The Royal Pavilion in Brighton, England, was designed by architect John Nash for the Prince Regent, who in 1820 became King George IV. Nash deliberately set out to echo the architecture of Britain's Raj in India.

frame. Inside, it contains a museum, a library, an auditorium, offices, and meeting rooms, all assembled within two wings separated by a courtyard that opens out toward the Cathedral of Notre-Dame. The translucent marble façade of the seven-story northern wing is elegantly curved to follow the sweep of the quay. At the west end of this wing is the 100,000-volume library, a spiral tower of books behind a transparent wall of glass that provides panoramic views. The principal façade of the 11-story southern wing consists of 113 photosensitive panels that operate like a camera's diaphragm, opening and closing to control the intensity of light in the interior. The southern façade's polygonal openings echo Islamic geometric forms, giving it the air of a gigantic *mashrabiyya* (carved wooden screen). The building is significant for its sensitive blending of French and North African Arab cultures.

Britain has had long links with the Muslim world; indeed, until India and Pakistan gained independence in 1947, the British Empire had more Muslim subjects than any other political entity in the world. Muslim potentates within the Empire sought for a long time to build a mosque in the heart of London, the imperial capital. Their efforts bore fruit in 1944, when the Central Mosque was formally opened by King George VI.

Designed by Frederick Gibberd, the building was completed in 1978. It is built in a traditional style, with a prominent golden dome. The main prayer hall holds more than five thousand worshippers. In line with Islamic principles, there is a separate space for women on a balcony overlooking the hall, whose only decoration is a chandelier, although the interior of the dome is embellished with geometrical patterns. Otherwise, the Central Mosque is a building of concrete and glass whose lines are clean and modern.

The golden dome and minaret of the Central Mosque in Regent's Park, London, completed in 1978.

See Also

Brief History of Islam
22–43 ❖ Holy
Places 174–193 ❖
Visual Arts 198–219 ❖
Jerusalem 194–197 ❖
Islam and Architecture
in the United States
246–247 ❖

Islam and Architecture in the United States

The distinctive features of Islamic architecture can be seen throughout the United States. In addition to mosques, many non–Muslim buildings incorporate aspects of Islamic design.

Architecture associated with Muslims in the United States may be divided into three categories: Orientalist buildings erected by non-Muslims to evoke the spirit of the East; buildings of Spanish-American style recalling the Mudejar architecture of Spain; and mosques built by Muslims since the 1950s.

ORIENTALISM

Beginning in the 19th century, architects in both the United States and Europe began to seek inspiration from the distinctive architectural styles of remote, exotic cultures such as those of China, India, and the Muslim world. These influences created a style known as "orientalism" that became popular during the late 19th and early 20th centuries in Europe and the United States. The influence of the architecture of the Muslim world created a style known as Moorish architecture. In the United States, the Moorish style was popularly understood as incomplete without at least one large spherical dome, arches of different kinds, minarets, towers of varying sizes, horizontal bands of colored bricks or tiles, and decorative terra-cotta.

The three most famous examples of domestic architecture inspired by the Muslim world are Longwood, a villa in Natchez, Mississippi, designed in 1861 by noted architect Samuel Sloan; Villa Zorayda (built in 1882) in Saint Augustine, Florida, which was designed by architect Franklin W. Smith as his own winter home; and the buildings of Opa-Locka—an area of suburban Miami—developed by Aviation pioneer Glenn Curtiss in 1926. Opa-Locka was conceived as the "Baghdad of southern Florida"; the buildings have horseshoe shaped windows, minarets, domes, and crenellations.

One of the most conspicuous uses for Moorish forms in the architecture of post–Civil War America was in the

In the United States, the Moorish style was popularly understood as incomplete without at least one large spherical dome.

synagogue. Jewish houses of worship appeared in American cities from New York to Galveston, Texas, with Moorish minarets rising above horseshoe-arched facades in fantastic combinations of historical and imagined

The city hall of Opa-Locka, Florida (built in 1926), with its assorted domes, towers, and minarets is a typical example of Moorish architecture from the early 20th century.

Longwood, a Moorish style villa, in Natchez, Mississippi. Construction began in 1861 but was suspended at the outbreak of the Civil War.

forms. These Moorish synagogues were inspired by the great synagogues of Islamic medieval Spain and by the ideas of 19th-century German architect Gottfried Semper. He believed that since the Jews originated in the Near East, the appropriate architectural style for their places of worship would be Eastern. This unlikely use of the Moorish style became an accepted architectural treatment for synagogues well into the 20th century, preferred by many congregations to the more traditional Gothic Revival style that had become associated with a period of anti-Jewish persecution in Europe. Since there were no notable mosques in the United States at that time, the synagogues were not confused with Muslim places of worship.

AMERICAN MOSQUES

Muslim populations in Europe and North America have grown rapidly since the 1980s due to conversion to Islam and immigration. As the Muslim communities grow, they require more mosques. There are over 2,500 mosques in North America, of which some 200 are purpose-built.

Mosques are becoming places of public gathering and socialization while retaining the primary role as a place of worship and religious education. In the design of mosque architecture in the United States, three approaches are influential in the final outcome of the building. The immigrant Muslim community retains a vivid visual link with its country of origin, desiring a traditional design. Examples of this approach can be seen in the Islamic Cultural Center in Washington, D.C.; Dar al-Islam mosque in Abiquiu, New Mexico; the Islamic Center of Toledo, Ohio; and the Islamic Center of Charleston, West Virginia. An approach to mosque design that seeks to reinterpret and accommodate features of the traditional with that of the site in America can be found in the examples of the Islamic Cultural Center in New York and the mosque in Jonesboro, Arkansas. Finally, there is the third approach, that of the innovative, unprecedented mosque. Examples are the Islamic Society of North America headquarters in Plainfield, Indiana; the Islamic Center of Albuquerque, New Mexico; the Islamic Center of Edmond, Oklahoma; and the Islamic Center of Evansville, Indiana. With a new generation of U.S.-born Muslims coming of age in the 21st century, it is safe to anticipate changes in mosque design.

نولغنی بمی اش فروخت | بهردند صلصال با از جای | پهردند کردن کی زا بیا

جوکوه اندر آمد میان سپا | جو صلصال نزدیک مالک رسید | بیکردار پس دمان برومیند

زمامون بابر اندر افشتش | برایکبخت بوالمجن اسب هنز | بیا بی مالک برو حمله

ابوالمجن جشیده دل را کم | کرفت و جدا کرد شاز پشت زین | سمی خواست بازم هردورا

بیامد بنز دیک آن دیوسار | کرفتش کمرگاه دیفتردهای | فرو داشت ظنی مرادر

248

LITERATURE

The diversity and global distribution of Islamic culture are nowhere more accurately reflected than in its literature. Muslim and Muslim-influenced writings have flourished since around the time of the Prophet Muhammad and are now in evidence in much of Africa and Asia as well as in Europe, North America, and South America.

The earliest Islamic literature was strictly concerned with the religion itself. Indeed, the holiest literary work of the faith, the Koran, is held to have been revealed to Muhammad—who was almost certainly illiterate—by Allah (the God of Islam) himself. This, in the view of many Muslims, is both the most important distinguishing feature of Islam and the religion's greatest miracle—the revelation of the Koran to the Prophet is as important to Islam as the resurrection of Jesus is to Christianity.

During the subsequent history of Islam, religion and the arts—particularly literature—became so intertwined that it was sometimes almost impossible to discern the dividing line between the two. The sacred and the secular became stylistically and thematically indistinguishable, not only in the cradle of Islam, the Arabian Peninsula, but throughout the widening Muslim world as the faith extended across Africa, Asia, and Europe and, eventually, into North America and South America.

The earliest Arab poetry could be straightforwardly divided into two categories—hymns of praise and satires.

The verse forms employed were highly formal in structure, with complex meter counterbalanced by simple rhyme schemes—typically, every line ended in the same rhyme. The original purpose of verse in every culture is generally agreed to have

> With the development of writing and the increasing availability of parchment, Islamic literature began to deal with nonreligious subjects, notably love and drinking wine.

been to help people remember it—an essential requirement in the time before poems and stories were written down.

With the development of writing and the increasing availability of parchment, Islamic literature began to deal with non-religious subjects, notably love and drinking wine. This thematic departure was a matter of great concern to pious Muslims because both the pursuits now commonly described were proscribed by the Koran. Indeed, any work of literature that was not

This illustration of a battle is taken from a medieval edition of *Shah-nameh* (Book of kings) by the 11th-century Persian epic poet Firdawsi.

The pre-Islamic oral tradition of the Arabian Peninsula still has echoes in the modern world. Here, a Bedouin storyteller recites his tale by firelight.

explicitly religious in theme and tone was in danger of condemnation by the strictest imams. The potential threat to the authors became so great that poets and prose writers increasingly veiled their true meaning in ellipsis, symbolism, and other forms of expression that deliberately made their intentions unclear. This was partly to make it difficult for any hostile critic to demonstrate conclusively that their work had any nonreligious or sacrilegious intention. That gave rise to a feature that may still be identified in the literature of the Muslim world today—a dreamlike quality that may or may not be allegorical. In many works, the distinction between

everyday preoccupations and the divine becomes blurred. This characteristic leads some religious readers to the conclusion that even the most apparently nonreligious works serve to demonstrate the immanence of Allah in all of creation.

THE IMPORTANCE OF WORDS

Muslim civilizations have strong traditions of both oral and written literature. The high value that they attach to the written and spoken word can be traced back to the story of the revelation to Muhammad of the Koran. The written and spoken word shaped the religious and cultural consciousness of the Muslim world.

Before and during the lifetime of Muhammad (570–632), poetry played an important role in the culture of the Arabian Peninsula. Poets were invested with the authority to chronicle histories, to promote or denigrate ideas and events, and to incite animosity toward or cement friendship with neighboring tribes. The poet (*sha'ir*) was an important personage who represented the tribe's prestige. Tribal clans often fought *zajal* (poetry battles) as an alternative to warfare. The root of the English proverb, "The pen is mightier than the sword," is sometimes traced back to this custom. In addition to an official poet, each of the nomadic Bedouin tribes of the Arabian Peninsula had a *rawi* (reciter), whose job was to memorize, embellish, and declaim orally transmitted poetry. *Zajal* battles over the custodianship of the Kaaba in Mecca—many families vied for control of the city's holy sites—were similar in many respects to modern poetry festivals.

According to Muslim tradition, after receiving the revelation of the Koran, Muhammad would recite the message of Allah in verse, the poetic and lyrical beauty of which matched and often surpassed the compositions of Mecca's greatest established poets. This would become, for the people of Arabia, one of the proofs of Muhammad's prophethood. Indeed, many Hadiths (sayings of Muhammad) describe how former opponents of the Prophet converted to Islam after hearing him recite the Koran. Consequently, Islam has created cultures and civilizations that attach sacred authority to the spoken and written word.

ANCIENT DIVERSITY

It is impossible to treat Muslim literature as a uniform, monolithic block. The world of Islam is too heterogeneous and, today, too widespread for generalizations to have any valid meaning. While all Muslim literature was originally in Arabic, it is now written in a host of languages—including Amharic, Hindi, Persian, Turkish, Somali, and Urdu—and translated into numerous other languages, including English.

QASIDA

Qasida (plural: *qasidah*) is an Arabic verse form that originally developed in pre-Islamic Arabia. It was later adopted by versifiers all over the Muslim world and reproduced in many languages other than the original Arabic.

Qasidah begin with formal preludes that describe the poet stopping at a Bedouin encampment to reminisce sadly about the loss of a lover. They typically end with a dedication to the poet's patron. The central section of each poem is devoted to one of three traditional main themes. The subject may be a eulogy or a paean (a poem of praise), an elegy (a poem lamenting the death of a person or the loss of a valued object), or a satire (a poem that criticizes someone or something, often in discourteous or bitter terms).

The *qasida* usually consists of between 60 and 100 lines. Throughout the poem, it maintains just one rhyme, which occurs not only at the end of the lines but also halfway through each line. This would be virtually impossible in English, and if it were to be achieved would likely be tedious for the listener, but the linguistic structures of Arabic, Persian, Turkish, and Urdu are well suited to this form. There are almost no restrictions on the meter that may be employed in a *qasida*.

As Islam spread from the Arabian Peninsula, it took with it the ritual of Koranic recitation and an aesthetic value system that acknowledged and acclaimed the spiritual power of poetry. However, this esteem for language changed and grew as it merged with localized cultural traditions of poetry and oral storytelling, thereby creating a diversity of regional styles and structures.

As already noted, pre-Islamic Arabia had a strong tradition of poetry. One of the most celebrated Bedouin poets of the time before the Prophet Muhammad was Imru al-Qays (d. 550), who often began his recitations with a lament for a lost beloved. Following the establishment of the early Muslim community in Arabia, and during the rule of Abu Bakr (632–634), the first Rashidun caliph, there was a decline in Arabic poetry, partly because of criticism in the Koran of the morality of poets.

Ghaylan ibn Uqbah (d. 735) was the last of the Bedouin poets to predate Islam. His poetry continued the stark desert themes and the *qasida* style (see box) of the nomadic tribes. The second Umayyad caliph, Yazid I (r. 680–683), who himself wrote verses, resurrected Arabic poetry by introducing it into the court culture. The more settled and luxurious life of the Umayyads brought about a great shift in poetic themes. Singers and musicians often recited and performed the compositions of court poets. This tradition of Arabic court poetry and performance was chronicled by Abual-Faraj al-Isbahani (897–967) in his *Kitab al-aghani* (Book of songs).

The preference of the Umayyads and the early Abbasid court for romantic and sometimes licentious verse was counterbalanced by the emergence of a new genre of religious poetry. The greatest exponents of this later form were Sufis (Muslim ascetics and mystics), such as Rabia al-Adawiyya (717–801), Abu Yazid Bistami (804–874), and Mansur al-Hallaj (858–922).

Arabic poetry written in the traditional style, using the structures of *qasida* or *ghazal* (a short lyric, often in rhyming couplets), is referred to as classical poetry. Modern Arabic poetry, while generally still composed in any of the 16 traditional, standardized rhythms, differs from classical Arabic poetry in its themes and content,

RABIA AL-ADAWIYYA

Rabia al-Adawiyya (717–801) is one of Sufism's best-known poet-saints. Little is known about her life, and much of her writing comes to us from secondary sources, especially the biography by the Persian poet Farid ud-Din Attar (1142–1220).

Born in Basra (a city in modern Iraq), Rabia was a free woman until the death of her parents, when she was sold into slavery. Legend has it that her master saw a halo of light above her while she was praying at night, and in the morning he freed her. She then lived an ascetic life of celibacy. Although Rabia did not leave behind any written texts, she was well known and respected during her lifetime as a wise and pious woman. As a result, her oral compositions of entreaties to God and her rhyming couplets were memorized and passed down from generation to generation of Sufis, poets, and scholars. It was Farid ud-Din Attar who finally recorded her poems in writing and assured her lasting reputation as one of the greatest poets in Arabic.

ADONIS

The Syrian poet Adonis, whose real name is Ali Ahmad Sa'id, is considered by many observers to be the greatest living Arab poet and literary critic. Adonis was born in French-occupied Syria in 1930 and exiled from his native country in 1951 because of his nationalist political activity. In 1956 he became professor of Arabic literature at St. Joseph University in Beirut, Lebanon. He began writing poetry that was similar to that of Nizar Qabbani and Mahmoud Darwish—that is, social and political commentaries—but, as his career developed, he became more interested in liberating Arabic poetry from the strictures of its form so that it could become free verse. Adonis brought international attention to modern Arabic poetry, often writing about the East and the West, affirming that "The West is another name for the East" and "I and the other are both the same."

Adonis has become one of the most widely published and influential literary and intellectual figures in the Arab world, translating works from the Arabic literary canon into English and French, writing critical reviews of contemporary Arabic writing, hosting radio programs, editing anthologies, and pushing the boundaries of Arabic writing and poetry into the avant-garde.

style, language, and structure. Modern Arabic poetry is often written in free verse rather than in standardized rhythms. It may consist of straightforward prose or unrhymed couplets. Unlike classical Arabic poetry—which often restricts itself to courtly, romantic, mystical, or satirical themes—modern Arabic poetry may address any subject.

During the period of colonialism, there was a revival of neoclassical styles of Arabic poetry, as writers strove to maintain native cultural identity in the face of European domination. This genre of Arabic poetry consciously evoked the themes and styles of the early Bedouin poets. However, at the same time, many poets of the colonial period rejected neoclassical revivalism and, instead, sought their inspiration from the romanticism of 19th-century English poetry and from the French symbolists.

The early 20th century brought with it a new poetic movement that used the *ghazal* form, traditionally associated with romantic or love poetry, to praise and express devotion to the homeland.

This rapidly intensifying sentiment of patriotism was directly linked to the numerous nationalist and pan-Arabist movements that arose in the 1950s and the 1960s.

Among the most famous of the nationalist poets was the Palestinian Mahmoud Darwish (1941–2008). Darwish used his writing as a tool of political resistance. In the early part of his career, he adhered to the classical forms. However, after the Israeli occupation of the West Bank and Gaza in 1967, his writing became directly political—short, staccato poems that were cries of outrage. Darwish's poetry is today taught in schools throughout the Arab world and has been set to music. His compositions have helped to shape the popular cultural identity and the literature of the modern Arab world.

Another well-known modern poet, a contemporary of Mahmoud Darwish and also a member of the Palestine liberation movement, was the Syrian Nizar Qabbani (1923–1998). Qabbani wrote about women, at first in a romantic style and then, later, after the suicide of his sister in protest at an arranged marriage, as a male feminist, urging women to fight against restrictive social conventions. Unlike the traditional classical poets, Qabbani used simple everyday language for his poems, eulogizing the common person. Much of his most easily accessible work was originally published in the Arabic newspaper *Al-Hayat*. It was then popularized by Syrian and Lebanese singers who wove his verses into thelyrics of their songs.

CLASSICAL PERSIAN POETRY

As Islam spread beyond the Arabian Peninsula, it attracted followers among the speakers of different languages and was expressed in new forms of literature. Persian poetry had perhaps the greatest influence, after Arabic, on the formation of a distinctly Muslim genre of literature.

The term *classical Persian poetry* is applied not only to the verse of the country that is now Iran but also to the verse produced in the historical Persian-

FIRDAWSI, THE FATHER OF PERSIAN LITERATURE

The Persian poet Firdawsi—the pen name of Abu ol-Qasem Mansur (935–1020)—was the author of one the most celebrated national epic poems of all time, the *Shah-nameh* (Book of kings). Firdawsi is sometimes described as the father of Persian literature. The *Shah-nameh* has been memorized, recited, and celebrated by Persian speakers for over 1,000 years. It remains unparalleled as a masterpiece of epic poetry.

Consisting of 50,000 rhyming couplets, the work took Firdawsi some 30 years to complete. The *Shah-nameh* recounts the tales of ancient Persia, based on the oral tradition of folktales that were narrated at social gatherings by official storytellers, who were the traditional custodians of the Persian literary heritage. The poem's heroes, who include Prince Rustam and King Jamshyd, face adversity, and their experiences contain important ethical lessons for them and for those listening to their adventures. Firdawsi had, in effect, compiled a history of Iran, using legends that straddled the boundary between fiction and fact in much the same way as contemporary historical fiction.

This miniature from a manuscript dated 1576 shows a Persian prince going hunting in an illustration of a scene from the *Shah-nameh*. Firdawsi's poem remained a favorite subject for artists for centuries after it was completed.

speaking provinces, including modern Afghanistan and parts of several nations of Central Asia. The rulers of the Delhi sultanate (the Muslim rulers of northern India from the 13th century to the 16th century) and the Mughals (the Muslim dynasty that ruled most of northern India from the early 16th century to the mid-18th century) brought Persian to northern India. Under their influence, a number of South Asian poets also composed their verses in Persian prior to the emergence of Urdu as the region's foremost Muslim literary language.

The Persians had a strong pre-Islamic heritage of poetry and oral literature. With the advent of Islam, Arabic poetry and literature came to dominate the scene until a host of mostly Central Asian poets began to write in a new "Islamic" Persian, thereby reviving the literary language. Many Persian writers also continued to write in Arabic and, in some cases, in Greek.

Abu Abdollah Jafar ibn Mohammad (859–941), who used the pen name Rudaki, was the first poet to write in the Persian language using the Arabic alphabet. Rudaki was in many ways the founder of the new Persian literary style. He served as the court poet of the Samanid dynasty (the first native rulers of Iran after the Muslim Arab conquest) until 937, when he fell out of favor. Rudaki composed 100,000 couplets of which only 1,000 have survived. He also translated from Arabic into Persian the *Kalilah wa Dimnah*, a collection of fables of Indian origin.

Mosharref od-Din ibn Mosleh od-Din Sa'di (1213–1291), better known as Sa'di, is the acclaimed author of *Bustan* (The orchard) and *Gulistan* (The rose garden).

RUMI

Jalal ad-Din ar-Rumi (1207–1273) is today reputed to be the most widely read poet in the United States. The popularity of his mystical love poems is largely due to the successful English translations of his work by the American poet Coleman Barks (b. 1937). Rumi was born in Balkh (a city in modern Afghanistan), where his father was a religious teacher. When Rumi was five years old, the family emigrated to Konya in present-day Turkey. After his father's death, Rumi became a disciple of Burhan ad-Din, a vizier and mystical poet, who told him that there was more to his father's teachings than met the eye. Rumi then took over his father's jobs as a teacher at the madrassa and as a preacher at the mosques of Konya.

An Iranian woman prays at the tomb of the Persian poet Sa'di in the city of Shiraz.

Bustan is composed entirely in verse. It is a moral treatise recounting stories and fables that illustrate Muslim virtues such as justice, liberality, modesty, and contentment. It is also a kind of guidebook for Sufis,

A woman mourner touches the tomb, in Shiraz, Iran, of Hafez, the mystical Persian poet of the 14th century.

reflecting upon the beliefs, practices, and comportment of dervishes.

Gulistan is written in prose and contains long tales and personal anecdotes, interspersed with a variety of short poems. Sa'di, who is himself often classified as a Sufi, writes profoundly about the trials and tribulations of the human condition, distinguishing between the inner spiritual life (*batin*) and the more mundane practical life (*zahir*).

Rudaki, Firdawsi, and Sa'di are among the masters of classical Persian literature. The tradition of oral poetry is still very much alive today in most Persian-speaking cultures. It is not unusual to hear a couplet or a proverb from these masters spoken or

sung in a rural bazaar or for an urban taxi driver to utter the first line of a *ghazal* and a general in the army then to respond with the second line.

Persian Sufi poetry often takes the form of romantic *ghazal*, fables, and instructional verses that use imagery in such a refined and sometimes obscure way that only those tutored by a spiritual master (*pir*) can determine the true meaning.

Mantiq al Tayr (The conference of the birds) is one of the best known and most widely read Sufi texts in the world today. It is one of the early works of Farid ud-Din Attar, a 13th-century pharmacist from northern Iran. It tells the story of 30 birds who embark on a great journey to meet Simurgh, the king of the birds. On their way, they cross seven perilous valleys, which symbolize the stages of awareness through which a Sufi must pass in order to understand fully the true nature of God. Each bird is symbolic of a moral weakness and each one, at a specific stage of the journey, refuses to go on, citing some worldly distraction as an excuse. The leader of the birds is the hoopoe and, at the journey's end, he realizes that Simurgh is actually *Si Murgh*—the Persian for "30 birds". Hence the birds themselves are the king they seek. Attar wrote more than 25 other books, including *Tadhkirat al Awilya* (The biographies of the saints).

Mohammad Shams od-Din Hafez (1325–1390) is often described as a poet's poet. The sublime collection of verses in his *Diwan* are, superficially, rhapsodies on love and wine but, at a deeper level, testaments of his personal spiritual journey. In the 21st century, most Persian-speaking households contain a copy or a recording of the *Diwan*. Most Iranians know at least a few of Hafez's couplets by heart, and his poetry is often used in calligraphy and set to music.

The *Diwan* has been translated into numerous foreign languages and is known to have influenced several leading Western writers, including the German Johann Wolfgang von Goethe (1749–1832), the American Ralph Waldo Emerson (1803–1882), and the Irishman Oscar Wilde (1854–1900).

In the view of many people, the greatest poet in the Persian language was Jalal ad-Din ar-Rumi (1207–1273; see box). Like many other poets of the period, Rumi was not a writer in the conventional, modern sense; he composed his works in his head and, when he recited them, a scribe would take them down. Rumi composed much of his poetry while whirling in ecstatic dance. Most of his work addresses religious topics and his main poem, the *Masnavi-yi Ma'navi*—consisting of more than 25,000 couplets and sometimes known as "the Persian Koran"—had a lasting influence on Sufism.

MODERN PERSIAN POETRY

The emergence of public printing presses and newspapers in Iran paved the way for political and literary magazines and the

In the view of many people, the greatest poet in the Persian language was Jalal ad-Din ar-Rumi (1207–1273).

consequent modernization of Persian literature. New attitudes toward poetry are reflected in the works of Iraj Mirza (1874–1925), Arif Qazvini (1882–1933), and Mirzadeh Eshqi (1893–1923). These three authors laid the foundation of what would culminate in the experimentation of writers such as Nima Youshij (the pen name of Ali Esfandiyari, 1896–1959), who revolutionized Persian poetry by changing the focus from form to content.

Having studied at a French school in Tehran as a boy, Nima Youshij was more familiar with French poetry than with Persian poetry. This gave him a unique perspective for composing poems in Persian, even though his linguistic training and formal versifying methods were considered to be weak. He was the first modern Persian poet to turn away from classical forms, devising his own structures. He was an innovative writer who used highly original figures of speech and explored new ways of embellishing syntax and sound. He inspired an entire school of poets and thus is often considered the founder of modern Persian poetry.

Nosrat Rahmani (1929–2000) and a host of poets of the next generation began to move even further away from classical forms and romantic subject matter, writing harsher, more realistic poetry. Rahmani was allegedly a drug addict who called himself "the Infamous Poet of the Town." He used vivid imagery to depict the everyday lives of the common people. Fereidoon Moshiri (1926–2000), on the other hand, adopted a more detached, philosophical tone, using beautiful images even when writing poetry that is sociopolitical criticism.

The most commercially successful of the modern poets was Nader Naderpour (1929–2000). His sentimentality is similar to that of Moshiri, but his themes delve deeper into the fabric of modern society. His Persian linguistic and literary training enabled him to improve the new forms with a classical attentiveness to rhythm and rhyme.

Ahmad Shamlou (1925–2000) began his career by writing lyrical and patriotic prose poems. He later abandoned the Persian classical tradition and sought inspiration in modern French poetry, as well as in the works of other European poets in French translation. He was particularly influenced by the Frenchmen Eugène Grindel (pseud. Paul Éluard; 1895–1952) and Louis Aragon (1897–1982), the Spaniard Federico García Lorca (1898–1936), and the Turk Nazim Hikmet (1902–1963).

NAZIM HIKMET

Nazim Hikmet is modern Turkey's most celebrated poet, playwright, and novelist. In 1921, at age 19, he went first to Inebolu in Anatolia and then to Ankara to fight in the Turkish War of Independence against the Greeks. In Ankara he met Kemal Atatürk, the father of Turkish independence, for whom he composed a poem that would inspire Turkish independence activists. Hikmet traveled to Batumi in Georgia, which in 1921 became a part of the Soviet Union. In July 1922, he went on to Moscow, where he studied economics and sociology at the Communist University of the Toilers of the East. There he was influenced by the experimental poetry of Vladimir Mayakovsky (1893–1930) and Vsevolod Meyerhold (1874–1940), as well as by communist ideology. On his return to Turkey, Hikmet became the charismatic leader of the Turkish avant-garde.

Many of Hikmet's poems have since been adapted into songs by the composer Zülfü Livaneli. Some of his work has also been translated into Greek by Yiannis Ritsos and set to music by the Greek composers Manos Loizos and Thanos Mikroutsikos. During the 1940s, Hikmet was imprisoned by the Turkish authorities. In 1949, a campaign for his release was led by international figures such as the Spanish painter Pablo Picasso, the American singer Paul Robeson, and the French philosopher Jean-Paul Sartre. In 1950, Hikmet went on an 18-day hunger strike and was released from prison in a general amnesty. In 1951, Nazim Hikmet was awarded the International Peace Prize by the World Peace Council. He died in Moscow in 1963.

TURKISH POETRY

According to Chinese sources, the earliest Turkish literary works date back to the 2nd century BCE. The oldest extant Turkish writings date from the 8th century CE and were discovered in the valley of the Orhon River, northern Mongolia, in the late 19th century. As the Turks moved westward from Central Asia, their languages changed and developed, most notably into Oguz and Chagatai. Oguz became the language of the Seljuks. Chagatai became a Turkic literary language; it was most notably used in the 16th century for the

Babur-nameh (Memoirs of Babur), the autobiography of the Mughal Emperor Babur (r. 1526–1530).

The period of Ottoman imperial literature began in the 13th century, just as Arabic poetry was declining and making way for Persian and Turkish literature to develop in the courts and capitals of the empire. Persian linguistic and literary forms were gradually adopted by Ottoman poets, leading to the creation of a new form of Turkish known as Osmanli—the language of the imperial court. Persian-inspired poetry flourished during the 16th century and reached its peak with the writings of Ahmed Nedim (1681–1730), the most prominent and celebrated poet of the so-called Age of Tulips (Laale Davri).

The 19th century brought increased contact with Europeans and Western literary forms. The poetry of Ahmed Hasim (1884–1933) combined Persian meters with themes and influences of the French Symbolists. Hasim tried to demonstrate that the Turkish language was somewhere "between simple speech and music." The emergence of the modern Republic of Turkey (founded 1923) produced a poetry that displayed a greater consciousness of its local, popular roots, turning to the syllabic meters of folk poetry. The old Osmanli literary style gave way to the more direct language characteristic of most Western poetry today.

URDU POETRY

Urdu literature first emerged in the courts of the Persian sultanates of northern India in the late 14th century. It derived from the classical traditions of Persian and Arabic Muslim literature. The flavor of Urdu—which is written in a modified form of Persian Arabic script and has a vocabulary split almost evenly between Sanskrit-Hindi and Arab-Persian words—was a synthesis of the cultural aesthetics of the Afghan and the Persian civilizations.

The poet Amir Khusro (1253–1325) is often cited as the midwife of Urdu language and literature. Khusro wrote

The emergence of the modern Republic of Turkey (founded 1923) produced a poetry that displayed a greater consciousness of its local, popular roots, turning to the syllabic meters of folk poetry.

in both Persian and Hindi, frequently engaging in ingenious combinations of the two languages. His influence on court viziers and writers was so great that, a century after his death, the poet Quli Qutub Shah (1580–1611) wrote in a new language that would later become known as Urdu.

Classical Urdu literature was generally composed more of poetry than of prose. The prose component of Urdu literature was mainly restricted to the ancient form of epics known as *daastaan*, which featured magical and fantastic creatures bound in events and plots that verged on myth.

Most Urdu poetry is written in the *ghazal* form, borrowed from the Bedouin Arabs, passed on to the Persians, and then bequeathed to the poets of South Asia.

The preeminent Indian poet of the 19th century, Mirza Asadullah Khan Ghalib (1797–1869), wrote in Persian and in Urdu. He was often accused of willful obscurity, but his most accessible poems remain popular today. Ghalib wrote mainly

THE TRAVELS OF IBN BATTUTAH

The first journey of the celebrated Moroccan traveler Ibn Battutah (1304–1368 or 1369) was to Mecca to perform the hajj, the holy pilgrimage that is the duty of all Muslims. He traveled via Algiers, Tunis, Egypt, Palestine, and Syria to reach the holy city. Like Ibn Jubayr before him, he also visited the thriving capitals of the period, traveling on to Baghdad, Shiraz, and around the Mesopotamian region. He then returned to Mecca to perform a second hajj, after which he set out via Jiddah and Yemen on a sea journey, landing at the port of Mombasa—in modern-day Kenya—and traveling along the eastern coast of Africa. He then performed a third hajj, returning to Mecca by way of Hormuz, Siraf, Bahrain, and Yamama. His third hajj was followed by another journey, this time to Cairo, Palestine, and Syria, from where he set sail to Anatolia and Sinope, crossing the Black Sea to reach Constantinople (modern Istanbul). He returned via Khurasan by way of Khiva, seeing all the important cities, including Bukhara, Balkh, Herat, Tus, and Nishapur.

Ibn Battutah then crossed the Hindu Kush into Afghanistan and northern India. He sailed to Goa, the Malabar coast, the Maldive Islands, and Ceylon (modern Sri Lanka). He went on to visit the Coromandel coast, Bengal, Malaysia, Cambodia, and China. He returned via Calcutta and Muscat through Iran, Iraq, Syria, Palestine, and Egypt to make his final hajj to Mecca. After 30 years of traveling, he returned to Fez in Morocco and was invited to the court of Sultan Abu Inan, where he dictated the accounts of his journeys to Ibn Juzayy (1321–1355). Ibn Battutah later visited Muslim Spain and Nigeria.

in three forms—*ghazal* (love lyric), *masnavi* (moralistic or mystical parable), and *qasida* (panegyric, or poem of praise)—and greatly expanded their thematic scope.

Muhammad Iqbal (1877–1938) was a Muslim poet, philosopher, and politician whose poetry in Urdu, Arabic, and Persian is considered to be among the greatestof the period. Iqbal's nationalistic versewas part of the inspiration for the foundation of Pakistan, which becamean independent state in 1947.

Close behind Iqbal—chronologically and in reputation—came Faiz Ahmed Faiz (1911–1984). Faiz was a highly political poet who was associated with communism and was a strong proponent of content over form and even style.

MUSLIM PROSE

Apart from verses of the Koran and the commentaries on them, one of the earliest forms of Muslim literature as text, rather than oral transmission, is the hajj journal, called *rilah* in Arabic and *safarnameh* in Persian. The precursors of modern travel writing, accounts of the hajj pilgrimage to Mecca have, since the earliest days of Islam, formed one of the religion's most widely read and compelling literary forms. From diaries of the intensely personal spiritual challenges faced by believers as they fulfill this most taxing of the Five Pillars of Islam, to the social and cultural adventures of setting out into new lands, to firsthand accounts and comparative analyses of prosperous ancient cosmopolitan centers, to the trade logs of merchants and the memoirs of philosophers and scientists, the hajj travelogue is a veritable compendium of Muslim civilization.

One of the earliest works in this genre is the *Safarnama* (Book of travels) by Nasir-i Khusraw (1004–1077), an account of the author's seven-year round trip from his native Yumgan (a city in modern Afghanistan) to Mecca and then on to Egypt. A great prose stylist, Khusraw wrote in an imaginative form of Persian that uses memorable phrases and coins new words.

Another master of the hajj travelogue form was Ibn Jubayr (1145–1217), whose *Rihlah* (English title: *The Travels of Ibn Jubayr*), written in Arabic, described his journey from his home in Granada (a city in modern Spain) to Mecca via Sardinia, Sicily, Crete, Egypt, and the Arabian city of Medina. Having completed the hajj, Ibn Jubayr went on to Mosul, Damascus, Acre, and Baghdad. Among the most interesting parts of his book are its descriptions of the cordial interpersonal relations between individual Muslims and Christians, in spite of the fact that Islam and Christianity were locked in combat over ownership of Jerusalem and Palestine.

In the opinion of some critics, the greatest travel writer of all was Ibn Battutah (1304–1368 or 1369), whose *Rihlah* (Travels) describes a journey of more than 75,000 miles (120,000 km) that included visits to the lands of every Muslim ruler of his time.

WESTERN INFLUENCE

The spread of European colonialism and, more particularly, the introduction of the printing press, brought Muslims into closer

Pakistani women celebrating National Day display a portrait of the national poet, Muhammad Iqbal (right), together with an image of Mohammed Ali Jinnah, the country's first president.

contact than ever before with Western literature. These developments introduced the world of Islam to the short story and the novel—forms that had previously been virtually unknown to Muslims. Particularly influential in the 19th century were translations into Arabic of the short stories of the Frenchman Guy de Maupassant (1850–1893) and the Russian Anton Chekhov (1860–1904), the historical novels of the Scotsman Walter Scott (1771–1832), and the vast epic novels of the Russian Leo Tolstoy (1828–1910).

The popularity of works by these and other Western authors changed forever the character of Muslim literature. The traditional preoccupation with artifice—

Naguib Mahfouz (1911–2006), an Egyptian, was a powerful author who, in 1988, became the first writer in Arabic to win the Nobel Prize for Literature.

art for art's sake—began to run in parallel with, and was in many areas superseded by, the use of literature as a vehicle for the expression of ideas. Writers in the Islamic world—religious and secular authors alike—increasingly addressed political subjects. Politics had been a part of Western literature since the Middle Ages, but in the Muslim world it was an almost entirely new departure.

THE RISE OF THE NOVEL IN ARABIC

The 20th century saw the rapid development and increasing popularity of the novel. The novel became a vehicle for Muslims from a variety of cultural and linguistic backgrounds to express the growing synthesis of their social, cultural, political, and religious identities. The Muslim novel, in its postcolonial form, bridges numerous divides, from class and gender to race, ethnicity, and political orientation. The novel has become simultaneously a window into the inner workings of cultures and societies whose voices, more often than not, have been left out of the broader historical narratives as well as a compelling public forum from which, at least in principle, no voices are excluded. The thread of Islam in these novels, with its many forms, permutations and interpretations, remains constant yet diverse, as in the changing patterns of a tapestry.

Throughout the 20th century and into the 21st century, the novel in Arabic has evolved principally as a testament to the Arab world's political and civil strife. Prose fiction has been used repeatedly to describe displacement, emigration, and refugee camps and to evoke the changing faces of society as it grapples with the redefinition of traditional gender roles within the Muslim context.

One of the leading novelists writing in Arabic is Hanan al-Shaykh, who was born in 1945 in Beirut, Lebanon, into a Shia family. Widely regarded as the most important female Muslim author of her generation, al-Shaykh addresses the shifting realities of women's lives as they progress through a changing society, facing civil war, exile, and migration while challenging traditional gender roles, the relationship between the sexes, and the institution of marriage. Al-Shaykh's novels have been translated into English and numerous other languages. She left her native country in 1976 to escape the civil war, emigrating first to Saudi Arabia and then settling in London, England.

Al-Shaykh's first novel, *Inthihar Rajul Mayyit* (Suicide of a dead man) was published in Egypt in 1970. Her third novel, *Hikayat Zahrah* (*The Story of Zahra,* 1994), brought her international acclaim. Hanan Al-Shaykh's work differs from that of other Arab feminist writers in that, while it imparts a strong sociopolitical message about the lives of women, it also uses allegories, metaphors, and lyrical language that can be interpreted in different ways.

Naguib Mahfouz (1911–2006), an Egyptian, was a powerful author who, in 1988, became the first writer in Arabic to win the Nobel Prize for Literature. He began his career as a short-story writer but won global recognition as a novelist with *The Cairo Trilogy*—*Bayn al-qasrayn* (1956; *Palace Walk,* 1989), *Qasr al-shawq* (1957; *Palace of Desire,* 1991), and *Al-Sukkariyyah* (1957; *Sugar Street,* 1992)—a sequence of novels that traced three generations of different families in the Egyptian capital from World War I (1914–1918) until the military coup that overthrew King Farouk in 1952. Mahfouz's next major work, *Awlad haratina* (1959; *Children of the Alley,* 1996) was banned in Egypt because of its depiction of the Prophet Muhammad and organized religion. In 1967, after the Arab-Israeli Six-Day War, Mahfouz wrote *Miramar,* a scathing sociopolitical criticism of the Arab regimes of the time.

PERSIAN PROSE

Modern Persian writing has been shaped to a large extent by the two Iranian revolutions of the 20th century—the first led by Reza Shah Pahlavi against the Qajar dynasty in 1925 and the second, the Islamic revolution of 1979. Iranian writers explore similar themes of mass migration and the consequent encounters with new lands and new cultures and the struggle to maintain a coherent sense of what it means to be an Iranian and a Muslim.

Simin Daneshvar (b. 1921) writes about modern and contemporary Iranian life. Rooted firmly in realism, her stories depict the drama of changing societies during the 1960s and 1970s. Daneshvar's *Savushun* (1969), about sedentary and nomadic life in and around her home city of Shiraz, became the best-selling Persian novel of all time.

Bozorg Alavi (1904–1997) was the founder of the Tudeh Party, the Communist Party of Iran, and, as a result, following the right-wing coup of 1953, spent the rest of his life in exile in Germany. His best-known novel, *Chashmhayash* (1952; *Her Eyes,* 1989)—about the love affair between a revolutionary man and an upper-class woman—was banned in Iran. In exile, Alavi remained a passionate Communist and wrote novels that were highly critical of modern society. His later writing revealed a deep nostalgia for his homeland.

TURKEY

Modern Turkish literature has been shaped predominantly by the social revolution of Kemal Atatürk (ruled 1923–1938), the founder and the first president of the Republic of Turkey. In line with his sweeping policy of Westernization, Atatürk changed the alphabet of the Turkish language from Persian script to Latin script. This was a highly significant development that made all forms of Turkish culture—particularly literature—more Eurocentric than ever before.

In addition to his work as a folk musician and a movie director, Ömer

The Turkish poet, academic, and nationalist Mehmet Akif Ersoy was as renowned for his patriotism and support for independence as for his mastery of the Turkish language. His most famous work is now the Turkish national anthem.

Zülfü Livaneli (b. 1946) was one of the most widely read novelists in Turkey at the start of the 21st century. A left-wing political activist, Livaneli was held in detention during the Turkish military coup of 1971. He was then forced into exile and lived in Stockholm, Paris, and Athens before returning to Turkey in 1984. Livaneli later advanced his literary career and became active in mainstream politics. His third novel, *Mutluluk* (2002; *Bliss*, 2006), was a popular hit that was subsequently turned into a movie. Also in 2002, Livaneli was elected a member of the Turkish parliament. In 2006, Livaneli's novel *Leyla'nın Evi* (Leyla's house) became a best seller that ran into 45 editions.

MODERN AFRICA

The single greatest external influence on the culture of the continent of Africa has been European colonial dominance. Consequently, much modern African writing in all languages has been preoccupied with the postcolonial struggle of recreating a national, ethnic, or tribal identity. As in the Arab world, many African nations have been severely damaged by civil strife and warfare, resulting in large-scale emigrations and mass dislocations. Many African authors confront the politics of identity and belonging in their writing.

Nuruddin Farah (b. 1945) is a Somali who was raised trilingually, speaking Amharic, Arabic, and Somali. He later learned English, and that was the language in which he chose to write, principally because he had a typewriter with English letter keys. Farah's novels—some of the later of which he wrote in Somali—deal with the politics of Ethiopia and with women's emancipation in modern Somalia. Central to his work is the postcolonial and postmodern conundrum of combining multiple cultures, multiple languages, and multiple histories in a single identity. Farah looks at how people navigate around such upheavals while trying to maintain a solid sense of self and of belonging. In 1974,

Farah was forced into exile and later lived in India and in Italy. He is widely regarded as one of the most important African writers of modern times.

Al-Tayyib Salih (1929–2009), an Arabic-language novelist and short-story writer, was born in the Northern Province of Sudan and was educated in Khartoum and London. He later worked in the BBC Arabic service. Typical of his writing is *Mawsim al-hijrah ila al-shamal* (1966; *Season of Migration to the North*, 1969), a novel that might equally well be described as a prose poem. It describes the experience of Africans who, like himself, came from rural backgrounds into cosmopolitan life abroad, where they faced sometimes irreconcilable conflicting emotions about the relative merits of commonsense and formal education, East and West, town and country, men and women, and the moment and eternity.

SOUTH ASIA

Like Africa, South Asia was dominated by colonialism and, after its nations achieved independence, by the legacy of European rule. The partition in 1947 of India, a mainly Hindu country, and Pakistan, a Muslim state, occasioned the largest movement of population in human history, during which around 14.5 million people crossed the newly defined borders in order to settle in the state that approved their own religion. In spite of these massive migrations, India still had more Muslims than all of Pakistan, and this painful experience informed much subsequent Urdu literature, as writers confronted questions of national and cultural identity.

Saadat Hassan Manto (1912–1955) is best known for his short stories, which include "Bu" (Odor), "Khol Do" (Open it),

"Thanda Gosht" (Cold meat), and, most famously, "Toba Tek Singh", which tells the harrowing story of the violence, anguish, and madness that accompanied the partition of India and Pakistan. Influenced by the controversial British author D. H. Lawrence (1885–1930), Manto wrote about subjects that were taboo in society, exposing the darker face of human existence. On more than one occasion, Manto was charged by the Pakistani

The grande dame of Urdu fiction, Indian-born Ismat Chughtai (1911–1991) was known for her indomitable spirit and fiercely feminist views.

authorities with obscenity and with disrupting social cohesion, but he was never convicted. He was famously quoted as saying, "If you find my stories dirty, the society you are living in is dirty. With my stories, I expose only the truth." Much of Manto's writing was, in fact, a scathing sociopolitical commentary on the governments of India and Pakistan just before and just after the end of the British Raj. His first short story, "Tamasha," was about the 1919 Amritsar Massacre, in which hundreds of Indian men, women, and children were shot dead by the British army at Jallianwala Bagh, Punjab.

The grande dame of Urdu fiction, Indian-born Ismat Chughtai (1911–1991), was known for her indomitable spirit and fiercely feminist views. Her outspoken and controversial style of writing made her the passionate voice of the unheard, and she became an inspiration for a younger

Assia Djebar

Fatima-Zohra Imalayen is an Algerian novelist who writes under the pen name of Assia Djebar. She is one of the most widely acclaimed writers working in French, having been elected to the Académie Française in 2005. She is the first writer from North Africa to achieve such recognition. Djebar has also published poetry, plays, and short stories, and has produced two films. She explores the complexities of the world of Muslim women, focusing in particular on their struggle for social emancipation. In addition to receiving praise and recognition, she has been criticized and vilified, particularly in her native Algeria.

Fatima-Zohra Imalayen was educated at her father's French school in Algiers. She attended the Lycée Fénélon in Paris, France, and became the first Algerian woman to be accepted at the École Normale Supérieure. She was an active participant in the Algerian student strikes in Paris in 1956, and it was these events that gave her the material for her first novel, La Soif (1957; The Mischief, 1958). Her second novel, Les Impatients (1958; The impatient ones) was published two years later, followed by Les Enfants du Nouveau Monde (The Children of the New World, 1962) and Les Alouettes Naives (The Naive Larks, 1967). All four works address the theme of young women who face political change, challenge patriarchy, and become entangled in love, war, and tradition. During the Algerian War of Independence (1954–1962), Djebar collaborated with the anti-colonial National Liberation Front newspaper El-Moujahid by conducting interviews with Algerian refugees in Morocco.

After independence, there was widespread criticism of Algerian writers working in French. Sensitive to this criticism, Djebar stopped writing and began to explore other media, such as film, theater, and radio. She also studied Arabic. Her films have won numerous international prizes.

In 1980, Djebar published her fifth novel, Femmes d'Alger dans leur appartement (Women of Algiers in Their Apartment, 1992), a title taken from that of a famous painting by Eugène Delacroix (1798–1863). She later explained: "I had just turned 40. It's at that point that I finally felt myself fully a writer of French language, while remaining deeply Algerian." Among her later novels were Ombre Sultane (1987; A Sister to Sheherezade, 1988) and Loin de Médine (1991; Far from Medina), which deals with the women in the life of the Prophet Muhammad. In 1995, she published an autobiographical novel, Vaste est la Prison (So Vast the Prison, 1999).

generation of South Asian fiction writers. In 1941, she published "Lihaaf " (The quilt), a short story about a love affair between two women and the needs of a woman in a cloistered household. The lesbian theme caused outrage, and Chughtai was charged with obscenity. Through her short stories, novels, and political essays, Chughtai explored such previously forbidden themes as feminine sexuality, the hypocrisy of the emerging Indian middle class, and the ongoing challenges of a modernist, traditional Muslim society. A member of the Urdu Progressive Writer's Movement, Chughtai produced a vast oeuvre that included hundreds of celebrated short stories, four novels—including Ek Qatra-e-Khoon (A drop of blood) and Terhi Lakeer (The Crooked Line, 1995)—and an autobiography entitled Kaghazi Hai Pairahan (The apparel is paper-thin). One of her 17 film scripts, Gharam Hawa (Hot air), won the 1975 Bollywood Filmfare Award for Best Story;

in 1974, Chughtai won the coveted Ghalib Award for Urdu Drama.

MODERN DIVERSITY

The diaspora of Arab and Muslim peoples, which largely began in the 19th century in response to the weakening and eventual dissolution of the Ottoman Empire, made it more difficult than ever to define their literature. The Arabs who immigrated to Brazil and the United States preserved the Arabic language in literary and religious groups and in newspapers such as *Al-Huda* (founded in New York City in 1898), but most of them were Maronite Christians from Lebanon, so their work, while it is obviously Arab, is not Islamic. Meanwhile, in the nations of North Africa that were ruled by France or in which French was the language of the educated classes—notably Algeria and Tunisia—most Islamic literature continued to be written in the language of the colonists even after independence. It is therefore normally categorized as French, rather than Muslim, in spite of the fact that much of it is clearly influenced by Islamic tradition and addresses the predominant themes that occupy modern Muslim authors around the world: ethnic and cultural upheaval and the immigrant search for new identities while remaining faithful to the cultural and religious heritage of native lands.

See Also

Scriptures and Doctrine 102–123 ❖ Mystical Islam 148–149 ❖ Visual Arts 198–219 ❖ Performing Arts 270–289 ❖ Philosophy and Science 312–331 ❖

ORHAN PAMUK

Orhan Pamuk was born in Istanbul, Turkey, in 1952. He first came to prominence with the novel *Cevdet Bey ve ogullari* (1982; Cevdet Bey and his sons). He consolidated his reputation as a writer with an international bestseller, *Benim adim kirmizi* (1998; *My Name Is Red*, 2002), about Ottoman and Persian artists and their ways of seeing and portraying the non-Western world, told through a love story. Pamuk's novels are very popular in his home country; the publication of each new work is a cultural event accompanied by advertising campaigns, interviews, and considerable media coverage.

Meanwhile, in the 1990s, Pamuk began writing critically about the contemporary Turkish government, citing human rights abuses and the lack of freedom of expression. *Kar* (2002; *Snow*, 2004)—which Pamuk described as his "first and last political novel"—tells the story of violence and tension between political Islamists, soldiers, secularists, and Kurdish and Turkish nationalists. In the year its English translation appeared, it was selected as one of the 100 Best Books of 2004 by *The New York Times*.

In 1999 a selection of Pamuk's newspaper and magazine articles on literature and culture, together with a selection of writings from his private notebooks, was published in English under the title *Other Colours* (2007). *Istanbul: Hatiralar ve sehir* (2004; *Istanbul: Memories of a City*, 2005) is a poetical memoir of early adulthood and an essay about the city of Istanbul, illustrated with photographs from his own album, Orientalist paintings, and photographs by Turkish photographers.

In 2005 Pamuk gave an interview in a Swiss newspaper in which he claimed that Turkey was responsible for genocidal massacres of Armenians and Kurds. He was put on trial by the government and accused of "denigrating Turkishness"—a criminal offense—but his trial provoked such international outrage that the charges were dropped. The following year, Orhan Pamuk was awarded the 2006 Nobel Prize for Literature, the second youngest person ever to be so honored. In Turkey the decision to award him the Nobel Prize was praised by writers and literary critics, but criticized by the popular press, who suggested it was awarded for political reasons.

Women Writers

Recent novels by Muslim women writing in the United States and Britain center on their female protagonists' adherence to Islamic values while living in a Western society.

Several Muslim women novelists—writing in English—have published critically acclaimed books in the United States and Britain in recent years. For many non-Muslim readers, these books offer them their first glimpse into Islamic life and culture. In general, the themes and characters in these books are fraught with anxieties. The writers appear to weigh their portrayals of Islam against the largely negative public perceptions in these two countries. In certain works, the writers stress only the positive aspects of the Muslim communities; in other works, they address what the authors view as negative aspects of Islamic life in the West. Many writers have openly expressed—in articles and interviews—their awareness of hostile public feelings toward Muslims and Islam, and it appears that this has strongly influenced their work.

The works discussed here are two American and two British novels: *Madras on Rainy Days* (2004) by Indian American Samina Ali (1971–), *The Girl in the Tangerine Scarf* (2006) by Arab American Mohja Kahf (1967–), *Brick Lane* (2003) by the British writer of English and Bangladeshi heritage Monica Ali (1967–), and *Minaret* (2005) by Sudanese writer Leila Aboulela (1964–). Themes in these novels include the concern over the alarming rise in Islamophobia and remaining faithful to Islam while living in the West.

NEGATIVE THEMES

The writers do not shy away from negative Islamic themes, but often in contexts that explain or dismiss these themes as aberrant. These negative themes appear only as blemishes that detract from what the writers see as true Islam or simply as un-Islamic notions and practices due to ignorance or bigotry. *The Girl in the Tangerine Scarf* exposes Muslims' racism and condemns it based on Islamic religious authority and tradition. For example, the young protagonist, Khadra, struggles with

Egyptian-born Sudanese writer Leila Aboulela spent many years living in Britain. Her works include the novels *The Translator* (1999) and *Minaret* (2005).

accepting a claim about a massacre by Muslims of the Assyrians (ethnic Christians originating in the western Asia) in 1914. A more complex situation emerges in *Madras on Rainy Days*, where the development of the action hinges on better knowledge of Islam, especially the Koran. Dismayed at the protagonist, Layla's, secular upbringing, her mother-in-law, Zeba, begins tutoring her in the Koran, and soon enough Layla uses that knowledge to expose the ignorance and hypocrisy around her. In *Minaret*, the closest to a negative theme is Doctora Zeinab's bewilderment at her son's austere Islamic observance and her resentment at his falling in love with the protagonist, Najwa, who is nearly twice her son's age.

POSITIVE IMAGE

These novels tend to focus heavily on giving Islam a positive image and little on the interactions between Muslims and non-Muslims. *Madras on Rainy Days* offers no significant interaction with non-Muslim Americans, and *Minaret* has just one scene of interaction, in which three British young men assault Najwa on a bus. *The Girl in the Tangerine Scarf*, on the other hand, does depict numerous encounters between Muslims, Christians, Jews, and Buddhists—among others. The novel is about Khadra's coming of age in the American Midwest. Many

The writers do not shy away from negative themes, but often in contexts that explain or dismiss them as aberrant.

of her encounters prove critical for her development, and many end up confirming common ground between Muslims and non-Muslims rather than differences. For example, Khadra is elated one day to see "halal candy corn" at a food store, and she and her Jewish roommate, Blu, prepare to feast on it. Blu recites a blessing (*berakhah*) to her Muslim companion: "And together they did eat of the candy corn. And it was good."

Madras on Rainy Days, *The Girl in the Tangerine Scarf*, and *Minaret* seem motivated by the urge for their

characters to speak up. Notions of marginalization, silencing, and reactive responses seem to dominate. However, in *Brick Lane*, Ali creates scenes in which her Muslim characters interact with and relate to the wider community. Ali, and also Kahf, present Muslim characters at home with their faith and militant enough to confront the hostile environment in their new homeland. Other Muslims in these novels revel in their religious identity and distance themselves from Western culture and values.

In all works, images and perceptions of Islam weigh on the characters' consciousness and play a central role in shaping their responses. For example, in *Minaret* and *Brick Lane*, the Koran is a significant part in the lives of the main characters. Ali's heroine, Nazneen—a Bangladeshi woman who moves to London at the age of 18 to marry an older man—cherishes the Koran and seeks in its verses comfort and guidance. Similarly, Najwa, in Aboulela's novel, recalls her first visit to the mosque and the deep interest she felt when she saw a woman reciting, an attraction that explains her later pursuit of the art of Koranic recitation.

Despite being part of a counterculture that to some extent curbs their participation in the cultures of their adopted homeland—be it the United States or Britain—many Muslims, especially women, manage to overcome their disadvantageous conditions and relate to the surrounding culture. In the novels discussed, writers present comparable protagonists who resort to assertiveness—not so much in reacting to marginalization—but in demanding a share in shaping mainstream culture. For example, Nazneen in *Brick Lane* teaches herself English, resists blackmail by Muslim acquaintances over her affair with young radical Karim, rejects justification of suicide bombing, stays in England, and supplies the novel's closing statement, "This is England . . . You can do whatever you like." Her husband, Chanu, in comparison, preaches assertiveness to his daughters and prompts them to take pride in their Muslim background, but he chooses to go back to Bangladesh rather than fight prejudice in the aftermath of 9/11.

Chapter 12

PERFORMING ARTS

In spite of a popular misconception in the Western world that Islam discourages or even forbids music, song, and dance in religious ceremonies and in ordinary life, the faith has a long tradition in all the performing arts, which have strengthened and diversified as Muslims have spread across the world.

While Muslim architecture and visual arts are now well-known in the West, there is still relatively little awareness of Islamic achievements in the performing arts. Nevertheless, Islamic traditions in live music, song, dance, and oral poetry are strong and as old as, or in some cases with vital sources older than, the religion itself.

Historically, great emphasis has always been placed in Islam on the beauty of the

❖

Historically, great emphasis has always been placed in Islam on the beauty of the human voice, particularly in the recitation of the Koran.

human voice, particularly in the recitation of the Koran. During the lifetime of the Prophet Muhammad (570–632), his companions labored hard to learn the Koran by heart in order to preserve the authenticity of its contents. (It should be remembered that, before the Koran was

first committed to paper sometime after its creation, there was no alternative method of transmitting or disseminating the work.) However, simply being able to recite the verses by rote was not seen as sufficient; of equal importance to Muslims has always been the beauty of the sound of the Koran when spoken. Proper performance of the recitation (*qira'at*) depends on the accurate pronunciation (*tajweed*) of each word. The art of *qira'at* is still taught at Islamic institutions around the world. Competitions are held regularly between leading exponents of *qira'at*.

Because Islam is today a multicultural, global religion, the forms of musical expression found in modern Muslim communities are diverse and incorporate at least some elements of the local styles of each of the regions in which they have taken root. In the western Asian heartland where Islam first emerged, the music of Islam has been influenced by a wide variety of traditional instruments, including different types of flutes and clarinets, stringed instruments such as the oud, and an assortment of percussion pieces. The

A dervish dances for tourists at a restaurant in Luxor, Egypt.

spread of Islam through the region in the seventh and eighth centuries had a significant effect on the development of music beyond the Muslim world throughout the centuries that followed. For example, the origins of the lute and even the guitar can be traced back to the oud. Similarly, drums from around the world share many common features with the *duf* and other types of Arab percussion instruments. The spread of Muslim influence from Islam's heartland in the Arabian Peninsula into northern Africa, central, eastern, and southern Asia, and Europe resulted in cultural exchanges, many of which occurred through artistic media, especially music.

ANASHEED

Anasheed is the Arabic word for traditional songs performed in the Arabic language. The lyrical content of *anasheed* typically reflects Islamic beliefs, history, and contemporary issues. *Anasheed* could be considered analogous to the hymns or psalms recited in many Christian churches. These songs have persisted throughout the ages and have been carried to almost every part of the world by Muslims who have migrated from their native lands. Young children are often taught popular *anasheed* in Islamic schools and sing them together in the classroom. Similar to nursery rhymes, they are often very simple and offer children an easy way to remember Islam in their everyday lives.

Anasheed may be performed in a wide variety of musical styles. With the rich heritage of music in western Asia, some modern *anasheed* are accompanied by an assortment of instrumental arrangements. It should be noted, however, that most *anasheed* are more conservative and are

performed either a cappella (by singers who perform without any kind of musical backing) or accompanied only by a single percussion instrument.

Throughout history and in ever more numerous parts of the world, singers have maintained the *anasheed* tradition in public performances attended by Arabic speakers. One prominent modern exponent of the art is the popular singer Muhammad Abu Ratib. Born in Aleppo, Syria, in 1962, Abu Ratib was immersed from an early age in the rich musical traditions of the Arab world. As he balanced his love of music with a growing interest in Islam, his work moved in an increasingly spiritual direction. By the beginning of the 21st century, he was established as one of the world's leading musicians of his type, performing *anasheed* solo and with bands live and on recordings throughout the world.

Abu Ratib is an active member of the Arabic arts community and is involved in numerous organizations to promote Islamic music and artist development worldwide. Since immigrating to the United States, Abu Ratib has become known as a pioneer of modern *anasheed*. He has traveled all over the country and abroad as a featured artist at community events, in mosques, and on college campuses.

EAST MEETS WEST

There is much cross-fertilization between Western and Islamic popular cultures. One of the most striking manifestations of this phenomenon has been the growing popularity in the Muslim world of talent shows in the style of U.S. television series such as *American Idol: The Search for a Superstar*. The leading Arab equivalents— *Munshid al-Shariqah* and *Munshid al-Sharjah*—are talent competitions to find the

next great *munshid* (*anasheed* singer). These programs, together with spin-off video clips on the Internet, have done much to popularize *anasheed* with a new generation of Muslims and, to an increasing degree, with non-Muslims.

Both *Munshid al-Shariqah* and *Munshid al-Sharjah* are recorded in the United Arab Emirates (UAE), a nation that has become one of the leading cultural influences on Islamic western Asia. The West has responded quickly to this development. Popular American performers, such as Ludacris and Justin Timberlake, have given concerts in Abu Dhabi and Dubai, the two most important states of the UAE. The American cable network Music Television (MTV) has launched a UAE-based subsidiary called MTV Arabia to serve this market. Much like MTV networks in other parts of the world, MTV Arabia features a varied assortment of programs including music, reality shows, and documentaries. Broadcast from Dubai, MTV Arabia aims to be more than just a music channel; it also provides a platform from which young people can address some of the social problems that concern them. In an effort to reconcile the wide cultural differences across the broadcasting region, MTV

The oud—played here in a recording studio by Turkish musician Erol Ciftci— has a deep, pear-shaped body and a fretless fingerboard. The classical oud has four pairs of strings, but 10- and 12-stringed ouds are not uncommon. The strings are made of gut and plucked with a plectrum.

The Egyptian businessman Naguib Sawiris is the owner of the Melody broadcasting network, a subsidiary of his main company, Orascom Telecom.

employs a team of executives from Iraq, Lebanon, Palestine, Saudi Arabia, and the UAE that has developed a conservative selection of music and reality programming, substituting the racy dating shows that characterize the Western MTV equivalents for celebrity interviews and coverage of a variety of extreme sports.

Although MTV Arabia is dominant in western Asia, it does not have a monopoly in the region. Among its leading competitors is the Rotana network, which has four music channels and is financed by Saudi billionaire Prince al-Waleed bin Talal. Another rival is the Melody network, which is controlled by the Egyptian telecommunications mogul Naguib Sawiris. MTV Arabia, however, aims to be different. While the other networks focus on established Arab stars, such as Nancy Ajram, Amr Diab, and Elissa, MTV Arabia concentrates on new features including Arab hip-hop, a genre that thrives in the western Asian alternative music scene but which has so far been largely ignored by

the mainstream music channels. MTV Arabia's *Hip HopNa* show travels to four cities looking for local talent; the winner is decided by an audience vote.

QAWWALI

Qawwali—a form of devotional music practiced by Sufis (Islamic mystics)—is particularly popular on the South Asian subcontinent. It originally developed from the fusion of Persian and Indian musical traditions dating back to the 13th century. The center of modern *qawwali* music is the Punjab Province of eastern Pakistan, where it has been developed into a mainstream art form. With its elegant poetic expression, *qawwali* is typically sung passionately and powerfully in Urdu or one of the Punjabi languages. As with most Islamic music, *qawwali* is commonly sung in praise of Allah and in remembrance of the Prophet Muhammad and other important historical figures of Islam.

Practitioners of *qawwali* are often enthusiastic students of the writings of famous Sufi poets including Rumi (c. 1207–1273), an Afghan who made a significant impact on the classical mystical literature of Islam, inspiring many with his use of rich, elevated language.

Whereas most musical groups are referred to as "bands," a group of *qawwali* performers is known as "a party." A *qawwali* party is analogous to a gospel church choir, inspiring and motivating the audience with its powerful sound and evocative language. It is not uncommon to find avid listeners clapping their hands and singing along enthusiastically at live performances. *Qawwali* typically evokes strong, emotional responses from its audience through the passionate nature of its content and the manner of its performance, which is said to induce a trancelike state of spiritual ecstasy that Sufis take as being a form of direct connection with God. Worldwide, Muslim communities with large Indian and Pakistani representation have maintained and cultivated their religious and cultural roots by organizing concerts featuring *qawwali* music. *Qawwali* is also often featured at religious festivals and at weddings.

A *qawwali* party normally comprises one or two main vocalists supported by a backing chorus following a call-and-response format; the chorus will repeat key verses and support the percussion with hand-clapping. This easy-to-follow arrangement is highly conducive to audience participation. *Qawwali* is commonly accompanied by a harmonium and, in India and Pakistan, by hand drums such as the tabla and the *dholak*.

Renowned performers, such as the Sabri Brothers, who emerged in the 1950s, and Nusrat Fateh Ali Khan (1948–1997), popularized *qawwali* with modern

audiences and exerted a wide-ranging influence on other musicians and styles. Nusrat Fateh Ali Khan, for example, established himself as a presence in the mainstream music industry with several worldwide releases on major record labels. As a result, *qawwali* has been adapted in many nonreligious contexts, from Bollywood (the Indian movie industry) to the hip-hop scene in Europe and North America; it has also influenced the work of Western popular musicians such as the British musician Peter Gabriel (formerly the lead singer of the rock band Genesis) and the American rocker Eddie Vedder of Pearl Jam.

WHIRLING DERVISHES

Dance is not commonly associated with the performing arts in Islamic culture. However, it is practiced by some Muslims, notably the dervishes, a sect of Sufi ascetics based mainly in Albania and Turkey, who lead lives of austerity and renounce material possessions.

The Mevlevi are a Sufi order founded in the 13th century by followers of the poet Rumi. Still active today, they are known as Whirling Dervishes for their gyrations in time to a musical accompaniment as a form of *dhikr* (remembrance of God). Their traditional ceremony, the Semâ, represents the spiritual journey of humans from self-absorption, through love, to fulfillment and a new maturity that enables them to be of service to all of creation.

Today, the dance is often performed as a form of entertainment for tourists. However, in its religious aspect, the ceremony is practiced in the Semâ *hane* (ritual hall) according to a precisely prescribed symbolic ritual. The Whirling

Egyptian Amr Diab (born 1961) is one of the most successful popular singers in the Muslim world. In this photograph, taken at the 2007 World Music Awards in Monaco, he is seen receiving his third trophy for the year's bestselling album in western Asia and North Africa—he had previously won the award in 1998 and 2002.

Dervishes spin in circles around their sheikh, a Muslim spiritual leader, who is the only dancer revolving on his own axis. The Whirling Dervishes traditionally wear long white robes with full skirts, which represent the shrouds of their egos. Over these garments, each dervish has a *hirka* (voluminous black cloak), which represents his worldly tomb. On their heads, the dervishes wear *kûlah*—tall, conical felt hats that signify the tombstones of their egos.

The Semâ begins with a chanted prayer to the Prophet Muhammad, who represents love, and to all the other prophets who preceded him. Next, a kettledrum sounds as a symbol of the divine order of the Creator, followed by a haunting musical improvisation on the *ney*, a traditional Middle Eastern reed flute, which symbolizes the Divine Breath that gives life to everything. The master bows, then leads the Dervishes in a circle around the hall. As they pass the master's ceremonial position at the head of the hall, they bow to each other, portraying the salutation of soul to soul.

After three revolutions, the Whirling Dervishes drop their black cloaks to symbolize deliverance from the cares and attachments of this world. One by one, arms folded on their breasts, they approach the master, bow, kiss his hand, receive instructions, and then spin out across the floor. The Dervishes believe that, through whirling, they relinquish the earthly life to be reborn in a mystical union with God. The Whirling Dervishes open their folded arms and extend their hands outward so that their right palms face upward and their left palms face downward. Blessings from heaven are thought to enter through the right palm, pass through the body, then transfer through the left palm and from there into the earth.

Eventually, the Semâ reaches a point at which all the Dervishes are whirling simultaneously and achieving a trancelike state. After about 10 minutes, they all stop and kneel. Then, rising, they begin again. This combination of whirling followed by saluting is repeated a total of four times. The conclusion of the whirling is followed by a recitation from the Koran. The Semâ ends with a prayer for the peace of the souls of every prophet and believer.

A dervish dances at the Wikala El Gourhi Theater in Cairo, Egypt. Such popular performances are based on, but different from, the religious ceremonies.

The Turkish government does not allow frequent performances by the Whirling Dervishes. However, they are permitted to perform once a year in Konya at the Mevlana Festival to commemorate the anniversary of Rumi's death on December 17, 1273. The Whirling Dervishes performed in North America for the first time in 1972; their return tour in 2007 was sold out nationwide.

MUSICAL PERFORMANCE IN ISLAM

The term *nasheed* has been adapted from the word *anasheed* to describe modern Islamic music and the artists who perform it. While traditional *anasheed* works are most commonly conservative in nature and performed either a cappella or accompanied only by one or two percussion instruments, a new generation of *nasheed* artists is incorporating a far wider variety of musical instruments and styles into a revised form of the art. This development has caused controversy within some sections of the Muslim community because of the vast range of scholarly opinions about the permissibility of music in Islam. These views range from absolutely forbidding music and singing to allowing the use of musical instruments as long as the subject matter is of an Islamic nature and does not encourage sinful acts. The Taliban government of Afghanistan in the 1990s forbade all music, for example, while

Musical performance has a long history in the Muslim world. This 19th–century print of women from the sultan's harem in Turkey shows a musician and two dancers.

other Muslim scholars say that music has a rightful place in the culture of Islam as long as it maintains appropriate standards of morality and does not divert people from the worship of God.

As increasing numbers of Muslims migrated to the West in the 20th century, they brought with them not only traditional understandings of Islam but also their own cultural norms. The ensuing assimilation process resulted in a clash between conservative Muslim views and increasingly liberal Western views of music, art, and general social expression. As a consequence, many Muslims developed a fear of music as an encouragement to immoderate behavior that outweighed their desire to maintain it as a part of their identity. It is probable that a fear of the transgressive aspect of music lies at the root of many of the current questions regarding the permissibility of music in Islam.

In strict Islamic culture, female singers are typically banned from public performance because it is considered immodest for women to sing in the presence of men. Muslim women will often host private "sisters-only" gatherings, at which they can sing and dance together in groups. These traditions, however, are changing. In Malaysia, for example, mothers looking to offer an alternative to Western musical bands formed a female *nasheed* group named Huda. The prominence of Muslim females in Western art is steadily increasing, especially in poetry and the spoken word.

MARKETING MUSLIM MUSIC

The Asian nation in which the greatest cross-fertilization between Muslim and Western artistic traditions currently occurs is Malaysia, the inhabitants of which come from a worldwide range of ethnic and cultural heritages. As a result, Malaysia has developed into a fertile environment for *nasheed*, which has grown there into a thriving industry. Among the leading Malaysian exponents of the form is the singing group Raihan, named for the Arabic word meaning "fragrance of Heaven." Formed in the early 1990s, this group, originally of five members, enjoyed worldwide success with its first album, *Puji-Pujian* (1996). Raihan changed the complexion of Islamic popular music, blending modern Eastern styles with a traditional performance style more commonly found in the Muslim world. The band's use of contemporary rhythms and its incorporation of close harmonies were, for many, a welcome change from the old-fashioned *nasheed* to which the audience had been accustomed.

Raihan's early success attracted the attention of Warner Music, which signed the band to a recording contract and then aimed its marketing at the Muslim world, releasing the title track of *Puji-Pujian* as a single during the Islamic holy month of Ramadan. During this annual period of increased spirituality and celebration, *nasheed* are given extensive airtime on radio stations, and the exposure Raihan received during the month helped the group to build a large fan base for what became known as "Muslim Pop," a commodity that appealed to all age groups.

Raihan's success on the Warner label encouraged other Western recording companies to introduce their own *nasheed* acts. This development improved the production quality of the *nasheed* groups' work. Raihan remained prominent, however, going on to consolidate its

YUSUF ISLAM (FORMERLY CAT STEVENS)

Yusuf Islam is a British musician and singer songwriter. Although he was an international pop star in the 1960s and 1970s under the name of Cat Stevens, he later became even better known as one of the world's most prominent converts to Islam, for which he now does extensive philanthropic work.

The man now known as Yusuf Islam was born Steven Demetre Georgiou in 1948 in London, England. He is of Greek Cypriot and Swedish heritage. As a singer-guitarist-songwriter, he adopted the stage name of Cat Stevens and in 1966 had the first of a string of hit singles in his native country. In 1970, he became established in the United States with his album *Tea for the Tillerman*, which reached the *Billboard* Top 10 and sold more than 500,000 copies. The single from the album, "Wild World," reached number 11 in the chart.

Stevens had further success with *Teaser and the Firecat* (1971), which was certified as a Triple Platinum album, and, above all, with *Catch Bull at Four* (1972), which sold 500,000 copies soon after its release and topped the *Billboard* chart for three weeks.

Throughout this period, Stevens took an interest in different religions, studying many in his quest to find a deeper meaning in life. In 1976, he was given a copy of the Koran by his older brother. Stevens accepted Islam in the following year and took the name Yusuf Islam. He immediately abandoned his musical career and devoted himself to his newfound faith. He set up a Muslim school in London and engaged in charity work for famine victims in Africa and orphans in the Balkans, Indonesia, and Iraq. He was the chairman of Muslim Aid from 1985 to 1993.

In 1985, Yusuf Islam performed on stage for the first time in more than 20 years at the Live Aid charity concert that was held to raise funds for the relief of famine in Ethiopia. By demonstrating that a sensible balance can be achieved between music and Islam, Yusuf Islam has paved the way for Muslim performing artists in a range of genres.

Yusuf Islam performs at the 2007 Live Earth concert in Hamburg, Germany, which was held to raise international awareness of global warming.

reputation and capture numerous international honors and awards.

THE VOICE OF A NEW GENERATION

The arrival of Islamic music in the mainstream commercial market opened the eyes of a new generation to the potential of this form. Today, young Muslims are increasingly breaking free of outdated constraints and using music as a medium for expressing their own preoccupations. Music is quickly becoming acknowledged as a common part of daily life. While there is undeniably a strand of liberal and hedonistic thought in modern mainstream popular music, the desire to use music as an alternative method of uplifting, motivating, and empowering society—much as *anasheed* and *qawwali* did for earlier Muslim societies—is gaining popularity among Muslim and non-Muslim artists alike.

The potential of music to convey Islamic ideologies sympathetically became especially important after September 11, 2001. The terrorist attacks on the United States on the day now known as 9/11 inspired widespread suspicion of Islam and hostility to Muslims, who were perceived by many Americans as a threat to the world. Hasty judgments based on stereotypes and misinformation led to discrimination and hate crimes. The peaceful majority of Muslims resisted the portrayal of Islam as a religion of terrorism. They denounced the perpetrators of 9/11 and tried to encourage non-Muslims to learn more about the true nature of their faith. There was a renewed emphasis on sharing knowledge of Islamic religion and culture in the United States. Many Muslims realized that music is a powerful tool for this form of communication. It offered a common language through which

stereotypes could be dispelled and the world's social climate could be transformed from one of tension to one of mutual understanding. Through music, Muslims could go back to the basics and share Islam's message of peace with anyone willing to listen.

Fundamentally, music with an Islamic message is free from vulgarity, profanity, and the glorification of drugs, violence, and illicit sex that is often linked with Western rock music. Like traditional *anasheed* and *qawwali*, explicitly Islamic contemporary music contains devotional lyrics, references to Islamic beliefs, or sociopolitical content pertaining to issues relevant to Muslim communities and humanity at large. In addition, some Muslim artists may use material that, while not overtly Islamic, addresses other important subjects, such as poverty, racism, sexism, and war. These are, indeed, functionally Islamic in nature because they promote the core Islamic moral values that encourage goodness and discourage wrongdoing.

POPULAR OR "POP"?

Following the emergence of groups such as Raihan onto the mainstream Western music scene, increasing numbers of Muslim artists set their sights on the commercial market. One of the most prominent musical figures associated with Islam is Yusuf Islam, formerly known as Cat Stevens. The British-born Stevens had been a conventional pop star in the 1960s and 1970s, selling millions of copies of his folk-rock singles and albums throughout Europe and North America. In 1977, he converted to Islam and became a leading charity worker for the faith. He established an Islamic-focused record label called Mountain of Light, promoting the development of new Muslim *nasheed* acts as well as his own work.

In October 2001, Yusuf Islam played at the Concert for New York City, condemning the 9/11 attacks and singing his 1971 hit "Peace Train," for the first time in more than 20 years. He also donated half of his box-office royalties to the September 11 Fund for victims' families, and the other half to orphans in underdeveloped countries.

Following in the footsteps of the early Muslim pop artists came Sami Yusuf and Seven8Six. British-born Yusuf ushered in a new era of Muslim music with the release of his first album, *Al-Mu'Allim*, in 2003. Sami Yusuf's formal training in classical music under his Azerbaijani father exposed him to a variety of influences from both East and West; he plays piano, violin, and numerous Arabic and Persian instruments. His classical stylings combine comfortably with traditional Islamic sounds, but the most striking quality of his work is its lyrical message. His hit song, "Hasbi Rabbi," begins with a call to God:

Oh Allah the Almighty

Protect me and guide me

To your love and mercy.

The accompanying promotional video shows Sami Yusuf in a suit, walking down a London street, and giving up his seat on a bus to an old lady. The symbolism of this juxtaposition of Islamic religious invocation and British social customs is, in context, intentional and clear: Sami Yusuf is a Muslim who espouses the values of Western society and sees no contradiction in his position. Both Yusuf Islam and Sami Yusuf have been at the forefront of Muslim efforts to counteract antipathy to Islam in the wake of 9/11 by redirecting popular

attention to the goodness and wisdom of the faith.

Seven8Six—a five-member *nasheed* group described as "the first Muslim boy band"—comes from Detroit, Michigan. Incorporating Arabic, English, and Urdu lyrics, they produce a distinctive vocal harmony that reveals a wide range of influences, including Indo-Pakistani *qawwali*, R&B, rock, and Tamla Motown. Their name is a popular numerical shorthand for the Arabic *bismillah*, an invocational word used at the beginning of all but one sura (chapter) of the Koran, meaning: "In the name of Allah, the beneficent, the merciful." Seven8Six's modern interpretations of traditional *anasheed* and *qawwali* music overcame initial opposition from conservative Muslims to gain enormous popularity, mainly but not exclusively among U.S. immigrants of Indian and Pakistani heritage. Seven8Six's first two albums—*786* (2003) and *Straight Path* (2005)—were international best sellers.

COUNTRY MUSIC, ROCK, AND FOLK

Muslims have also made their presence felt in country music, rock, and folk, three genres that, until the late 20th century, were distinctive identifiers of American nationality. The emergence of Muslim performers in these areas is evidence of Islam's ability to adapt to the cultural experience of its adherents, no matter where they may live. It also demonstrates the willing adaptability of U.S. society to new influences.

Popularly, if not necessarily accurately, known as "Islam's first country singer," Kareem Salama (b. 1978), the son of Egyptian immigrants, was raised in Oklahoma and Texas. He speaks and

OUTLANDISH VOICE OF INTERNATIONAL ISLAMIC MUSIC

Based in Denmark, Outlandish is a hip-hop trio comprising Isam Bachiri (born in Denmark of Moroccan descent), Waqas Ali Qadri (born in Denmark of Pakistani descent), and Lenny Martinez (from Honduras). All three members are deeply committed to their faiths—Bachiri and Qadri are devout Muslims, Martinez is a dedicated Catholic.

The group's first album, *Outland's Official* (2000), was typically hip-hop, with raw lyrics and stories from the street in several languages, including Arabic, Danish, English, Spanish, and Urdu. The songs featured a balanced blend of rap and soulful melodies with an undertone of spirituality that periodically worked its way to the surface and broadened the band's appeal. Muslim audiences quickly tuned in to the group as its popularity increased throughout Europe.

Outlandish's subsequent releases showed increasing maturity, deeper meaning, and softer language. The band sang of religious struggles, family, and politics. The highlight of Outlandish's third album, *Closer Than Veins* (2005), is "Look into My Eyes." This song, which was also released as a single, features lyrics based on a poem by Gihad Ali, a Palestinian, about the suffering of people of all religions in Gaza and the West Bank.

With its refined style, Outlandish has become a voice for a new generation of Muslims seeking an identity that balances Islamic ideals and Western culture.

The three members of Outlandish—(left to right) Lenny Martinez, Waqas Ali Qadri, and Isam Bachiri—arrive at the 13th annual MTV Europe Music Awards held in Copenhagen, Denmark, in November 2006.

sings in a strong Southern accent and his material is a synthesis of both the "down-home" and the *nasheed* traditions. Most of his lyrics have a universal meaning and no single influence. In the song "Baby I'm a Soldier," for instance, he tells the tale of the shared humanity of two combatants on opposing sides of a battle. Salama's narrative introduces the listener to both sides of the story and builds an emotional connection with each character. The first verse tells of a man close to home, telling his wife that he must leave home to defend his country. In the second verse, Salama introduces a mother and her son, who is leaving home to fight to protect his land.

In times of tension between India and Pakistan during the late 1990s, Junoon's song "Dosti" (Urdu for "friendship") became an anthem for young peace-seekers in the region.

Salama claims that country music and traditional *nasheed* are strongly linked by common preoccupations such as respect, love, and religion. By emphasizing these connections in his own work, Salama has been able to integrate Islamic ideas into his music while managing to ensure that the product retains a broad appeal that goes beyond the Muslim world. Salama's commercial success demonstrates his belief in the shared values of Islam and the American way; his music has gained many fans among Muslims and non-Muslims alike.

Other performers of Muslim heritage have also tapped into the American music scene with impressive results. Dawud Wharnsby Ali (b. 1972), a Canadian singer-songwriter, uses classic folk stylings to deliver unifying messages of peace and hope. He has pioneered the use of guitar and piano in *nasheed*, which traditionally shunned the use of such instruments. Since the 1990s, Wharnsby Ali's live performances have attracted a diverse audience from Muslim and, increasingly, non-Muslim backgrounds. He has also become well-known for his children's songs and educational television programming featuring his writing, acting, and musical soundtrack contributions through Islamic media distributors.

Another notable talent is Salman Ahmad (b. 1963), a native of Pakistan who composes and plays what might be termed spiritual rock-'n'-roll; he performs both solo and as a member of Junoon, a band that has been popular since the early 1990s in Pakistan and with young people with Pakistani roots in other parts of the world. Junoon's music is remarkable for its spirituality and awareness of modern issues. In times of tension between India and Pakistan during the late 1990s, Junoon's song "Dosti" (Urdu for "friendship") became an anthem for young peace-seekers in the region.

PERFORMANCE POETRY

Poetry is of particular significance in Islam because it has historically provided a way for authors to circumvent the ban on fictional literature in traditional Muslim societies. Writers and performance artists have taken one of the most basic poetic frameworks—the rhythmical declamation of raw emotions—and subverted it in order to disguise ideas and messages that would have been unacceptable if expressed directly. Thus, for example, there are throughout Islamic literature numerous poems that appear to be expressions of the love of God but which may, on closer examination, be oblique and covert statements of sexual desires. In Arabic— and, by extension, in the languages of all Muslim civilizations—poetry is an effective vehicle for irrational ideas that are difficult or impossible to convey in prose, either because of the limitations of the language or because of laws that forbid their free expression.

In the modern Muslim world, poetry remains a powerful medium for telling stories of love, faith, and struggle. In particular, spoken word performances have come to the forefront, not only for Muslims but also for activists and storytellers of all cultural and religious backgrounds. College campuses feature regular appearances by Muslim poets, both amateurs and professionals, reciting works that express their political beliefs and social concerns. Most performances are in a style that is rhythmical and powerful, with an inherent musical nature that does not require a background beat or other musical accompaniment. Most such works address Islamic faith, politics, social issues, and the performers' personal convictions.

Spoken word performance has seen the rise of some prominent Muslim voices. The popular and influential television program *Def Poetry Jam*, developed for the Home Box Office (HBO) network by hip-hop executive Russel Simmons, has featured a range of Muslim performance poets,

Russel Simmons (third from the right) and fellow members of the cast of *Def Poetry Jam* are honored at the 2003 Tony Awards at Radio City Music Hall in New York.

including Suheir Hammad, Amir Sulaiman, Liza Garza, and Mos Def. Other poets in the same tradition, including Brother Dash, have toured the world as guest performers and lecturers at poetry readings, conferences, and concerts hosted by both Muslim and non-Muslim organizations.

Suheir Hammad (born 1973), a Palestinian American, has acquired a committed following of Muslims who identify with her work. Her breakthrough came with "First Writing Since," a rumination on 9/11 she first performed on *Def Poetry Jam* in November of 2001. The work—which features the line: "Please God, after the second plane, please, don't let it be anyone who looks like my brothers"—was so well received that Hammad became a regular guest on the show.

HIP-HOP

Today, the spoken word is widely regarded as one of the most elegant forms of expression of Islamic thought, not least because it avoids much of the debate that

Now a U.S. citizen, performance poet Suheir Hammad was born in Amman, Jordan, three weeks after her mother had fled Palestine to escape the 1973 Yom Kippur War.

BROTHER DASH

Born Dasham Brookins in 1971 in New York City, Brother Dash is a spoken-word poet whose work focuses on society, spirituality, and the inner self.

Brother Dash began writing and performing his poetry while studying at Rutgers University, New Jersey. It was at this time that his interest in Islam began. Impressed by the clarity of the faith and the solace that it offered, he embraced the religion. Today, Brother Dash's poetry is influenced by his Islamic faith, his love of humanity, and his belief that poets are the observers, commentators, and "word activists" of society.

According to Brother Dash, "Poetry is therapeutic." He explains his live performances in the following terms: "I enjoy sharing my work with young people in particular because poetry can inspire people to channel their energies, wants, hopes, dreams, even hate, in a nondestructive yet very constructive way. Upset about something? Put it in a poem. You'll be amazed at how it helps you and others."

In addition to featuring on several compilation albums, Brother Dash has produced two full-length solo discs: *Poetically Speaking: Savory Spoken Word . . . Spiritually Served* (2007) and *Spoken Soul* (2009).

Acutely aware that some Muslims disapprove of public declamations of Islamic faith, Dash responds to their criticisms by saying that every religion has to accommodate itself—and, of course be accepted by—new and changing cultural environments. Although Islam originated in the Arabian Peninsula, it is now established in many countries worldwide, and Dash believes that it is wholly appropriate for it to adapt itself to different surroundings.

has been focused on music in Islam. As such, it has developed a substantial following and is thought to have had a significant influence on hip-hop.

In spite of the fact that Islam has been practiced in African American society for centuries, its rise to the forefront of the mainstream music scene was undetectable until hip-hop offered a mode of expression for the thoughts of rappers about social issues and spirituality. Islam is now sometimes known as "the official religion of hip-hop."

The effect of Islam on hip-hop has been demonstrated repeatedly as prominent mainstream stars such as Mos Def and Lupe Fiasco have started to rap about their religious influences. However, as hip-hop became established on the world music scene in the late 1990s, a new genre of Islamic rap emerged that rejected the misogynistic, materialistic overtones of its antecedents, such as gangsta rap. Many Muslim artists began to concentrate their efforts on using hip-hop as a new form of *dawah* (teaching about Islam).

Hip-hop music has been an active vehicle for social protest in the United States. Its targets have been racism, discrimination, police brutality, poor education, and other social ills. The hip-hop cultural movement has united Muslim and non-Muslim artists in their opposition to misguided thought and misunderstanding. This musical genre is now a global phenomenon that is popular with young people in countries as diverse as Algeria, Australia, Brazil, China, Colombia, Cuba, Egypt, France, Germany, Japan, Lebanon, Mexico,

Salman Ahmad salutes the audience after performing at the 2003 MTV Indian music awards in Mumbai, India. With Ahmad is Palash Sen (left), the lead vocalist of the Indian band Euphoria.

Norway, Palestine, Senegal, and South Africa. Some commentators have even suggested that hip-hop may be the leading modern U.S. export; that is a contentious claim, but what is not disputed is hip-hop's power as a unifying force of global youth culture.

Rappers often draw parallels between the musical and lyrical flow of hip-hop and the poetic nature of the verses of the Koran. They claim that the music and the book share rhythms and rhyme schemes and that they have the common purpose of imparting knowledge to listeners and readers. Whether the medium is Arabic, English, or any other language, these principles apply universally. As rapper Mos Def has said: "Do you know how much information—vital information—you could get across in three minutes [the typical length of a rap number]?... The Koran is like that. The reason that people are able to be *hafiz* [an honorific title given to anyone who has memorized the entire Koran] is because the entire Koran rhymes... and it holds fast to your memory. And then you start to have a deeper relationship with it on recitation.... Hip-hop has the ability to do that—on a poetic level."

Another well-known American Muslim rapper, JT the Bigga Figga, was born in 1973 in San Francisco, California. He has elaborated on the same idea about the power of the spoken word: "It's almost like with Allah how he'll describe his prophets as moonlight. He'll describe his word that he speaks in a metaphoric phrasing."

FUTURE POSSIBILITIES

Hip-hop performers, both Muslim and non-Muslim, are increasingly incorporating Islamic thoughts and language into their work. By infusing Islamic knowledge into familiar rhythms and striking and memorable language, hip-hop artists are reaching out to a global audience with inspiring and empowering messages. Growing numbers of major hip-hop artists cite Islamic concepts regularly and spontaneously, a development that reflects their increasing interest in studying Islamic ideologies and applying them to their everyday lives. This is a widespread, sophisticated, cultural movement with the potential to reshape modern thought. It increasingly appears as if, after centuries of mutual ignorance, Western civilizations and the world of Islam are currently experiencing a growing awareness of each other's artistic heritage.

It increasingly appears as if, after centuries of mutual ignorance, Western civilizations and the world of Islam are currently experiencing a growing awareness of each other's artistic heritage.

It is in some ways ironic that this rapprochement should have been hastened by a popular reaction against the widespread hostility toward Muslims that was aroused in the United States and elsewhere by 9/11. Nevertheless, the terrorist atrocities perpetrated on that day in 2001 have catalyzed a move toward a greater cross-cultural understanding which, like so many influential movements in history, is driven upward from the grassroots through, in this case, popular performing arts striving to inform the political agenda.

See Also

Mystical Islam 148–149 ❖ Visual Arts 198–219 ❖ Arts Festivals 220–221 ❖ Literature 248–267 ❖ Comedy and Islam 290–291 ❖ Media 292–309 ❖

Comedy and Islam

Comedy is one of the main methods of artistic expression through which Muslims describe their interactions with the modern world.

Religion is seldom associated with humor, and Islam is conventionally regarded as a solemn faith. This is perhaps unsurprising; the Koran, like the Judeo-Christian Bible, is not a treasury of jokes any more than a comedy club is an obvious source of moral precepts. However, the holiest book of Islam contains an abundance of good humor in the broad sense of the term and the Hadiths (stories of the life of Muhammad) feature many tales that reflect the importance of amusement in the life of the Prophet.

Muhammad valued humor highly and explicitly counseled his followers to "mix with the people on the condition that your *deen* [religion; way of life] is not jeopardized, and be jestful with the family." One of his closest companions was known as "the jester of the Prophet." Muhammad ordered another of his followers, who reported that his parents had cried when he left home, to "return to them and make them laugh as you made them weep."

Humor is as important in modern Islam as it is—and always has been—in all areas of human life, regardless of geographical location or religious persuasion.

Comedian Dave Chappelle converted to Islam at age 25 and has incorporated jokes about his experiences as an American Muslim into his popular stage act.

Although Muhammad expressed enjoyment, he did so within bounds. He discouraged humor that was at the expense of others or in any way deceitful. He was always moderate in the way that he expressed his own pleasure. Several Hadiths report that the Prophet smiled while his companions laughed. Aisha, the third wife of Muhammad, said: "I never saw the Prophet laugh fully to such an extent that I could see his uvula. He would rather smile."

PRESENT LAUGHTER

In the 21st century, the hostility of Muslims to satirical criticism of Islam has been adduced as evidence of their humorlessness. The best known case in point is the violent response to the publication in the Danish newspaper *Jyllands-Posten* on September 30, 2005, of 12 cartoons of the Prophet Muhammad. More than 100 people were killed in the riots that flared in many parts of the world as Muslims denounced these depictions as Islamophobic and racist. Some commentators claimed that this reaction was an assault on freedom of expression and showed an inability to take a joke. Other observers pointed out that the affront to Muslim sensibilities was exacerbated by the fact that the insult came, not from an agnostic, neutral perspective but from people raised in other—and, in this context, rival—faiths.

Humor is as important in modern Islam as it is—and always has been—in all areas of human life, regardless of geographical location or religious persuasion. In the West, the prominence of Muslim humor has increased since the terrorist attacks on New York and Washington, D.C., of September 11, 2001. This is one of the classic, general responses to tragedies and inexplicable events—to try to make them more bearable and comprehensible by laughing about them.

LEADING MODERN EXPONENTS

When the popular American comedian Dave Chappelle (b. 1973) revealed, in a 2005 interview with *Time* magazine, that he had converted to Islam in 1998, the news came as a surprise to many people. Chappelle explained, "I don't normally talk about my religion publicly because I don't want people to associate me and my flaws with this beautiful thing. And I believe it is beautiful if you learn it the right way." Chappelle was also the executive producer of *Allah Made Me Funny*, a touring stage production that featured himself and two other top American Muslim comics, Azhar Usman and Preacher Moss. One of Moss's jokes typified the show. He told audiences: "I'm African American and a Muslim, which basically means that when I'm pulled over by the police, I get two tickets instead of one."

The Canadian sitcom, *Little Mosque on the Prairie*, was premiered in 2007 and has since been shown in

Albert Brooks's movie *Looking for Comedy in the Muslim World* was dropped by the original production company, Sony Pictures, because they feared that the title was too controversial. The film was later distributed by Warner Independent Pictures.

more than 100 countries. It was created by Zarqa Nawaz (b. 1968), a British Canadian of Pakistani heritage. The drama derives from the interactions between an Islamic community and the non-Muslim residents of a small, rural Canadian town.

An independent American film, made in 2006, was based on the idea that Americans tend not to think of Muslims as people with a sense of humor. In *Looking for Comedy in the Muslim World*, the Jewish American comedian and actor Albert Brooks (b. 1947) is hired by the U.S. government to write a 500-page report on what makes Muslims laugh. He travels to India, where more than 150 million Muslims live, and sneaks into Pakistan, a majority Muslim country, for secret meetings with comedians. While Brooks does not find any answers, he reaches the conclusion that laughter is universal to all cultures and faiths.

Chapter 13

MEDIA

There is no strictly delineated entity that can be described as Muslim media. Muslims in Asia, Africa, Europe, Australia, and North America are served by a wide variety of media. Nevertheless, some of the characteristics of Muslim print journals, radio, and television are more or less common around the world.

The term *media* describes the many institutions and technologies used to distribute information and entertainment to the public. The term applies to many forms of mass communication, including newspapers, magazines, radio, television networks, movies, and the many services available on the Internet.

In the last decade the media industry in the Muslim world has grown exponentially; many countries have gone from having just one, state-controlled television and radio station to hundreds of competing commercial television and radio stations. Similar increases in the number of websites, newspapers, and magazines have been recorded. This growth is due to several factors, including technological advances, rising literacy rates, economic success, and a reduction in government interference.

The rapid expansion of the media industry has had a dramatic impact on the politics and culture of the Muslim world. It is now much harder for a government to control the flow of information to its people, who can access online news services, international satellite television networks, such as Al-Jazeera and Al Arabiya, and read first-hand accounts of important events on social networking websites.

Headlines on a newsstand in Tehran announce the 1980 death in exile of the former Shah beneath an image of the leader who deposed him, Ayatollah Khomeni.

COMMON THEMES

General issues that can be observed when discussing media in Muslim countries include: the intersection of politics with media; freedom of expression; and the legacy of colonialism. Around the world, it is not unusual for media and politics to influence one another. However, in some Muslim-majority countries, governments may control, manipulate, and censor media

❖

Some of the new media that have reshaped Western society, particularly the Internet, may not be as influential throughout the Muslim world.

for their own purposes. This is often more explicitly acknowledged than in Europe or North America. It is not unusual for journalists in Asian countries to limit their criticisms of the government or to avoid controversial topics to escape the inevitable unfavorable reaction.

Like entertainment, however, journalism finds ways to evolve in spite of constraints. After years of tightly restricting media

Dubai has positioned itself as the media hub of the Arab world, partly through the establishment of the free media zone at Dubai Media City.

outlets or limiting access by foreign media, governments in Jordan, Egypt, Lebanon, and the United Arab Emirates have moved toward the establishment of free media zones, in which various media outlets from abroad and from neighboring regions may have tax-free privileges and full operating control. Such privileges are granted to operations such as CNN, Reuters, Sony, and MBC in Dubai Media City, for example—but the situation may be less positive for media shut out of the free zone.

To some degree, the circumstances typified by Dubai Media City may be seen as an extension of a global imbalance.

Media flows often tend to come from Western countries and to be one-way. Media infrastructure continues to be stronger and more concentrated in places such as North America and Europe than in areas such as western and southern Asia or northern Africa.

All the same, changes have come to these regions, and the type and quantity of media continue to grow. Some change may be prompted by a cataclysmic event, such as the 1991 Gulf War, which demonstrated the power of satellite media and 24-hour news channels such as CNN. Other changes may stem from political leaders.

King Abdullah II has allowed more press freedom in Jordan, although it is hardly unrestricted, and King Mohamed VI relaxed some restrictions on journalists in Morocco following his accession in 1999. In 1999, the newly installed emir of Qatar lent money and support to the news channel Al-Jazeera, which has had an enormous impact on the way that media are perceived.

Critics who believe that the media in Asian countries demonstrate a bias against North America often oversimplify the climate within which those outlets operate. Many journalists in these countries are accustomed to seeing images of Arabs or Muslims in Western media that they consider unrepresentative or untruthful. If, in turn, they offer a more positive image of Arabs and Muslims, they may see this as a way of providing balance rather than bias. Still, some Muslim-run news organizations do express opinions that may be seen as extreme or anti-Semitic. The Israeli-Palestinian conflict informs an underlying current in many media outlets, although not all Islamic media are anti-Semitic or even anti-Israel.

Steps have been taken to change the pattern of communication in many Muslim-majority countries, but issues still persist with censorship and state control, varying approaches to human rights and freedoms, and a lack of audience research, which would help to plan for the future. Differing economic resources, as well as the legacy of colonial education and language, engender competition between national and foreign media.

Staff in the Al-Jazeera International newsroom prepare to launch the first English-language news and current affairs channel based in western Asia in November 2006.

The different Arabic dialects impeded the creation of pan-Arab media for some time. Many Muslim-majority countries, particularly former colonies, also commonly use French, English, or other European languages. Dialects and languages may be so different that it is difficult to meet the needs of all readers and listeners. As the mass media have grown, modern standard Arabic (MSA) has become more commonly used.

EARLY FORMS OF COMMUNICATION

As elsewhere, traditional forms of communication in Muslim societies tended to rely on word of mouth. Imams and town criers disseminated important information, and marketplaces and mosques were arenas for the exchange of news and gossip. Even today, the marketplace, or souk, continues to be a place where people meet regularly to disclose information or gossip. The same is often true of the mosque, although it may cater to a more specific population.

In the 19th century, colonial powers wished to bind together their empires. Beginning in 1857, the British worked with the Ottoman Empire to create a national telegraph system and later helped connect the Persians and the Ottomans. Cable lines ran from London to Tehran, while others joined India and England. Reuters opened its first news bureau in Bombay in 1870. Within the colonies, the telegraph allowed for better news flow, facilitating the creation of private newspapers and the inclusion of international news items.

Afghan men exchange views in a street in Kabul. Face-to-face communication is still an important way for news to spread.

PRINT MEDIA

Despite varying rates of illiteracy in countries where Muslims live, print media occupy an important place in many societies. Print was originally especially valued for its ability to capture and spread religious information. Later, colonizers were likely to promote newspapers as a way to consolidate their empires, often using the language of, and news from, the mainland. During his brief reign over Egypt, from 1798 to 1801, the French leader Napoleon Bonaparte started Egypt's first newspaper—in French—which was soon followed by the first Arabic-language newspapers. Countries such as Lebanon, Morocco, Algeria, and Tunisia quickly followed suit, with Kuwait and Bahrain joining much later. A distinctive press tradition tended to rise in countries where colonial influence was strongest. In places such as Egypt, Lebanon, Syria, and Algeria, the nationalist struggle became a key driver of print journalism in the early 20th century, as newspapers devoted themselves to opinionated commentary.

Some observers suggest that the Arab press, in general, tends to be less grounded in data and information than Western media and to be invested more in the promotion of ideas, literature, and culture. In the early 20th century, newspapers often relied on funding from political parties, which had certain expectations regarding the kind of coverage they could expect. Newspaper reading took place primarily among middle-class or upper-class citizens, who could be influential.

Countries that reclaimed their governments from colonizers, dictators, or other perceived oppressors did not normally inherit a free press. In a number of Arab countries, licenses are required for newspapers to publish and for journalists to work. Journalists are also aware of the influence of media, and some place their responsibility to the nation above all, believing that they should avoid creating conflict that would fracture national unity. Others may be critical, although sometimes selectively. For instance, the London-based *Al Sharq al-Awsat* offers more balance than other news outlets but has demonstrated strong bias on occasion, as with its antipathy toward the late Egyptian president Anwar Sadat. In Iraq, the United States funds outlets such as the newspaper *Al Sabah* (The dawn) to promote U.S. policies.

It is not unusual for newspapers to be created or operated outside of western Asia, even if their primary audience is located there. *Azzaman*, for example, was started in London by a journalist who left Saddam Hussein's Iraq. International newspapers such as *The Arab Times* offer news to Arab emigrants; the same trend is found with newspapers such as *The Times of India*, an English-language daily read by people of Indian origin all over the world.

India, like many Arab countries, is no stranger to censorship, but overall its press tends to operate within less strict confines, if only because laws regarding libel or access to information are not clearly defined. While radio and television are state-owned in India, print remains private, as is also true in Pakistan. In both countries, the press is sometimes viewed as responding too obviously to special interests or to political influence. In Pakistan, the media have been accused of promoting Taliban messages; in India, the media are often seen as supporting religious or political factions.

Even within these countries, however, media outlets may support divergent positions. Newspapers in Pakistan, for example, do not hold uniform views. *Nawa-e-Waqt* tends to be more supportive of opposition parties, while *Jang*, with a higher circulation, generally favors the governing party. *Dawn*, Pakistan's leading English-language paper, was founded by independence leader Muhammad Ali Jinnah and can be more critical of the government than the two Urdu newspapers, as it is viewed as an outlet

In a significant example of the impact of print media, the 1979 Islamic Revolution in Iran was spurred at least partly by leaflets distributed by activists.

for the elite rather than the masses. Similarly, Indonesia has two major newspapers: *Jawa Pos* is more commercial, while *Kompas* is both more intellectual and more influential.

In a significant example of the impact of print media, the 1979 Islamic Revolution in Iran was spurred at least partly by leaflets distributed by activists. Countries like Turkey—which has a number of strong, privately owned newspapers—have a long-standing literary tradition where novelists may write social commentary, as in the case of Nobel Prize-winner Orhan Pamuk. Pamuk has, however, been put on trial for expressing "anti-Turkish" opinions.

NEWS AGENCIES

If newspapers are meaningful ways to promote government policies and power, so too is the establishment of news agencies to gather information. In the 19th century,

Reuters established itself in Egypt and in India. Until World War II (1939–1945), only European news agencies were found in many countries with large Muslim populations. This was not initially a source of conflict; people often welcomed the import of foreign news as a sign of modernization or cosmopolitanism. Foreign news was also less likely to attract government ire than domestic news. Following the war, however, Associated Press (AP) and United Press International (UPI) offered alternatives to Reuters and the newly renamed Agence France-Press; domestic news agencies also appeared.

The first Muslim news agency was established in Sudan in 1945. It was followed in 1956 by Egypt's Middle East News Agency (MENA). The Iraqi News Agency, Tunis Afrique Press, Maghrib Arab Press, and Lebanese National News Agency were founded before 1960, and other bureaus of the same kind were later set up elsewhere. India is served by two agencies, United News of India and Press Trust of India. Despite this increased diversity, large agencies such as AP, UPI, and Reuters still tend to dominate international news flows.

RADIO

More than newspapers, radio and television have been key transmitters of propaganda and are frequently used by governments to send out sponsored messages. The United States has expressed concern about this, especially since its own long-standing station in the region, Voice of America (VOA), does not have notable influence. Following the terrorist events in New York, Washington, D.C., and Pennsylvania on September 11, 2001, the United States set out to reach Arab youth through a brand-new station, Radio Sawa (Together), which features Arab and U.S. pop music as well as news and caters to a younger demographic than VOA.

Radio has been an enormous internal political influence in the region. A station such as Voice of the Arabs, owned by Egyptians but broadcasting into many regions, urged political action in a number of areas, to the concern of local politicians.

Radio is influential for a number of reasons: It is cheap and easy to broadcast over a wide range; it overcomes issues of illiteracy; and it exploits aspects of the oral tradition prized in many Muslim cultures. Such a medium lends itself well to promoting a cult of personality, and Muslim countries have had numerous strong leaders who have been expert

orators. Just as U.S. president Franklin D. Roosevelt exploited the radio in the 1930s and 1940s with his famous fireside chats, the dominant figure in western Asian radio during the 1950s and 1960s was Egyptian president Gamal Abdel Nasser. Nasser's ability as an orator, combined with smart management of radio and a strong belief in pan-Arab policies, led other governments to fear his influence.

Egypt pioneered radio broadcasting in the early 1930s, when the government took an active role in the industry. An agreement with Marconi in the United Kingdom helped establish a radio service in 1934. Following Egyptian independence in 1936, the new government took control of broadcasting. Today Egypt is home to a well-developed radio system, based mainly in Cairo and Alexandria. Radio stations

The main studios of Radio Sawa are in Dubai in the United Arab Emirates (UAE).

have included Radio Cairo, the Middle East Program, and the Egyptian Radio and Television Union.

Jordan's broadcasting system also had connections to the British. Its roots lay in the Palestine Broadcasting Service (PBS), founded by the British in 1936, and English and French radio services continue to cater to many people in Jordan. Lebanon's media systems have also been affected by colonial influences. The first radio station's existence can be credited to the French government, which wanted to counter Italian and German propaganda. Later broadcasting projects stemmed from Lebanese initiatives, and a station such as Voice of Lebanon, founded in 1975, has been praised for forging success independent of the government.

Syria's broadcasting system advanced partly through Egypt's assistance and echoed Egypt's propagandistic model. In its nascent stages, Syrian radio broadcasting benefited from an exchange program that allowed Syrians to train in Egypt.

Egyptian radio spurred the start of broadcasting in southern Yemen, where British officials were frustrated by its influence. They set up local stations but found it difficult to compete with Voice of the Arabs. Similarly, Iraq's radio service could not provide strong opposition to Voice of the Arabs, although Saddam Hussein did try to use broadcasting as a propaganda tool.

Saudi Arabia is one of the most complex subjects in regard to broadcasting. In the 1960s, conservative religious leaders refused to countenance radio until the king had set up a demonstration in which a recitation of the Koran was broadcast. However, music was still forbidden. In an effort to influence the listening patterns of its citizens, the government created its own station, which leaned heavily toward religious programs.

Like other countries in the region, however, Saudi Arabia was compelled to react when Voice of the Arabs began to generate dissatisfaction with the Saudi royal family. In response, the government launched two new radio stations to compete more aggressively with Egypt and also eased restrictions on broadcasters. By the early 1960s, the government had realized that it was impossible to ban music

AUDIO- AND VIDEOCASSETTES

Nowadays, audiocassettes are among those technologies that are less commonly seen in many Western and Muslim countries; they have been replaced by CDs and MP3 technology. However, they do deserve mention, given the importance of their circulation during the Islamic Revolution in Iran. Living in exile, with attempts at mass communication curtailed by the shah's regime, the Ayatollah Khomeini transmitted his message through sermons that were taped and disseminated by his followers.

In more mundane ways, audio- and videocassettes have been used to circulate sermons or banned music in many Middle Eastern countries, to such an extent that the Arab Postal Union at one time prohibited the mailing of any cassettes. Not surprisingly, such recording media are also central to problems with piracy, damaging the profitability of industries such as India's Bollywood. More recently, however, piracy issues tend to be centered more in the Internet and DVDs rather than videocassettes.

or female announcers entirely when Saudis could hear both on Egyptian radio.

The ability to transmit beyond borders, or to transmit in an unofficial capacity, has been key to radio's development in western Asia. Transmissions from the Palestine Broadcasting Corporation can be heard in parts of Jordan, Syria, and Egypt, as well as Saudi Arabia, and illegal radio transmissions also abound. Tunisian radio became available online in the late 1990s, marking a first both for the Arab world and for Africa. Like Tunisia, Morocco also began radio early. Broadcasts in Arabic and Berber continue to be important for those who cannot read or speak French, or afford television. Sudan's population, aside from being widely dispersed, also includes many non-Arabic speakers. The national program that is intended to blanket the country broadcasts in Arabic only.

Iraq faces challenges of its own, a fact recognized by the United States, which has founded the Iraqi Media Network as a radio and TV network along the lines of PBS or the British Broadcasting Corporation (BBC). The latter is already popular in parts of the developing world, but in the Arab region, Radio Monte Carlo (RMC) is also well-established. RMC can be heard in various areas in the region and is very popular.

India was one of the first countries to broadcast to western Asia in Arabic, in 1941, to reach guest workers living in Arab countries. Indian and Pakistani guest workers are still found in large numbers throughout western Asia, and some radio stations operate an Urdu service. Various countries have attempted to gain a foothold in broadcasting in the region, and Christian stations also use radio as a way to attract converts.

Radio remains popular but does not have the widespread influence that it held in the early 1950s, perhaps because citizens are less likely to accept without question the version of events being broadcast.

TELEVISION

Many Muslim-majority countries have their own TV stations and some form of domestic programming, but foreign channels are also popular. Estimates suggest that 10 million Indonesians receive MTV, for example, while a million Iranians have access to CNN, and BBC is widely available. At the same time, numbers alone do not tell the tale. The BBC is important because it is considered credible; in Pakistan, where many citizens have lost faith in state-owned television, BBC's Urdu service is the preferred source for reliable information. CNN is important because its format influenced other broadcasters and because it played a key role in the 1991 Gulf War, a fact that was not lost on observers in western Asia. Similarly, the international reporting of CNN, BBC, and now Al-Jazeera serves as a reminder of how interconnected the world is. The development of television in many countries has been a response to the citizens' attachment to and respect for foreign media. National TV stations are also a symbol of national unity, development, and modernity.

The television industry in Northern Africa has its origins in the late 1950s and early 1960s. During its early years, television was used as a form of cultural and political propaganda by both nationalist governments and former colonial powers of Europe. In Algeria, for example, the national television station was established as a propaganda instrument by the French government, broadcasting in French. After Algeria gained its independence, the television station became an important part of the government's Arabization policy, broadcasting in Arabic despite its largely French-speaking staff. Television in Tunisia has a similar history; the national television station was established in the 1960s in response to the growing number of households who watched television broadcasts from Italy. Private or partly private stations have opened across the region in more recent years, but governments have maintained a significant stake in the television industry.

Egypt moved into television in the 1950s when the United Arab Republic and the Radio Corporation of America (RCA) helped provide a service for both Egypt and Syria. Egypt had personnel from radio, as well as from film, to create a significant

amount of its own programming. Egyptian film and television programming still constitute a valuable export. Cable News Egypt (CNE), founded in 1991, demonstrates the fusion of West and East through its partnership between CNN and ERTU, the Egyptian Radio-Television Union. While government controls of media persist, they have been relaxed somewhat under President Hosni Mubarak.

In the last 15 years several countries in the Arabian Peninsula have developed large and influential television industries. In 1996 Qatar was the first country to launch an international television station, the news station Al-Jazeera. Al-Jazeera now operates a network of different channels providing news, sports coverage, documentaries, and children's programming. The rise of Al-Jazeera spurred Qatar's neighbors to invest in their own television industries, resulting in the launch of the news channel Al Arabiya, based in Saudi Arabia, in 2003, and the entertainment station Dubai TV, based in Dubai's media city, in 2004. Although most countries in the region have largely ceased officially censoring the media, both Al-Jazeera and Al Arabiya have been accused of ignoring stories that would portray their host countries in a negative light. A high proportion of households in the region have access to international satellite television; in Bahrain, for example, surveys suggested that as many as 99 percent of households have a satellite television receiver.

India and Pakistan both have state-owned television channels, but they operate in different economic and political circumstances. Doordarshan, India's state-owned network, was dominant until the early 1990s when India embarked on a policy of liberalization. By 2004,

THE VOICE OF THE ARABS

Historically, the Voice of the Arabs radio station has played a significant role in Middle East politics, due in no small part to the careful exploitation of the medium by Egypt's President Nasser. Founded in 1953, Voice of the Arabs used music, entertainment, and news to bookend more political programming that was openly hostile to neighboring regimes of which Nasser disapproved. Voice of the Arabs' influence extended into 1950s Iraq, where the station's vociferous campaign against Iraq's prime minister, Nuri as-Said, may have contributed to the 1958 overthrow of the royal family. The propaganda issued from Voice of the Arabs alienated a large part of the Egyptian population, however, during the 1967 Six-Day War, when rapid defeat by Israel confirmed that the station's optimistic view of Egypt's success was unfounded. From that point onward, the tone of the station's broadcasting became less strident and its influence was not as great.

Doordarshan faced competition from a variety of commercial 24-hour news channels. Just as some developing countries complain about the influence of U.S. programming, so places such as Pakistan and Bangladesh are influenced greatly by Indian programming, which is easily accessible and may have superior production values. Pakistan's own PTV is not seen as objective, being clearly influenced by the government.

In Central Asia, television was introduced in the 1950s when the region was part of the Soviet Union. There were typically three channels offered during the years of Soviet control. The first two were the same for all the states in the region, and were broadcast from Moscow; the third was run by the local government of each state. The majority of the programming was in Russian, and local customs and religious practices were ignored or actively criticized. Although some progress has been made since the countries of the region gained their independence in 1991, the state of television broadcasting varies considerably from one country to the next. In Tajikistan, for example, the television industry has expanded since 1991 to include regional and privately owned stations, as well as a variety of state-run channels. By contrast, in Turkmenistan, there is still just one, state-controlled television station—Turkmen TV—that broadcasts only heavily censored propaganda material.

Television is the most popular form of media in the Muslim countries of Southeast Asia. Both Indonesia and

A Muslim family in Indian Kashmir talk to relatives in Pakistani Kashmir on a video link organized for a BBC Urdu program in 2004.

TV DRAMA

In Saudi Arabia, religious leaders were even more opposed to television than they had been to radio. However, as Saudi Arabia worked to combat Egyptian propaganda, the government became determined to build sophisticated telecommunications facilities. In response to a request for help, the U.S. Army Corps of Engineers helped establish television infrastructure. In the 1950s, a television station debuted with mainly American programming directed at U.S. military in the region. A subsequent station mixed American and local programming, but by the 1960s, the Saudi government knew that it had to develop its own system. Some of its citizens had already experienced television through visits to neighboring countries, and the government realized that providing its own system would allow it to exercise more control over what Saudis saw; it would also allow Saudi Arabia to have the same symbols of modernism as other leading Arab nations.

Ironically, the antagonism that conservatives in Saudi Arabia felt toward television indirectly ended the reign of King Faisal and his attempts at moving the nation forward. Khalid ibn Musad, King Faisal's nephew, gathered protestors in a public expression of opposition to the construction of television equipment. Soon after, Khalid was killed in a mysterious struggle with an official from the Ministry of the Interior. Almost a decade later, Khalid's younger brother, Faisal ibn Musad, assassinated King Faisal in an act that many believe was rooted in revenge for Khalid's killing.

King Faisal's death did not halt the progress of television, which by that time had become well-established. By 1975 the system was managed by Saudis, some of whom received broadcast training in the United States under the supervision of the Army Corps of Engineers. Taking seriously its position as the kingdom that houses two of Islam's most sacred sites, Saudi Arabia began broadcasting from Mecca during Ramadan and hajj and generally reserved a high percentage of its programming for religious matters. Saudi Arabia does import programming from other Arab nations and from the West, but it follows strict censorship guidelines; those guidelines have only tightened since the 1991 Gulf War. Sexually provocative scenes, blasphemy, scantily dressed women, alcohol, and gambling are just a few of the items that are not allowed on Saudi television. While the government has been careful to limit any programming that may undermine its authority, in 1979 it learned a lesson from the attempted takeover of the Grand Mosque, when officials tried to control the story only to realize that citizens suspected the government of minimizing the extent of the damage. In an about-face, the media then found that it was more helpful to broadcast accurate details, since withholding them merely sparked concern.

Malaysia have several private- and government-owned television networks. Under the military dictatorships that controlled the country from 1967 to 1998, television in Indonesia was heavily censored, but today it is largely unrestricted and reflects the cultural diversity of the country. In Malaysia, however, television is strictly monitored by the government, which imposes Islamic rules of decency on all programming. Furthermore, while there are plenty of television networks, the public's access to international satellite television networks is limited.

FILM

Movies of interest to Muslims are produced both within and outside Muslim-majority countries. Indigenous film industries such as Pakistan's

Reporter Farah Nourentin checks her notes in the offices of the TV channel Al-Manar (The beacon), set up by the political movement Hezbollah in Beirut, Lebanon, to broadcast throughout the region and in Europe. Some Western governments ban Al-Manar for promoting terrorism.

Lollywood (based in Lahore) attempt to offer images through which Muslim South Asians can recognize themselves, as well as stories that uphold cultural and religious values, as interpreted by the filmmakers. Lollywood is careful to maintain cultural norms that distinguish it from its major competitor, India's Mumbai–based film industry, Bollywood. Bollywood also depicts Islam and Muslims at times and employs a large number of Muslim actors, screenwriters, lyricists, and others.

However, most Bollywood films tend to valorize Hindu nationalism, culture, and rituals, marginalizing Islam and Pakistan to at least some degree.

Given the tense history between India and Pakistan, which is embedded partly in religious differences, Pakistan has chosen to operate its own industry and attempts to prevent its citizens from viewing Bollywood films. Despite this, Bollywood films continue to be very popular in Pakistan, where they remain accessible

Hala Sarhan, a talk show host on the private Egyptian station Dream TV, caused great controversy in 2002 when her live satellite show discussed sexuality and masturbation, which are widely considered taboo in the Arab world.

through black-market satellite dishes, videos, and DVDs, and among Muslim South Asians in diaspora. This may be due partly to the close cultural affinity between the two countries, but also simply to Bollywood's bigger budgets and glossier productions.

As Bollywood, marketing vigorously to audiences in North America and Europe,

increasingly incorporates sexually explicit scenes and other departures from its traditional conservatism, Lollywood has tried to define itself as more conservative and better-suited to Muslim values.

In parts of the Arab world, Muslim values are interpreted as requiring opposition to public cinemas; therefore, many countries do not invest in film development. In Morocco, investors find films a risky proposition. In places such as Algeria, women cannot visit a cinema. Some countries rely instead on imported movies, although they tend to censor those that are seen as explicit or immoral.

Countries such as Egypt have experienced both foreign influence and indigenous development, moving from privatization to nationalization and back again. Although Egypt's film industry is not as large as India's and has sometimes drawn criticism from those who dislike signs of Westernization or what is considered to be common vulgarity, it has demonstrated more strength than most in the region. Just as Egypt and Lebanon have been leaders in broadcasting, Lebanon joins Egypt in having a relatively strong film industry.

Pakistan has chosen to operate its own industry and attempts to prevent its citizens from viewing Bollywood films.

However, some commentators argue that the real story for film and the Muslim world has to do with the many movies that address themes related to Islam but are not produced in the Muslim world. Iranian filmmakers living in exile following the Islamic Revolution have been especially productive, but also Algerians, Lebanese, Palestinians, Turks, Moroccans, and Tunisians living outside their countries of origin have produced films that are seen around the world and that may explore political or social issues with a freedom that is lacking in their native countries.

THE INTERNET

Although film can appeal to Muslims living outside their native countries, the Internet has been described by some as the truly global medium. While Internet penetration rates remain low in many Muslim-majority countries compared to rates in North America, Europe, and Australia, it is rising. In 2008 an estimated 180 million of the world's Internet users lived in the Muslim world, compared to only 40 million in 2002. This rapid growth has been mostly limited to towns and cities so far, but the number of users in rural areas is expanding.

As the proportion of Internet users in the Muslim world increases, so too does the number of websites that cater to their interests and cultural backgrounds. While in the past, an understanding of English was considered necessary to use the Internet, websites in languages such as Arabic, Persian, and Turkish have become more and more common in recent years as demand increases. This change has been helped by the development of internationalized domain names (IDNs). IDNs allow Internet addresses to be written in languages that use different alphabet systems.

The relatively unmonitored nature of the Internet has also made it an important tool for Islamist militants. They can attract publicity with videos of terrorist acts; promote their ideology through articles, sermons, and speeches; and can distribute guides and instructions for others planning terrorist acts. In many Western countries, viewing websites that encourage or celebrate terrorist acts is against the law and can bring a prison sentence or placement on a terrorist watch-list.

THE INTERNET AND POLITICS

The Internet has taken on a special importance in Muslim countries where the government controls or censors traditional forms of mass media. Although some governments do monitor and block access to certain websites, there are many ways for users to work around these restrictions.

There are many services on the Internet that allow users to post pictures, videos, and text that they have created themselves; once online, this content can be viewed by anyone, anywhere. These services have enabled ordinary Muslims to report on events that larger media organizations are either unable or unwilling to report.

The first prominent example of this phenomenon was a 2003 blog (online journal) kept by an Iraqi translator who wrote under the name Salam Pax. Dubbed the "Baghdad Blogger" in the Western media,

Salam Pax's daily reports gave a first-person perspective on what the 2003 Iraq war was like for ordinary Iraqis. As few reporters

> The Internet has taken on a special importance in Muslim countries where the government controls or censors traditional forms of mass media.

stayed in the country during the invasion, his reports provided a perspective on the war that was otherwise absent from media reports. In the aftermath of the invasion, he continued to write about the conditions that Iraqis faced each day, describing the shortages, power cuts, and bomb attacks that became part of everyday life in Baghdad.

Billboards of movie stars at a movie theater in Karachi, Pakistan.

In neighboring Iran, the Internet has become a vital means of expression. One 2005 study found that Iran had one blog for every ten Internet users—one of the highest rates in the world. Activists used their blogs to organize protests and political campaigns, switching hosts and identities constantly to work around government censorship. During the disputed Iranian elections of 2009, the Internet became even more important as a tool for opposition activists, both as a means of communication and as a way to publicize their cause. In the days following the disputed election, social networking websites such as Twitter and Facebook were used by opposition supporters to spread news of upcoming protests and appearances by opposition leaders. Such was the importance attached to these online tools that the United States government requested that Twitter's owners

During the disputed Iranian elections of 2009, the Internet became even more important as a tool for opposition activists, both as a means of communication and as a way to publicise their cause.

postpone some scheduled maintenance until 2 a.m. Iranian time so as to not disrupt opposition activities.

Despite its perceived importance at the time, however, many analysts have subsequently concluded that social networking sites were actually not widely used to coordinate opposition activities. They cite the fact that Internet access is monitored and restricted in Iran, so the number of Iranians able to use such

ISLAM ONLINE

Many websites targeted specifically at Muslims are used to promote religious knowledge, analyzing the Koran, allowing debate, or providing guidance on religious issues, often from noted scholars. The Internet can thus be seen as belonging to the Islamic tradition of exchanging viewpoints. Muslims around the world also use the Internet and other electronic media to report on current events or to protest against governments or social injustice. In 2009, news of protests against presidential election results in Iran were widely disseminated by mobile phone and Twitter. Some observers note that e-mails and text messages present a way of evading government restrictions just as photocopies and faxes once did—even if specific messages are not permitted, the technologies cannot be completely shut down. The Internet and other digital technologies provide Muslims with forums to explore religion, society, and politics, and ways to forge communities and movements, although not all Muslims currently have access.

websites was restricted to the small number with Internet access and the technical skills required to circumvent government censorship. However, while social networking sites played only a relatively small role in the coordination of opposition, they were an important stage in the process of getting information to people and governments outside Iran.

With Western news agencies banned from reporting the protests within the country, opposition groups turned to the Internet to publicize their cause. Pictures and video footage, shot on mobile phones, was posted to websites such as YouTube and Flickr, and quickly picked up by international news agencies. One piece of footage, showing the fatal shooting of a female protester, Neda Agha Soltan, led to international condemnation of the Iranian government and raised the profile of the opposition movement around the world.

See Also
Visual Arts 198–219 ❖
Performing Arts
270–289 ❖ Al-Jazeera
310–311 ❖

Al-Jazeera

In the aftermath of the 9/11 attacks of 2001, Al-Jazeera was widely criticized in the West for acting as a mouthpiece for terrorism. Supporters of the station argue that it merely redresses the usual anti-Islamic bias of the broadcast media.

Founded in 1996 with an investment of $150 million from the emir of Qatar, Al-Jazeera (which translates as "the Peninsula") has introduced a transformative and controversial style of broadcasting to the Arab world. In a region where TV networks are often subject to control, Al-Jazeera has offended many through its candor, its airing of gruesome images, and its willingness to discuss issues that are normally taboo for Arabs and Muslims, often from different perspectives.

Already established with Arab viewers, Al-Jazeera came to international attention in 2001 with its coverage of the war in Afghanistan and broadcasts of videotapes featuring Osama bin Laden. While critics, especially U.S. officials, have expressed suspicion of Al-Jazeera as a mouthpiece for terrorism and dangerous Arab causes, the channel has been criticized by Arab governments for giving airtime to Americans and Israelis. Despite complaints from regional and Western governments to Qatar, which still funds the channel, the state has usually refused to become involved in editorial decisions. In turn, critics note that Al-Jazeera's famous frankness does not apply to Qatar itself, which is rarely featured.

Qatar's larger neighbors may find themselves the subject of impassioned debate, sometimes on popular

On an unannounced visit to the station's unprepossessing headquarters, Egyptian president Hosni Mubarak reportedly exclaimed, "All this trouble from this matchbox!"

shows such as *Al-Ittijah Al-Mua'kis* (Opposite direction), which uses figures with very different positions on an issue. Al-Jazeera is often criticized for employing commentators who hold extreme views and offer inflammatory feedback. Al-Jazeera makes no apologies for this or for broadcasting polarizing figures such as bin Laden or Israeli officials. Its proud slogan is "The opinion, and the other opinion." While some North Americans see the network as pro-Arab and anti-American, other observers note that Al-Jazeera is bound

A still from an Al-Jazeera report shows a child injured in a U.S. airstrike in Afghanistan. Widely condemned in the West for showing such images, Al-Jazeera argues that they are important in the cause of balance.

Ghida Fakhry (left) and Dave Marash (right) anchor the first live news bulletin on the opening day of Al Jazeera's English-language service from Washington, D.C., in November 2006.

to have a western Asian perspective, just as U.S. media have a North American perspective. The bulk of Al-Jazeera's programming is international, rather than local.

In November 2001, the United States destroyed the al-Jazeera headquarters in Kabul, Afghanistan, with an airstrike. The U.S. government suggested that the office was a site for al-Qaeda activity, but the fact that an Al-Jazeera office in Baghdad was also attacked in 2003 during the war in Iraq—killing a correspondent—has led some to believe that the United States was deliberately targeting the network. More recently, U.S. and British officials seem to feel that they are better served by embracing the network. High-profile figures such as former British prime minister Tony Blair and former U.S. secretary of state Condoleeza Rice have both appeared on Al-Jazeera.

In an attempt to build its global audience, Al-Jazeera started using English subtitles in 2002 and shortly after, launched an English-language network with offices in Doha, Kuala Lumpur, London, and Washington.

Al-Jazeera maintains more than 25 bureaus, although diplomatic problems have caused temporary closures, as in a 1998 dispute with Jordan. Al-Jazeera's staff are drawn from a range of Arab countries and many are trained by the BBC. Its visual appearance echoes that of the BBC, as it captures a quick-moving aesthetic familiar to Western viewers. Although the network has not been a huge commercial success and occasionally struggles to attract advertising, it has had a remarkable global impact given the smallness of its base. On an unannounced visit to the station's unprepossessing headquarters, Egyptian president Hosni Mubarak reportedly exclaimed, "All this trouble from this matchbox!" Operating out of a country of roughly 900,000 inhabitants, Al-Jazeera attracts an estimated audience of 35 million people, including more than 200,000 subscribers in North America.

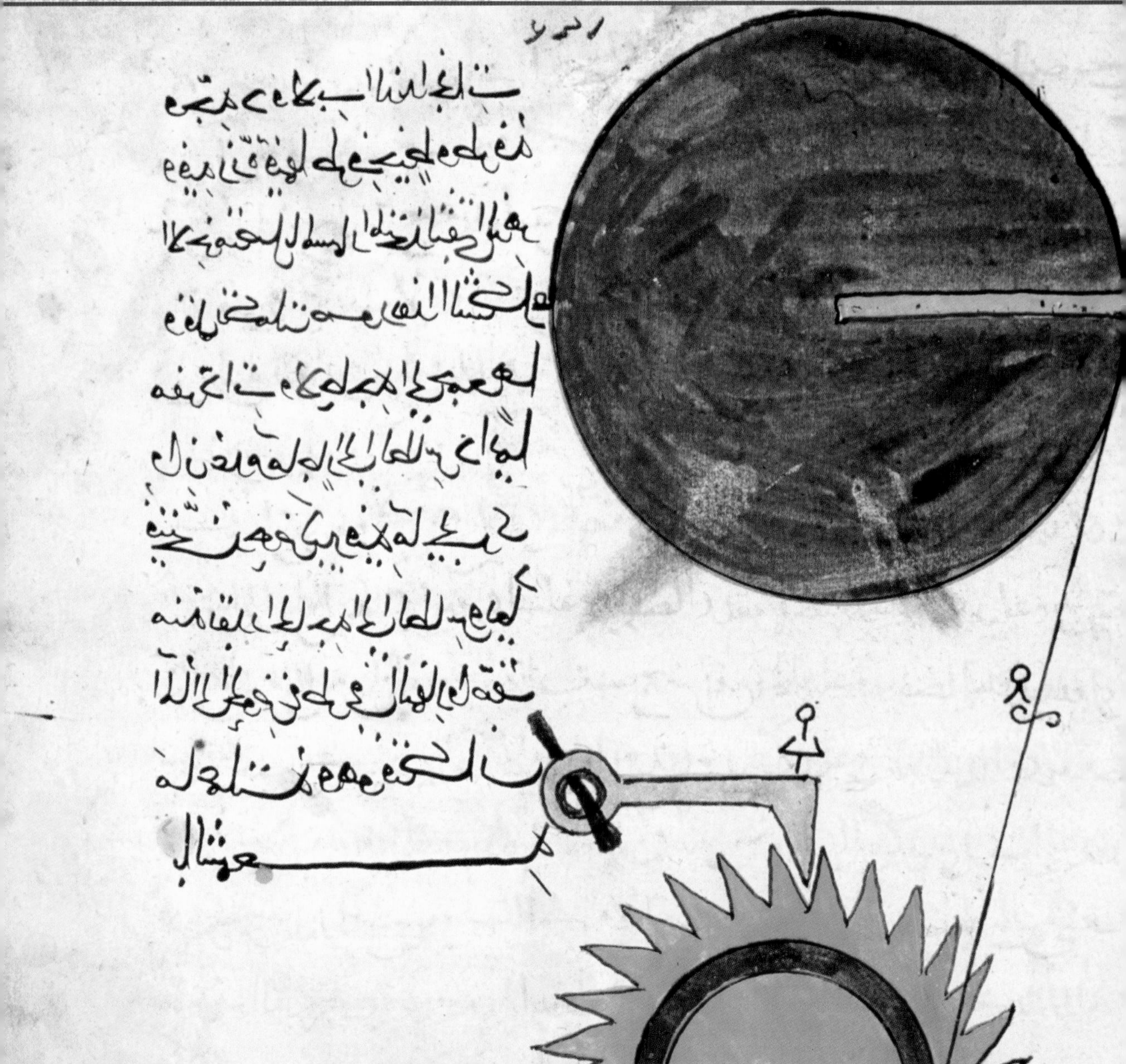

Chapter 14

PHILOSOPHY AND SCIENCE

The history of ideas in the emerging Muslim world was subjected to two main influences. The first was the teachings of the Koran and the other sacred works of Islam. The second was increasing contact with non-Arab cultures, most notably with the philosophy and science of Greek civilization.

The development of Muslim philosophy is strongly linked to the emergence of Islam as a major religion. Islam was based on the revelations received by Muhammad between 610 and 632 and recorded in the Koran. Although divine revelation is central to the Koran, the holy book of Islam was supplemented by a collection of documents that reported the Hadith (sayings) and deeds of the

---

❖

The early Muslim community was preoccupied with determining the precise meaning of the texts: Which practices did the revelation permit? Which practices did it forbid?

Prophet. This collection, known as the Sunnah (Prophetic way), together with the Koran, make up the core of the Muslim tradition. The reception and interpretation of these documents are crucial to understanding the subsequent history of Islamic philosophy.

The early Muslim community was preoccupied with determining the precise meaning of the texts: Which practices did the revelation permit? Which practices did it forbid? Numerous interpretations emerged through variant readings of the holy works, and those interpretations are among both the causes and the effects of the great importance attached to grammar and linguistics in the development of knowledge in Islam. Later, religious clerics specialized in interpreting the Koran and applying its strictures to day-to-day matters. Some scholars even used the Koran and the Sunnah to adjudicate legal matters.

Gradually, as Muslim society evolved and its problems became too complex for straightforward resolution by reference to the key Islamic texts, theologians became increasingly involved in interpreting the will of God and applying it to a host of situations and problems that had emerged long after the revelation and the composition of the texts.

The earliest Islamic theologians were the Mutazilites, who emerged in the eighth

This manuscript illustration comes from *Book of Knowledge of Ingenious Mechanical Devices*, written in 1206 by the Arab scholar al-Jazari.

century. The name in Arabic means "those who stand apart" and refers to their refusal to take either side in the dispute between the Sunnis and the Shiites over the rightful heir of the Prophet. The Mutazilites used rational arguments in support of their view that all humans have free will under God and that God's justice is absolute.

In the middle of the eighth century, the original Islamic ruling order, the Umayyad caliphate, was overthrown and replaced by the Abbasid dynasty (750–1258). The Abbasids presided over the first full flowering of Muslim culture, as Islam developed from a religion into a way of

The Mutazilites used rational arguments in support of their view that all humans have free will under God and that God's justice is absolute.

life. The growth of Islam was accelerated after the Abbasids moved their capital from Damascus (the capital of present-day Syria) to Baghdad (the capital of present-day Iraq), a city that had previously been colonized by people from the area of southeastern Europe that is now mainly Greece. The Abbasids were thus strongly influenced by Greek learning and culture.

The Muslim rulers of Baghdad rapidly absorbed Greek scientific expertise, a process that was accelerated by an immense translation project that made most of Greek learning available in Arabic. Particular attention was paid to the disciplines that appeared to have the greatest practical potential, principally astrology (which was related to, but at that time took

precedence over, astronomy), mathematics, and medicine.

Muslims were also influenced by Greek philosophy, but their interaction with it was sometimes controversial. The main difficulty was in reconciling the revelation of God's word to Muhammad with the strict rationality of Greek thought. The ensuing intellectual difficulties brought Arab thinkers into conflict with the imams (religious leaders).

Orthodox Muslim resistance to Greek philosophy was based on two main objections. First, Greek rationalism was perceived as an unwelcome intrusion into Islam that would dilute the purity of the Koran. Second, the Greeks were pagans and, as such, lacked the piety required fully to comprehend the Prophet's experiences. The subsequent history of Islam was characterized by the divisions that emerged between those Muslims who were willing and able to reconcile divine revelation with rational philosophy and those who adhered strictly to the belief that rational philosophy would inevitably corrupt the word of the Prophet.

The Muslim opponents of Greek philosophy based their arguments on their belief that the revelations in the Koran were, in themselves, sufficient to guide individuals and society both in this world and in the world to come. In addition, there were certain features of Greek philosophy that were in contradiction to strongly held Islamic beliefs. It is because of these contradictory beliefs—together with philosophy's claim to explain the nature of the universe by reason alone—that philosophy's status was always fragile under Islam. For philosophers, questions about the nature of truth could always be resolved rationally. However, for strictly orthodox

Islamic scientists, whose education had been grounded in the Koran and the Sunnah, it was the revelation to Muhammad that ultimately determined whether something was true.

NEOPLATONISM

The most important philosophical school of the period—and the one that exerted the greatest influence on early Islamic thought—was Neoplatonism, a development of the ideas of Plato (428–348 BCE) and his student Aristotle (384–322 BCE). According to Neoplatonism, the cosmos had a hierarchical structure, with a singular intellect at the top and the world inhabited by humans at the bottom. This scheme of things offered an innovative solution to the philosophical problem of "the One and the Many"— the attempt to understand the single being responsible for the whole of creation. The Neoplatonic solution was that "the Many" were the products of a series of emanations from a singular, pure unity— "the One." The theory of emanations maintained the link between the One and the Many while clearing the former of responsibility for the faults of the latter. This neat solution to the age-old problem of how a perfect being can have created such an imperfect world was easy to reconcile with the foundational beliefs of Islam.

The man commonly regarded as the first Islamic philosopher and the first Muslim thinker to engage seriously with Greek philosophy was al-Kindi (died c. 870). Al-Kindi's scholarly output was not restricted to Neoplatonism; he wrote on a wide range of other subjects, including arithmetic, astrology, cooking, medicine, and sword making. He was the first in a long line of Muslim polymaths—scholars who concerned themselves with anything and everything that might increase their own and their readers' understanding of the universe.

Al-Kindi often worked in opposition to traditionalist theologians and jurists who were suspicious and fearful of any knowledge that was not clearly grounded in divine revelation. One of his most important treatises, and the first of its kind in Islamic thought, is known in English as *Exhortation to Study Philosophy*. Although the manuscript is lost, the major points of al-Kindi's argument can be reconstructed by reference to his other surviving works. Al-Kindi praises philosophy as the highest of the human arts, defining it as the knowledge of the reality of things. He distinguishes between several branches of philosophy and identifies metaphysics as the highest branch of all.

The main aim of metaphysics—which al-Kindi calls "first philosophy"—is to comprehend the meaning of the True One (an extension of "the One"). The True One is eternal and infinite and therefore cannot be compared to other classes of existing things. The True One is incorporeal (has no body) and is beyond the categories of time and space. The True One is the cause of all existing things and the force that maintains them in all their widely varied forms.

Without the principle of unity, according to al-Kindi, nothing would exist. Contrary to the claim of Aristotle that the world is eternal, and contrary to the Neoplatonic notion that the world is the result of an eternal process of emanations between different levels of being, al-Kindi claimed that the True One is the originator of all things through creating the world out of nothing. Here al-Kindi is faithful to the Koran, which also states that the world was formed out of nothing by the Creator.

Al-Kindi regards all sources of knowledge, regardless of their cultural origins, as equally valuable for the pursuit of the one truth. He also warns of the danger of using religion as an excuse to hinder people from the search for truth. The pursuit of philosophy is essential because even those who claim that it is unnecessary are obliged to provide an argument to support their claim and, in doing so, they are necessarily engaged in a philosophical act. Moreover, philosophy illuminates the truth of religion and is an important aid to understanding the Koran.

In the work of al-Farabi, the links between the truths contained in the revelations to Muhammad and the truth of philosophical inquiry became much looser.

Al-Kindi acquired a large following that included the Christian philosopher Yahya ibn Adi (d. 972?). Among Ibn Adi's students was al-Farabi (c. 878–950), one of the most important Islamic philosophers.

In the work of al-Farabi, the links between the truths contained in the revelations to Muhammad and the truth of philosophical inquiry became much looser and were often severed altogether. Al-Farabi, the major Neoplatonist thinker in Islamic philosophy, specialized in logic, political philosophy, and metaphysics. One of his major works, known in English as *Enumeration of the Sciences*, introduced a

Muslim audience to the structure of the Greek philosophical education system, which provided a classification of the various sciences of the day.

The first group of al-Farabi's classification system comprised the philosophical sciences, which included mathematics and its subdivisions (arithmetic, astrology, astronomy, geometry, mechanics, and music). The next group featured the natural sciences, of which al-Farabi identified eight subdivisions, each corresponding to a separate work of Aristotle on the physical sciences. Al-Farabi's third category was divine science, a common name for metaphysics in Arabic. Divine science was divided into three subcategories: ontology (the study of being); epistemology (the study of knowledge); and another subdivision that focuses its investigation on immaterial substances and their grades, from the lowest levels of existence to the perfect being.

Al-Farabi's most radical suggestion was that logic had primacy over language. That was a direct contradiction of the conventional wisdom of the time. Traditional thinkers felt that this was a dangerous idea because it tended to undermine the status of the Koran as the foundation of all knowledge and thought.

Al-Farabi's best known work is in political philosophy. In *Principles of the Opinions of the Inhabitants of the Virtuous City*, al-Farabi presents his version of the emanationist scheme of the creation and preservation of the universe. He discusses the ideal form of the state and the ways in which political organization helps the soul toward its ultimate destiny. Al-Farabi rejects the solitary life that was advocated and adopted by the Sufis. He favors Aristotle's view of humans as political animals.

Happiness, according to al-Farabi, can be achieved only through associating with others in society. Such associations may be made in three ways: socially; through the *ummah* (nation); or through the *madinah* (city-state). Of the three, al-Farabi prefers the last, which he designates as the place where human happiness is ultimately attained. In his development of the idea of what he calls "the virtuous city," al-Farabi lists the undesirable alternatives. These include the ignorant city, the corrupt city, the perverted city, and the erring city. The inhabitants of the virtuous city have understood the true meaning of God, the afterlife, and what al-Farabi calls the "Active Intellect." Their ruler—a philosopher and a prophet—is able to foretell the future.

Al-Farabi's virtuous city is a combination of Plato's ideal city and the Islamic political ideal in which the caliph–imam is supposed to be guided by the law (Sharia), which is itself grounded in divine revelation.

Ibn Sina (980–1037), known in the West as Avicenna, developed and refined al-Farabi's Islamic Neoplatonism. He was one of the greatest polymaths, and the only subject that seems to have perplexed him was metaphysics. By his own account, he read Aristotle's work on the subject 40 times but failed to understand it fully until he turned to a treatise by al-Farabi, *On the Intention of Metaphysics*. Ibn Sina was an extraordinarily prolific author, and his masterpiece was *Kitab al-Shifa* (Book of healing), a 15-volume work that attempts

This detail from *The School of Athens* by the Italian Renaissance painter Raphael (1483–1520) shows Plato (left) in discussion with Aristotle (right).

This 10th-century woodcut from Germany is a portrait of Ibn Sina, the Iranian polymath known in the West as Avicenna.

to encompass all the known disciplines and learning of his day.

In philosophy, Ibn Sina was most interested in logic and metaphysics. He refined al-Farabi's brand of Islamic Neoplatonism while remaining faithful to its fundamental tenets. He believed that the human soul's ultimate goal is to merge with the Active Intellect and thus be subsumed into absolute good and absolute beauty. It is in this state that the human soul finds fulfillment in happiness.

After Ibn Sina, there was a strong critical reaction in Islamic theology (*kalam*) against Neoplatonic thought. At the head of the countermovement was Abu al-Hasan al-Ash'ari (873–936), who founded the theological school that later produced al-Ghazali (1058-1111). Al-Ghazali was a stern critic of the Islamic Neoplatonists, especially of al-Farabi and Ibn Sina. In his influential *Refutation of the Philosophers*, he condemned various of their philosophical positions as heretical. Among the Neoplatonist notions that al-Ghazali denounced were the eternity of the world, the limitation of God's knowledge to universals rather than particulars, and the denial of the resurrection of the body.

In al-Ghazali's view, the philosophy of his time had strayed dangerously far from the Koranic revelation. He objected in particular to the notion that the world was uncreated because such an idea undermined the possibility of demonstrating the existence of God. Al-Ghazali was also unhappy with the Neoplatonists' arguments against God's knowledge of particulars. Ibn Sina, the main target of al-Ghazali's discontent, had argued that God's knowledge of particulars would implicate God in the world of change and therefore lead people to the conclusion that God changes. Al-Ghazali took issue with that, saying that the will of God was sovereign and free to break at any time the normal link of causes to effects (necessary causation). Cause and effect are connected in the human mind because they are what people normally experience. However, in al-Ghazali's view, the sole agent in the world is God, and all things in the world are directly caused by him. The ultimate purpose of al-Ghazali's argument was to preserve the centrality of belief in miracles—divine interventions—which the Neoplatonist idea of necessary causation would make impossible.

Al-Ghazali's attack on philosophy was hugely influential and inspired an antirationalist movement in Islamic thought. The backlash took two main forms. One form—a rejection of all philosophical, even theological learning— was a return to the traditions established by the Hanbali legal school of Ahmad ibn Hanbal (780–855) and consequently became known as neo-Hanbalism. The other form was a renewed emphasis on direct contact with God through Sufism (Islamic mysticism). The main proponents of the neo-Hanbalite position were Ibn Hazm (d. 1064), Ibn Taymiyah (d. 1328), and Ibn Quayyim al-Jawziyah (d. 1300). Ibn Hazm, born in Córdoba, Spain, wrote an epic poem on the art of courtship (*The Ring of the Dove*), as well as *The Book of Ethics and Ways of Life* and an important treatise (*The Book of Rebuttal*), in which he attacked all forms of theological and legal reasoning and discourse. The only legitimate methods of reasoning that Ibn Hazm accepted were those based either on sensual experience or on statements in the Koran and the Hadith.

The most influential voice in the attack on philosophy and theology—a voice that continues to feed traditionalist and fundamentalist sentiments in the Muslim

The main proponents of the neo-Hanbalite position were Ibn Hazm (d. 1064), Ibn Taymiyah (d. 1328), and Ibn Quayyim al-Jawziyah (d. 1300).

world today—was that of Ibn Taymiyah. Ibn Taymiyah advocated a return to the piety of the earliest Muslims and believed that religious truth can be found only in the Koran and the Hadith as interpreted by the contemporaries and immediate successors of the Prophet Muhammad. According to Ibn Taymiyah, the meaning of the holy books of Islam had been diluted and obscured by subsequent generations. He was especially virulent in his attack on the philosophers, denouncing as elitist their claims that the masses lack the capacity to

The arches inside Córdoba cathedral reveal its original identity as a mosque built by the Umayyad rulers of Spain in the eighth century and expanded over the following 200 years. It became a place of Christian worship in 1236.

particulars and could therefore produce only falsehoods about God. He concluded that true knowledge, of God and of particulars, can be attained only by strict adherence to the literal meaning of the Koran and the Hadith. Ibn Taymiyah's advocacy of a return to the piety of the earliest Muslims (*salaf*) became highly influential among Islamic traditionalist movements and found a receptive audience in the revival of the extreme traditionalism of the Wahhabi movement, founded in the 18th century by Muhammad Ibn Abd al-Wahhab. Wahhabism has, in turn, became the official state ideology of the modern rulers of Saudi Arabia.

SPAIN AND NORTHERN AFRICA

While most of the activity described above was concentrated in western Asia, the Muslim lands of Spain and northern Africa did not fall behind in their philosophical, scientific, and cultural achievements. One of the greatest centers of Muslim learning was in al-Andalus (modern Andalusia, Spain). Córdoba, the capital of the region, became a center of philosophical and scientific learning under al-Hakam II (r. 961–976) and his successors. Throughout this period, the city rivaled Baghdad in importance and prestige in the Islamic world.

arrive at truth through the use of reason. In his *Refutation of the Logicians*, Ibn Taymiyah attacks every element of Aristotelian logic, including syllogisms. (A syllogism is a formal structure of argument comprising one major premise, one minor premise, and a conclusion based on the two of them: for example, "All men are mortal; Julius Caesar was a man; therefore Julius Caesar was mortal.") Ibn Taymiyah argued that philosophy and logic were incapable of producing any tangible knowledge of

The first important philosopher to emerge in Andalusia was Ibn Bajjah (1095-1138), who wrote several commentaries on Aristotle and a major work of political philosophy, *Conduct of the Solitary*, in which he uses the Platonic influences of al-Farabi's virtuous city to determine the type of political state that was in harmony with the philosophical life. Ibn Bayyah realized that the ideal state often does not exist, which makes it necessary for the philosopher to seek happiness in the contemplative life, an ultimate union with the Active Intellect.

Another important figure in the philosophical tradition of Muslim Spain was Ibn Tufayl (1109–1186), whose popular novel, *Living Son of Wakeful*, tells the story of Hayy, a fictitious character born on a desert island with no known human parents and raised by animals. At various stages of his life, through his observations of the world, Hayy arrives at important conclusions about the meaning of death, the necessity of a Creator, the nature of his soul, and the means of finding happiness.

By far the greatest philosopher of Andalusia, and perhaps of all medieval Islamic philosophy, was Ibn Rushd (1126–1198), known in the West as Averroës. He was born in Córdoba and, after extensive studies in several sciences, he was commissioned by the caliph Abu Yusuf Yaqub al-Mansur (ruled 1184–1189) to produce a series of commentaries on the works of Aristotle. The resulting masterpieces were influential in the Muslim world and, when they were transmitted to Christian Europe, contributed greatly to the revival of philosophy in the West, where it had been stagnating for several centuries. In addition to these original and creative commentaries on Aristotle, Ibn Rushd wrote *The Incoherence of the Incoherence*, a refutation of al-Ghazali, in which he argues for more nuanced interpretations and applications of philosophy. Ibn Rushd claimed that, in interpreting ambiguous passages of the Koran—which are often taken at face value by the masses and accepted literally by the traditionalists—it is philosophers who are best equipped to provide a satisfactory interpretation.

For Ibn Rushd, the relationship between philosophy and theology is more complementary than contradictory. Whereas al-Ghazali denounced the philosophers' view of the eternity of the world as heretical, Ibn Rushd pointed to the ambiguity of the Koranic passages regarding creation. According to Ibn Rushd, it is open to interpretation whether the world was created out of nothing or whether it is eternal, and it is philosophy that is best equipped to weigh the relative merits of each standpoint and interpret the true meaning. Ibn Rushd also rejects al-Ghazali's charge that philosophers deny God's knowledge of particulars. Finally, Ibn Rushd embraces the importance of the metaphysics of causation, which had been called into question by al-Ghazali, who claimed that God is beyond the system of cause and effect and creates and acts according to his sovereign will.

Ultimately, in Islamic thought, al-Ghazali's attack on the philosophers won the day. However, in western Europe, it was the ideas of Ibn Rushd—transmitted through translations into Latin of his commentaries on Aristotle—that set the stage for the revival of philosophy. Averroism was the dominant philosophy in the 13th century, during which thinkers almost routinely defined themselves as being either for or against Ibn Rushd's philosophy. Certain misinterpretations of Ibn Rushd's understanding of the relationship between theology and philosophy led to further controversies in Christendom; in 1270, his books were publicly burned at the entrance to the Sorbonne university in Paris.

The philosophy of Ibn Rushd represented the high point of Islamic

This statue of Ibn Rushd—the Arab philosopher known in the West as Averroës—stands in his native city of Córdoba, Spain.

philosophy in the Arabic-speaking world. On his death, his philosophical style, which drew heavily on the Greeks, went out of fashion. The traditionalist viewpoint prevailed and became generally accepted without dispute in most parts of the Muslim world.

PERSIA

Unlike developments in other parts of the Muslim world, there was no interruption in philosophical activity in the Persian-speaking Muslim world. There, the

philosophical tradition established an enduring presence in the curriculum of the theological schools. This tradition derived from *The Wisdom of Illumination*, the major work of As-Suhrawardi (1155–1191), which expanded Ibn Sina's philosophy. The work was an attempt to define philosophy in an organic manner that amalgamated the wisdom of the Greeks with the mystical orientation of western Asia. As-Suhrawardi wrote about the science of light, in which all things find their meaning through their relation to the power of light. He envisioned a hierarchical cosmos in which different levels of being were distinguished by their proximity to the source of light, the Light of Lights. As-Suhrawardi's philosophy, a blend of Neoplatonism and the Islamic mystical tradition, established the Ishraqi (Illuminationist) tradition in Persia, and it survived both the frontal assault of al-Ghazali on philosophy and the immense destruction left behind by the Mongol invasions of large parts of Muslim Asia in the 13th century. Because of the patronage and active support of philosophical and theological learning by a succession of Persian rulers, the region's philosophical tradition flourished throughout the Middle Ages and beyond. The most important philosopher of the Persian school was Sadr ad-Din ash-Shirazi (c. 1571–1640), widely known as Mulla Sadra. His lasting influence lies in the creative integration of philosophy and Sufi mysticism into the Shiite tradition.

ISLAM AND SCIENCE

In the West, a common modern view of the Muslim world is of an impoverished and underdeveloped society in which science and technology do not play significant roles. Although there is some truth in that perception, it should not conceal the fact that numerous scientific and medical discoveries that are now taken for granted came originally from the Islamic world. During the Middle Ages, there was a great surge of scientific activity in the region, leading to the emergence of new fields of study and numerous important inventions.

The world's first physicists and chemists worked in Baghdad, and the city was also home to the best medical scientists, who made important advances in surgery and in the understanding of human anatomy. Baghdad was the capital of the Abbasid Empire, where the caliph al-Ma'mun (ruled 813-833) devoted vast resources to the pursuit of philosophical and scientific knowledge. Al-Ma'mun established an academy called the House of Wisdom (Bayt al-Hikmah) and instructed the leading academics of his empire to focus on translating the wisdom of the Greeks into Arabic and then to advance the frontiers of knowledge.

The ensuing flurry of activity was, at least in part, a reaction against the previous period, during which philosophical and scientific inquiry had stagnated. The Arabs did not just translate scientific works from the Greek and then imitate them and follow their instructions. The scientists,

The scientists, recruited from all over the world by the caliph, learned from the Greeks and then made their own discoveries and new contributions to science.

recruited from all over the world by the caliph, learned from the Greeks and then made their own discoveries and new contributions to science.

Another center of intellectual activity was Basra (present-day Iraq), the native city of al-Jahiz (776–868), the author of the multivolume *Book of Animals* in which he recorded his observations about the organizations of ant colonies and wrote about methods of communication between various species of animals. Al-Jahiz was a prolific author. According to legend, he was killed when a pile of all the books that he had written fell on top of him. Another Muslim scholar who was active in Basra was al-Masu'di (died 957). Al-Masu'di relied on his extensive travel experiences and observations to write about the history, geography, and sociology of the places and peoples he encountered, using an objective and descriptive style that later became a staple element of scientific writings in the Muslim world.

In the developing and expanding Islamic civilization, science had an important function and was regarded as an autonomous institution that benefited all of society. Although there were scattered voices from religious circles that expressed misgivings about certain scientific endeavors, academic study remained largely undisturbed by religious discourse. In contrast to Islamic religious knowledge, which was regarded as an exclusively Muslim preserve, the scientific quest was considered to be the property of all nations, regardless of their religious beliefs. The advances made in the Muslim world were greatly facilitated by the establishment of Arabic as the international language of scientific discourse; Arabic even superseded Latin to a great extent in the Western world.

ASTROLOGY AND ASTRONOMY

In the Muslim world during the Middle Ages, astrology and astronomy were of comparable importance. Although astrology is no longer regarded as a science, it is founded in astronomy because its basic assumption is that the movement of the heavenly bodies affects human life. The two fields of study coexisted at medieval Islamic courts, although a clear line was drawn by the astronomers themselves

between their own science and astrology, which was used habitually by rulers to predict events. Arab astronomers were initially influenced by the works, newly translated into Arabic, of Persian and Iranian astronomers. However, the real breakthrough in the development of Arab astronomy was the translation of Greek works into Arabic. In particular, one Greek work, the *Almagest*, written by Ptolemy (100–170), had an immense influence on Arab astronomy that lasted until his geocentric theory (that the earth was at

The advances made in the Muslim world were greatly facilitated by the establishment of Arabic as the international language of scientific discourse.

the center of the solar system) was finally discredited. The first original work of Arabic astronomy was *Zij al-Sindhind* by al-Khwarizmi (780–850), which was completed while Ptolemy's *Almagest* was being translated into Arabic. Ptolemy's astronomy was therefore received by an already eager audience of astronomers who then fashioned significant refinements of the Greek author's theories. The Muslim astronomers integrated new discoveries in mathematics, such as trigonometry, into their work and, through the cross-fertilization of scientific disciplines, came up with new concepts and theories and made more accurate computations than ever before. The late 10th century and the early 11th century were especially vibrant in the development of astronomy, and it was during this period that the

This early-16th-century illustration depicts Ptolemy, the Greek scientist whose work had an immense influence on the development of Arab astronomy, using an astrolabe to measure the heavens. Ptolemy also had a lasting effect on the study of geography and mathematics in the Islamic world.

famous polymath al-Biruni (973–1048) was active. His most important work in astronomy was *al-Qanun al-Masudi* (The Masudi canon), which many people compared to Ptolemy's *Almagest*. Al-Biruni's integration of trigonometry into the science of astronomy helped him to arrive at a very close estimation of the circumference of the earth. The rigorous application of mathematics led to the realization that astronomy was a science that is independent of the theories of the universe propagated by philosophy. The breaking away from philosophy, and the extensive use of mathematics to describe nature, resulted in the emergence of a new school of Muslim astronomers who began to question the basic, philosophical presuppositions that had formed the basis of Ptolemaic (geocentric) astronomy.

MATHEMATICS

The Arabs also restructured mathematics through algebra—the use of abstract symbols rather than specific numbers in arithmetical operations and formal manipulations. Due to the generalizing method of algebra, all mathematical disciplines, including geometry and arithmetic, were radically reconfigured. Algebra initiated a new way of calculating by introducing a general way of treating equations. The first work that approached equations in this manner by the use of algebraic expressions was al-Khwarizmi's *Kitab al-Jabr* (The book of algebra). Written in the early part of the ninth century, this book is an outstanding landmark in the history of mathematics. Al-Khwarizmi founded an entirely new discipline in mathematics that produced a general

This astrolabe was made by Arab craftspeople around 1300. Astrolabes are used by astronomers and navigators to compute time and geographical position.

theory of solving linear and quadratic equations by means of radicals. His new discipline was then applied to geometry and arithmetic, where old problems found new solutions through the use of algebraic expressions. The achievement of al-Khwarizmi was extended by a long line of outstanding mathematicians who further expanded their subject through the interaction between arithmetic and algebra. Abu Bakr Muhammad al-Kajari (d. 1010) applied the laws of arithmetic to algebraic expressions. Al-Kajari worked at the same time as several Greek mathematical works appeared in Arabic, notably the first seven books of *Arithmetica* by Diophantus (third century), which was translated by al-Balabakki (820–913) under the title *The Art of Algebra*. Al-Kajari's work was used as a reference source by Arab mathematicians for the next 600 years.

The creative and systematic application of arithmetic was only one dimension of the evolution of mathematics in the Islamic world. The work of the Persian mathematician Omar Khayyam (1048–1131) represented the high point of the creative use of geometry to expand the algebraic theory of equations. Omar offered a geometric theory for solving polynomial equations of up to three degrees. He offered a classification of three-degree equations and worked out a method of solving them by means of the intersections of conic sections. His achievement was later developed by Sharaf al-Din al-Tusi (d. 1213), whose work established the foundation of a new discipline in mathematics, algebraic geometry. Al-Tusi was able to use algebra and a system of equations to find the intersections of curves and further expanded the understanding of third-

degree equations. These mathematicians were part of a larger community that was engaged not only in commenting on the older traditions of Greek and Indian mathematics, but also in innovative work that led to the birth of separate subdisciplines of mathematics. Moreover, the achievements of these mathematicians greatly accommodated the development of other natural sciences and led to practical applications in engineering and other disciplines.

MEDICINE

Medicine is the most extensively documented of all the sciences in the Muslim world. The sources record not only particular scientific achievements but also the social organization and institutions that fostered the discipline. As with other sciences, the original center of research and practice was Baghdad but, by the ninth century, its preeminence came under challenge from other cities. By the 13th century, Syria in general and Damascus in particular had become the most vibrant places for medical activity, attracting the best physicians from all over the Islamic world. As with the other sciences, Greek learning was instrumental in the development of medicine in the Islamic world. Hunayn Ibn Ishaq (808–873) translated, with the help of collaborators, all available Greek works on medicine into either Syriac or Arabic. The first significant original Arabic work of this period was *Firdaws al-Hikma* (Paradise of wisdom), by Ali ibn Sahl Rabban al-Tabari (783–858). In this book, al-Tabari compares all the various known medical traditions, including those of India and Greece. Although it was Indian medicine that gave the initial impetus to the development of Islamic medicine, it was the Greek tradition that proved dominant and helped to develop Islamic medicine into a uniform system. The work of the Greek physician Galen (129–200) was hugely influential on Islamic medicine. Of particular importance was Galen's understanding of the four humors (blood, phlegm, yellow bile, and black bile), and their relation to the four elements (air, water, fire, and earth), and to the four qualities (hot, moist, cold, and dry). Reflecting the medical orthodoxy of his time, Galen contended that diseases were caused by a lack of equilibrium between the environment and the body, and that they should be treated by the manipulation of the humors and the external elements. In addition to studying theoretically the causes of disease (pathology), early Muslim physicians greatly expanded empirical (observation-based) medical knowledge. The great representative of the clinical-based approach to medicine, which focused on particular cases, was the ninth-century scholar Abu Bakr ar-Razi. His writings included discussions of the practice of diagnosis and the process of selection of various options of treatment. Ar-Razi's expansive work in clinical medicine was based on his experience as the chief physician in the hospitals of Baghdad and Rayya (a town in the Punjab, India). For example, ar-Razi wrote a treatise, based on his own clinical experience, on the diagnosis and treatment of smallpox and measles. His most important work, however, remains *al-Hawi fi al-Tibb* (The comprehensive book on medicine), a treatment of clinical medicine in which ar-Razi describes the symptoms of diseases, options for their treatment, and descriptions of the effectiveness of those

treatments. A further importance of this book was that ar-Razi, following his own observations as a practicing physician, frequently disagrees with or ignores Galen. Ar-Razi's main aim was always to rely exclusively on his own observations and experiments to find effective treatments for illnesses. Although ar-Razi's work contained a wealth of information, it was soon supplemented by the more organized and accessible late-10th-century works of Ali ibn Abbas al-Majusi—notably, *Kitab al-Malaki* (The royal book)—and of Abu al-Quasim al-Zahrawi (936–1013), the author of *Kitab al-Tasrif li man Ajiza an al-talif* (Manual for medical practitioners). The most important part of al-Zahrawi's 30-volume work—which was published in Córdoba—was his discussion of surgery. This section of the book, often reproduced separately from the larger work, contained descriptions of surgical interventions and of the various tools used in surgery. Al-Zahrawi believed that practice in surgery was a basic requirement for a better theoretical understanding of medical science.

The most important theoretical work in Islamic medicine, a book that remained influential until the 17th century, was that of Ibn Sina, who was often compared to Galen and became known as the Prince of Physicians. Ibn Sina was a child prodigy and, by the age of 16, his knowledge of medicine was so extensive that even qualified physicians were said to turn to this teenager for instruction. Ibn Sina wrote *al-Qanun fi al-Tibb* (The canon of medicine) with the intention of providing a major reference text in the theory of medical science. Ibn Sina presented a rigorously organized synthesis of medical history and theory, yet his work and its enormous

Muslim physician and polymath Ibn Sina (980–1037) made significant contributions to medicine, philosophy, and the physical sciences during his lifetime. This engraving is from an 18th-century Western collection of his work.

influence should not be permitted to overshadow the immense accomplishments of early Muslim physicians in the field of practical medicine.

The practical orientation that most Arab physicians brought to medicine was reflected in the growth of pharmacology, the development of medicines to treat illnesses. From the 10th century, physicians in northern Africa and Andalusia were also often pharmacologists. The most important people of this period were In al-Jazzar (d. 980), Abu Marwan in Zuhr (1090–1162), Abu al-Ala ibn Zuhr (d. 1131), and Abu Jafar al-Ghafiqi (d. 1165). These names

were associated with a practical, hands-on approach to medicine in which physicians were often involved in developing and experimenting with new drugs. The empirical method was also successfully applied to anatomy, in which al-Baghdadi (980-1037) and Ibn al-Nafis (d. 1288) made important contributions, in spite of the fact that anatomical dissections were frowned upon for religious reasons. However, the general prohibition against dissections did not prevent physicians from performing them, and their work contributed greatly to the understanding of human anatomy.

Founded in 970, al-Azhar University in Cairo, Egypt, is the oldest educational institution of its kind in the world.

The efforts of these and other scholars contributed to a rapid rise in the status of medicine. The medical establishments of Cairo (the capital of present-day Egypt) and Damascus attracted large numbers of physicians. In Damascus, a special center of learning was designated exclusively for the study of medicine. Instruction in medical science also made its way onto the curriculum of religious schools (madrassas). Medical science gradually became a part of the everyday life of society through hospitals, the widespread construction of which was one of the greatest achievements of medieval Islamic society. The first hospitals were built in Baghdad; more soon followed in other major population centers. The most important were the Nuri hospital in Damascus (built in the 12th century) and the Mansuri hospital, built in Cairo in the 13th century. These hospitals were open to every member of society, free of charge. They were well funded, administered by professional staff, and created an environment in which the science of medicine could be further developed.

MODERN TRENDS IN PHILOSOPHY

The two most significant thinkers who ushered Islamic philosophy into the modern era were Jamal ad-Din al-Afghani (1838–1897) and his disciple Muhammad Abduh (1849–1905). Together, they attempted to reconcile the basic principles of Islam with modern science. Their reformist movement initiated a continuing discussion and struggle within the Muslim world with the manifold challenges presented by modernity.

Al-Afghani was more of a social visionary than a professional philosopher. Through his travels in the Muslim world and across Europe, he realized the backwardness of his people and began to propagate the idea of pan-Islamism, proposing the union of all Muslims in a bid to shake off foreign rule. Al-Afghani's philosophical and theological ideas found a comprehensive expression in his *Refutation of the Materialists*. In this work, he extols the positive role of religion in the progress of humanity. He attempts to demonstrate that the decline and fall of all the great empires of history were caused by their political leaders' neglect of religion. The systemic elimination of religion from the moral fabric of society is described by al-Afghani as a final catastrophe of humanity.

> The systemic elimination of religion from the moral fabric of society is described by al-Afghani as a final catastrophe of humanity.

Al-Afghani's ideas were perpetuated by his disciple, Muhammad Abduh. Abduh studied at Al-Azhar University in Cairo and then lectured there in philosophy and theology, two subjects that were considered dangerous in the late 19th century. In his theological treatise *Risalat al-Tawhid* (Epistle of unity), Abduh demonstrates the importance of reason and rationality in upholding the traditional Islamic beliefs in the existence of God and Muhammad as His final prophet. These were not revolutionary propositions but, in the context of the intellectual and scientific stagnation prevalent in the Muslim world of his day, they offered a new possibility to modernize Islam. On the contentious issues of moral responsibility and God's justice, which had divided the Muslim community into rival schools, Abduh struck a conciliatory note, arguing that God is neither a servant of the dictates of reason nor a ruler whose rule is beyond rationality. On the question of free will, Abduh follows the rationalists (Mutazilites) in claiming that humans naturally make their choices on the basis of reasonable deliberations. However, he also acknowledges that there are situations in which reason reaches its limit and realizes that it needs to follow a divine directive. However, Abduh says little about the mechanics of how and under what circumstances this realization takes place in the human mind.

Abduh's acknowledgment of the importance of revelation lay in pointing out its importance as an aid to the moral development of humans and in providing an ultimate source of justification for the claims of reason. Unlike many observers who looked at the Koran as an exclusive source for answering specific scientific questions or for providing insights into particular historical situations, Abduh saw in the astronomical, geographical, and historical references of the Koran a simple textual aid to demonstrate the majesty of the divine. The foundation of Muslim renewal lies in the realization that Islam perfectly unites human aspirations in this world with the world to come, providing guidance, through its legal framework, for every aspect of human life, both individually and socially.

In this view, because of its comprehensive nature, Islam is superior to all other religions. The modern Salafiya movement—followers of which call for all Muslims to unite and return to the teachings of their pious ancestors—had its origins in the pan-Islamism of al-Afghani and Abduh and was later instrumental in the development of the now numerous Islamic fundamentalist movements.

See Also

Brief History of Islam 22–43 ❖

Scriptures and Doctrine 102–123 ❖

Literature 248–267 ❖

Contemporary Trends in Islamic Philosophy 332–333 ❖

Contemporary Trends in Islamic Philosophy

Islamic philosophy is influenced by various schools of thought. The most far-reaching Muslim thinkers of recent times have championed Islam as the way forward in today's world.

The work of many contemporary Muslim philosophers is concerned with how Islam should react to the constantly changing social, political, and cultural climate of the modern world. Over the course of the 20th century the conditions in which the global Muslim population live have changed dramatically. In addition to the political upheavals of the last 60 years, there have also been major demographic shifts. For example, many millions of Muslims now form minority communities in non-Muslim countries.

Muslim philosophers have proposed many different responses to these changes. These responses typically attempt to reconcile the need to adapt to the circumstances in which many Muslims now live with the need to maintain traditional practices and the integrity of the faith. There is another group, which has been brought to global prominence through its association with terrorism, that argues for the total rejection of modern cultural, sociological, and political ideas and the adoption of a fundamentalist interpretation of Islam.

ISLAMIC KNOWLEDGE

One of the most significant ideas in contemporary Islamic philosophy is the "Islamization of knowledge," a concept proposed by Palestinian-American philosopher Ismail al-Faruqi (1921–1986). In his writings, al-Faruqi argued that Islam should not reject modern Western ideas but seek to reshape and understand them within the framework of Islamic ethics. This process of Islamization, it is argued, was once a common part of Islamic philosophy. Writers such as Ibn Sina (Avicenna) and Ibn Rushd (Averroës), for example, incorporated the ideas of Greek philosophers in their theological works. Al-Faruqi hoped that this process would invigorate the intellectual culture of both the West and the Muslim world.

His own discussions of Islamization were largely limited to the humanities and the social sciences, however, leaving the status of the physical sciences open to debate. Some followers of his philosophy have asserted that scientific knowledge is neutral and so does not require

Qutb blamed Christianity for abandoning its traditional involvement in people's lives on Earth and for turning instead to an idealized spiritual world.

Islamization, while others have argued that although scientific knowledge is neutral, the philosophy of science is not, and so needs to be Islamized.

Another important Muslim philospher is Muhammad Abid al-Jabiri (b. 1936), a Moroccan professor who recognizes in Arab thought a synthesis of Muslim and Greek traditions but is critical of what he regards as its current failure to reconcile the conflicting aspects of each main influence. Al-Jabiri's views are in sharp contrast to those of the better known radicals and extremists. However, many commentators have acclaimed al-Jabiri as the outstanding modern champion of the moderate Arab philosophical tradition established by the Muslim polymath Ibn Rushd (1126–1198), known in the West as Averroës.

QUTBISM

The most influential voice of the fundamentalist movement as a whole, a voice that gave this movement intellectual legitimation, was that of Sayyid Qutb (d. 1966). Qutb was a proponent of secularism until he went to study in the United States, after which he became increasingly critical of the West and what he saw as its decadent values. In *Islam and the Problems of Civilization*, Qutb blamed Christianity for abandoning its traditional involvement in people's lives on Earth and for turning instead to an idealized spiritual world. His assessment was that the West, with its Christian heritage, had allowed the development of a kind of schizophrenia in modern society. The cure for this illness, in his view, was to reunite the spiritual and temporal realms. The medicine is provided by Islam, which, according to Qutb, never acknowledged a split between religion and politics. Islam, through its call to jihad (struggle), liberates people both physically and spiritually from their unbelief.

Photographed at his trial in 1966, radical fundamentalist Sayyid Qutb (right) was the leader of the Egyptian Muslim Brotherhood. He was executed after the trial.

Obstacles that stand in the way of true belief should be removed by any means possible—that is the main tenet of Qutb's thought. Qutb's life reflected his philosophical and ideological commitments and, after years of imprisonment, he was executed in Egypt on the orders of President Gamal Abdel Nasser (1918–1970).

The fundamentalist ideologies of Qutb, and then of Sayyid Abu'l-A'la Mawdudi (1903–1979), a Sunni Pakistani who founded Jamaat-e-Islami, the Islamic revivalist party, became notorious in the West for their strong anti-Western sentiments and their use of the concept of jihad to justify military resistance to or even hostile attacks upon the enemies of Islam. These have become the most highly publicized trends in contemporary Islamic philosophy, but they represent the view of only a small group.

GLOSSARY

Allah (Arabic: "God") Muslims believe that the god of Islam is unique (*wahid*), omnipotent, and omniscient. Allah has 99 names that are known to humans and a 100th name that will be revealed when the world ends on the Day of Judgment.

ayatollah a high-ranking Shiite Muslim cleric. Holders of the title are experts in various aspects of Islam, particularly law, ethics, and philosophy.

dhimmi (literally, "protection") any non-Muslim living in a state governed by Sharia law. *Dhimmi* status afforded holders various rights, such as the freedom to practice their own religions, but also imposed several restrictions— for example, *dhimmi*s were not permitted to bear arms.

Eid al-Adha ("Festival of Sacrifice") the second of the two great Muslim festivals, the other being Eid al-Fitr. Eid al-Adha lasts for three days, starting on the 10th of Dhu'l-Hijja, the last month of the Islamic calendar. Eid al-Adha commemorates Abraham's son Ishmael (Ismail) and marks the culmination of the hajj.

Eid al-Fitr ("Festival of Breaking Fast") the first of the two great Muslim festivals. Eid al-Fitr is held on the first three days of Shawwal, the 10th month of the Islamic calendar. It celebrates the end of Ramadan.

fatwa a legal opinion. In the West, the term has been widely taken to mean "death sentence." This incorrect translation arose after the fatwa of 1989 in which Ayatollah Ruhollah Khomeini (ruler of Iran, 1979–1989) publicly condemned the Indian British author Salman Rushdie (b. 1947) for his book *The Satanic Verses*.

fiqh Islamic jurisprudence. *Fiqh* expands and develops Sharia law on the basis of the judgments and rulings of Muslim jurists. The term is used particularly with reference to judgments concerning the observance of rituals and morals, and with social legislation.

Hadith sayings and narratives attributed to Muhammad or his companions. Hadith collections are the second most important source of religious law and moral guidance in Islam, after the Koran.

hajj a pilgrimage to the holy sites of Mecca, performed during the month of Dhu'l-Hijja. The hajj is considered a religious duty that all Muslims should perform at least once in their lifetime.

halal generally, anything sanctioned by Islamic law. The adjective is applied particularly to foods that have been specially prepared so that they may be eaten by Muslims in accordance with religious requirements—for instance, the animals from which meat is obtained have to be slaughtered using a special method known as *dhabiha*.

haram in Arabic, a sacred place or territory that is the focus of pilgrimage and a place where divine blessings are bestowed. The principal *haram*s are in Mecca, Medina, Jerusalem, and, for Shiites, in Karbala (Iraq). The Arabic word for "forbidden" derives from the same root and can be transliterated as both *haram* and *haraam*.

hijab a veil that covers the hair and usually the neck of Muslim women. The term is used generally for any form of modest Islamic dress, including the burqa (which covers the entire face and body) and the chador (an outer garment or open cloak thrown over the head and held closed in front). The *jilbab*—a long, loose-fitting coat that covers the entire body, except for hands, feet, face, and head—may be complemented by the *khimar* (a wraparound scarf) and the *niqab* (a veil). The notion, common in the West, that Islam requires believers to cover their bodies almost completely has no basis in the Koran, which requires only the wearing of the *khimar* (head scarf).

hijri the Muslim calendar. The Islamic year is either 354 or 355 days long and consists of 12 lunar months, each of which begins at the appearance of the new moon. While the months of the Gregorian calendar always fall in the same season of any given year, the months of the *hijri* calendar come at different stages of every year in a cycle of 32.5 solar years.

imam the head of a Muslim community, typically the leader of prayers in a mosque. The two main divisions of Islam view the imam's function in different ways. To the Sunnis, the imam is a caliph, a successor to Muhammad in the Prophet's temporal role but not in his spiritual role. He is appointed by men. To the Shiites, the imam is a spiritual authority of paramount importance.

jihad usually translated as "to strive" or "to struggle," the term has often been misapplied by non-Muslims who have taken it to be synonymous with holy war.

Kaaba (Arabic: literally, "cube") the shrine in Mecca that Muslims face during prayer. Muslims believe that the Kaaba was built by Abraham and his son Ismail, known in the Judeo-Christian tradition as Ishmael.

madrassa in the Islamic world, any school, college, or university, regardless of whether it is religious or secular.

minaret (from Arabic *madhanah*, "beacon") a tower that forms a part of, or is immediately adjacent to, a mosque. It is from the minaret that the muezzin (crier) traditionally summons the faithful to prayer five times daily. There is a wide variety of designs, but a typical minaret has a square base beneath a round tower with several floors, each of which has its own projecting balcony.

mosque a Muslim house of worship. The prayer area of a mosque can be a hall or an open courtyard. The focal point of this space is the mihrab, which indicates the direction of Mecca. Close to the mihrab is the *minbar*, a raised seat from which the imam addresses the congregation, similar to the pulpit in a church. No statues, ritual objects, or pictures are permitted in a mosque; the only decorations that are allowed are inscriptions of verses from the Koran and the names of Muhammad and his original companions.

mufti an Islamic legal authority who can deliver fatwas (formal legal opinions). Historically, muftis were often the highest-ranking authorities, with wide-ranging jurisdiction in spiritual and temporal disputes. However, the development of civil codes in most modern Muslim countries has limited the power of the muftis to matters of marriage, divorce, and inheritance, and not even all of those.

Pillars of Islam the five duties incumbent on every Muslim—*shahada* (the profession of faith); *salat* (the five daily prayers); *zakat* (almsgiving); *sawm* (fasting during the month of Ramadan); and hajj (pilgrimage to Mecca).

Ramadan the ninth month of the Muslim lunar calendar, throughout which believers fast and abstain from sinful thoughts and deeds between dawn and dusk. The end of the fast is marked by Eid al-Fitr.

salat a strictly defined set of actions and phrases that are performed and recited in a specific order at designated times. Personal prayer (*dua*) is also permitted, but most images of Muslims praying show the *salat*, which is the preferred form of worship. Muslims observe the following five prayers on a daily basis: the *fajr*, performed after the break of day but before sunrise; the *duhr*, performed around the middle of the day; the *asr*, which must be performed sometime before sunset; the *maghrib*, performed after sunset but before dark; and the *isha*, performed after the *maghrib*, which must be completed before dawn.

Sharia (Arabic: literally, "the path leading to the watering place") the religious law of Islam, originally codified in the eighth century. There is no one Islamic law—rather there are several different schools of

Islamic law. The main division is between the Sunni and Shiite branches of Islam, which have further divisions within them.

sheikh an honorific title that predated Islam in the Arabian Peninsula and was later applied by Muslims, first to any male older than 50 years, and later to heads of state, religious leaders and theologians, college principals, and learned men.

Shiite a member of the smaller of the two main branches of Islam; the larger branch is the Sunni. The schism between the two groups was caused by a dispute in the seventh century about who should succeed the Prophet Muhammad. The Shiites believe that the founder of Islam ordained al-Husayn ibn Ali (626–680)— the son of Ali ibn Abi Talib and the grandson of the Prophet Muhammad. The Sunni believe that the legitimate heir was Abu Bakr, Muhammad's father-in-law.

Sufism Islamic mysticism. Although often mistaken for a distinct sect, Sufism is more accurately described as an expression of the mystical, meditative dimension of Islamic belief. Sufis work to achieve *taqwah* (consciousness of God) though solitary prayer, meditation, and chanting.

Sunna (Arabic: "custom") the record of the Prophet's deeds. The Sunna is second in authority only

to the Koran in shaping Muslim worldviews and behavior. As a result, the literature recording it, while not technically scripture, functions in much the same way as holy writ. The Sunna is articulated in the Hadiths (the sayings or deeds of Muhammad).

Sunni a member of the larger of the two main branches of Islam; the smaller branch is the Shia. The schism between the two groups was caused by a dispute in the seventh century about who should succeed the Prophet Muhammad. The Sunni believe that the legitimate heir was Abu Bakr, Muhammad's father-in-law. The Shiites believe that the founder of Islam ordained his grandson al-Husayn ibn Ali.

sura any of the 114 chapters in standard editions of the Koran. All but one of the suras are arranged in descending order of length. The exception is the first sura, the *fatiha*, which is only seven *aya* (verses) long. Every sura but the ninth begins with the *basmalah*—the phrase "*bism Allah ar-rahman ar-rahim*" (in the name of God, the Merciful, the Compassionate). Some Muslims divide the Koran not into 114 suras but into 30 equal sections, known as *juz*, so that the entire work can be read in a single lunar month.

ulama Muslim legal scholars. Most ulama are experts in jurisprudence but some are

specialists in other fields. Among the groups who comprise the ulama are the mufti (Islamic legal authorities entitled to deliver fatwas), the *qadi* (judges), and the *faqih* (those who expand and develop Sharia law on the basis of the continuing judgments and rulings of Muslim jurists).

ummah the Muslim community. The term is commonly used to mean either all the Islamic nations or all the Arab world, regardless of the constitution of the countries in which the members reside.

Wahhabism an ultraconservative interpretation of Sunni Islam characterized by a very strict adherence to Islamic law as well as to the practices of the early Islamic *ummah* (religious community). Its restrictions include the mandatory covering of women in full-length black cloaks. The ruling royal family of Saudi Arabia is Wahhabi.

wudu ritual purification before prayer, traditionally performed in a bathhouse adjacent to a mosque. The ceremony involves washing the hands three times, rinsing out the mouth and putting water into the nostrils three times, and then washing the whole head, from the chin to the nape of the neck. The feet must also be washed. At the end of this process, Muslims recite a pledge to Allah and the Prophet Muhammad and then make their way into the mosque.

FURTHER READING
AND RESEARCH

Reference

Esposito, John L. *What Everyone Needs to Know about Islam*. New York: Oxford University Press, 2002.

Esposito, John L. (ed.). *The Oxford Encyclopedia of the Islamic World*. New York: Oxford University Press, 2009.

Martin, Richard C. (ed.). *Encyclopedia of Islam and the Muslim World*. New York: Macmillan Reference USA, 2004.

Robinson, Francis (ed.). *The Cambridge Illustrated History of the Islamic World*. New York: Cambridge University Press, 1996.

Ruthven, Malise. *Islam in the World*. New York: Oxford University Press, 2006.

History

Ansary, Mir Tamim. *Destiny Disrupted: A History of the World through Islamic Eyes*. New York: PublicAffairs, 2009.

Casale, Giancarlo. *The Ottoman Age of Exploration*. New York: Oxford University Press, 2010.

Goldschmidt, Arthur. *A Brief History of Egypt*. New York: Facts On File, 2008.

Gordon, Matthew. *The Rise of Islam*. Indianapolis, IN: Hackett Publishing, 2008.

Lewis, David Levering. *God's Crucible: Islam and the Making of Europe, 570 to 1215*. New York: W. W. Norton, 2008.

Madden, Thomas F. *The New Concise History of the Crusades*. Lanham, MD: Rowman and Littlefield, 2006.

Marozzi, Justin. *Tamerlane: Sword of Islam, Conqueror of the World*. London: HarperCollins, 2004.

Mukhia, Harbans. *The Mughals of India*. Malden, MA: Blackwell, 2004.

Sonn, Tamara. *A Brief History of Islam*. Malden, MA: Blackwell, 2004.

Walker, Paul E. *Exploring an Islamic Empire: Fatimid History and its Sources*. London: I. B. Tauris, 2002.

Walker, Paul E. *Fatimid History and Ismaili Doctrine*. Burlington, VT: Ashgate, 2008.

Beliefs and Practices

Bravmann, M. M. *The Spiritual Background of Early Islam: Studies in Ancient Arab Concepts*. Boston: Brill, 2008.

Caner, Emir Fethi. *More than a Prophet: An Insider's Response to Muslim Beliefs about Jesus and Christianity*. Grand Rapids, MI: Kregel Publications, 2003.

Caner, Ergun Mehmet. *Unveiling Islam: An Insider's Look at Muslim Life and Beliefs*. Grand Rapids, MI: Kregel Publications, 2002.

Dawood, N. J. (trans.). *The Koran*. New York: Penguin Books, 1990.

Farah, Caesar E. *Islam: Beliefs and Observances*. Hauppauge, NY: Barron's, 2003.

Gordon, Matthew. *Understanding Islam: Origins, Beliefs, Practices, Holy Texts, Sacred Places.* London: Duncan Baird, 2002.

Hazleton, Lesley. *After the Prophet: The Epic Story of the Shia-Sunni Split in Islam.* New York: Doubleday, 2009.

Kabbani, Muhammad Hisham. *Encyclopedia of Islamic Doctrine.* Mountainview, CA: As-Sunna Foundation of America, 1998.

Ramadan, Tariq. *The Messenger: The Meanings of the Life of Muhammad.* New York: Penguin Books, 2008.

Rippin, Andrew. *Muslims: Their Religious Beliefs and Practices.* New York: Routledge, 2005.

Schwartz, Stephen. *The Other Islam: Sufism and the Road to Global Harmony.* New York: Doubleday, 2008.

Swarup, Ram. *Understanding the Hadith: The Sacred Traditions of Islam.* Amherst, NY: Prometheus Books, 2002.

Culture

Broug, Eric. *Islamic Geometric Patterns.* New York: Thames and Hudson, 2008.

Burckhardt, Titus. *Art of Islam: Language and Meaning.* Bloomington, IN: World Wisdom, 2009.

Goodman, Lenn Evan. *Avicenna.* Ithaca, NY: Cornell University Press, 2006.

McCaughrean, Geraldine (ed.). *One Thousand and One Arabian Nights.* New York: Oxford University Press, 1999.

Michell, George. *The Majesty of Mughal Decoration: The Art and Architecture of Islamic India.* New York: Thames and Hudson, 2007.

O'Kane, Bernard. *The Treasures of Islamic Art in the Museums of Cairo.* New York: The American University in Cairo Press, 2006.

Ruggles, D. Fairchild. *Islamic Gardens and Landscapes.* Philadelphia: University of Pennsylvania Press, 2008.

Welzbacher, Christian. *Euro Islam Architecture: New Mosques in the West.* Amsterdam, Netherlands: SUN, 2008

WEBSITES

Aga Khan Archnet
www.archnet.org
Website that provides profiles of sites of architectural interest in the Muslim world, with numerous diagrams, photographs, and academic papers.

Islam
www.bbc.co.uk/religion/religions/islam
Website that provides a comprehensive outline of Muslim beliefs as well as an account of the religion's historical development.

Islamic Philosophy Online
www.muslimphilosophy.com
A site covering the history of Muslim thought.

Online Hadith Collection
www.hadithcollection.com
Website providing translations of the full text of all the major collections of Hadith; also includes introductions that explain the origins of each collection and its author.

Online Koran Project
www.al-quran.info
Website that provides searchable translations of the Koran in many languages.

Tariq Ramadan
www.tariqramadan.com
Website of Swiss Muslim intellectual Tariq Ramadan; includes lectures, debates, and essays by Ramadan and other Muslim intellectuals.

INDEX